Praise for *Arise*

"Elena has done it again. *Arise* is a literal masterpiece. Full of deeply personal reflections, radically supportive scripts, and loads of opportunities to explore one's patterns, beliefs, and experiences, this book is a game-changer for any human being. I even used the strategies with my teenagers and partner; this content is not just applicable in a professional setting, but in a personal context as well."

—*Maia Heyck-Merlin, founder and CEO, The Together Group; author of* The Together Teacher, The Together Leader, *and* The Together Teammate

"Since the pandemic, schools and organizations have often struggled to rebuild community and trust. *Arise* builds on the foundations of Elena Aguilar's impactful prior work, giving practical strategies and case studies to support the well-being of students, teachers, and administrators alike."

—*Liz SoHyeon Kleinrock, author*

"Want change? No one knows more about leveraging the human side of change than Elena. In her deeply optimistic new book *Arise*, Elena shows how Transformational Coaching—yes, coaching that is literally transformational—is the key to improving teacher practice and creating a school community where we all thrive. This book is exactly what we need so our students and our schools can flourish."

—*Jenn David-Lang, founder, THE MAIN IDEA and Learn & Lead Masterminds*

"*Arise* is an incredible compilation of *all* of Elena's best work. This book will help any coach or supervisor continually practice becoming a better coach for their team and help any organization get closer to actualizing the full potential of each human being. To "Arise" means to put in the effective effort and reflection necessary to improve yourself as a coach and immensely transform the lives of those who work with one another to improve systems for all of us. If we believe in ourselves and others and desire to bring and become our best selves, we will all Arise!"

> —*Shanie J. Keelean, deputy superintendent of schools, Rush-Henrietta Central School District*

"*Arise* should be required reading for all coaches and instructional leaders! It addresses the too often overlooked nuisances and soft skills of being an instructional coach head on, in an authentic way. It provides its readers with emotionally intelligent strategies and mindset shifts that are vital if you are serious about becoming a transformational coach."

> —*Deidra Fogarty, Black Girls Teach*

"Elena Aguilar has beautifully and cogently unpacked the 'behind-the-scenes' thinking and skills that will assist any coach who desires to transform education through her coaching conversations. With its use of real-world scenarios and practical coaching language supports, *Arise* will support every reader, no matter her role, in developing her coaching mindset (and skill set). Brava and thank you, Elena, for another wonderful contribution to our field."

> —*Jennifer Abrams, communications consultant; author of several books, including* Having Hard Conversations *and* Stretching Your Learning Edges: Growing (Up) at Work

Arise

Arise

The Art of Transformational Coaching

Elena Aguilar

JB JOSSEY-BASS™

A Wiley Brand

Published by John Wiley & Sons, Inc., Hoboken, New Jersey.
Published simultaneously in Canada.

ISBNs: 9781394160396 (paperback), 9781394160419 (ePDF), 9781394160402 (ePub)

For general information on our other products and services, please contact our Customer Care Department within the United States at (800) 762-2974, outside the United States at (317) 572-3993 or fax (317) 572-4002. For product technical support, you can find answers to frequently asked questions or reach us via live chat at https://support.wiley.com.

Wiley also publishes its books in a variety of electronic formats. Some content that appears in print may not be available in electronic formats. For more information about Wiley products, visit our web site at www.wiley.com.

Library of Congress Cataloging-in-Publication Data:

Names: Aguilar, Elena, 1969–author.
Title: Arise : the art of transformational coaching / Elena Aguilar.
Description: First edition. | San Francisco : Jossey-Bass ; Hoboken, New
   Jersey : John Wiley & Sons, Inc., [2024] | Includes index.
Identifiers: LCCN 2024014073 (print) | LCCN 2024014074 (ebook) | ISBN
   9781394160396 (paperback) | ISBN 9781394160419 (adobe pdf) | ISBN
   9781394160402 (epub)
Subjects: LCSH: Mentoring in education. | Personal coaching. |
   Teachers—In-service training. | Teachers—Professional relationships.
Classification: LCC LB1731.4 .A4225 2024 (print) | LCC LB1731.4 (ebook) |
   DDC 371.102—dc23/eng/20240511
LC record available at https://lccn.loc.gov/2024014073
LC ebook record available at https://lccn.loc.gov/2024014074

Cover Design: Paul McCarthy
Cover Art: © Getty Images | Shunli Zhao
SKY10076554_060624

This book is just the start. I've got so much more to offer you.

On my website, you'll find dozens of free downloadable tools, including all the tools in this book, and much more to help you become a Transformational Coach. There you'll also learn about our virtual and in-person workshops, webinars, and retreats and many other ways that the Bright Morning team and I can support you. Scan the QR to explore how to keep learning with me.

For my parents,
Linda and Gilbert,
whose imperfect love was perfect.

Love is the bridge between you and everything.

—Rumi

CONTENTS

ABOUT THE AUTHOR

Elena Aguilar, one of education's leading voices on coaching and cultivating resilience, is the author of *The Art of Coaching*, *The Art of Coaching Teams*, *Onward: Cultivating Emotional Resilience in Educators*, *The Onward Workbook*, *The Art of Coaching Workbook*, *Coaching for Equity*, *The PD Book*, and *Arise: The Art of Transformational Coaching*. She also hosts the *Bright Morning Podcast* and is the CEO of Bright Morning.

Elena's organization, Bright Morning, brings the ideas in Elena's books to life by providing world-class professional development to educators and mission-driven leaders across the globe. You can learn more about Bright Morning at brightmorningteam.com.

Elena is a sought-after keynote speaker and contributor to major education publications. Her contributions can be found on Edutopia, EdWeek, and in Educational Leadership. Her "Weekly Wisdom" newsletter provides bite-size doses of inspiration, practical strategies, and tools for transformation to tens of thousands of educators.

Elena lives in northern California with her husband and son. She enjoys being in nature, writing fiction, cooking soup, traveling abroad, reading, going to therapy, and exploring what it means to be a human being.

ACKNOWLEDGMENTS

Writing acknowledgments is my favorite part of writing a book. I love reflecting on those who have contributed to who I am and what I do. However, I also always feel woefully unsatisfied—my attempt at expressing gratitude never feels complete. I'm also limited in how much I can write and struggle to keep my acknowledgments concise. I hope you will feel the love behind these words.

I am tremendously grateful to everyone who has read my books, attended a workshop with me, or listened to a podcast episode, and who has shared questions, feedback, and appreciations. Your questions have pushed my thinking and contributed to the development of my work; your appreciations buoy me and help me remember the extensive community that surrounds me.

Liz Simons, my coach at ASCEND way back in 2001, will forever hold a special place in my heart and mind. I might have quit teaching that year had it not been for Liz's curious and compassionate coaching; she made me want to be a coach.

Leslie Plettner, the first Transformational Coach I experienced, still exemplifies who I want to be when I grow up. She lives a life devoted to exploration, self-knowledge, kindness, healing, and justice. I'm also grateful that our coaching relationship became a friendship.

My creativity coach, Elana Bell, guided me to connect with the spirit of this book, and back into coherence over and over. In being her client, I was also reminded of the incredible vulnerability of being coached, and I am grateful for her compassionate and courageous space-holding.

This is the eighth book I've published with Jossey-Bass. Amy Fandrei is a dream editor—she is attentive and responsive, she gives me permission to write anything, and she makes every part of this process as easy as possible. Her team is also a delight to work with, and I couldn't ask for anything more from a publisher.

Caitlin Schwarzman has been my content editor for seven of my books. She's carefully read every word I've written in its messy draft form and provided kind, meaningful, direct feedback that greatly improved the final product. I'm so grateful for her commitment to Transformational Coaching and to me as a writer.

The following people crossed my professional path at crucial moments and provided friendship, guidance, partnership, encouragement, and inspiration: Shannon Carey, Davina Goldwasser, Kristina Tank-Crestetto, Matt Duffy, Lisa Jimenez, Ken Yale, Zaretta Hammond, Shane Safir, Kate Gagnon, Maia Heyck-Merlin, Raiza Lisboa, Chiara Kupiec, Charlotte Larsen, and Rebecca Crook. Thank you, all.

Sarah E. Hughes made the first couple years of teaching so much easier with her lesson-planning companionship and her enthusiasm for music and dance.

I am honored to have witnessed the courageous, heart-centered, transformative leadership of Steve Sexton, Javier Cabra, Alexandrea Creer Kahn, Tina Hernandez, Drea Beale, Kathrina Mendez, Tiffany Cheng-Nyaggah, and many others. I am grateful for the friendships that developed from these encounters, and also grateful for Alexandrea's beautiful testimony in the foreword to this book.

Since 2013, I've been delivering workshops on my books around the world. A group of presenters, who have since moved on to other pursuits, helped me share this work, and they deserve recognition. I am grateful to Lettecia Kratz, Noelle Apostol Colin, Lori Cohen, Jessie Cordova, Janet Baird, and Maria Dyslin for their commitment to Transformational Coaching and to transformative professional development. I am also grateful for the dedication of other former teammates, including Jeanne Carlson, Debbie Raymond, and Maya Haines, who helped me build Bright Morning into what it is today.

Lettecia Kratz deserves additional recognition. She became a coach before I did, and I've learned so much from her about how to listen and hold space for someone. She also read and offered extensive feedback on the manuscript for *The Art of Coaching*, and her friendship has bridged several decades of my life.

I am grateful for Nick Cains, who presents my workshops with tremendous competence and with a huge heart and who contributed invaluably to one part of this book.

Laurelin Whitfield helped me get my work out into the world in a number of ways. She collaborated with me on several projects, including on an old version of the Transformational Coaching Rubric, and *The Art of Coaching Workbook*. She also pushed my thinking about the content of this book into directions I might not have gone. I'm grateful for her friendship and partnership.

My heart and soul overflow with gratitude for the Bright Morning team, which currently consists of Becky Barstein, LesLee Bickford, Nita Creekmore, Jess Levasseur, Jennifer Liu, Cary Meyers, Antoinette Strain, and Nyesha Trusty. We should all be so fortunate to work with people who are this skillful, thoughtful, self-aware, courageous, and committed to individual and collective thriving. I'm often amazed by the fact that I've got these people supporting me, and I feel humbled by their dedication. Also, they are a lot of fun, and I love spending time with them.

An additional appreciation goes to Becky Barstein who provided feedback on drafts of this book that made it a stronger, clearer, and more coherent final product. LesLee Bickford also provided feedback, input, and suggestions that greatly improved this book's message, organization, and potential for impact.

Everyone deserves to have someone like LesLee in their lives. While LesLee is Bright Morning's president, her contributions extend far beyond her job description. No one else understands my mind the way she does or the vision that I hold for this work. LesLee has been my primary professional champion in the last five or so years, skillfully coaching, nudging, and encouraging me to expand in ways I want to expand (or not) and to include my needs in my work. LesLee is the easiest person I've ever collaborated with, as well as someone whose presence I deeply enjoy. This partnership has convinced me that we can create organizations in which everyone (including the leader!) thrives and in which relationships can transcend power dynamics.

Since 1987, my two closest friends, Kathy McKay and Kristen Guzmán, have helped me navigate the 10,000 joys and sorrows of life. When they listen to me with their enormous, open hearts, I heal. When they encourage me onward, I thrive.

I am blessed to have chosen family in Nairobi, Kenya. My *dada*, Carol Owala; my *kaka*, Dennis; my nephews, Jeff, Larry, and Louie; my niece, Nala; and my kids, Sharon, Barlin, Vyette, and Denis—I love you all and can't wait for our dance party.

My deepest gratitude goes to those who have extended a hand to walk me home: Anais, Cynthia, Lisa, Meridel, and Shane. I could not do what I do without your care and guidance. You are the teachers I didn't know I needed and the role models who show me a new way of being and doing and living.

My husband, Stacey Goodman, makes me laugh like no one else, gives me the best hugs, reminds me of what's most important, opens new paths for exploration, and is the truest companion I could ever imagine. He constantly reminds me of what is possible, of my own magnificence and areas for growth, and of the exquisite delights of being a human. The only reason why I started to write about education, back in 2008, was because he encouraged me. The only reason why I became an entrepreneur was because he encouraged me. Regardless of what I say I'm interested in or aspire to do, Stacey believes I can do it and supports me. His partnership is my oxygen.

My son, Orion, is my joy and my heart, and mothering him has been the greatest gift of my life. He also inspires me, teaches me, and keeps me honest. As our relationship becomes one between adults, I'm profoundly grateful to know him. He's become a role model for me in the way he lives his life and in how he aspires to be in the world. Also, I'm grateful for his interest in health and for his research skills: I may not have finished this book had it not been for his recommendation of some supplements.

This book is dedicated to my parents, Linda and Gilbert. Like all humans, my parents were imperfect, and I know that they did the very best they could. They modeled living with curiosity and compassion, they taught me to question authority and challenge power, they encouraged me to pursue my passions, they cultivated my agency, and they loved me tremendously. I hear them in the words I write, I feel them when I speak, and I know that my conviction that all we need is love was seeded by their love for me.

FOREWORD

At a time when teaching shortages remain persistently high, creating and sustaining adult learning spaces that ensure psychological and identity safety is essential. Research finds that the most important factors influencing teacher satisfaction beyond salary are their professional learning conditions (Sutcher, et al, 2016). *Arise: The Art of Transformational Coaching* offers a comprehensive, concrete, and nuanced theory-to-practice guide for coaches and leaders to foster the identity-affirming conditions that allow teachers to stay in the profession, meet the needs of every child, and thrive.

I first encountered Elena's work in 2016 when I became a school network leader overseeing teaching and learning for secondary high schools. Elena's book, *The Art of Coaching*, offered a strengths-based coaching approach for supporting teachers serving our most underestimated students. Over time, I found that the woman behind *The Art of Coaching*, and the courageous and humanistic coaching she embodies, is even more incredible than her published works.

My story with Elena began after I picked up her book and attended one of her Bay Area workshops. There was a buzz among the attendees around this phenomenal woman and this book that had fueled great shifts within the instructional coaching sphere. While an eager learner, I was unsure about what this "PD day" would look like. As an experienced leader of color, I began the day expecting a workshop in which you receive information, leave with some ideas, and have little time to process your learning. Yet the workshop modeled adult "learning by doing" and forced me to examine my biases as a coach. I left feeling renewed, hopeful, and equipped with tools to create compassionate learning conditions for adults.

Through serendipitous events, Elena became a consultant for my organization, and then my leadership coach. During those two years, Elena held space for me to think deeply about problems within my work, challenged me to think creatively and introspectively, and grounded me in my values. This was during a time of incredible personal and professional change. I was a newly married, newly mothering, and newly ascended chief academic officer in an organization with predominantly white leadership. Returning from maternity, I was full of self-doubt. I was uncertain about my ability to do the role, whether people would believe in my leadership, and whether this work was worth time away from my baby.

During the time we worked together, I navigated many professional peaks and valleys. I remember in one tearful coaching session in which I doubted my abilities, Elena calmly said, "And what if all of the things you believe are true? What then?" Her question shocked me out of my train of thought and helped me shift from disempowerment to agency.

What was always steady was Elena's ability to see and value my wholeness, to create a space of unhindered learning, and to believe in my ability to reach my greatest potential—in whatever direction that took me. Elena believed in me when I applied for a superintendency, when I removed myself from the hiring process to prioritize my family, and when I made a major career change. A Transformational Coach creates the space for you to tackle your hardest challenges and create new possibilities—whether outside or inside of you. Working with Elena made me a better coach, a better leader, and a better person.

If you've picked up this book, you may be wondering, will this book answer my burning questions about coaching? How can this book top Elena's other books about coaching? Having read it, I can guarantee that this book will not only answer all your questions about coaching but that, somehow, it does top Elena's other books.

Arise makes visible how we can center the humanity of adults and coach with courage, compassion, and, most importantly, love. Elena flawlessly weaves in her experiences as an educator, mother, and advocate, thus revealing her authenticity, courage, and fallibility. In doing so, Elena continues to pave the way for how we best support adults who teach the next generation of TK-12 students. This book will be another go-to resource that I will use to support my practice and that I will highly recommend to others at all levels of the educational continuum.

Alexandrea Creer Kahn
Senior Director of Academic Programs,
Alder Graduate School of Education
Co-author of *Identity Safe Classrooms, Grades 6-12,*
and *Belonging and Inclusion in Identity Safe Schools:
A Guide for Educational Leaders*

INTRODUCTION

Every human being desires belonging and connectedness, autonomy, mastery and competence, genuine self-esteem, trust in oneself, and purpose and meaning. These are *core human needs*, and just about everything we do is an attempt to meet these needs. When our needs are met, we thrive. When they're not, we don't.

Overwhelmingly, educators are not thriving.

This book will help them thrive. It will also help you thrive.

I know that when you thrive, the teachers you support will be far more likely to thrive, and when those teachers thrive, they will be far more likely to meet the social, emotional, and academic needs of students. And when children's needs are met, there's a greater likelihood that they will thrive.

Transformational Coaching is a values-centered philosophy and methodology for relating to others. Transformational Coaches pull from an expansive set of strategies that create the conditions where core human needs can be met. This book will guide you through the skills, beliefs, and dispositions that will enable you to thrive at work and in life—and to create the conditions in which all those around you thrive as well.

Every Child, Every Day

Transformational Coaching is radical in its scope. This model is teacher- *and* student-centered; it centers our *collective well-being*. Students cannot thrive unless the adults who spend all day with them are also thriving; teachers cannot thrive unless the coaches and administrators who support them are also thriving. The reason that this approach is transformative, and the reason it works, is because it is holistic and inclusive of all the humans in the system. This is a human-centered model.

I know that you're here—working in the field of education—because you want to positively impact young people. I'm sure you believe that all children are born deserving of love and care, that all children deserve to thrive. You might just not know *how* to make this a reality.

All of the work that I do is in service of the conviction that every child deserves to thrive every day in school. *Educational equity* means that every child receives whatever they need to develop their full academic and social potential and to thrive, every day. Every child deserves to thrive *academically as well as socially* and *emotionally* every day. Every child has a right to feel loved and cared for and to feel that they belong to a community. In this definition of educational equity, emotional well-being is as valuable as academic success.

Educational equity means there is no predictability of success or failure that correlates with any social or cultural factor. In other words, a child's educational experience or outcomes is not predictable because of their race, ethnicity, linguistic background, economic class, religion, gender, sexual orientation, physical and cognitive ability, or any other sociopolitical identity marker. Here are some examples of educational equity:

- A Latine child who enters kindergarten speaking only Spanish performs as well on reading assessments in third grade as their native English-speaking counterparts.
- A Black teen is just as likely as their white or Asian classmates to enroll and thrive in an engineering program in high school.

- Girls and nonbinary children are equally represented in advanced math courses—and are equally as successful as their male classmates.
- A Latine male with a learning difference is just as likely to graduate from high school on time as his white counterparts and is prepared to pursue the career or college path of his choice.
- There's proportionality in the demographics of kids "sent to the office": if a district's Black population is 20 percent, then at most 20 percent of office referrals are for Black students.

Beyond the predictability of success and failure, educational equity means that every child is seen for who they truly are, and their unique interests and gifts are surfaced and cultivated. For every child to cultivate their unique gifts, they need access to an extensive range of learning opportunities, activities, and materials. This means that when Prentis Jr. discovers in first grade that his love and skill for drawing surmounts all of his other skills, he has the opportunity and encouragement to pursue this passion. This means that in fourth grade, when Thui's verbal abilities are recognized, her public speaking skills are developed. When done right, education is a vehicle to full expression, self-realization, and liberation.

Educational equity means *every* child, *every* day. Period.

This is a high bar.

And it is attainable. Transformational Coaching is a systematic, holistic, comprehensive method to help us create educational equity.

I've coached hundreds of educators using Transformational Coaching, and I've trained tens of thousands of people in the art of coaching. Over and over, I've witnessed how the strategies I'll share with you transform individuals, teams, and organizations.

I want this for you. I know you ache to feel more effective in your work, that you long to have deeper impact on schools and children.

I know you've got the will to work hard. I suspect you need more skills and knowledge.

This book might be the start of a journey of transformation, or perhaps you're already on this journey and this book will catapult you forward. In some ways, the process will be simple: I'll offer frameworks, sentence stems, and sequential actions to take. In other ways, it might be challenging: I'll ask you to look inward at who you are being, at your deeply held beliefs, and at the shadow parts of yourself—the thoughts, feelings, and beliefs that feel uncomfortable to look at. But don't fear the discomfort; it's a gateway for growth. The inward examination might reveal old wounds that deserve healing, opportunities for empowerment, and areas for expansion.

An Overview of This Book

My first book, *The Art of Coaching*, was published in 2013. As the 10-year anniversary approached and book sales continued to be strong, my publisher encouraged me to write a second edition. But as I began what I thought would be a light revision of the content, I realized that I was writing a whole new book.

In the decade since writing *The Art of Coaching*, I have learned so much about coaching and teaching others how to coach. I've figured out new ways to organize material, concepts, and resources so that they're more accessible and actionable. I've also learned a tremendous amount about how to coach emotions, how to explore beliefs, and how to coach for equity.

While the central principles in this book are the same as those in *The Art of Coaching*, this book is an expanded and refined presentation of the skills, knowledge, dispositions, and values required to implement a transformative approach to educator development. As such, the 2013 *Art of Coaching* and *The Art of Coaching Workbook* (2020) will go out of print as this book makes its way into the world.

The Core Human Needs as the Central Framework

In the last 20 years, the biggest shift in my thinking about coaching, leading teams, and transforming organizations has emerged from the concept of core human needs. My motivation to learn about emotions came from a quest to figure out how to coach seemingly resistant teachers. That exploration led to the understanding that humans have basic social and emotional needs. We are motivated by the desire to meet these core human needs, and we struggle (or experience uncomfortable emotions) when one or more aren't met. This resonated personally, and when I thought about educators who were struggling, I immediately saw that the root cause of the problem was that they weren't getting their needs met.

Psychologists classify core human needs in various ways. Table I.1 captures Dr. Gabor Maté's (2022) categorization.

Table I.1: Core Human Needs

Core Human Need	Description
Belonging	Connectedness, relatedness, interpersonal relationships, being part of a group, friendship, intimacy, trust, acceptance, giving and receiving affection, and love
Autonomy	Having a sense of control in your life, being able to make choices, and having agency
Competence	Self-fulfillment, personal growth, and feeling masterful at something
Self-Esteem	Having a sense of genuine self-worth that's not dependent on achievement, attainment, acquisition, or valuation by others

(Continued)

Table I.1: (Continued)

Core Human Need	Description
Trust	Believing you have the personal and social resources needed to sustain yourself through life (trust in yourself)
Purpose	Knowing yourself as part of something larger—spiritual or as part of nature; living a life of meaning; and experiencing transcendence

Pause and consider which of your needs feel like they're being met in your life right now, and perhaps which feel unmet.

So much of the suffering that people experience—both at school and at home—stems from unmet core human needs. In contrast, the definition of thriving is that our needs are met. If we were to coach with no other goal but to empower people to get their core human needs met, our schools would be different places. I'm willing to bet that we'd see less burnout and turnover, and more kindness, joy, and learning.

Transformational Coaching has always centered these needs—but now, since learning more about core needs, I have the framework to pull many ideas together. As you read, you'll recognize the centrality of this concept and the simple way it can help us transform organizations. On my website, you'll find a graphic representation of this framework that you can print and post somewhere to help you remember. In Chapter 8 you'll learn how to coach using the core human needs.

What Is and Isn't in This Book

This book is organized around how to coach the Three Bs—behaviors, beliefs, and ways of being. This concept is a central and defining framework of Transformational Coaching. We'll begin digging into the concept of the Three Bs in the next chapter by exploring the set of beliefs and ways of being that can empower you to be a Transformational Coach. Then we'll dive into Transformational Coaching behaviors that enable you to guide someone to explore and shift their behaviors, beliefs, and ways of being.

In this book, among many other things, you'll get direction on:

- How to have meaningful coaching conversations that result in a change of practice
- How to manage your triggers and frustration
- How to listen deeply and expansively
- How to coach teachers you perceive as being resistant
- How to guide someone to examine and deconstruct their beliefs
- How to support someone in the midst of an emotional crisis
- How to reinvigorate a disengaged educator
- How to build relationships that are meaningful and satisfying to you and your client
- How to cultivate leadership capacity
- How to do a classroom observation
- How to discuss student data
- How to be who you want to be as a coach

There's so much more to share than what can fit in the book you're holding—which is why I've built an organization around teaching Transformational Coaching and why I create supplemental content that I share in podcast episodes, newsletters, workshops, and my learning library. You can access all of these resources via my website.

In this book, you won't find an exhaustive explanation of the technical elements of coaching, such as how to structure coaching cycles, how long to meet for, how to take notes, or how to manage the relationship with the client's supervisor. Those elements are important for a coach, and you'll find resources to support you in acquiring those skills and knowledge on my website.

There's also a lot to consider around the coaching program. Coaches don't work in isolation—they are embedded within a system. Many of the challenges that coaches experience in schools are the result of less than optimal systems. When coaches describe dilemmas they're grappling with, I often ask, "What's the definition of coaching in your school or district? What are the coaching program's goals and values?" And I'm met with a blank stare. More often than not, there is no definition, or goals or values. There's no systematized, intentional coaching *program*. On my website, you can find more information about how to create a coaching program and how to align systems.

In Appendix A, you'll find a Transformational Coaching Mini-Rubric. A rubric guides you toward mastering a complex set of skills. In this book, I've chosen to include a short version of my Transformational Coaching Rubric. This mini version is a distillation of the complex art of Transformational Coaching and includes the essential competencies. The longer version, available on my website, is triple the length and contains all of the competencies and indicators required for enacting Transformational Coaching with fidelity.

This rubric is not designed as a tool for evaluation. Rather, it is meant as a guide for development—to point you toward the highest-leverage coaching skills and to the critical beliefs, ways of being, and behaviors of a Transformational Coach. You could use this for your own growth or as a resource to structure professional development for coaches.

Here are some ways you might use the Transformational Coaching Mini-Rubric, or the full version:

- **As a tool for personal reflection:** Note which competencies come easily to you and which you struggle with. Set intentions and goals based on indicators.
- **As a tool for practice:** Role-play with a colleague and focus on demonstrating certain indicators. An observer could also provide feedback on the indicators you identify as focal skills.
- **As an organizing structure for professional development (PD) sessions:** Specific PD sessions could focus on a single domain, competency, or set of indicators.

A Springboard for Learning

Some years ago, I worked with a nonprofit organization in which all the coaches who participated in the training I provided read *The Art of Coaching* and attended a two-day workshop. After that, they proclaimed themselves to be Transformational Coaches. But in the schools and offices where they attempted to use the strategies, they didn't see the outcomes they'd hoped for. When I observed them coaching, and debriefed with them, we agreed that they struggled to use the skills, anchor in the beliefs, and embody the dispositions. The coaches and their leaders were frustrated. I realized the problem was in their expectations—they assumed that reading a book and attending 14 hours of PD would be sufficient. I realized I hadn't made the learning journey clear.

I want to manage your expectations. I am sure that you will learn a whole lot from reading this book, and I hope it will be a springboard for learning. And if you want to thrive as a Transformational Coach, you need to be prepared to engage in a lot of practice and refining of your skills. After many years of writing and teaching about coaching, I've observed that the most powerful learning happens in community—both at in-person events and at live-virtual events. This is in part because humans are social creatures, and we need each other to make sense of the world and be encouraged and motivated. An in-person or live-virtual PD can be transformative and catalytic. I've also learned that people need short, asynchronous learning experiences so that they can pace themselves, rewind when necessary, and honor their unique learning needs. This is what you'll find on my website in my learning library.

The Intended Audience

Anyone can use Transformational Coaching strategies. Regardless of your title or role, you can use these strategies to cultivate reflection, growth, and resilience in others. You can be a principal, superintendent, director of human resources, teacher, and, of course, a coach. You can work within the education system or in an unrelated field. You can also use these strategies with your students, children, partners, friends, family members, and so on. When I say "a Transformational Coach . . . ," know that I'm talking about you whenever you choose to use Transformational Coaching strategies, regardless of your title.

This book will be essential for new and novice coaches who sense the potential of coaching and are overwhelmed by the magnitude of skills to acquire. But it'll also be invaluable for those who have coached for years and who have thought, *I know that coaching could have a greater impact, but I don't know how to make that happen.* Seasoned coaches will find a wealth of opportunities for growth and expansion in this book.

I have worked with countless leaders and school administrators who consider developing the adults they support to be a central part of their role—but they don't know how to do this, especially how to navigate the tricky power dynamics that arise when you supervise or manage someone and you want to help them grow. I'll address that dynamic and guide you through it in this book.

This book supports educators in any context. Transformational Coaching is content neutral—you can use these strategies whether you are a new teacher coach, an English Language Development coach, an early literacy coach, a secondary math coach, an arts integration coach, an equity coach, or something else. At their core, *coaching strategies are communication strategies*, which means not only can you use them across context and content, but you can also use them with your partner, children, friends, family, neighbors, and so on. One of the most meaningful compliments I've received about *The Art of Coaching* was from my father. Decades after his second divorce, in his mid-70s, he fell in love with Olga, a retired school teacher. Around that time, *The Art of Coaching* came out. My father read it and began using the listening and questioning strategies with Olga. With gratitude, and sadness, he said, "If I'd only known the things you write about when I was married to your mom, my life would have been different." Coaching strategies help us connect with others.

How to Make the Most of This Book

Although the ideas in this book are sequenced and build on each other, you don't have to read the chapters of this book in order. First, preview the table of contents, and if there's a chapter or a section that grabs your attention, go read it. Of course, all the ideas in this book are critical to the successful implementation of Transformational Coaching, but allow yourself to be pulled into sections as they feel most relevant.

Second, find learning partners. I hope that you have colleagues with whom you can discuss this book and share how you're applying the ideas. I also hope you have colleagues with whom you can practice the skills. We can't read our way into new behaviors—we have to *do* new behaviors in order to internalize them. When we don't practice the behaviors we want to acquire, we often end up with what's called a *knowing-doing gap*. We might *know* something, but we can't *do* it. Learning in community supports meaning-making and application.

Third, listen to the *Bright Morning Podcast*. On the podcast, you'll hear examples of real coaching conversations, short episodes that provide deeper explorations of many of the concepts in this book, and a whole lot more, such as a series called *What to Say When You Hear Something Racist*.

On Language, Anonymity, and Anecdotes

A few notes:

- I mostly use the term *client* to refer to the person we coach. Although that may sound corporate or clinical, I don't like the alternative, *coachee*, which I think sounds like a diminutive of a coach.
- I use the traditional pronouns *he* and *she*, and in recognition of nonbinary gender identification, I also use *they*.
- I use *Latine* as a gender-neutral alternative to Latino or Latina.
- To protect the identities of people I've coached, I've changed all names and identifiers.

- Some of the stories in this book are almost exact transcripts of coaching conversations edited only for brevity and readability. Other stories are composite conversations—necessary to preserve anonymity or to provide useful examples.

From London to Oakland to Nairobi

I was born in 1969, in the East End of London, to parents who did not want to be living in the United Kingdom but, for complicated reasons, had no other choice. My father is Costa Rican. With the exception of a brief stint in Europe, he has always lived in Costa Rica. My mother was Ashkenazi Jewish, born in San Francisco and raised in East L.A.

Spanish was my first language. After entering school in London and learning that none of my peers spoke it, I refused to speak Spanish. When I was six, my parents divorced, and my mother became a single parent. Prior to their separation, money had always been tight, but when my father returned to Costa Rica, our financial situation became really difficult. When I was 10, my mother, brother, and I moved to a white, wealthy, conservative community in Southern California. Although we felt alienated there because of our economic status, we had a free place to live. In school, my teachers made assumptions about my skills and ability based on my non-Anglo name, my non-white phenotype, and the obvious indicators of my lower-class status; they slotted me into the low tracks and generally ignored me.

My younger brother had physical and emotional special needs. He was brutally bullied, his teachers disliked him, and he was shuffled into Special Education classes. On the day he turned 16, he dropped out of school. The circumstances of my birth, my early childhood, my experiences in public schools, and my brother's experiences shaped the educator, coach, and leader I've become. I see the world through the frame of race, class, and other socially constructed identity experiences, and with an eye on privilege and access.

Our sociopolitical identities shape how we see the world and how we respond to it. I identify as Latina and Jewish and with being an immigrant—culturally, I've often felt like I don't belong in the United States. I'm also a cisgendered, heterosexual, able-bodied, neurotypical, college-educated woman. At the time of writing, I've been married for 25 years. My husband is an artist, an educator, and a Black man from the South. Finally, I'm the mother of a Black son, which has afforded me an experience that has profoundly influenced my work in schools. When I go into classrooms, my attention is drawn to the quiet and ignored girls (who remind me of myself), to the boys who are seen as a problem (who remind me of my brother), and to any student who has identity markers that are currently marginalized in our world, be these based on race or ethnicity, gender or sexuality, ability/disability, or anything else. I have experienced and witnessed so much marginalization that equity is ingrained into the way I see, hear, and think.

My foray into education began in 1994, when I taught high school English Language Development in Salinas, California. I loved working in a rural community of migrant farm workers, but a year later, I moved north to Oakland to teach second grade at a bilingual English/Spanish school in the Oakland Unified School District (OUSD). In 2001, I helped start a small, autonomous K-8 school in OUSD, and I taught middle-school humanities. As our school grew and hired staff, we needed someone to guide new teachers in our unique instructional approaches. I was nominated to be this coach and began my journey into the field of adult learning.

As a teacher, I was fortunate to have had a fantastic coach. By the time I met Liz Simons, I'd been teaching for seven years, but she saw my full potential as a teacher and helped me navigate challenges I faced in the classroom. I felt like I could confess all the things I was feeling that I wasn't supposed to feel (*I really dislike that kid* or *I don't think I'm going to make it through this year*), and she pushed me in the way I wanted to be pushed so that I'd grow. When challenges arose as I began coaching, I often asked myself, *what would Liz do?*

After being in a hybrid coaching and teaching role for a few years, I decided to take a full-time instructional coaching position at another

Oakland public middle school. This school was different. I felt unprepared to support teachers when they cried and cried and cried or pushed back on my nudges or shut down and smiled disingenuously and told me that "everything is fine" or refused to meet with me or told me they didn't need me or asked me what I did all day or said that I couldn't help them because I'd never taught eighth-grade math. It wasn't only coaching that I was unprepared for—I also had to lead teams and facilitate PD, and I felt equally ineffective in those realms.

The greatest challenges I faced, however, came from not being prepared to respond to my own feelings—to the anger that surged, to my sense of inadequacy and powerlessness, or to the grief that I felt when I witnessed children suffering. I doubted my decision to leave the classroom where I'd felt effective, appreciated, and impactful. I wondered if I'd made a huge mistake in going into coaching.

The overwhelming majority of coaches that I've met have been catapulted, as I was, into coaching with little training in facilitating adult learning. But despite the difficulty of the work, many find it compelling. As I did. Even though I struggled as a coach, something kept drawing me in. As a coach, I could indirectly influence hundreds of students. Furthermore, in those first years, I *did* coach a handful of teachers who were receptive and who grew with my support. I quickly hit the limits of my abilities when they became overwhelmed by their emotions, when the practices they implemented weren't sustained, or when issues around race and equity came up. But I was engrossed by the puzzle of coaching adults.

As an instructional coach, I saw how our district's administrators desperately needed their own coaching and high-quality professional development—I saw how so many of the things that teachers struggled with had roots in ineffective or nonexistent systems and structures in the school or with a struggling organizational culture. Although I didn't have experience as a site administrator, I had learned a lot about how to guide adults in reflection and growth, and I became a leadership coach in the district. I loved this role—it gave me deeper insight into systems, organizational culture, and leadership development and an opportunity to create and refine those necessary elements. I felt honored to coach principals and district leaders.

Like so many large school districts, OUSD was and is a place of constant change, and it seemed like every other year, there was a massive "reorg" in which departments and roles were eliminated and I had to reapply for a position. After the leadership coaching department was dissolved, I found myself in the now-defunct Office of School Transformation. Working with a massive federal grant, our office served some of the most struggling middle and high schools in the district. In this department, I proposed that I lead a team of instructional and leadership coaches who would offer coaching and PD. My pitch was accepted, and the following years were a highlight of my tenure in OUSD. I hired 10 coaches, trained them in the model of coaching I'd developed, and implemented many of the strategies I describe in my books. Our team saw significant impact on the schools we supported, and my leadership skills expanded.

I wrote *The Art of Coaching* as my personal PD project during this period. Coaching has always felt so intuitive for me, and I wanted to identify the strategies I was using and make them accessible to other coaches. I wrote every Sunday for a year and enjoyed the process of writing. I had no plans to leave OUSD—I loved my work, my colleagues, and the Oakland community that I'd been part of for 15 years. I imagined I'd retire from OUSD after a few more decades of service. But when *The Art of Coaching* came out in 2013, my email inbox started filling with inquiries: They all said something along the lines of, "Do you provide trainings on coaching?"

The following six years were a whirlwind of airplanes and presenting and speaking and eating my homemade kale-lentil dinners in hotels and also writing—*The Art of Coaching Teams* (2016), *Onward: Cultivating Emotional Resilience in Educators* (2018), *The Onward Workbook* (2018), *Coaching for Equity* (2020), and *The Art of Coaching Workbook* (2020).

During this period, in 2017, in response to the demand for my trainings, I founded Bright Morning. My team and I traveled around the United States and abroad, presenting workshops to thousands of educators every month. One of the most meaningful professional experiences I had was an opportunity to collaborate with Kenyan educators and work in Nairobi with marginalized communities. My dreams of impacting children were realized when I observed Kenyan coaches utilizing strategies from *The Art of Coaching*. I was humbled by the conditions in which they worked, inspired by their passion and commitment, and amazed that the strategies I taught in the United States were so relevant and applicable in East Africa. I came to see how the core beliefs of Transformational Coaching and the Transformational Coach's way of being were transferable—that a commitment to compassion is universal, as is a longing to create a more just, equitable world.

And then COVID hit.

The pandemic was profoundly destabilizing and horrifying for so many reasons, and it changed all of our lives in some way. Bright Morning pivoted to being an online service provider. Our outreach expanded, and we have been able to train educators across the United States and in more than 40 countries. My work has also found an audience outside of education—coaches have passed on my books to social workers, political activists, and astronauts. Former educators who moved into the corporate world have shared my resources and brought me in to present these strategies.

The pandemic also compelled us to start the *Bright Morning Podcast* as another vehicle through which to connect to our expanding community and to offer content on coaching. In 2022, *The PD Book* was published, and that same year, *Onward* was translated into Korean, reflecting a growing global interest in educator resilience. As of late 2023, my previous books have sold more than half a million copies, and the podcast has been downloaded more than one million times.

On the personal front, since *The Art of Coaching* came out, I also became a certified meditation teacher, my son entered college, and I've embarked on a personal quest to heal from childhood trauma and chronic stress. As I've dug into my own stuff, I've become a far more effective coach and leader. As I've cultivated self-awareness; unpacked my social, emotional, and identity experiences; deepened my compassion and curiosity; and amassed a robust set of communication skills; my relationships with friends, family, and loved ones have improved. My life has become more meaningful, satisfying, and fulfilling—in great part due to the process of becoming a Transformational Coach.

It's said that we teach what we need to learn. I teach how to thrive, how to listen, how to connect, and how to build community, because that's what I aspire to do well. Know that I speak to you as someone who is also on a learning journey—who is alongside you. I've learned a bit about how to live a life where I'm meeting my core human needs and contributing to every child thriving every day, and I'm still learning. I'm grateful for your company.

The Bridge to Everything

While I've changed a lot since *The Art of Coaching* was published in 2013, the world has also changed. Ongoing political, humanitarian, social justice, environmental, and health crises have countless implications for schools, teachers, and young people. The cumulative effects of stress and exhaustion mean that each year has been harder than the previous year, and, unfortunately, as a whole educational institutions and organizations haven't responded effectively.

I see tremendous opportunities these days—opportunities to do school, learning, leading, and being differently. In recent years, in response to the multiple crises that we face in the United States and around the world, there's been an upsurge in social justice movements including #metoo, Black Lives Matter, the movement for trans rights and the embracing of gender diversity, the increased attention to Native rights and the Land Back movement. This time period is scary, but there's also a deep desire for healthy connection among people, for figuring out how we get to the root of the dysfunction in our schools and society, and for understanding ourselves and how we can change. Yes, there's been a backlash—attacks on critical race theory, book banning, anti-LGBTQIA+ legislation, and more—but this backlash confirms that the status quo really is being challenged, as it needs to be.

Many educators are asking about how we can fight the backlash, how we can step into opportunity in our schools, and how we can stay the course toward justice for every child, while remaining curious and compassionate. This book offers responses to these questions and presents a cohesive approach to facilitate educator growth and create equitable schools.

And it offers much more.

My aspirations for *Arise* are vast. I hope it will activate your optimism and agency. I hope that you will learn more about how to meet your core human needs, how to connect deeply with others, and how to live into your values. And at the risk of seeming too corny before you know me, I'll reveal my deepest desire: that this book will be a call to love—to love yourself, to love others, to explore love, to know love, to be love. I hope that as you read this book, you'll sense the undercurrent of love in all of my work. I hope you'll allow yourself to be carried by it.

The epigraph for this book is by the 13th century Persian poet, Jalal ad-Din Muhammad Rumi, who wrote, "Love is the bridge between you and everything." I hope you'll step onto this bridge or continue traveling it—it might be the only way for us to close the gap between where we are now and where so many of us want to be.

Pause and Process

Reflect:

- As you read this introduction, when did you feel a sense of connection to the ideas?
- Which of your core human needs are you able to meet right now, at work? Belonging? Autonomy? Competence? Self-esteem? Trust? Purpose?
- What do you hope to learn from reading this book?

Next steps:

- Download and print the Core Human Needs framework from my website. Post this on your office wall, tape it into your coaching notebook, or put it on your computer desktop so that you can reference it regularly.

- Listen to *Bright Morning Podcast* episode 197 on the core human needs.
- If you're reading this with colleagues, download "The *Arise* Book Study Guide" from my website.
- Listen to the Spotify playlist that I made for this book. You can find it at https://bit.ly/ariseplaylist.
- Sign up on my website for my weekly newsletter to get invitations to free webinars, notifications about upcoming workshops and retreats, and weekly tips on coaching and leading.

CHAPTER 1

Transformational Coaching

Why No One Can Learn from You If You Think They Suck

Common misconception: Coaching is telling people what to do.	*Transformational Coaches know:* Coaching requires exploring behaviors, beliefs, and ways of being.

In my first years as a coach, I didn't realize that my beliefs were limiting what was possible. These beliefs ran rampant and without my awareness until my coach, Leslie Plettner, instigated the biggest wake-up call of my professional life when she said, "No one can learn from you if you think they suck."

In a flash of painful awakening, I realized that *I had indeed* thought that some of the teachers and administrators I coached sucked. I thought they were incompetent and even committed to oppressing children. The belief had been running unconsciously through all my work as a coach. As this awareness crystallized, I felt ashamed. Why would *anyone* want to work with a coach who thought that they were incompetent? No wonder they didn't want to meet with me! No wonder they were defensive and resistant.

Reflecting on Leslie's observation, I had a hard conversation with myself: "Either you quit this job right now—*today*—or you shift these beliefs. They're not serving you, they're not helping kids, and you're contributing to anger and pain in the world." I realized that the beliefs I'd been holding about the teachers I worked with did not align with my core values—I was living out of integrity with what mattered most to me. If I were to have this hard conversation with myself now, I might be kinder to myself, but I'd be at least as clear about the importance of attending to my own beliefs and ways of being in order to coach others.

The belief that my clients sucked was tangled up with a whole bunch of feelings that I hadn't explored. These included fear that I wouldn't be effective as a coach, fear of other people's fear and anger and sadness, and grief and rage about what I'd experienced as a child in school. To truly shift the belief that my clients sucked, I needed to process and release feelings.

In the months and years after Leslie's stinging wake-up call, I processed my cynicism and sadness. I interrogated my belief system, and I realigned with who I truly wanted to be. I also committed to learning about how to coach effectively and began a deep study of communication, behavior change, and emotional intelligence. As my skill set expanded, I saw my clients' skills increase and their beliefs shift. This, in turn, helped me settle into the new beliefs I was adopting—that my clients wanted to change, that they were capable of growth, and that there was something good and worthy in every one of them.

The shifts I made during and after my coaching with Leslie contributed to the development of the Transformational Coaching that I now use. The following vignette provides a snapshot of what this approach looks and sounds like, and of the contrast to traditional coaching approaches.

A Transformational Coaching Conversation

About 10 years after I started coaching, I sat in a molded plastic chair at a student desk across from Carmen, a new third-grade teacher. It was the end of a hot day in mid-September, and Carmen looked tired. "How are you?" I asked.

Carmen unwrapped a granola bar as she thought about my question. "I don't know how I am," she sighed. "I am so exhausted. I have no idea how teachers do this year after year. I just want to go home and get in bed and sleep for a month."

Okay, I thought. *It's going to be* this *kind of conversation.* Even though 18 years had passed since I'd been in Carmen's shoes, I remembered the feelings she described, and my empathy shot up. I'd also been coaching long enough to have had countless coaching conversations with exhausted first-year teachers, and I knew which strategies worked to help them process the emotions and feel more empowered to address their situation. I took a slow, deep breath and noticed how my body relaxed; I rested my hands in my lap and looked at Carmen.

"Tell me more," I said.

"I don't know how I'll ever get enough sleep. I have piles of grading to do, and the principal asked me to stop by his office today. I have calls to make to parents, and if I don't clean up the science experiment we did last week, my classroom will become a health hazard. Do you mind if I clean up as we talk? I can multitask. I mean, how am I supposed to do all of this? I still have to finish my plans for tomorrow—can we work on those together? I need to cut out 100 triangles from construction paper."

"Oh, Carmen." I exhaled audibly. "I'm glad we're meeting."

"I thought about canceling our session," Carmen said, "but I don't think I have a choice about meeting with you if I want to clear my credential, so here I am."

"I'm glad you're here," I said. "What would be most useful for us to talk about?"

Carmen's expression looked a little frustrated. "You tell me what we should talk about," she said. "I don't know. I'm overwhelmed, I feel like I'm doing everything poorly, and like I said, I have so much more to do this evening. And then, when I do get in bed, I can't sleep. I can't even remember why I wanted to be a teacher. I'd appreciate it if you would just tell me what to do. I can't think clearly."

"Okay, I hear that you're open to help. Can I make a suggestion?" Carmen nodded. "Let's stand up for a moment." We stood. "Now reach your arms out and open your chest and take five deep breaths." Carmen looked dubious, but she followed my lead. Two minutes later we sat down. "How do you feel?" I asked.

"A little tiny bit better," she said. "But I realized how achy my body feels. I haven't been to the gym in months. I used to go almost every day. Exercise really helps with my anxiety, and I miss it."

"It's good that you recognize that ache and you feel a tiny bit better," I said. "Carmen, I am wondering if you've ever felt this overwhelmed in your life. Was there a time in college, in high school, or another time in your life when you felt anything like what you're feeling now?"

Carmen thought for a long moment. "I had some rough semesters in college. There was one year when my dad was sick and I had to go home a lot to take care of him. That was hard."

"Do you see any more similarities between that time and this one? Either in terms of what was hard or how you coped?"

"Caring for someone you love who is sick is horrible," Carmen said, her voice cracking a little. "I couldn't sleep then either. I don't know how I coped—I just got through it. I did what I had to do every day, and my dad got better. My grades weren't the best that year, but I passed all my classes."

I nodded and took in what Carmen shared. After about 15 seconds, I asked, "What did you learn about yourself from that experience?"

Carmen thought, and I noticed her hands relaxing a bit. "I guess that I'm stronger than I think I am. I remember crying a lot that year and saying to myself, *I don't think I can do this.*"

"Hmm," I said, pausing to allow a little more silence. "What else?"

"I learned that I didn't need to get As in every class. I'd always been a really good student, so getting Bs and Cs was hard—but it wasn't the end of the world."

I nodded again, holding a few seconds of silence. "What else?" I asked. "What else did you learn about how you cope with hard situations?"

"I had to just put one foot in front of the next and do what had to be done." Carmen sighed audibly.

"When you recall that year and how you got through it," I said, leaning forward a little, "do you see any lessons that you can apply to this hard time? To help you get through this time?"

"I guess the reminder that I don't need to always be perfect. The reminder that I do persevere during hard times. The reminder that hard times pass." Carmen paused. "But that was different—I was only responsible for me and my dad then. Now I'm responsible for 30 people. And they're children!"

"Ah," I said, "that must feel like a tremendous responsibility."

"It is! I know what the implications are for my kids if they don't learn to read well this year. I know how that will affect them going forward. It'll shape the rest of their lives!"

"Oh, Carmen. That must feel overwhelming," I said.

"It *is* overwhelming, and it's also terrifying," The pitch of Carmen's voice had risen. "I didn't become a teacher so that I could fail kids. But that is what I'm doing."

I intentionally shifted my tone to one that was slightly more authoritative than empathetic as I responded: "I'm hearing two things right now, Carmen. First, I hear that *you do* remember why you became a teacher, you know why you made this choice; and second, I hear that the hardest thing about this moment right now is that you feel like you're failing children and like you're not being who you want to be—an effective teacher."

Carmen nodded as her eyes welled with tears. "It's just so hard," she said. "Is it always going to be this hard?"

"What do you think? Given how you've experienced challenges before, given what you know about teachers and teaching, do you think it'll always be this hard?"

"No, I guess not," Carmen said.

"Say more about that," I responded.

"I mean, if it was always this hard, there wouldn't be any teachers. So it must get easier. And yes, I know I've dealt with challenges before."

"What else?" I said.

"I guess I need to lower my expectations for myself," Carmen said as she looked down at her hands and rubbed them together. "But I believe in high expectations! If I lower my expectations for myself, it's like I'm saying it's okay if my kids don't learn to read."

I smiled very slightly. "Are those the only two options?" I said. "Either you keep super high expectations for yourself *or* you lower them and your kids don't learn to read?"

Carmen shook her head. "I hear what you're saying. Maybe it's not all or nothing."

"What else?" I asked.

"I guess I could tell myself that this year it's okay if I get a B as a teacher. I don't need to get an A my first year."

I nodded slightly. "I'm also hearing—correct me if I'm wrong—that it's really important to you that your kids learn to read this year. Is that right?"

"Yes, it is. Of course," Carmen said.

"So, let's see if we can figure this out together," I said. "This year, you want to be a 'B teacher,' meaning a good teacher, right? Maybe not an exemplary teacher, which I think is realistic given it's your first year and it's inevitable that you'll make some mistakes. But you want to be a really good teacher." Carmen nodded. "And you want your kids to learn to read, right?" Carmen nodded again. "And I'm going to assume you'll measure their reading skills with a set of assessments, and you'll measure their growth, and that'll be a key indicator of their success and yours too. Right?" Again, Carmen nodded, now more energetically. "So teaching reading is your top priority."

"Well, I guess so," she said, "but what about math? They also need to learn math. And I want them to learn science. And I also want them to have art because we can't take that out of the curriculum—that does them a disservice."

"Prioritizing something doesn't mean you cut other things out," I said.

Carmen nodded. "Okay," she said. "I'm just so anxious."

"I hear that," I said. "And we'll continue to explore your fears because they deserve attention—I think if we explore them, you'll sleep better. We'll also focus on how to teach reading really well. Okay? How does that sound?"

"I guess that sounds good," Carmen said. "I didn't expect you to talk to me about anxiety. Do you think I'm overly anxious?"

"You're experiencing a great deal of the emotions that first-year teachers experience," I said. "What you're feeling is completely normal. I encourage you to talk to some of your colleagues here about their first year. Ask them about how they got through their first year."

"I've wanted to do that," Carmen said, "but I'm afraid of hearing horror stories."

"Ask them what helped, what they learned about themselves, and what they'd do differently if they could go back and do it over," I said. I paused for a few seconds and then continued. "Carmen, what have you learned about yourself in our conversation today?"

"I guess I remembered that I'm stronger than I think I am. I don't like to think about that year in college because it was so hard. But remembering it made me realize that I have been through hard times."

"What else?"

"I know why I became a teacher. I do want to be here. I want to teach." Carmen's voice had a full range of tones.

"What else?" I asked, again.

"I love my kids. I'm afraid of letting them down." Her voice cracked a little.

"What else?" I said.

"I need to go to the gym tomorrow," Carmen said enthusiastically. "I want to go."

"Okay," I said, my tone of voice shifting again into a more authoritative tone. "In the time we have left, what do you feel would be most useful to talk about?"

"I'm overwhelmed with grading," Carmen said. "Can we talk about that?"
"Of course," I said.

How did you feel while reading this conversation? How do you think you would have felt if you were the teacher? If you were the coach? How was this conversation similar to and different from coaching conversations that you've been a part of as coach or client?

The portion of the conversation that you just read took about 12 minutes. In the subsequent 40 minutes, we explored the reading assessments Carmen was giving her students, the systems she had established for documenting student learning, and how she spent her prep time. In this conversation, I recognized a number of *knowledge* and *skill gaps*. You'll learn more about identifying gaps in Chapter 14, "How to Coach Behaviors," but basically, I learned that there was knowledge about assessments that Carmen didn't have, and that she needed to develop skills around grading—which was normal, given that she was a first-year teacher. We ended the session by making a few agreements about what Carmen would do next, and I promised to text her the next day and ask if she'd made it to the gym.

Here's what is most important to know about the conversation you just read: I was using *Transformational Coaching* strategies *to create the conditions* in which Carmen could solve some of her own problems and get some of her needs met. I did that in the following ways:

- I regulated my nervous system and brought awareness to my emotional state. This prevented me from becoming distressed by Carmen's distress, allowed me to feel calm, and relieved the pressure I can sometimes feel to solve other people's problems. Feeling calm allowed me to remember to trust the process. As a result, I felt fully present with Carmen.

- I used stems such as "Tell me more," "What else?" and "What would be most useful for us to talk about?" These phrases help a coachee reconnect with their agency and remind them that they have the capacity to respond to whatever is going on. Such phrases carry the message that the coach does not hold the answers and that the coach is not there to fix the client.
- I used my body language, pitch, pace, and tone of voice to communicate empathy, connect, validate, and indicate shifts in the conversation. I paused frequently to cue Carmen to slow her speech and process her thoughts and feelings.
- In asking Carmen about previous experiences, I helped her remember that she had been through hard times and that she had the capacity to deal with a tough situation. I helped Carmen reconnect with her resilience.
- I reminded Carmen of her vision for herself as a teacher—of who she wants to be. I helped her anchor in that vision and refine it.
- I acknowledged and normalized the emotions that Carmen expressed. I didn't try to fix them; I didn't try to push her through them.
- I guided Carmen to identify learnings. Doing so reminded her, again, of her ability to make sense of the challenges she was facing.
- I helped Carmen determine next steps.

Before I further define the Transformational Coaching approach, I want to be sure we're on the same page by defining the concept of coaching and offering a few key points about how it works.

Coaching Is Professional Development

There's generally an agreement that educators need more knowledge, skills, practice, and support after they enter the profession. Malcolm Gladwell, the author of *Outliers: The Story of Success* (2008), calculates that it takes 10,000 hours of deliberate practice—*practice that promotes continuous improvement*—to master a complex skill. Ten thousand hours translates into about seven years for those working in schools. Teachers want this professional growth. They want to be more effective, implement new skills, and see students be successful.

In many schools, professional development (PD) takes the form of a three-day training, say in August before school starts, and then perhaps a couple of follow-up sessions throughout the year. This kind of PD by itself, which just about every teacher has experienced, rarely results either in significant change in teacher practice or in increased learning for children. According to a 2009 study on professional development, teachers need close to 50 hours of PD in a given area to improve their skills and their students' learning (Darling-Hammond and others, 2009). This is why we need coaching.

It's essential to realize that coaching is professional development; in fact, coaching is a particularly effective form of professional development. As either a stand-alone structure or a component of a comprehensive professional development plan, coaching helps people grow because it is *job-embedded* and *ongoing*—two requirements for sustained learning. Furthermore, because it's individualized, it's inherently *differentiated*.

Unfortunately, I've visited countless schools and districts where coaches have been plunked into classrooms with little training and less vision. In these settings, professional growth is haphazard at best, and everyone involved becomes frustrated. Ideally, every school or organization would have a clear, shared definition of coaching—one that every teacher, administrator, and coach is aware of and has bought into. Not having one is at the root of all kinds of breakdowns in understanding and at the root of many people's frustration with coaching. There's a whole lot to say about how to develop an effective coaching program, and you can find resources to do so on my website.

Coaching Isn't the Same as Mentoring

Coaching and mentoring are different things, although the terms are sometimes used interchangeably. A mentor is an insider or an expert in a field who supports a novice. A mentor shows a novice the ropes, shares tricks of the trade, or helps the newcomer get through a career transition. A mentor helps someone develop by closing gaps in their knowledge and making them feel like they're not alone.

While a coach helps someone develop professionally, coaching is more formal and structured than mentoring. Coaching is also anchored in goals (client's goals, school's goals, and/or student goals). Formal agreements around meetings, confidentiality, and processes are established at the start of the coaching relationship. A coach will usually have (and should have) a more robust skill set than a mentor. Teachers can benefit from having both a coach and a mentor—they complement each other.

The Core Principles of Transformational Coaching

For as long as I can remember, I felt like my reason for being alive was to contribute to healing and transforming the world. But for years, I grappled with *how*. After 20 years as a coach, I've come to see Transformational Coaching as the vehicle through which I can have the greatest impact on the education system—and thus, the world. My hope is that Transformational Coaching can offer you this entry point as well.

Transformational Coaching is a methodology for organizational change that I created and that I've practiced, written about, and taught for two decades. In conceiving this way of coaching, I've drawn from traditional instructional coaching, life coaching, ontological coaching, mindfulness and meditation, neuroscience and psychology, and systems thinking, as well as from my own experiences as a teacher, coach, and leader. So what is Transformational Coaching? I'll begin at the highest level—with core principles.

Transformational Coaching is centered around two core principles: a conviction that we all deserve to thrive and an understanding that our purpose (as coaches who work in schools) is to meet the needs of every child, every day.

We All Deserve to Thrive

The children in the schools we support deserve to thrive. Their parents deserve to thrive. Custodians deserve to thrive. Superintendents deserve to thrive. You deserve to thrive. I deserve to thrive. It is our birthright to thrive.

We thrive when we feel challenged and competent at doing something. We thrive when we feel a sense of belonging and our skills and gifts are appreciated by others. We thrive when we trust ourselves, when we feel genuine self-esteem, and when we feel like we're being our best selves. We thrive when we have choices and feel that we can create the life we want. We thrive when we feel a sense of purpose and can find meaning in our lives. We thrive when our core human needs are met.

Because humans are social beings, our primary human need is for connection. And so we thrive when our connections to others are strong, healthy, and authentic. We thrive when we can communicate with others—when we are listened to deeply, when we can share what's on our minds and in our hearts without fear of judgment. Transformational Coaching enables educators to get their core human needs met and to thrive. And when adults thrive, children are far more likely to thrive.

Every Child, Every Day

Transformational Coaches work in service of the social, emotional, and academic well-being of every child. As such, our work is focused on educational equity and on serving the most vulnerable members of society. A commitment to equity means that we recognize the larger systemic issues at play. We hone our ability to recognize and interrupt inequities that reflect marginalization and dehumanization of groups of people, including of people of color, women, and queer people.

Doing this work requires us to look inward at our own beliefs, to look outward at the inequitable beliefs propagated by the dominant culture, to scrutinize our actions and ways of being, and to commit to *every* child, *every* day. We acknowledge the feelings that may arise with such an ambitious commitment—perhaps the fear that this goal is unattainable, perhaps the sense of responsibility that can feel weighty, perhaps the grief over the current conditions that so many young people experience. Effective educators feel those feelings, honor them, learn from their wisdom, and then release them. A Transformational Coach is comfortable standing at the intersection of equity and emotions. Navigating this experience requires ongoing learning. We welcome this learning, and in doing so, we embrace our full humanity.

Four Theories of Action That Drive Transformational Coaching

Transformational Coaching is rooted in a set of core beliefs about *how* we can use the long lever of coaching to intervene in a system. Four theories drive Transformational Coaching: coaching teachers is the greatest leverage point in transforming our education system; transformation happens when we coach behaviors, beliefs, and ways of being; coaching happens in conversations; and transformation requires attending to the core human need for connection and belonging.

Coaching Teachers Is the Greatest Leverage Point in Transforming Our Education System

I'll stand by this statement until my final days: *if we take care of teachers, they will be able to take care of children.*

If we honor teachers in their full, complex humanity, they will do the same for children. Teachers are not machines that can be programmed. Mandates, scripted curriculum, threats of job loss, or humiliation will not transform education. Teachers are not obstacles or problems to solve—such a technical and transactional view has not worked and will never work because it violates our needs for autonomy, connection, and purpose. But if we love teachers, and believe in their capacity to change, and if coaches develop the skills to facilitate that change, *we can serve children*.

These concepts deserve repetition and elaboration. Most educators recognize that teachers need to develop a massive instructional skill set to teach well. Transformational Coaches support such development. We also understand that it's far more likely that students' social, emotional, and academic needs will be met if teachers have a trusted person who sees their potential, who doesn't judge them, and who helps them sort through their thoughts and feelings. We know that in addition to traditional pedagogical knowledge and skills, teachers need emotional intelligence skills and cultural competency—and that they need spaces in which to be vulnerable and to refine their reflection and decision-making capacities.

Furthermore, if teachers belong to healthy, resilient communities within their school buildings and if these communities deal with conflict in healthy ways, make informed decisions, and collectively address the systemic injustices within their organizations, then it is far more likely that students' social, emotional, and academic needs will be met. We can create these teams and communities by using Transformational Coaching.

If teachers had Transformational Coaches, they'd be more effective and resilient. If teachers worked in healthy teams, they'd have the collective resources to address systemic issues in their schools. If all of this were true, we'd be able to address issues at the social, economic, and political levels that impact children, such as school funding, legislation, school board elections, state-level decisions about curriculum and testing, and so on. And then children would be better served—young people would be far healthier in every sense than they are today.

Providing Transformational Coaching is the single best way to care for teachers while also centering the needs of children. This approach to development is holistic and human-centered and addresses the three domains of who we are—what we think, how we feel, and what we do. As such, it is the key to transformation.

Transformation Results from Addressing the Three Bs: Behaviors, Beliefs, and Ways of Being

Coaching behaviors is not enough. Transformation happens when we coach behaviors, beliefs, and ways of being. People's underlying beliefs and ways of being drive all of our behaviors. If we coach beliefs and ways of being, then our behaviors can shift—for good. This concept sets Transformational Coaching apart from other coaching models in schools. A Transformational Coach attends to and addresses a client's Three Bs. The bulk of this book teaches you how to coach a client's behaviors, beliefs, and ways of being. But before going deeper into the *how*, let's understand what this means. Figure 1.1 is a simple representation of this concept.

Beliefs

In my first visit to Annie's classroom, I observed 34 eighth graders sitting in rows, silent for almost the entire period, and with an all-too-familiar glazed look in their eyes. Annie stood at the front of the class and read aloud from a textbook. During the 50-minute period, she asked four questions. After each question, she called on a student who had raised their hand to respond. There were no tasks given to students, no turn-and-talks, and no formative assessment.

Annie, who had taught for a decade, would be participating with me in a 12-week coaching cycle focused on student engagement. Although I'd

Figure 1.1: The Three Bs

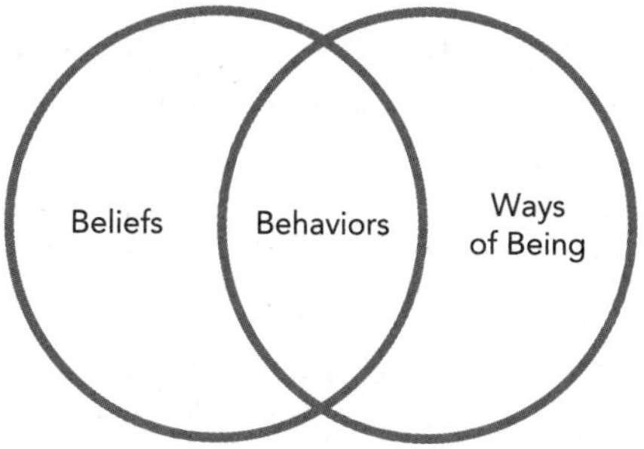

anticipated some resistance, I found her receptive to implementing new structures, and 12 weeks later, the desks were clustered in groups, students used protocols to discuss texts, and Annie spent most of the period circulating through the classroom and asking higher-order thinking questions. I patted myself on the back and mentally checked Annie off of my list of teachers to fix. It felt like a transformation.

When I stepped back into Annie's classroom that spring, I anticipated the buzz of students talking about history. But I walked into a silent classroom. The desks were back in their sterile rows, and Annie stood at the front reading aloud from a textbook.

"What happened, Annie?" I bluntly said when the last student had shuffled out. "Why did you move them back into rows? Why did you stop using the discussion protocols?"

Annie's voice was warm—not defensive as I'd worried it might be—as she said, "I realized I didn't really *believe* that students needed to be in small groups or needed to be talking to each other to learn." Annie shrugged. "And they got noisy again. You know how eighth graders are. It's easier to control them when they're in rows."

Annie's comments prompted me to reimagine how I coached. When I'd worked with Annie during the first cycle, I'd been purely instructive in my coaching—I'd explained new strategies, demonstrated them, and given Annie feedback on her implementation of the strategies—but we'd never unpacked *why* these strategies could be effective or her beliefs about what students need in order to learn. Basically, I'd told Annie, *do this, this way.* She'd complied, but her beliefs hadn't changed. When her motivation for using the strategies I'd introduced diminished, she went back to what she'd always done—rows, reading textbooks, silence—because those strategies had worked for her for 12 years, or so she thought.

The second coaching cycle that Annie participated in was much harder for both of us, but it resulted in sustained, transformational change. We dug into the beliefs she held about students, learning, classroom management, and discussion. As she identified those beliefs, I guided her to unpack them and understand how she had developed them (which you'll learn how to do in Chapter 11, "How to Coach Beliefs"). I also shared research about student learning, took her to observe classrooms where students engaged in rigorous small-group discussions, and guided her through the challenging phase of internalizing new practices. I had realized that in the first coaching cycle I hadn't accurately assessed Annie's Zone of Proximal Development (ZPD), and I'd released her into new practices before she was ready to execute them independently. Most critically, I hadn't excavated her belief system or scaffolded a shift into new mindsets.

It's been more than a dozen years since I coached Annie. She's still teaching, and her classroom has never returned to being a silent place of rows and checked-out eighth graders. I attribute this to a transformation of her beliefs.

All of our actions emerge from beliefs, whether we are conscious of those beliefs or not. I eat kale, for example, even though I don't really like the taste and it takes so long to chew, because I believe that it makes my body healthy. I eat very little sugar because I believe it harms my body. If I didn't believe this, I would eat a lot of sugar—I love the taste and the dopamine surge. These beliefs about health shape my actions.

Here's another personal example: as a child, I adopted a belief that I couldn't count on anyone else to take care of me and I needed to solve every problem on my own. As an adult, this translated into predictable behaviors—I tried to deal with everything by myself. I took on too much. I rarely asked for help. I was often overwhelmed and resentful.

Unless coaches address beliefs, we often see only superficial, unsustainable change. Sometimes we may see compliant behavior, but compliance will not change this world. If we want to truly change behaviors—and see transformation—we have to surface and explore the beliefs at the root of behaviors.

Ways of Being

Our ways of being are how we show up in the world. When we talk about ways of being, we're referring to demeanor, character, disposition, and sense of identity.

It can be hard to completely differentiate a *way of being* from a *belief*, because our ways of being create beliefs, and our beliefs create ways of being. Behaviors emerge, then, from both beliefs and ways of being. Both our beliefs and our ways of being have their origins in childhood, where our personalities, coping mechanisms, relationships to emotions, mental models, values, and behaviors developed.

When I sit down for a coaching session with a new client, I aspire to show up as curious, compassionate, and humble. This is a way of being. I do this because I believe that this is the stance I need to take to develop a relationship with my client. My beliefs about my client's needs commit me to a way of being from which I enact the following behaviors: I ask facilitative questions, I speak far less than my client, I hold silence and rarely interrupt, and I consciously position my body in a way that communicates receptivity—shoulders back, arms open, face relaxed. In doing so, I strive to create alignment between my way of being, my beliefs, and my behaviors.

However, when I give a keynote address to thousands of people, I aspire to show up as confident. That's another way of being. I do this because I believe confidence is key to communicating a message that will provoke new insights and understandings. When I walk onto the stage, I take long strides, I stand tall and look directly into the eyes of the people in front of me, my breath fills my voice, my tone is assertive, and my statements are declarative and authoritative.

When we're intentional about who we want to be, it's more likely that we'll be successful in whatever we're doing—be that teaching, coaching, speaking, parenting, or anything else. We will also feel better. During the decades when I thought I had to take care of everything, alone, I often felt resentful, physically and emotionally exhausted, lonely, and afraid. Sometimes old beliefs arise when I'm emotionally activated, but now I hold a belief that I don't need to solve everything by myself. As this belief has gotten stronger, my way of being has become calmer, more confident, and more self-accepting.

Behaviors

Behaviors are exactly what they sound like: the actions we take, the things we do. Our behaviors are the result of what we believe and of who we are being. Ultimately, this area is where we want to see changes in schools—in behaviors such as how teachers respond to students, in the design of lessons and units, and in how teachers build relationships with families and caregivers.

Philosopher Danah Zohar thinks of radical change metaphorically: "Most transformation programs satisfy themselves with shifting the same old furniture about in the same old room. But real transformation requires that we redesign the room itself. Perhaps even blow up the old room" (Zohar, 1997, p. 243). I worked in a few schools where we were constantly moving the furniture—in an effort to meet student needs, we tried different master schedules, new intervention programs, and tiered systems of support. But it always felt like the room was still the same room, and we didn't see the results we wanted for children.

On the other hand, I did see dramatically different results for students when I worked in a school in which teachers had a tremendous amount of autonomy—we radically redesigned our schedule and staffing assignments, we had flexibility in which standards we taught, and students and parents had a great deal of decision-making. It felt like we'd truly created a new room because we operated from a different set of beliefs about children and adults than schools usually hold. As a result, we could *be* different—our relationships with students, with their guardians, and with each other were characterized by a lower power differential, by openness and care. Student outcomes were remarkable. We created a school in which children thrived.

The purpose of Transformational Coaching is to both improve teaching and transform schools into places where all members of the community thrive. The impact of coaching must be evident in student achievement data and in the quality of connection between a student and teacher, a teacher and administrator, and a coach and their colleague. After a coaching session, a teacher should be able to do something different the next day, should feel more empowered and resilient, and should have new insights into their thoughts.

Coaching Happens in Conversations

Systems thinking analysts work by identifying leverage points in a complex system where a small shift can produce big changes in everything else. For those of us working in schools—and any organization—the most powerful leverage point for us to address is our conversations. If educators had different conversations with each other, our schools would be different places. If our schools were different, our world would be different. We need to have conversations that address behaviors, beliefs, and ways of being; that are "hard" or "courageous" and that create resilient communities.

Conversations are a key leverage point for several reasons. How we have conversations is within our sphere of control, the skills are learnable, it's not expensive for us to learn how to have different conversations, and the ripple effect would be tremendous. If a coach could have different conversations with their clients, or a principal with a teacher, or a teacher with a student's parent, we might also apply these skills in our personal lives: in conversations with partners, children, parents, and neighbors. We might be able to have conversations with people who hold vastly different beliefs than we do—and we might be able to bridge those ideological gaps with authentic human connection. In this book, I focus on acquiring the skills, knowledge, and will to have conversations that change practice and change systems.

Transformation Is Possible When We Attend to Connection and Belonging

The final theory of action behind Transformational Coaching emerges from recent findings from neuroscience, psychology, and sociology. As I discussed in the introduction, human beings have core needs. The great majority of our behavior is an effort to meet those needs or preserve them. Of these needs, our longing for connection and belonging is paramount, likely because, as a social species, humans simply cannot survive without each other. If we attend to this core human need, then transformation is possible.

As you read this book, you'll find I often return to this need. There is skill required to coach toward meeting the need for connection, but doing so is also intuitive and simple. Sometimes I think we've made things far more complicated than they need to be. Coaching for connection is supported by heaps of data convincing us, for example, of the importance of psychological safety among groups, but the skills required to create connection is ancient and innate knowledge. As such, when I nudge you to coach for belonging, I trust that it will resonate—the strategies I'll suggest might feel easier because you carry this desire within you too. If we focused on creating connection and belonging, so much conflict could be avoided, and so many efforts could be streamlined. Data analysis protocols are helpful, but they don't address the core human need for connection. And so, Transformational Coaches prioritize creating connection. I'll come back to this over and over in this book.

A Transformational Coach's Essential Beliefs

Every action emerges from a belief. As such, we need to ensure that as coaches we're holding beliefs that support everyone to thrive. What follows is an overview of the beliefs that a Transformational Coach needs to hold about themselves and their clients.

Beliefs We Hold About Ourselves as Coaches

Transformational Coaches hold a set of core beliefs about themselves, beliefs that enable us to implement Transformational Coaching strategies with integrity and fidelity. To begin unpacking this statement, as you read the following statements, notice how you feel:

- "The system is so messed up that what I do doesn't make much of a difference."
- "It's impossible to make change here. Everyone is stuck in their ways."
- "As long as this administration is running the show, my hands are tied."
- "Those teachers will never change their ways. I can't coach them."

Beliefs are strongly held opinions. Sometimes they feel like the absolute truth, but really they're simply thoughts we hold onto. Fortunately, we can have a tremendous influence on our thoughts. The first step is to identify our current beliefs. Then we can choose to continue to hold those beliefs or to shift or even abandon them.

When I believed I worked in a school that was so messed up that I couldn't have any kind of positive impact, I stopped taking meaningful action. I didn't talk to my assistant principal because I thought it was pointless. I thought, *These teachers will never be open to trying anything new*, so I didn't coach toward new behaviors. I avoided having hard conversations with some teachers, and I had contentious debates with others. I was grumpy and cynical a great deal of the time. My beliefs shaped my actions and my way of being.

An effective Transformational Coach holds the following beliefs about themselves:

- I deserve to thrive
- I start with myself
- I have agency
- I can be effective
- I am a facilitator.

Let's explore why each of these beliefs matters.

I deserve to thrive. A Transformational Coach values their own well-being. This is based on a deep belief of inherent worthiness. If we believe that we are born worthy of love, joy, ease, satisfaction, and belonging, then we believe that we deserve to thrive.

So many of us have experiences, often in childhood, that lead us to feel like we aren't worthy. These core wounds shape the beliefs we adopt and then the actions we take. If we don't believe we deserve to be in a job where we feel effective and satisfied, we will put up with all kinds of things that undermine our ability to thrive. If we believe we deserve to thrive, we will take action and work to make that a reality.

Your clients will be able to thrive only if you are thriving too. To be an effective Transformational Coach, you've got to cultivate the belief that you deserve to thrive.

I start with myself. Transformational Coaches explore and attend to our behaviors, beliefs, and ways of being. This means we advocate for our own professional development and take ownership of developing our skills. It means that when we perceive a teacher's resistance, we turn inward and explore our resistance to that teacher. Starting with ourselves means that as we begin noticing and addressing racism in schools, we look at our own biases and work to dismantle them. It means that we attend to our core human needs—that we prioritize our need for community, emotional healing, and connection. To be a Transformational Coach, you must start with yourself, feel your feelings, cultivate awareness of your beliefs, and engage in practices to transform your behaviors.

I have agency. Transformational Coaches believe that we have agency—the ability to take meaningful action to create the lives we want. Many of us have experiences, often in childhood, that lead us to feel like we can't influence our lives. When we don't believe we have agency, we feel like nothing we say matters. When speaking with a client or with a supervisor, we might fear that we won't be heard or understood.

When we believe in our agency, we see many options, even when we encounter massive obstacles. We feel optimistic. When we feel like we have agency, we experience uncomfortable emotions, and we know that they'll pass and that our ability to effect change is always accessible. To impact a teacher's development, a coach has to believe that they have the ability to influence the situation—that they have agency.

I can be effective. Transformational Coaches believe that we can be effective in our work. This means we believe we can find the resources to build our skills, knowledge, cultural competency, and emotional intelligence—and that we can have a positive impact.

Many of us experience self-doubt and perhaps imposter syndrome. In my first years as a coach, I believed that I could be effective with one kind of teacher, but with other kinds—the "resistant teachers"—I was less confident. "I just can't work with them," I'd say to colleagues. "They're not open to coaching." This belief undermined my efforts. I didn't attempt to build a relationship with those teachers or refine my coaching skills. My erroneous belief curtailed my impact.

The importance of believing in our own potential for efficacy aligns with the research on growth mindset. As I shifted out of a fixed mindset that I was unable to work with "resistant teachers," my coaching skills expanded quickly, my sense of agency grew, and I had greater impact.

I am a facilitator. Transformational Coaches believe our job is *to facilitate* someone's learning journey. A Transformational Coach doesn't believe that people are broken and need fixing but rather that clients need a skillful guide in order to grow.

This belief runs counter to messages from the dominant culture. The dominant culture tells us that we improve through doing what experts and authority figures tell us to do, and that the wisdom that leads to growth lies outside of an individual, rather than within. Transformational Coaches believe the wisdom to change is within, and we help clients access it. To be a Transformational Coach, you need believe that clients can solve their own problems when the conditions are right—and that your job is to create those conditions.

Beliefs We Hold About Our Clients

Just as a Transformational Coach holds certain beliefs about themselves, they also hold a set of beliefs about clients: that a client deserves to thrive, that a client has agency, and that a client can be effective. While these mirror beliefs that Transformational Coaches hold about themselves (and could be generalized to apply to all people), in restating them as beliefs we hold about clients, we reinforce their importance.

My client deserves to thrive. A Transformational Coach knows that a client deserves to thrive because they are inherently worthy. There has never been a newborn baby who did not deserve to thrive, and this extends to adults: a client deserves the support, care, and kindness they need to flourish— because they are a human being.

Sometimes it can feel hard to hold this belief, especially when people make choices that hurt others. I've coached teachers who expressed dehumanizing opinions about children, who screamed at students and publicly humiliated them. The most effective way to shift student experience is to stay in relationship with a client. Anchoring in this belief allows me to act with compassion and curiosity.

My client has agency. A Transformational Coach recognizes the core human need for autonomy. When a client doesn't seem to remember that they have power to act, it's our job to facilitate a return to agency. This may feel hard when a client presents as passive, resigned, or cynical; it can feel hard when your client blames students, parents, admin, and the district for the situation they're in.

When I believe that my client has agency, it means that I know that they can solve many of their own problems *given the right conditions.* The right conditions include a coach who asks good questions, who listens without judgment or attachment to outcome, and who cares deeply about them.

When I coach a client deeper into their agency, I ask a lot of facilitative questions. I recognize that my client is the expert on their situation, that

I will never know who they are or what they're going through as deeply as they do, and I embrace my role as a facilitator of learning. My job is to help my client feel empowered to explore their situation, tap into their inner reserves of insight and wisdom, and make intentional choices.

My client can be effective. A Transformational Coach believes that a client can learn, change, grow, and be effective as an educator. To believe this, we have to believe that a client *wants* to learn and change. Far too often, we can slip into thinking that someone else doesn't want to change—they even act in ways that make it seem like they don't. However, even people who are doing something that's ineffective or generating harm want to change. I know it can be hard to believe that—but coaches have to. When we don't believe a client can be effective, we may not take the actions required to cultivate a trusting relationship with them. We might give up on them.

When you believe that your client can be effective, you continuously search for their strengths and potential. You know that the desire for growth lies within them (because it lies within all of us) and that they can build knowledge, skill, and will.

Beliefs We Hold About What We *Do* (Our Behaviors)

A Transformational Coach working in education is deeply informed about all things teaching and knows how to guide a teacher to respond to challenging student behavior, to create rigorous learning targets, and to incorporate strategies to teach neurodivergent children. A Transformational Coach has developed traditional coaching skills such as those needed to observe classrooms and disaggregate and analyze data, and they also know how to help a distressed teacher explore and process strong emotions, how to guide a teacher toward deeper understanding of the impacts of their racial identity experiences in the classroom, and how to guide a teacher toward new behaviors that reflect all this awareness and understanding.

The work we do to help another person grow emerges from a set of beliefs about our behaviors. We believe our work is to create the conditions in which people change; engage emotions, prioritize relationships;

unpack beliefs about equity, identity, power and privilege; and make every conversation count.

We create the conditions in which people can change. A Transformational Coach believes that people desire change, that people *can* change, and that, given the right conditions, people can solve many of their own problems. Every strategy in this book contributes to creating these conditions. You will learn strategies to build trust, to listen deeply, to be attuned to and responsive to someone's emotions, to ask questions that elicit new insights, to scaffold learning new skills, and to set up a classroom observation, among many others. In some ways, all we can do is create conditions—but the right conditions are powerful.

We engage emotions. Emotions are a normal part of being human, and they arise more intensely when we are in a growth process. A Transformational Coach knows that emotions contain insight and wisdom and that we can engage with them in healthy ways. We acknowledge and welcome emotions—both our own and our clients'—and we coach toward emotional resilience.

Furthermore, coaches committed to equity know that addressing emotions is essential. Emotions are not an obstacle to coaching for equity. In fact, when we have the skills to respond to them, emotions help us to confront inequitable systems and ideologies. They can galvanize us and energize us.

We prioritize relationships. A Transformational Coach knows that because humans are a social species and because our core human need is for belonging and connection, we must prioritize building and maintaining relationships with clients. We know that trust is essential in relationships, and we continuously assess levels of trust and repair trust when it breaks down. We are exceptionally skilled in building connections with clients—and accept that relationship-building is the only place to start in coaching.

We unpack beliefs about equity, identity, power, and privilege. Transformational Coaches examine sociopolitical identity—both our own and our clients'—and unpack the way identity experiences influence our work.

This conviction requires that we explore power and privilege and have conversations about race and other identity markers.

Equity issues are present in every situation—that's the nature of living in a society in which systems of oppression are embedded in our mindsets, behaviors, and institutions. We often don't recognize the prevalence of systemic oppression, because that's precisely how it works—systems of oppression seem "normal," part of how things are, how we think, and how we feel. A Transformational Coach works from these assumptions and therefore seeks all opportunities to surface and explore beliefs about identity.

Comparing Traditional Instructional Coaching with Transformational Coaching

When I became a literacy coach, I was trained as an instructional coach. I attended PD where I learned specific skills—for example, how to guide teachers through protocols to analyze student work, how to use video in the classroom, and how to conduct classroom observations and collect data on student engagement. I also participated in professional development on such topics as early literacy acquisition, fluency and phonemic awareness, academic literacy, English Language Development, learning targets, formative assessment, and classroom management. These trainings offered useful content. But they didn't prepare me to respond to the new sixth-grade teacher I was assigned to coach who cried through every single coaching session. Or the eighth-grade English teacher who refused to meet with me. Or the open and receptive science teacher who regularly made dehumanizing comments about her students of color.

It's painful to remember my first years as a coach. Every week, I emailed the distraught new sixth-grade teacher dozens of resources—things I'd created when I taught the same content, articles, and templates for lesson plans. I did battle with the resistant English teacher and complained about her to anyone who would listen. When I heard the science teacher express biases, I alternately avoided confronting her beliefs or tore them down. I missed teaching and feeling like I was doing something useful in the world. I often felt frustrated and considered a dozen other life paths. I was clumsy, well-intentioned, and ineffective. The training I received in instructional coaching was insufficient for what I encountered in schools.

Traditional instructional coaching fails to fully consider and address the reality that a teacher is not a person performing a role; they are a fully formed human. As a result, traditional instructional coaching, I'd argue, comes from the same "banking concept of education" that Paulo Freire condemns in his classic, *Pedagogy of the Oppressed*, a concept in which students are seen as empty receptacles that need to be filled by teachers. Aligned with a transactional, industrial model of education, traditional instructional coaching is experienced as something that's *done to* teachers, as a response to poor performance, or as an indicator that a teacher is ineffective. No wonder so many teachers flinch when a coach shows up at their door. Certainly, some traditional coaches have found ways to coach effectively, but more often, the interactions are limited at best and harmful at worst.

Transformational Coaching, on the other hand, is a model that supports teachers to thrive. It is a collaborative process where the coach is a supportive guide. To be clear, Transformational Coaches do need content knowledge and knowledge of the disciplines in which they work. They do address teacher behaviors. But Transformational Coaching is far more expansive and holistic than traditional instructional coaching. Table 1.1 outlines key differences between instructional coaching and Transformational Coaching.

Transforming our schools, and creating the conditions where every educator can thrive, requires Transformational Coaching.

What teachers do is critical to the success of students. Both traditional instructional coaching and Transformational Coaching address teachers' behaviors—the way they design units and lessons, the kinds of questions

Table 1.1: Differences Between Instructional Coaching and
Transformational Coaching

	Instructional Coaching	Transformational Coaching
Purpose	• To improve a teacher's instructional practices—their behaviors. • To address what a teacher doesn't do well. • To help a teacher make growth as measured on an evaluation.	• To boost a teacher's emotional resilience and create the conditions for them to thrive. • To surface and celebrate a teacher's strengths and tap into their inner wisdom. • To make sustained changes in behaviors by exploring underlying beliefs and ways of being.
Beliefs	• Teachers need fixing; they are receptacles to be filled. • The coach is an expert and provides answers. • The coach's subject-matter content knowledge is essential and most valued. • Student well-being and outcomes are the end goal.	• Teachers can find solutions to their problems with skilled guidance; they possess a great deal of knowledge and wisdom. • The coach facilitates a learning process. • The coach's content knowledge is secondary to the knowledge of facilitating a learning process. • Student well-being and outcomes *and* educator well-being and outcomes are the end goals.
Professional Development for Coaches	• Coaches are trained in instructional practices and coaching on those practices. • The focus is on gathering and analyzing data.	• Coaches are trained in instructional coaching strategies, exploring beliefs, and addressing ways of being. • Development provides opportunities for coaches to reflect on their own beliefs and ways of being. • Practicing coaching conversations is a primary focus.

teachers ask students, the curriculum that's selected, the assessments that are given, and so on. The difference is that Transformational Coaching also results in transformative shifts in underlying mindsets and boosts teachers' emotional resilience. If we aspire to interrupt educational inequities, then we'll need to explore beliefs. If we aspire to help teachers navigate the inevitable emotional fatigue of teaching, to avoid burnout, and to find joy and meaning in the career they've chosen, then we need to explore ways of being.

What coaches do is critical to the success of teachers. Both traditional instructional coaching and Transformational Coaching provide development around what the coach *does* and the tools the coach *uses*—the question stems, data analysis protocols, forms for documenting coaching meetings, real-time coaching techniques, and so on. But Transformational Coaching provides much more, building from an understanding that the coaches, like the teachers they support, are multidimensional human beings. We have thoughts (beliefs) and feelings—*lots* of thoughts and *lots* of feelings. To support our clients in their own transformation, we must also tend to our own.

The Impact of Transformational Coaching

The far-ranging impact of Transformational Coaching can be found at the classroom level, school level, systems level, and personal level.

At the Classroom Level

Marta was a veteran third-grade teacher who disrupted staff meetings and refused to implement new curriculum; parents complained about her regularly. Within a year of beginning work with her coach, Marta was a different person. In the classroom, she delivered engaging lessons and built warm rapport with students; in PD sessions she was open and curious; with parents she listened and was responsive to feedback.

"How do you explain this?" I asked Lupe, her coach.

"I listened and listened," Lupe said. "I communicated care and confidence in her ability to keep learning. I didn't give up on Marta, and I didn't give up on my ability to figure out how to help her grow."

Marta is just one of countless teachers who have shifted their behaviors, beliefs, and ways of being through Transformational Coaching. You'll read about others in this book, and when you start using these methods, you'll see teachers change and compile your own databank.

At the School Level

For several years, I worked with a small group of public school educators in a city in the Pacific Northwest that aspired to interrupt educational inequities for Black and Brown high school students in the sciences. My team and I trained and coached the coaches and their leaders. As in many schools across the country, most of the coaches and teachers in the schools were white, and the coaches had a lot to learn about coaching cultural competency and interrupting racial inequities. If we had simply told them what to do, we would have failed.

Instead, we trained the coaches in the Three B's of the Transformational Coaching model—we explored beliefs and worked on our ways of being as well as practicing coaching behaviors. We had many conversations with each other about power dynamics, racism, and children. Then the coaches went into schools, where they had more conversations—sometimes hard conversations, but often healing conversations, about race and class and expectations and children. Because this district received a large grant for this work, they had an external evaluator who compiled research each year on the impact of the coaching program. And so, in addition to changes we saw in the behaviors, beliefs, and ways of being of the coaches, and inspiring anecdotes we heard about what was happening in the science classrooms, we received reports that described significant changes in teacher practice. The impact of those changes was also illustrated in Black and Brown students' achievement in science, their interest in advanced science courses, and their success in those courses.

At the Systems Level

When I train educators in Transformational Coaching, I witness them wrestling with beliefs, developing new ways of being, and practicing refined ways of communicating. As they do this, their hope and optimism surge. They realize that they *can* have conversations that might feel uncomfortable at the moment but that change a teacher's practice.

At school after school, Transformational Coaching shifts teacher practices in ways that result in better outcomes for students, supports increased teacher retention, reduces student discipline issues, and improves attendance of both teachers and students. Time and again, I hear from coaches who, in practicing Transformational Coaching, find greater access to their own power to impact education.

Transformational Coaching is a set of proven strategies to change conversations and organizations. It is effective because it addresses the entirety of the human experience—from what we do, to what we think, to how we feel—and because compassion and curiosity are the primary tools to facilitate growth. This holistic approach to change intervenes in the complex education system at the leverage point of conversations between adults. At this point, we can quickly and fairly easily acquire new skills to communicate more effectively. This model answers our needs for healthy connection and belonging, meaning and purpose, autonomy, competence, genuine self-esteem, and trust.

At the Personal Level

Finally, Transformational Coaching changes and impacts the practitioner. I will speak for myself only, now, and share that I am a much happier person because I've committed to using the strategies in this book, to holding the beliefs of Transformational Coaching, and to embodying the ways of being you'll explore in the next chapter. Many of my core human needs are met simply by being a Transformational Coach. In so many ways, I am thriving because I've traveled this path.

It would be disingenuous to say I'm thriving solely by practicing Transformational Coaching. It was only after a therapy session, many years after I started coaching, that I came to a deep understanding of what was below my belief (mentioned at the start of this chapter), that all the teachers I coached sucked. What I realized was that I had been *projecting* things that I didn't like about myself onto the teachers I coached. I didn't really think they sucked—I thought that *I* sucked.

I'm going to include a plug for therapy a number of times in this book, because if you want to really unearth and shift your beliefs, a therapist can help in ways no one else can. Our beliefs are shaped by our life experiences, especially those in early childhood, as well as by dominant culture. It's a major undertaking to explore our beliefs and even harder to shift them. Many of our beliefs carry strong emotional charges. For example, if you don't believe you're worthy of being treated with kindness and respect, you may tolerate behavior that undermines your well-being. But luckily, no one has to sort through the morass of experiences, events, and feelings alone.

I'm also a big believer that coaches need coaches. A coach can help you better understand yourself. They can acknowledge emotions and hold space for you to process and release them, but a coach doesn't probe into your psyche or childhood. A coach is not trained to do this kind of work, and it's unethical to do so; therefore, there are limits to what coaches can do and should do.

Therapists are trained to guide someone to explore their psyche. While the impact of working with a skilled therapist can be life changing, I recognize that there are hurdles to finding a therapist. In many communities there is still a stigma around therapy and a belief that seeking out therapy means someone is "crazy" or that it's self-indulgent or a waste of time. Therapy also costs money. Many health insurance plans are insufficient when it comes to covering mental health services. It can feel hard to find a therapist with whom you feel comfortable—and if you're a person from a marginalized group and want a therapist who shares that identity, the search for the right therapist can be harder. Finally, it can take time to discover the modality that works for you—some people benefit from traditional psychoanalysis or cognitive behavioral therapy, while others respond to EMDR (Eye Movement Desensitization and Reprocessing) or psychedelic-assisted therapy.

I resisted therapy for many years. Between the difficulty of finding the "right" therapist and the expense, it was easy to rationalize my resistance. But I knew that there were events in my childhood that I hadn't explored and behaviors and beliefs that emerged from those events that were undermining my well-being. I suspected that therapy could help. When I finally found modalities that worked for me and therapists with whom I connected, I experienced healing that I'd been unable to imagine. I am a much better coach, leader, teacher, mother, partner, and human as a result of what I've learned in therapy; I'm much more present and much happier. On many days, I know I'm thriving.

I hope that as you learn about Transformational Coaching, as your commitment to these strategies deepens, and as you recognize how central you are to the whole endeavor, and as you remember your inherent worthiness and right to well-being, you'll find the care you deserve. Everyone deserves to know themselves. Everyone deserves to heal from the inevitable pain we experience as human beings. Everyone deserves a guide in this process.

Pause and Process

Reflect:

- Given what you've read so far, what feels compelling about Transformational Coaching?
- Which ideas in this chapter evoked an emotional response, perhaps doubt or discomfort? How do you understand your response?
- Which questions or concerns would you want to explore in order to embrace Transformational Coaching?

Next steps:

- Listen to *Bright Morning Podcast* episode 149 to hear an example of a coaching conversation in which I coached a resistant teacher.
- Ask your clients, colleagues, and supervisors how they define coaching and listen for alignment.
- Listen to *Bright Morning Podcast* episode 83 on how to set up coaching at your site.
- Download the resource from my website, "Crafting a Coaching Vision," and begin drafting a vision for yourself as a coach.

CHAPTER 2

A Transformational Coach's Ways of Being

How to Create the Conditions for Transformation

Common misconception: The advice I give and questions I ask matter more than the conditions I create.	*Transformational Coaches know:* I create the conditions for transformation when working from compassion, curiosity, courage, humility, and trust.

Jason arrived at the department meeting 10 minutes late, looking frazzled and sweaty. "I was just leaving my classroom," he said, "and then Kayla's mom showed up. I told her I couldn't talk, but she just started complaining about how much homework I give and saying that Kayla hates me. I can't do anything right for that kid, and I am so sick of her mother." Jason sat down and looked around at the teachers who were engaged in a community-building activity. "Oh, sorry, I didn't realize you all had started without me."

If you were to describe Jason based on this snapshot, what would you say about him? In this, and the following vignettes, you'll notice *behaviors*, but you'll also get a sense of a person's *way of being*. As you read, consider how you'd describe that way of being:

- Lupe had just started working with a small group of students at a table in the back of the classroom when Juanito began crying and screaming. He threw himself onto the floor while the other first graders in his group backed away. "Teacher!" One of them shouted, "He's doing it again!" Lupe rose and walked over to Juanito. She crouched down next to him and spoke softly and slowly. "Juanito," she said quietly, "you're safe. Can you put your hands on your chest and take two deep breaths?" Lupe turned to the class, "I know this is upsetting, children, but right now, I want to ask you to return to your group work while I help Juanito, okay?"

- Elsa sat down with her coach, sighed loudly, and dropped her head into her palms. "I really messed up with DeAndre's father," she said. "I am so embarrassed to tell you about what happened, but I need your help. I mean, I've had a lot of Black students in my years, but I keep saying stupid things. In the past, when someone called me out, I'd get defensive. But I'm starting to think this is my problem. I'm ignorant or something. I don't want to be this way."

There are many ways to describe a way of being. Perhaps you thought Jason was being rude or that he was stuck in a victim mindset. Maybe Lupe seemed calm and confident in the face of a challenging situation. Perhaps you perceived Elsa as being vulnerable and courageous.

If I were coaching these educators and I'd witnessed the scenarios I described, my debrief with them would include these questions:

- How were you feeling?
- Who were you being?
- Who do you want to be?

These questions invite reflection on values, emotions, and aspirations, and they are a place from which we can unpack beliefs and make changes to behaviors. They help us coach a way of being.

When we coach only behaviors, we see limited change. When we coach beliefs, there's greater likelihood that we'll see transformational, sustained change in behaviors. And when we coach behaviors, beliefs, *and* ways of being, there's a far greater likelihood that we'll see individual transformation, as well as an increase in individual and collective resilience.

In Chapter 10, "How to Coach Ways of Being," I'll explain how to coach a client's way of being. In this chapter, you'll learn about what defines a way of being and read about a Transformational Coach's ways of being.

The Primary Role of Emotional Intelligence

The concept of *ways of being* can feel abstract. However, understanding the role that emotions play in our experience of being human is the starting point. From there, we can incorporate additional contributions to a way of being and the nuances of the concept. What follows are the key ideas behind a way of being:

- *Emotions are entwined with ways of being*: Emotions can reflect ways of being, or emotions can generate ways of being. Emotional intelligence is essential to "be" who and how you want to be.
- *Core values feed into our ways of being*: A way of being can reflect the core values we hold or aspire to live into. Our core values have emotional qualities to them, and they can generate feelings.
- *Challenges can shift our ways of being*: Our ways of being are tested, or can shift, when we experience challenges or change; in these moments we may experience what feels like an "identity crisis." Ways of being are not permanent, and shifts can be opportunities for growth.

- *We crave alignment between our behaviors and our ways of being*: We feel good when we act in alignment with who we want to be.

Let's unpack these ideas.

Emotions Are Entwined with Ways of Being

If you want to coach ways of being, you have to understand emotions. You need to be able to guide someone to recognize the emotions they're experiencing and, if feelings create obstacles or generate a way of being that doesn't serve students, to guide someone to process and move through those feelings. Learning to coach ways of being starts with understanding the role of emotions in our lives and the need for emotional intelligence.

Feelings frequently generate ways of being. Often the words we use to describe a way of being are words to describe emotions. For example, I can say *I want to be courageous, calm, confident, and curious*; or *I was being fearful, defensive, and arrogant*. These words describe both an emotion and a way of being. (See Appendix B, "The Core Emotions," for words that describe emotions.) We can see how emotions can give rise to ways of being in a statement like this: I felt empathy and concern for my students, and as a result of those feelings, I wanted *to be* a role model.

Cultivating Emotional Intelligence

Emotions are a part of being human. Like it or not, we experience emotions all day, every day. When we cultivate emotional intelligence, we develop skills to navigate our emotions, processing those that are uncomfortable and savoring the pleasant ones. Sometimes the way we express emotions can be challenging for ourselves and for others. Often, we talk about "managing," "controlling," or "regulating" emotions—as if they are problems. But we need to remember also that as we build emotional intelligence, we gain more consistent access to the emotions that feel good and allow us to thrive.

Emotional intelligence is comprised of four competencies: self-awareness, self-management, social awareness, and relationship management. These competencies create the foundations for healthy, satisfying connection with others, as well as for our own physical and emotional well-being. Table 2.1 provides an overview of the competencies of emotional intelligence and some of the indicators. The indicators are not an exhaustive list—they're meant to begin providing descriptors of the competencies.

Self-awareness is the starting point for emotional intelligence, the primary competency that makes developing the other competencies possible. Self-awareness enables you to recognize when you're experiencing an emotion and to name it. When your heart rate accelerates and your face

Table 2.1: Components of Emotional Intelligence

Competency	Indicators
Emotional self-awareness	• I know when I'm experiencing an emotion. • I know which physical sensations reflect which emotions. • I recognize thoughts that indicate that I'm experiencing an emotion, and I can identify the emotion. • I have a wide vocabulary to label my emotions. • I know the way I express emotions affects others.
Emotional self-management	• I explore what gets me emotionally activated; I can anticipate when/where/how I might be triggered. • I have strategies to regulate myself when I'm triggered or experience uncomfortable emotions. • I'm adaptable when things happen that I didn't expect, even if I'm disappointed. • I have a positive outlook on life; I don't deny or suppress sadness, anger, or fear, but I have perspective and know that nothing is permanent. • I cultivate self-compassion.

(Continued)

Competency	Indicators
Social awareness	• I infer other people's emotions by reading body language and facial expressions, as well as by interpreting tone, pitch, pace, and volume. • I recognize alignment or misalignment between someone's words and body language. • I anticipate other people's reactions to what I say and do. • I intuit how other people feel about me. • I infer how other people feel about other people. • I predict how my words and actions will influence others. • I refrain from making assumptions about what people are thinking or feeling. • I perceive power dynamics between people. • I anticipate other people's perspectives.
Relationship management	• I cultivate trusting relationships. • I build relationships across lines of difference. • I repair trust when it breaks. • I engage in healthy conflict and respond to unhealthy conflict. • I access my courage to have challenging conversations. • I problem-solve when challenges arise in relationships. • I navigate power dynamics. • I respond to other people's needs. • I set appropriate boundaries.

gets hot in response to someone cutting you off in traffic, for example, you recognize that response as anger. Or when your principal walks past you in the hallway and doesn't say good morning, you recognize that fear comes up—you might notice the thoughts that follow—*Did I do something wrong? Is she mad at me about something?*—and you say to yourself, *Ah, I'm feeling afraid.*

If we don't know that we're experiencing emotions or we can't name the emotions we feel, we can get stuck in a whirlwind of sensations and thoughts. With awareness, our experience of an uncomfortable emotion such as fear, anger, sadness, shame, or envy doesn't trap us—we can respond to the physical sensations and the cognitive aftermath in a way that aligns to who we want to be. This means you could experience anger, for example, and employ strategies to process and release the anger in a healthy way, rather than in a way that hurts yourself or others. It means that you tell yourself, *I'm not going to jump to conclusions about why my principal didn't say good morning. Maybe she's having a hard day. I'll check in later. And I also know that this is a trigger for me—when someone doesn't acknowledge me, an old emotional injury is activated.* An ineffective way to handle that fear would be to spend the day worrying about what you did wrong, or to avoid your principal for the whole week or to complain about her to other teachers. Well-developed self-awareness allows us to self-manage.

A person with high emotional intelligence has acute awareness of what activates them emotionally. When a person with high self-awareness is activated, they can follow their emotions to the source—often to an unhealed wound. As we cultivate self-awareness and while we're healing, we can learn to anticipate situations in which we might be activated or the words or phrases that trigger us. For example, I'm still activated when someone uses the phrase "these kids can't. . . ." While I likely can't keep from hearing this phrase again, self-awareness allows me to control my response. I can feel the *ouch*, employ a strategy to calm myself, and recognize that something within me—probably an old wound—deserves attention. There's a saying, "Triggers are friends to follow," meaning that triggers help us see our areas for healing.

With self-awareness, you can also notice when you experience joy. You might notice a sensation of lightness or openness in your chest, or a quiet calmness in your mind, or you might find yourself grinning. You can say to yourself, *I'm feeling joy, and this feels so good.* You might notice the adjacent thoughts: *This conversation is going so well. I feel connected to my client. I feel effective as a coach. I love coaching.* Cultivating self-awareness and developing self-management skills is essential for emotional resilience. Without these key components of emotional intelligence, we are unlikely to get our core human needs met and to thrive.

Self-awareness and self-management allow us to be effective at social awareness and relationship management—the competencies necessary to build good healthy connections with others. The first of these, social awareness, is the ability to read other people's emotions, to know how to influence them, to anticipate reactions, and to understand different perspectives. Social awareness is a precursor to the final competency—relationship management—which includes cultivating trust, developing healthy relationships, and dealing with conflict.

It is virtually impossible to meet the primary human need for belonging and connection without developing emotional intelligence. But what's most important—and empowering—to know is that *emotional intelligence is something you can learn*. Emotional intelligence is *skill and knowledge*, and it can be acquired. You can learn to have an easier experience of emotions, to learn from the uncomfortable ones, to more frequently experience the ones that you enjoy, and to allow them to support you to be who you want to be.

Core Values Feed into Our Ways of Being

Determining who you want to be includes identifying what matters most to you. Often, our core values represent what matters most. Values, ways of being, and beliefs are entwined. For example, if I value respect and believe that teachers deserve to be respected by students because of positional authority, then I might show up with students in a way that seems demanding. My behaviors with students would reflect this belief and would be expressed in my way of being, which could be stern or strict.

Sometimes values generate ways of being, which, in turn, generate beliefs. If I value kindness and strive to be compassionate with everyone, then I may develop beliefs about why people deserve compassion and about what it means when people are cruel. These beliefs feed my way of being; my way of being leads me to seek out beliefs that support it.

Our personal values usually emerge from larger dominant social and cultural values or from familial values—or sometimes in response to them. Families, cultures, and societies communicate values that we often experience and absorb unconsciously. For example, I was raised in a family that deeply valued service. I appreciate this value. However, I was also raised in a family, and in a society, that communicated that my needs, as a woman, were secondary to those of others, that service to others came before taking care of myself. This is a value that I've rejected.

It's worth identifying our core values to make sure that we haven't unconsciously absorbed social, cultural, or familial values that we don't believe in. To fully embrace the values I want to live into, I need to know that they are truly mine and not a reflection of dominant culture or a dysfunctional family dynamic. Once I own them, my values become a way of being. For example, I've incorporated my family's value of service as part of my core value of compassion. I aspire to show up with compassion, and I work to alleviate my own suffering and the suffering of those around me.

Challenges Can Shift Our Ways of Being

Our ways of being can feel tested when we experience challenges or change. When I became a literacy coach at a large, traditional middle school in Oakland and I was assigned to coach teachers who presented as disengaged and cynical, I felt like I became a different person—I hadn't yet developed effective coaching skills, and I showed up as defensive, angry and hopeless. I said to my coach, "I feel like I'm not myself anymore. This isn't me." This was a statement about who I was being and how I felt unmoored from myself.

We can experience what feel like identity crises when faced with life transitions. As external circumstances change, we can question who we are, who we want to be, and who we need to be. In moments like these, we see that ways of being aren't permanent. Just as our behaviors and beliefs change, our ways of being will also likely change. They change because our emotions and beliefs change, because our values shift, and because big transitions can reshape our identities.

We Crave Alignment

People aspire to act in alignment with who we want to be. The overwhelming majority of us want to show up in ways that are "good"—we want to be kind, compassionate, empowered, confident, humble, and so on. When we're not being who we want to be, it doesn't feel good.

The Dispositions of a Transformational Coach

One morning many years ago, I was summoned to a three-hour meeting for coaches in the central office. I didn't want to go. I anticipated that it would be a waste of time and I'd have to cancel several classroom observations at the last minute. As the meeting opened, I made a note at the top of the agenda: *My intention is* not *to be grumpy.* Setting an intention was something I'd learned in yoga classes, and I figured that identifying one might help.

An inner voice spoke up: *Frame it in the positive, Elena. How do you want to be experienced?* I scribbled an addendum: *I want to be open and receptive.*

The little voice spoke again: *What will that look or sound like?* I drew an arrow down the side of the paper and wrote, *My facial expressions will express curiosity; I'll make eye contact with the leader; I'll refrain from jumping to conclusions and ask truly open questions.*

The voice asked one more question: *Why does this matter?* I paused. I realized that unless I could answer that question, it would be hard for me to truly communicate curiosity. *Because I care how I'm experienced,* I thought. *And I want to be of service.*

Setting those intentions and identifying how I might live into them shifted my attitude and emotions. The time passed quickly, my questions were well-received and helpful, and I left the meeting feeling energized. I was so surprised that I'd been able to create a different kind of experience from what I'd anticipated, and I recognized that it was because of the commitment I'd made to who I wanted to be.

I began setting intentions before every coaching conversation. When my schedule was tight and I ran from meeting to meeting, I'd stand outside a school or classroom, close my eyes and take two deep breaths, and ask myself, *How do I want to show up today?* Most often, I landed on the simplicity of, *I want to be compassionate* or *I want to be curious.* When I was coaching someone and I felt stuck or insecure, I'd tell myself, *I want to trust the process*—I wanted *to be trusting.* When I entered a conversation anticipating that I'd explore issues around equity or when I was coaching someone in crisis, I'd make an intention to coach from courage. Slowing down for just a moment, turning inward, and connecting with my core values and aspirations allowed me to articulate an aspirational way of being. That felt good.

I started noticing that when I set intentions, I felt more present and focused during coaching conversations. I noticed that I listened more attentively; I felt less judgmental, more hopeful, and more connected to my client. I also noticed an increase in clients saying things like, "Oh, that's such a good question!" Or, "I can't believe you asked me that—I've been wanting to talk about that. It's like you can read my mind." Over time, I discovered which intentions were most conducive to doing transformational work. On the days when I was tired or frustrated, setting intentions to be compassionate, curious, courageous, humble, or trusting elevated my conversations with clients. As I articulated these ways of being to myself, I began noticing how these values were core to so many of the world's traditions and by leaders whom I admired including Harriet Tubman, Desmond Tutu, the Dalai Lama, and many others.

These five ways of being—compassion, curiosity, courage, humility, and trust—are the Transformational Coaching dispositions. After 20 years of coaching and a decade teaching others how to coach, I am convinced

that it is only when we work from these five dispositions that we create the conditions for transformation. Therefore, intentionally cultivating our ways of being is the most powerful work we can do. Fortunately,
that is entirely within our sphere of control. I'll describe each of these
ways of being and then offer an affirmation you can use to anchor in that
disposition.

Compassion

Compassion is empathy in action. When we are empathetic, we feel another
being's emotional experience—be that the experience of a child, a puppy, or
even a tree. When we take action based on that understanding, we demonstrate compassion. Acting compassionately centers the humanity of others
and preserves their dignity. When we act compassionately, we discover that
kindness is our greatest power.

A coach can demonstrate compassion for a client in these ways, among
others:

- Asking open-ended questions
- Refraining from making assumptions
- Acknowledging uncomfortable emotions
- Bringing awareness to strengths
- Affirming growth and change
- Appreciating vulnerability

To act compassionately toward others, we need to have compassion for ourselves. Imagine that you coach a new teacher to recognize
that making mistakes is normal, but when you stumble as a coach, you
berate yourself. If you can't accept the fact that you make mistakes, you
can't actually accept that others do too. Many of us who aspire to be
compassionate run aground on our own lack of self-compassion and
self-acceptance.

Another key to the practice of compassion is understanding that you can feel empathy for someone—and act compassionately toward them—*without agreeing* with what they think or do. For example, when I heard Rhea yelling at a kindergartner who was meandering back to class after recess, asking him if there was something wrong with his legs, I was angry. She'd made her student cry, and I was not okay with that. Then I imagined myself in Rhea's shoes and wondered what she was feeling—perhaps she realized she was going to be late to get back to her students, perhaps she had hoped to run to the bathroom before her next class, or perhaps she hadn't slept well or was hungry. While I knew she could do better, I suspended my judgment about Rhea for a moment.

That afternoon, during Rhea's coaching session, I raised the interaction with the child that I'd observed. Over the course of the conversation I asked a series of questions that I sourced from a place of compassion: "I wondered what was going on for you?" and "How do you think your student experienced that interaction?" and "Were you being who you want to be?"

As I posed the questions, I could sense my care for Rhea, and she received them well. She responded thoughtfully and expressed regrets about the way she'd acted. From a commitment to a different way of being, I coached her to recognize when she was feeling impatient or agitated, and we worked on what she could do to regulate those emotions. We also talked about strategies to get students back to class after recess, a conversation that could have fit into any new teacher coaching session.

Sometimes it feels like compassion is love. I'm tempted to declare love to be the primary aspirational disposition of a Transformational Coach, but I'm not sure that our institutions are ready for us to be talking about love. I wish they were. Consider this permission to integrate love—the concept and the word—into your personal reflections, conversations, and intentions. For now, in most places, I primarily talk about compassion, which is a good start toward creating more loving organizations.

Compassion Affirmation: My compassion arises from an unconditional positive regard for others: we are all connected, we have been dealt different cards in life, everyone is doing the best they can, and it is not my place to judge others. I can be both compassionate and discerning; compassion does not mean I agree with what someone does or thinks. Finally, there is no true compassion without self-compassion.

Curiosity

Curiosity is a state of openness, wonder, and receptivity. When we feel truly curious, we are willing to be surprised and let our beliefs change.

Not too long ago, I realized there have been times when I *thought* I was curious, but I wasn't. I realized that I used faux-curiosity as a mechanism of control. I would tell myself, *I'm really curious about why my client believes X, Y, or Z,* but actually I wanted to understand what they believed *so that* I could steer them in the direction I thought they should go. I've done this as a coach, as a leader, and with my husband and son. I don't judge my inclination to steer, but I'm recognizing that I was seeking a pathway to control, which is hard to admit.

Recently, a school leader shared his thoughts about a book we were both reading. His perspective was very different from mine and challenged my opinions. As he began speaking, I noticed that I relaxed, and my mind wasn't formulating counterarguments—I really wanted to hear what he had to say. I noticed that I felt truly curious. Along with that feeling came patience, openness, and care.

True curiosity is exhilarating and sometimes feels scary. It requires a willingness to give up everything I've ever known or believed. *Everything.* It's hard for me to be in that state. True curiosity demands courage and requires the willingness to be afraid. But the rewards are incomparable: when I'm in a state of true curiosity, I connect more deeply with others, I discover solutions to perplexing problems, and I'm more effective as a coach and leader. I feel alive and energized and aligned to my purpose in life.

Curiosity Affirmation: True curiosity requires that I suspend judgment and all that I think I know. True curiosity requires that I befriend my fear. When I am truly curious, I feel alive, accepting, and compassionate. When I am truly curious, I connect deeply with others, learn, and fulfill my purpose in life.

Courage

Many people see me as a courageous person, but I can tell you I also experience a great deal of fear. When I reflect on the actions I've taken that appear courageous, I recall how I was simultaneously terrified. When I proposed to lead a coaching department in my district, my imposter syndrome threatened to swallow me whole. When I offered a supervisor hard feedback about her management approach, I was sure I'd be fired. And when I stepped onto a stage to speak to 1,000 educators for the first time, I wasn't sure I could do it.

Many people think being courageous requires getting rid of fear. But being human means having fear—and being courageous means accepting fear and giving it just the right amount of influence in our lives. Fear helps us know where to set boundaries, how to get our needs met, how to keep ourselves safe, and how to take effective action. Accepting and working with fear allows me to take on big challenges. When I'm in a healthy relationship with fear, my courage fills me with energy and clarity to make decisions about what to say and do.

Here's how courage shows up when I'm coaching:

- I don't worry about whether I'll offend someone with a question.
- I effectively use the confrontational approach (see Chapter 5, "Fifty Questions to Ask").
- I listen to my intuition.
- I suggest activities that might be at the edge of my client's comfort zone.
- I share data that my client might struggle with.

- I name the elephants in the room—especially elephants that relate to educational inequities.
- I ask questions about emotions like, "What's coming up for you? I noticed that when I asked that last question, you crossed your arms and looked away."
- I recognize when I'm emotionally activated in a conversation and acknowledge my need for growth.

A Transformational Coach taps into a deep well of courage. It's hard to get up every day and commit to being compassionate and curious for others. It's hard to acknowledge our own shortcomings and practice self-compassion. Courage enables us to persevere and keep our eyes on the prize of a more equitable school system. When we work with courage, we feel belonging and connectedness, we access our agency, we gain competence, and we trust ourselves. Working courageously makes transformation—of ourselves, our clients, and the system—possible.

Courage Affirmation: Courage provides me with energy to take risks every day. When I'm aware of my fear, I can speak up on behalf of children, as well as on my own behalf, because I'm clear that we all deserve to thrive. I accept my fear, and I am committed to knowing it so that I can access the power of courage.

Trust the Process

When I trust the process, I accept that I can't know what will happen in the future, I can't know what's going on inside another person, and I can't predict the best outcome for the situation we're in—and I do the work anyway. To trust the process, I often have to wrangle with my ego, which tries to control the process.

Here's an example of when I didn't trust the process. Katia was a new teacher who struggled more than most. At 22, she was teaching seniors in a school in turmoil, and, though she was terribly unprepared, I was convinced that Katia could become the teacher the students needed her to be. My conviction was complicated by the fact that I'd interviewed her and lobbied hard for the principal to hire her—I thought she'd be fantastic.

The first time Katia quit, six weeks into the school year, I pursued her with a vengeance. I offered all kinds of coaching support, including co-teaching some of the classes. She came back, taught for a few days, and quit again. I'd had a fixed idea of what was best in that situation. I thought it was the worst thing in the world when she quit for good—the story I told was that it was because I was a bad coach. But three weeks later, we hired a long-term substitute who turned out to be a stable, competent teacher. Katia went on to teach younger children in a parochial school, where she thrived.

Here's an example of when I did trust myself and the coaching process. Initially, I was intimidated by Jackson, an older, veteran math teacher with a reputation for being cranky. Because my secondary math content knowledge is weak, I couldn't offer content-specific coaching, but I recognized how my lack of content knowledge could level the power dynamics between us (as a district coach, I was perceived to have more positional power). "My background is in teaching humanities," I explained. "But I feel confident that I can support you to think through the decisions you make in the classroom, I can guide you to deeper reflection on your teaching, and I can help you find ways to better serve your students. I'll rely on you to know best practices in math instruction." Jackson's eyebrows shot up when I said this. He thanked me for my honesty, although he admitted that he was still apprehensive about coaching.

For the first six weeks or so, our meetings were superficial and tedious. I would ask a reflective question such as, "How did you know that students were ready to engage in independent practice?" and he would respond with something like, "I just knew. I've been teaching for 23 years." I was intentional about building a relationship with Jackson—I'd uplift his strengths, ask questions about his aspirations as a teacher, and try to unearth personal connections—and yet these efforts seemed to fall flat. As the semester progressed, part of me worried that I wouldn't be successful with Jackson. *Trust the process*, I reminded myself.

Coaching Jackson successfully depended on acknowledging my own fears. I reminded myself that change doesn't always happen on the timeline I want, that I could trust the process because I trusted my coaching skills, and that I could depend on my ability to navigate my own emotions. I engaged my curiosity about what was going on, which helped me find new strategies to try. Little by little, Jackson softened to coaching. He began trying new things in his class, asking me questions about what I observed, and exploring his ways of being.

I've been in countless situations like this one with Jackson in which I feared that I wouldn't be effective as a coach and worried that a teacher wouldn't change. In some of those situations, fear blocked my ability to be curious and find a pathway forward. However, as I've strengthened my trust in myself and in the process, I've found I don't have to work as hard. As I've surrendered to the coaching process, which I facilitate but don't direct, I feel held by a hard-to-describe flow of things happening. Whenever my fear surges and I worry that I'm not helping my client—or that they won't change or that I won't know what to do with someone—I tell myself, *the story isn't over yet*. This reminds me that I don't know everything and that all I can do is trust in the unfolding of the experience.

There's a Zen parable that I return to again and again to remind me that the story isn't yet over. It begins a long time ago, with an old farmer who had worked his crops for many years. Then one day, his horse ran away. Upon hearing the news, his neighbors came to visit.

"Such bad luck," they said sympathetically.

"Maybe," the farmer replied.

The next morning, the horse returned, bringing with it three wild horses.

"How wonderful," the neighbors exclaimed.

"Maybe," replied the old man.

The following day, the farmer's son tried to ride one of the untamed horses, and he was thrown and broke his leg.

The neighbors again came to offer their sympathy for his misfortune.

"Maybe," answered the farmer.

The day after, military officials came to the village to draft young men into the army. Seeing that the son's leg was broken, they passed him by.

The neighbors congratulated the farmer on how well things had turned out. "Maybe," said the farmer.

Trusting the process might be the hardest disposition to live into. It's the hardest one for me to explain and teach. There is also an element to this disposition that borders on what some call *faith*. When I am truly in a state of trust, I feel a sense of trust in the universe or in the great mystery or something else. I encourage you to take my reflections on this disposition and consider this an inquiry for yourself. See where this exploration takes you. Trust in that process. The story is never over.

Trust Affirmation: I trust myself to build skills, find resources, create connections, and be the person I want to be. I trust that when I encounter inevitable challenges, I'll learn and emerge from the adversity more skilled and confident than before. Because I know that I can't know everything, I trust the coaching process and the timeline in which everything unfolds.

Humility

Many years ago, I had a principal who was exactly my age. She was a new principal, and I thought she was making a lot of mistakes. I accessed my courage and confronted her on her leadership, offering what I thought was clear, precise, actionable feedback that aligned to our school's mission and goals. I felt proud of myself. She received my feedback well and asked me a number of follow up questions. She invited me to problem-solve around some of the areas I was frustrated with. Then she shared context about those problems that I hadn't been aware of. She explained budget issues, federal laws, and the district's decision-making process. As my principal spoke, I realized that there was so much I didn't know and that I'd come to inaccurate conclusions. I recognized that below my intention to confront my principal were feelings of righteousness. I felt a wave of humility wash over me, and then I felt feelings of empathy for her, and then I felt a burgeoning curiosity.

Many of us have a tendency to overestimate how much we know, how right we are, or how special we are, a tendency that's exacerbated by dominant culture that values accomplishments and status.

Humility shows up as a value across many religions and cultures. Often depicted as a virtue, it also contributes to emotional resilience. Humility allows you to see yourself accurately, have perspective on your place in the world, acknowledge personal mistakes and limitations, have an open mind, focus less on yourself, and appreciate the value of all things. It's important to know that being humble does not mean having a low opinion of yourself. It means seeing yourself accurately and putting your accomplishments into perspective. You can think of humility as knowing your strengths and talents and also knowing that you are one of many people with strengths and talents.

When you embody humility as a coach, you know that the young teacher, fresh out of college, has strengths. You know that the veteran teacher, whom you perceive at times as resistant, has talents. When you know that others have talents, when you recognize that you don't know everything, you can be more curious, open, and empathetic. You likely find that it's a relief not to have to know everything—and that you have a lot more energy when you don't feel like you have to solve every problem.

When you're coaching, humility means you can authentically engage your client in figuring out how to address the challenges they face in the classroom. It is a way to communicate confidence in your trust in the process—since the success of an experience is not entirely contingent upon you. Humility also creates the conditions in which your client can trust you. It takes courage to be humble, and it is also an expression of compassion as you communicate your interdependence. Perhaps you're seeing how the dispositions of a Transformational Coach intersect and overlap. As you deepen your embodiment of one, you'll find that others are more accessible.

Humility Affirmation: I know that I am not better than anyone else, that I have made mistakes and am a developing person, and that I don't know everything. I recognize that I have strengths and talents and other people do too.

People Remember How You Made Them Feel

Not long ago, I demonstrated a challenging coaching conversation for a group of coaches. Afterward, I asked the coaches to generate a short statement to describe what they'd observed. One woman said, "You were kind, but not nice." I bristled and asked her what she meant. "I mean that as a compliment," she said. "You were kind, but firm and clear. You were direct, but compassionate. I felt like you truly wanted the teacher to grow, and you were respecting her process." I felt relieved: this was how I'd intended to be experienced.

There's nothing better than being experienced in the way you aspire to be experienced. Although you can't determine another's experience, you can control how you show up. With intentionality, practice, and awareness you can show up with compassion, curiosity, courage, trust, and humility, and your questions, facial expressions, feedback, words, and tone of voice will reflect those dispositions.

Let me be clear: embodying the dispositions can feel hard. It can feel challenging to trust the process when a teacher is resistant; it can feel almost impossible to be compassionate with a teacher who isn't serving children. But if you provide feedback from a place of superiority or righteousness or if you respond to resistance from frustration and annoyance, you will not change schools. You will simply replicate the inherently unequal status quo. Never underestimate the power of kindness, courage, and humility.

You may not remember all the words I write or say, but I hope you'll feel optimistic and empowered. As you develop coaching skills and strategies, remember that how you show up is within your sphere of control.

Pause and Process

Reflect:

- Consider the Transformational Coach's ways of being: compassion, curiosity, courage, trust, and humility. Which of these align most closely with your core values? Which come most easily to you?
- Which of the ways of being challenge you? What might be gained by embodying one of these ways of being?
- How might your own spiritual or personal belief system support your growth in the Transformational Coach's ways of being?

Next steps:

- Listen to *Bright Morning Podcast* episode 15 in which I coach Pearl Garden, an educational leader, around who she is being, and in the process, I'm pushed to reflect on who I need to be in the conversation.
- Download the core values tool and identify your core values.
- Spend a week paying attention to how you embody the Transformational Coach's ways of being. When are these easier to live into? When are they more challenging?

CHAPTER 3

The Foundational Abilities

The Cornerstones of Transformational Coaching

Common misconception: I don't have time for this type of coaching.	*Transformational Coaches know:* With strong skills and will, transformation can occur in 15 minutes.

When I became an instructional coach, I attended a few workshops on skills such as how to facilitate a data conversation, how to probe a teacher's thinking around assessments, and how to ask open-ended questions. During the breaks, I asked the trainers questions like these:

- What do you say when a new teacher can't stop crying and says she's going to quit?
- How do you decide where to start and what to coach on when you go into a classroom and see two dozen critical areas for improvement?
- What do you do when a teacher refuses to use the new curriculum?
- How do you respond when a teacher says, "These parents don't care about their kids"?

These situations require that a coach have a robust set of skills. Most traditional instructional coaching programs emphasize technical coaching skills such as how to give feedback or guide a teacher through lesson planning—but these alone are insufficient to respond to the complexities of guiding an adult learner.

This chapter introduces the foundational abilities of Transformational Coaching, namely the skills needed to:

- Coach the Three Bs—behaviors, beliefs and ways of being (which includes coaching emotions)
- Build, repair, and maintain trust
- Cultivate a client's agency—their sense of being able to take action
- Navigate power dynamics—because power is *always* present between people

Every additional coaching skill and strategy that we'll explore rests on your ability to enact these foundational abilities. Without them, you can't effectively facilitate a reflection on data, provide constructive feedback, or respond to resistance. I'm tempted to say that all you really need to do to be a powerful Transformational Coach is these foundational abilities.

To explain these foundational abilities, I'll tell you about a teacher I coached many years ago. After I share a portion of our first conversation, I'll describe the foundational skills and then highlight how I used those skills in my conversation with this seemingly resistant teacher. By deconstructing a segment of a coaching conversation, I'll reveal what the foundational skills look and sound like in action.

How to Coach a Teacher Who Opposes the New Curriculum

Isaac was a mid-career, fifth-grade math teacher who staunchly opposed the adoption of a new math curriculum that I'll call Perspective. He made his stance known at every staff meeting, in front of district leaders, and to me, even before I began coaching him. Although we'd taught in the same school some years before and we had a warm relationship, Isaac didn't want coaching. "With so many struggling new teachers," he explained, "I don't understand the decision for every teacher to engage in a coaching cycle." He grudgingly agreed to meet with me, but also insinuated that because his evaluations were always good and his students performed well on standardized tests, he planned to do what he'd always done in his classroom.

"You're wasting your time if you think you can convince me to teach Perspective," he said.

"Thanks for your honesty," I said. "There are some things I appreciate about the curriculum, but I'm really curious to hear more about your opinion of it. And I'm really not here to convince you to teach it. That's not my job."

"Elena," Isaac said, gesticulating as he spoke, "this curriculum is way too hard for our kids. There are more words in the workbook than numbers—this is an English text, not a math book. Maybe kids in the suburbs can do this, but our kids aren't ready for it."

"I'm kind of surprised to hear you say that, Isaac," I said. Isaac was the child of Central American immigrants and had attended public schools in Los Angeles. He'd always espoused high expectations for his students, and his instruction was generally known for being rigorous. "Can you say more?"

"They need a really strong foundation in the basics—that's what they're tested on. Perspective assumes they got good math instruction in the early grades and that they're going to get this same kind of instruction in middle and high school." Isaac leaned back and crossed his arms but maintained intense eye contact. His thick facial hair made it hard for me to see whether there was any hint of a smile, and I felt a little intimidated.

"Isaac," I said, taking an audible breath, "What's your biggest fear about teaching Perspective?"

He looked away, out the open window. The September heatwave had broken, and the air felt good. "That I'll fail my kids. That they won't be prepared for what they're heading toward." Isaac's voice softened. "You know what they'll get with other math teachers."

"I know how much you care about your kids," I said. "I've always seen that from you."

"That's why I can't teach this. It isn't right. It's not fair to them." Isaac sighed.

"I'm hearing that you're holding a firm belief about what they need, what they can do, and what this curriculum offers," I said. "I also hear fear about taking a risk. I'm wondering if you'd be willing to unpack this belief?"

Isaac looked at me and didn't say anything for what felt like a long time, but it was probably a few seconds. I couldn't read the expression in his eyes and felt a little nervous. "Look," he said, "*I made it out*. And it wasn't because I had great teachers. It's not fair for me to risk their future by teaching a curriculum that they're not ready for."

I nodded and paused for a few seconds, taking in what he'd shared. "So what enabled you to be successful as a kid?" I asked. "And to enjoy math enough to teach it?"

"My parents always encouraged me. They pushed me, and my uncle tutored me in math and made it fun. He was always giving me math problems to work out in his store—making me create profit predictions and calculate losses. In school, I probably only had one math teacher who challenged me."

I raised my eyebrows and made an expression that I hoped communicated empathy. "Thanks for sharing that," I said. "It helps me understand who you want to be as a teacher."

"I want to be the teacher who makes sure they're ready for middle school. That they've got more than the basics so that if they don't get a good teacher in sixth grade, maybe they won't fall too far behind." Isaac sighed. "I hate knowing that I can't control what happens to them after they leave here," he added.

"That's really painful," I said, nodding. I remembered that feeling well. "Your commitment to your kids is incredible."

"It's infuriating," Isaac responded. "What can I do?" His hand gestures, again, emphasized his frustration.

"Yeah," I said. "I hear your anger. I get it. And I hear your sense of powerlessness." I exhaled and paused. "Isaac, how do you think your experiences as a child affect the decisions you make as a teacher?"

"I mean, I think that's obvious, right?" he said. "I want to challenge them. I don't want to let them down. I feel like the decisions I make are high stakes."

I nodded and held silence for a few seconds. "Isaac," I said, as I shifted my tone to be more authoritative and bolder. "I want to challenge the conclusion you've come to about Perspective. And feel free to disagree, but it sounds like you've concluded that if you teach Perspective, your students will not be prepared for middle school, and they'll fail, and they'll meet some bad educational end. It's like a linear equation. Is this the only possible outcome? Is there any other way this could go?"

Isaac looked down at his hands and rubbed them together. He exhaled loudly and said, "Okay, I see what you're saying. But they aren't ready for this curriculum."

"Well," I said, "the interesting thing is that you recognize that Perspective is a really challenging curriculum—and I'm hearing that you were successful as a kid because you were challenged, and you are committed to rigorous instruction for your students."

"Yeah," he said. "But I don't know how to make Perspective accessible to them."

"Ah, okay," I said, nodding enthusiastically. "I'm curious if that's something you think you *might* be able to figure out? I mean, you've been teaching for over a decade."

"I probably could. I mean, if I have to be honest, I guess I admit that Perspective offers the kind of math that they need if they want to do advanced math in high school or in a real-life situation. I don't hate the program. I just know my kids couldn't do it."

"Okay," I said, "I'm not disagreeing with you necessarily. I'm just wondering if you might be able to figure out how to scaffold your lessons so that they could build toward engaging in at least some of Perspective?"

"Yeah, I mean, yeah. I know I can do that."

"Would you be willing to look at the first unit for five minutes or so? I'm really curious what thoughts come to mind about how you'd make it accessible."

Isaac nodded. I slid the Teacher's Guide across the table. Isaac flipped through the first few pages. "Well," he said, "I'd have to start by front-loading a lot of vocabulary." He identified half a dozen words that his students, most of whom were English Learners, wouldn't know. "I mean, do kids in the suburbs even know these terms?" he asked. I shrugged.

"What else?" I said.

"I doubt they'd know this concept or be able to do this process," he said, pointing at different parts of the page, "and without that knowledge, they wouldn't be able to do this lesson."

"Could you teach them those concepts?" I asked.

"Yeah, I'd need a few days, but of course."

Isaac continued skimming through the first unit. Occasionally he'd nod or make an affirmative sound.

"Isaac," I said, "If you *could* scaffold this unit and if your students *could* access this content, what do you think that would provide them?"

"I see what you're getting at, Elena. Because, yeah, of course, there's some good stuff here. This is complex, definitely a lot of higher-order thinking, and it's real-world math. I see that, and I know they'd probably be more engaged with this than with some of our old-school lessons. But . . ."

"Wait," I interrupted Isaac. "Hold on just a second." My tone of voice was playful and light. "Isaac, you mean you see some nuggets in Perspective? Did I hear that?"

Isaac nodded.

"Listen," I said, my tone becoming warm, but firm again. "Your fear is normal. It's understandable. It reflects deep love and commitment. It speaks to your life and experiences." I leaned across the table, toward Isaac. "And I'm also hearing that you recognize that this curriculum might serve some learning needs that aren't being met right now. Is that right?"

"Yeah, but I know you've seen the district's pacing guide. There is no way especially considering all the scaffolding that I'll have to do, that I'll be able to stay on track with that guide. No way!"

"I agree." I nodded. "So let's figure out what that means for how you teach this," I said, my voice confident. "But I want to clarify that I'm hearing that *you're willing* to try this curriculum?"

"You win, Elena," Isaac laughed. "You got me. I'll try."

"Okay, but I really wasn't wanting to convince you to do this. I just wanted to understand your perspective on Perspective."

"I know, I'm just messing with you," Isaac laughed again. "I *have* been closed off to this—I think it's also that I feel like the district makes so many random decisions and they'll probably only want us to teach this curriculum for three years and then there'll be something else. It's exhausting."

I nodded and raised my eyebrows. "I know. It *is* frustrating. And I'm excited to see what you do with Perspective. I'm excited to learn along with you and to support you in figuring out the pacing that makes sense. I'm even wondering if you might be able to share what you learn with the math department and maybe advise on next year's pacing guide. But let's take one step at a time. How about if we start plotting out the first unit and identifying the supplementary lessons you'll need to design?"

Isaac nodded. "That sounds good. I appreciate your ideas about how I might influence the district," he said. "I've thought about something like that, or being the math lead or something."

"I think your leadership is needed in our district," I replied. "And I'd love to work with you on exploring pathways into leadership."

"I thought you're just coaching me on Perspective?" Isaac said.

"Would it serve our students if you took a bigger leadership role in math instruction in our district?" I asked.

Isaac nodded.

"Then I can also do some coaching around developing your leadership," I said.

"Okay," Isaac said. "You've got a deal. Let's crack open this Teacher Guide and identify all the things my kids aren't ready to do yet."

Isaac and I spent about half an hour creating a supplementary scope and sequence with the additional content he predicted his students would need. As we went through the lessons in the first unit, Isaac made appreciative comments about the curriculum, noting that it pushed student thinking, encouraged divergent methods to solutions, invited collaborative problem-solving, and made connections to real situations students would encounter. Before we closed, I asked Isaac two final questions.

"Isaac, how have your beliefs about this curriculum changed as a result of the work we just did together?"

"I guess I see how my belief that my students couldn't access this was connected to my inability to know how to present it to them in a way that would make it accessible. I'm embarrassed to admit that I blamed them, or I made it something about them, rather than something I didn't know how to do."

"That's what we humans do," I said, "when we're afraid or don't know something. We tend to blame." I paused and then, in a softer tone, asked, "One more question: how are you feeling right now?"

"How am I feeling?" Isaac asked. "I guess I feel good. I was annoyed that you wanted to meet, and I felt like coaching was a waste of time. I only met with you because we go way back. But I'm glad you challenged me. I'm a Capricorn, and I can be a stubborn old goat. I'm feeling good, though. I actually feel excited to teach this. It's been some time since I've tried a new approach, and maybe I was getting a little stuck or even bored. I feel hopeful—also still skeptical—but I have to admit, I feel hopeful."

Coaching the Three Bs

As I described in Chapter 1, "Transformational Coaching," a Transformational Coach addresses a client's behavior, beliefs, and ways of being to create sustained, transformative change in practice. Because this work is at the heart of Transformational Coaching, it is the first of the foundational strategies. Given that the skill set needed to coach the Three Bs is vast, we'll spend many chapters exploring it.

Before you continue reading, if you'd like, skim through the transcript of the conversation with Isaac and see if you can identify places where I was coaching his behaviors, beliefs, and ways of being. Think of this as a pre-assessment; at the end of this chapter, you can return to the conversation one last time and see how much you learned about coaching behaviors, beliefs, and ways of being.

Breaking Down the Conversation with Isaac

The portion of the conversation with Isaac that's included in this chapter took about 15 minutes. It occurred during a period when I was intentionally focused on developing my coaching skills, and I recorded the conversation on my phone with his permission. I later transcribed the conversation, and I analyzed what I said. Take a few minutes to read my analysis in Table 3.1, paying attention to the ways the strands of coaching beliefs, behaviors, and ways of being are braided throughout the conversation.

Table 3.1: Analyzing the Coaching Conversation for the Three Bs

Elena's Words	Coaching Behavior, Belief, or Way of Being?	Explanation
"There are some things I appreciate about the curriculum, but I'm really curious to hear more about your opinion of it."	Belief	I wanted to surface his beliefs—"opinions" are beliefs.
"What's your biggest fear about teaching Perspective?"	Being	Ways of being show up in our emotions.

(Continued)

Table 3.1: (Continued)

Elena's Words	Coaching Behavior, Belief, or Way of Being?	Explanation
"I'm hearing that you're holding a really firm belief about what they need, what they can do, and what this curriculum offers. I also hear some fear about taking a risk. I'm wondering if you'd be willing to unpack this belief?"	Belief and Being	I wanted to reflect that I heard *beliefs*, and I wanted to guide him into understanding where the belief came from. I heard how his fear generated a belief and a way of being.
"Isaac, how do you think your experiences as a child affect the decisions you make as a teacher?"	Behavior	I wanted to guide Isaac into the awareness that the behaviors he engaged in were based in his experiences.
"I want to challenge the conclusion you've come to about Perspective. And feel free to disagree, but it sounds like you've concluded that if you teach Perspective, your students will not be prepared for middle school, and they'll fail, and they'll meet some bad educational end. It's like a linear equation. Is this the only possible outcome? Is there any other way this could go?"	Beliefs	I wanted Isaac to see the possible consequences of the beliefs that he was holding, and to recognize that his thinking was narrow.

Table 3.1: (Continued)

Elena's Words	Coaching Behavior, Belief, or Way of Being?	Explanation
"I'm just wondering if you might be able to figure out how to scaffold your lessons so that they could build towards engaging in at least some of the lessons?"	Behavior	I knew that Isaac was a skilled teacher, and I wanted to remind him that he knew what to do—the actions to take.
"Would you be willing to look at the first unit for five minutes or so? I'm really curious what thoughts come to mind about how you'd make it accessible."	Behavior	I wanted Isaac to look at the curriculum and envision the skills needed to supplement it.
"If you *could* scaffold this unit and if your students *could* access this content, what do you think that would provide them?"	Beliefs	I was challenging his thinking—his mindset—by inviting other possibilities.
"Your fear is normal. It's understandable. It reflects deep love and commitment. It speaks to your life and experiences. And I'm also hearing that you recognize that this curriculum might serve some learning needs that aren't being met right now. Is that right?"	Being	Acknowledging emotions is a way to coach a way of being.
"How about if we start plotting out the first unit and identifying the supplementary lessons you'll need to design?"	Behavior	I guided Isaac into taking action on next steps.

(Continued)

Elena's Words	Coaching Behavior, Belief, or Way of Being?	Explanation
"Isaac, how have your beliefs about this curriculum changed as a result of the work we just did together?"	Beliefs	I wanted Isaac to be aware of how his behaviors were connected to his beliefs and how a shift in beliefs could positively impact behavior.
"One more question: how are you feeling right now?"	Being	I wanted Isaac to be aware of how a shift in beliefs contributes to a positive shift in emotions and a way of being.

I hope you see how I fluidly moved among the Three Bs and how I cultivated Isaac's awareness of the connections among what a person believes, the actions they subsequently take, and how they feel.

In this conversation, the strategies I used to coach the Three Bs included active listening and using the cathartic, catalytic, and confrontational approaches (see Chapter 5, "Fifty Questions to Ask"). I also used emotional intelligence to build trust, I cultivated Isaac's agency, and I navigated the power dynamics between us and inherent in the district mandate. These are the foundational abilities we'll dig into next.

Building Trust

Cultivating trust is part of relationship management, but because it is such an essential skill, I've extracted it from the broader domain of emotional intelligence and elevated it as a foundational ability. *You must cultivate trust in order to coach anyone on their behaviors, beliefs, or ways of being*: this is a non-negotiable skill.

To create the conditions for trust, you need to do the following:

- Believe that you (the coach) deserve to thrive, that you can be effective, and that you are a facilitator of a learning process
- Believe that your client deserves to thrive, that they have agency, and that they can be effective
- Be compassionate, curious, courageous, humble, and trustful of the process
- Cultivate exceptional emotional intelligence
- See your client's strengths and potential
- Coach your client's way of being
- Listen deeply and expansively

In this section, we'll explore *interpersonal trust*. There's another kind of trust that's useful to know about—*situational trust*. When I talk about "trusting the process," this is what I'm describing—trusting the situation, meaning the context and process of coaching. As coaches, our focus is on building interpersonal trust, but we also tap into situational trust whenever possible.

What Is Interpersonal Trust?

Call to mind a person you trust. Imagine being with them and talking to them. Visualize their facial expressions and mannerisms. Listen to how they offer advice or share their experiences. How do you feel as you recall this person?

Trust is an emotional state in which we feel relaxed, receptive, seen, and cared for. When we trust someone, we ascribe positive intent to their actions—if someone gives us hard feedback, we assume it's because they want to help us grow. We trust people who we feel see our potential, who recognize that we are not our mistakes, who don't judge us, who listen to us, and who keep their word. In the presence of such people, we're more willing to take risks and be vulnerable.

Think back to the person you trust. Does this description of trust align with your experience? Can you recall a time when you asked them a vulnerable question or received challenging feedback from them?

Perhaps another scenario has come to mind, one in which you trusted someone and then they violated your trust. This has happened to everyone, and it hurts. Trust is not a permanent state—it can be created, broken, and repaired.

When we're in a place of positional power, such as being a coach or school leader, we can forget that we need to cultivate trust or check in on levels of trust. Furthermore, we can forget that it's our responsibility to regularly tune into the quality of trust between us and our clients, and repair any breaches in trust. Doing this requires the ability to listen well and to engage our emotional intelligence.

What Enables Trust?

You create the conditions in which trust can develop by demonstrating the Four Cs: care, consistency, congruence, and competence. These are skills and ways of being. Let's explore how the Four Cs show up for coaches.

You care: You demonstrate care through your compassion, curiosity, courage, and humility. You show an interest in who someone is beyond the role they're in. You maintain confidentiality; breaching confidentiality reflects a lack of care and is a surefire way to undermine trust. You are mentally and emotionally present in sessions. You listen deeply and expansively and ask nonjudgmental questions. Finally, you hold unconditional positive regard for your clients.

You are consistent: You do what you say you'll do. You honor your agreements. You walk your talk. Many new coaches over-promise—in an effort to appear helpful, they make more commitments than they can fulfill. This approach backfires when their clients inevitably perceive them as inconsistent and unreliable. Commit only to what you can do, ensure that your client understands your commitments, and uphold them. This is the baseline for consistency.

You demonstrate congruence: Your outsides match your insides: you behave in ways that align to how you feel. For example, if you feel grumpy, but you smile and ask questions about your client's weekend, they will perceive this—consciously or unconsciously—as a lack of congruence. This can generate distrust. One of the reasons it's essential to pay attention to body language (both your own and others') is because congruence or incongruence often shows up most clearly in our nonverbal communication.

You are competent: You use coaching skills well. You listen deeply, facilitate reflection, ask open-ended questions, and so on. You also regulate yourself emotionally and respond to other people's emotional states appropriately. Finally, to be perceived as competent, you need to take responsibility for clarifying expectations for coaching. You might believe, for example, that your competence lies in your ability to facilitate a learning process, but a client might expect you to have expertise in a particular math curriculum. This breakdown in expectations can weaken trust. A competent coach takes responsibility for ensuring that everyone is on the same page about what coaching is.

Back to the Conversation with Isaac

Because emotions are internal experiences, the transcript of the conversation with Isaac doesn't tell you everything I was feeling. There's more to understand about how I felt and how I managed my emotions, as well as about the conscious choices I made in response to the emotions I perceived in Isaac. As I share some reflections on the conversation, I hope you'll recognize how engaging my emotional intelligence allowed me to build trust with Isaac—and how that made all the difference in this conversation.

Before a coaching conversation, whenever possible, I reflect on how I'm feeling, how I anticipate my client will be feeling, and what I hope will happen in the conversation. Here's what I wrote before I met with Isaac:

I'm nervous about meeting with Isaac. He's been so vocally opposed to Perspective, he sees me as a district coach responsible for ensuring fidelity to the curriculum, and he's often sarcastic. There's also our age difference [he is about 20 years older], and sometimes I feel like he's been paternalistic with me. I'm afraid that if he's sarcastic, I'll get triggered—I remember being little and being with family who were sarcastic, and I didn't feel safe.

If I notice this happening (I'll feel a tightening in my body or like I'm recoiling or pulling back), I'll take a deep breath, tell myself that I'm safe, remind myself that if I feel really uncomfortable, I can leave, and then I'll remember that Isaac and I go way back. We worked together in my first years of teaching, and he was always kind to me. I'll remember when we took our third graders on a field trip and Martha got lost, and he was so worried he almost cried. I'll remember the time he gave me good advice about dealing with a parent who was upset. I'll remember how he brought his toddler to school once and how sweet he was with him. These things will help me remember our connection, the things I appreciate about him, and his commitment to kids.

But I'm also worried that, because he's still in the classroom (he's taught for three years longer than me), he might see me first as an emissary from the central offices. I'm afraid that this power dynamic will make him more difficult to work with. Also, his knowledge of math is much deeper than mine. He knows that I haven't taught math beyond third grade, and I think he'll doubt me as a coach.

I'm most worried that if I can't get him to consider Perspective, my competence as a coach will be questioned, and I'll be seen as a failure by my manager. Or maybe I'm most worried that I'll lose my patience and say or do something I regret. Because I don't actually think my goal is to get him to consider Perspective. Maybe it is, but I really just want to talk to him and hear what he's thinking. I remember him as being really thoughtful, and I don't understand what's going on with him. I hope that our relationship will let him trust me a little and allow for an honest conversation. My intention is to be open, to assume he's coming from a good place, to see his humanity and potential, and to listen.

This conversation will be a success if our relationship stays as it's been or even gets better. It will be a success if I understand what's going on for Isaac. It will be a success if I can coach him to reflect on what he's doing, thinking, and feeling.

Writing for 10 minutes in preparation for a coaching conversation is incredibly powerful. You can surface your hopes and fears. You can activate your empathy for your client. You can identify who you want to be. This reflection sets you up to walk into the conversation feeling far more confident than you might otherwise. I know, it's hard to find the time to write, especially if you coach a lot of teachers. If that's the case, then pick one teacher each week for whom you'll spend 10 minutes preparing.

Given that you've read my conversation with Isaac, you've likely generated opinions about whether the conversation went well and whether I achieved my objectives. I left the conversation feeling elated, to be honest, and I could feel this joy in the spring in my step and in the spaciousness in my chest. Our coaching session went far better than I could have imagined. I left feeling excited to coach Isaac. I felt like he would be open and receptive to coaching, I hadn't been emotionally activated (triggered), and I appreciated his trust.

Coaching Isaac that semester *was* delightful—it was fun, challenging, and invigorating. No one believed me when, after two months of coaching him, I said that not only was Isaac fully onboard with Perspective, but he was creating a supplemental curriculum for other teachers. I also squeezed in some leadership coaching, as I'd promised, and a few years later, Isaac became a district math coach. It was when I'd offered him leadership coaching, Isaac told me later, that he began thinking he could trust me.

The trust that emerged in our conversation hinged largely on a few moments when I coached from emotional intelligence. As you read Table 3.2, notice what coaching from emotional intelligence can look like and sound like and consider how this kind of coaching allowed me to build trust.

Table 3.2: Using Emotional Intelligence in a Coaching Conversation

What Happened	Emotional Intelligence Competency	Comments
The first thing Isaac said was, "You're wasting your time if you think you can convince me to teach Perspective." I said, "Thanks for your honesty. There are some things I appreciate about the curriculum, but I'm really curious to hear more . . ."	Relationship management	I appreciated Isaac for his honesty (my tone of voice reinforced this). I was transparent about my stance, saying there were things I appreciated, but I expressed interest in hearing from him. I know that my body language and tone were congruent with the words I spoke. I was conscious about how these actions might build trust.
When Isaac said that his kids couldn't do the work, I said, "I'm kind of surprised to hear you say that," and then I asked, "Can you say more?"	Social awareness and relationship management	I refrained from jumping to conclusions about the belief that Isaac was expressing, which sounded like a deficit mindset. I expressed curiosity.
I asked Isaac about his greatest fear in teaching Perspective.	Self-awareness, social awareness	Because I sensed that there was some fear present for Isaac, I decided to be bold and ask what it was about. I felt a little nervous asking this (my palms were sweaty), but I recognized that the potential benefit of asking the question outweighed the risk.

What Happened	Emotional Intelligence Competency	Comments
Isaac looked away from me, out the window, and his voice got soft when he said, "That I'll fail my kids. That they won't be prepared for what they're heading towards."	Self-awareness, social awareness, and relationship management	I felt so much empathy for Isaac at this point—I've had those same feelings about my students. I said, "I know how much you care about your kids. I've always seen that from you." In saying that, I was also reminding him of our relationship and my longstanding respect for him. This was intended to build trust.
I validated Isaac's care for his students and centered their needs.	Relationship management	I knew that Isaac was deeply committed to his students' success, and by affirming that commitment I hoped to build trust.
I appreciated Isaac for sharing how his childhood experiences helped me understand who he wanted to be as a teacher.	Relationship management	Isaac responded by sharing his vision for who he wanted to be. I heard how his deep commitment to his students originated in his childhood, and I knew that it probably felt good to remember why he became a teacher.

(Continued)

What Happened	Emotional Intelligence Competency	Comments
Isaac said, "I hate knowing that I can't control what happens to them after they leave here."	Social awareness and relationship management	I heard the sadness in his voice and validated it by saying, "That's really painful. Your commitment to your kids is incredible." I also validated his anger when he said, "It's infuriating."
At the very end of our conversation, Isaac said, "I feel hopeful, and also still skeptical, but I have to admit, I feel hopeful."	Self-awareness and relationship management	I noticed how happy I felt when he said this. I felt light and energized. I wanted to communicate my appreciation, and said, "I'm so glad to hear that." I know that my facial expression, body language, and tone also communicated my care, appreciation, and happiness.

I hope you might skim through the transcript again and identify additional points where you suspect that I drew on emotional intelligence to guide my decision-making and how those moves built trust. Every time Isaac spoke, I registered both his words and his nonverbal communication. Every choice I made during the conversation took into account his emotions, my own, and our relationship.

Cultivating Agency

Agency is the feeling that you can do what you want to do. It means you have a sense of control over your actions and their consequences. It's similar to feeling empowered or experiencing a sense of autonomy (one of our core human needs), and I use the terms *agency, empowerment,* and *autonomy* synonymously.

When people feel they lack agency, they might feel like things happen *to* them, that they have no say in the whirlwind of life, or that they're at the mercy of the fates—or the administration or the district. It's a horrible feeling, one that we all succumb to at some point. Feeling a sense of agency, on the other hand, contributes to the sense that we're thriving. A Transformational Coach listens for and notices the places where a client feels disempowered and then coaches them toward a sense of control over what happens in their life.

How to Coach Toward Agency

Coaching toward agency includes:

- Inviting a client to have input into the focus or goals for coaching
- Providing options for a client to take the lead in directing the conversation
- Communicating confidence that a client can solve their own problems
- Guiding a client to use their energy within their sphere of influence and control

These actions rest on the foundational beliefs that a client doesn't need to be fixed, that they have competencies, and that they act for reasons that may not make sense to you but that make sense given their life experiences. When you anchor in those beliefs, you invite a client to make decisions about the conversation or about problems they're facing.

When we coach toward agency, we listen carefully for victim stories (see Chapter 11, "How to Coach Beliefs"). We recognize these problematic narratives as soon as they pop up and we name, surface, and interrupt them. Sometimes this requires using confrontational coaching (see Chapter 5), and usually it requires coaching emotions. Someone who feels disempowered experiences fear, sadness, and anger, and sometimes regret, doubt, disgust, and envy. Often a sense of powerlessness has deep roots in the person's psyche and life experiences. While a coach doesn't probe into those roots (that's what a mental health professional does), we can skillfully acknowledge them and help our client recognize that their history might contribute to current feelings of victimization.

Coaching your client toward agency requires that you feel a tremendous amount of agency yourself. If you move through the world feeling disempowered, blaming others, saying things like, "I can't do Transformational Coaching even though I really want to because I've got 30 teachers to coach," then you can't coach toward agency. If you want to release a belief that upholds a victim story, you have to do your own work—you have to excavate and examine your beliefs and ways of being. Once you're reconnected to your power, coaching others toward agency follows naturally.

When you hear someone express powerlessness, your first move is to name it: "I hear that you want to be a Transformational Coach, and it sounds like you don't feel like you have power in this situation." Your client may feel relief at hearing this named. While some clients might then spiral deeper into disempowerment, more often clients begin questioning their own stories, saying something like, "Well, it's true that the district made this decision and I have to follow it, but they haven't told me that I can't coach a teacher on their legacy or talk about their beliefs. So I guess I could do that." Your client may begin to clarify their sphere of influence and control—a key step toward recovering a sense of agency. We'll explore coaching spheres of influence, an invaluable tool for cultivating agency, in Chapter 8, "How to Coach Emotions."

As we unpack victim stories, we need to be mindful of context. Some (or many) people have faced real harm or the threat of harm—both interpersonal and sociopolitical. This makes it hard to clearly assess risk. For example, Marta coached in a district where she was the only Latine leader and in a right-to-work state where she could be fired without cause. When her principal added standardized testing coordination to her responsibilities, she disagreed with his choice, but she was afraid of having a conversation with him to understand his decision-making. "If I speak up," she explained to me, "I could be fired." I wasn't sure about the real danger, and it wasn't my place to decide whether Marta was telling a victim story.

In contrast to Marta, a coach in another district, Emma, had frequently expressed fears about her principal that seemed exaggerated. "I can't ask him anything," Emma said. "He'll fire me." Emma's principal had never fired anyone, and she taught in a district with a strong union. When Emma shared that she'd grown up in a home with physically abusive parents, her fear of authority made sense. She had been a victim as a child, and she hadn't healed from that trauma. When people live within restrictive victim stories and struggle to tap into their agency, there's likely more going on. As you surface victim stories with clients, be mindful of how they respond. In Chapter 7, "What You Need to Know to About Emotions," we'll explore trauma-informed coaching.

Another strategy for coaching agency is reframing. When you ask a client, "Is there any other way to see this situation?" you nudge them to broaden their perspective. You remind them that they know the situation and that they can explore pathways forward. When you point to possibility, many people reach to grab it. If someone pushes back, they may need to work through some emotional blocks—probably fear and grief. We'll explore how to do that in Chapter 8.

A third strategy for coaching toward agency is deconstructing beliefs. Often when people are in a victim mindset, they hold fixed, and sometimes inaccurate, beliefs. You can begin to shake up a fixed belief by asking questions like the following:

- I hear you're frustrated and feel like admin doesn't take into account your views on coaching. I'm wondering how you came to this conclusion?
- What do you think went into the decision that admin made?
- Would you be interested in having a conversation with the administration about the coaching model?
- What do you think your administrators know about effective coaching programs?

These questions help someone recognize that they are holding *beliefs* (strongly held opinions, not truths), and this recognition makes space for reflection and change.

I have three goals for any coaching conversation: that the client feels more empowered, feels a little more hopeful, and can do something different or better. These goals are interconnected—when someone taps into their agency, they feel better and often subsequently take different actions. We all want to be seen as competent and capable of solving our own problems. Coaching toward agency serves that need.

Back to the Conversation with Isaac

I knew Isaac was stuck in a victim story before I sat down for our conversation. He'd been voicing it for weeks, a typical behavior when we feel powerless. Isaac's story is a common one in hierarchical systems: people with more positional power make decisions without input or agreement from those with less positional power. I had told this same story about district and site administrators in the past when I had bemoaned initiatives that were adopted or abandoned and last-minute shifts in my role. I knew that it felt really bad to tell this story, and I empathized with Isaac—I knew he was suffering.

I also remembered what it took to interrupt my victim story. I began moving away from those unsatisfying narratives when my coach didn't engage with my complaining or contribute their own misery and when I was invited to acknowledge the underlying emotions. I wasn't told that my victim stories were wrong; I was just shown a door through which I could exit if I wanted. Recalling times when I sank into victimhood grounded me in compassion and humility.

Navigating Power Dynamics

There's nothing wrong with power—it's not good or bad. It just is. And it's always present. Transformational Coaches focus on how we relate to power and how we use it. We can use power to find fulfillment in life, connect with others, and live our purpose, or we can use it to harm others. Sometimes the presence of power can generate uncomfortable emotions, including fear.

The most important thing to know about power is that you must pay attention to it. You must cultivate awareness of how it shows up, and you must learn how to use it skillfully. You can do this by exploring how you source power and how you leverage or use power. To unpack how power manifests in coaching conversations, we need to step back and understand how power shows up in a wider context.

Sources of Power

When I took my first full-time coaching role at a school I'll call Wilson Middle School, teachers questioned my credibility. I was introduced at the August staff retreat, which I co-facilitated with the principal, and so I was perceived as part of the administration. When asked about my qualifications for the role, I felt defensive, perhaps because I thought I had none. I spoke about my experience teaching and coaching at one of the highest-performing schools in the district, a school that had been nationally lauded for the work we'd done with previously underperforming students. That was not the right move, I quickly saw. Wilson was notoriously struggling, and I was comparing our two schools and saying one was better than the other. The teachers heard in my words: "Y'all suck. I'm great. I know how to teach. I'm going to fix you."

I shot myself in the foot on the first day of my new job. I didn't know how to establish credibility or authority as a coach. I didn't know that I needed to clarify my role in relationship to the administrators—to describe how I'd work with administrators, boundaries around confidentiality, and which decisions I'd be a part of. An entrenched us-versus-them mentality existed at this school— "us" being teachers, "them" being administrators. Because I didn't know how to navigate power dynamics, I was perceived as one of "them."

There is so much I wish I'd known when I took this coaching job. I've been extremely self-critical about how I showed up in the first months of that job—I can list 100 things I wish I'd done differently and all the beliefs that undermined me. And yet, I also have a lot of compassion for myself. I had received minimal training in coaching, the school was in crisis, the culture was toxic, and I had no support or other coaches to lean on. In 2012, when I wrote *The Art of Coaching*, I thought of it as the book I wish I'd had when I started coaching. In fact, all of the books I've written are for myself as a new coach as I struggled to work with teachers, facilitate teams, present PD, and cultivate my resilience. In particular, I wish I'd known more about power.

Social psychologists identify six sources of social power: position, coercion, rewards, expertise, relationships, and information (French and Raven, 1959). None of these sources is inherently good or bad, although coercive power can undermine health and well-being more directly than the other types of power. Power based on rewards can be similarly limiting. Table 3.3 describes these sources of social power.

Navigating power requires you to be clear on where you're drawing power from. Often, we draw from multiple types of power simultaneously, although it's not uncommon for someone to lean heavily on one source. When I began coaching at Wilson Middle School, I attempted to draw from positional power. But because I wasn't leading from relational power, I undermined myself and wasn't able to draw on my expertise.

Table 3.3: Sources of Social Power

Source of Power	Description
Position *(Positional power or legitimate power)*	• Comes from a formal right to issue directives or make key decisions because of position in an organization. • Granted by a title, role, and/or status.
Coercion *(Coercive power)*	• Comes from the ability to punish someone for noncompliance. Consequences can be losing a job, public shaming, being kicked out of class, or being socially ostracized. • Often relies on punishments that are vague and obtuse. • Relies on fear to induce compliance. • Can be explained as "the ends justify the means." • Typically tied to positional power, but not always.

Source of Power	Description
Rewards (*Reward-based power*)	• Comes from the ability to issue rewards such as a promotion, high grade, public compliment, or group approval. • Can be coercive if rewards are used to achieve compliance. • Typically tied to positional power, but not always.
Expertise (*Expertise-based power*)	• Comes from someone's experience or knowledge, and/or from reputation or qualifications. • Expertise doesn't have to actually exist, but the perception of expertise must exist.
Relationships (*Relational or referent power*)	• Comes from being trusted or respected. • Based on personality and interpersonal skills. • Isn't contingent on positional power.
Information (*Informational power*)	• Comes from access to facts and knowledge that others find useful or valuable. • Can result from and indicate relationships with power holders. • Builds credibility.

How to Establish Credibility and Authority

We associate credibility with being granted positional power. So what makes you credible or gives you authority as a coach? Can you coach a seventh-grade science teacher if you've only taught grades 1–3? Surfacing your beliefs about credibility will help you understand how you relate to power.

I wish all coaches could say this:

I'm qualified as a coach because I know how to guide adult learners. I know how to facilitate a reflective process that helps teachers cultivate their own resilience and meet the needs of every child, every day. I've been trained in these strategies, I practice them regularly and get feedback on my coaching, and I use data from my clients to improve my coaching.

I wish credibility came from knowledge about and experience in facilitating learning for adults and from a coach's commitment to their own growth and learning. Implicit in this wish, in case you don't hear it, is the wish that all coaches would receive substantive training *before* they take on a role as a coach, as well as ongoing PD, and that they belong to an active professional learning community of coaches.

Here are concrete ways to establish credibility and authority when you begin a coaching role, or perhaps along the way if you missed an initial opportunity. Department meetings, whole-staff PD sessions, and one-on-ones with teachers are all settings in which you might introduce your orientation to the work and establish credibility:

- *Introduce yourself in a way that conveys both confidence and humility.* This can sound like, "I'm thrilled to be part of this school. I can't wait to get to know all of you and to hear about your pathways into education and what matters most to you these days. I'm always reflecting on how my childhood impacts the teacher and coach I am today, and these reflections motivate me to figure out how we can better meet the needs of kids and also adults. I recognize now that my teachers might have been better able to care for their students had they been cared for themselves. I've been teaching for 12 years, and I'm both nervous to be moving into this position and also really excited."
- *Show up as a learner.* This can sound like, "Although I feel confident in teaching kids, I've been doing a lot of reading about how to coach adults, and I attended several workshops this summer in which I did a lot of practice. That was hard—I felt stretched, but I learned so much. I've also joined a coaching professional learning community (PLC) so that I can continue to practice. I'm eager to try out some of the coaching strategies I've been working on and to get your feedback."
- *Share your learning journey.* This can sound like, "Last year I got feedback that you wanted to have longer pre- and post-observation conversations and that you wanted me to ground my feedback in specific data points.

That was really helpful, and it resonated. This year I'll be implementing those suggestions in the following ways. . . ."

- *Be honest about what you know.* Don't be embarrassed to say you don't know something. This can sound like, "I'm glad you're asking about what role I'll play in determining the master schedule and teaching assignments. This is something I haven't talked about with our principal, so I'm going to check in with her and I'll get back to you."

- *Emphasize your commonalities and connections.* We rarely respect people just because they got this or that award or because their students scored high on an exam—in fact, boasting can lead others to withdraw respect. Activate your empathy, find points of connections, and share those when you do. This can sound like, "Although I've never worked in this community or faced the specific challenges that you're dealing with here, I'm reminded of the times when I felt overwhelmed by the magnitude of the work that had to be done. I remember how I found ways to work within my sphere of influence and be successful. I hope to share some of what I learned, and I hope that together we can figure out how to support our students."

Imposter Syndrome

Feeling like an imposter is a common experience for coaches, especially at first. Imposter syndrome is the feeling that you don't have the skills or expertise to be in the position you're in, even if you have been or can be effective in the role. At its core, imposter syndrome is a stew of emotions that results in a sense of inadequacy. Often this includes anxiety about how different you are from people who have traditionally been in your role or who are in a comparable role. You feel inadequate as a coach; you think, *someone else should be here, not me!*

The antidote to imposter syndrome is to redefine your authority and credibility in terms that resonate for you and for the people you're coaching and to continue to uproot unconscious beliefs that there's something inherently inferior about you. This is easier said than done. Here are a few strategies that can help you combat imposter syndrome:

- Surface, name, and explore the emotions that come up when you feel a sense of inadequacy.
- Identify the link between your thoughts and emotions. For example, you may think that you're not equipped to be a middle-school coach because you only taught elementary school, and that thought makes you feel insecure and afraid.
- Find evidence to counter your thoughts. For example, remember that you know a lot about instruction and curriculum and you can transfer that knowledge to working in a middle school, or acknowledge what you know about facilitating adult learning.
- Decide whether you want to believe your thoughts. Do you want to believe that someone else could do whatever you're doing better? Or do you want to believe that you can acquire the skills you need to do a good job?
- Create new thoughts and beliefs and recite those affirmations to yourself over and over. For example: *I am a curious and compassionate person, and I can guide someone into reflection on who they are being and how they are teaching. This is what's most important for a coach.*

When Positional Power Is Murky

Coaches are often in positions where their power is murky, stuck somewhere between administrators and teachers. On paper, your position might be "Teacher on Special Assignment," and you belong to the teacher's union, but because you are part of the Leadership Team, and you meet regularly with the principal, teachers see you as an administrator. If this is the case, know that it's a reflection of a dysfunctional or even toxic culture. When distrust runs rampant, especially of new staff and administrative decisions, and when there's suspicion about who talks to whom and who does what, deep problems exist in culture and systems.

While you shouldn't take this situation personally, there are things you should do to mitigate it. When there isn't clear and direct communication, suspicion and distrust flourish. To counter this, do the following:

- Get clarity from your supervisor/principal on everything. Why did they hire you? What are your roles and responsibilities? What will they consider as indicators of success for your work? What do they expect you to share with them about what you observe in classrooms or hear from teachers? What are the parameters around confidentiality? Will you play any role in evaluation? Will they ask you to share your opinion on whether a teacher should be retained or released? Which decisions will you have input into? Which decisions will you make on your own?
- Share all the information you receive about these questions with teachers. If they have clarifying questions, answer them—and if you don't know the answers, find them. Remember that if you're confused about an aspect of your role, teachers will be even more confused.
- Be impeccable in maintaining confidentiality and don't gossip, ever. Never say things about a teacher to another teacher or an administrator that you wouldn't say directly to them.

We live and work within many overlapping hierarchical systems. Our political, economic, and educational systems are all hierarchical, and we are socially and culturally conditioned to play into these systems—to assume our roles as those with more or less power. While this isn't always the case, power is frequently abused in hierarchical systems. What this means is that we need to cultivate an acute awareness of power: how we relate to it, how we source it, and how we leverage it.

How to Leverage Power

In hierarchical settings, which most schools are, we're often especially aware of how power plays out when it feels controlling or manipulative or when it is challenged and a struggle erupts. As facilitators and coaches, we might notice power most glaringly when it shows up as resistance. Once power manifests as resistance, it can be challenging to address. But as coaches learn how to source from and use power intentionally, we can avoid most resistance.

Sociologists explain that, regardless of where we source power, we can choose how to use it. They describe three ways to use our power: power-over, power-with, and power-to. As you read Table 3.4 about the ways we yield power, try to recall times you tried each—perhaps as a teacher, as a leader, or in interpersonal relationships.

Table 3.4: Ways to Use Power

Way to Use Power	Definition and Examples
Power-over	Power-over relies on force, coercion, or threats, either concealed or overt. An individual or group typically makes decisions for others and ensures compliance by threatening consequences. Power-over rests on the beliefs that power is finite and must be protected and that one individual or group is superior to another. Those who use power-over often source from coercive power. Those who use power-over are often enabled by well-established systems and institutions and/or have high levels of social capital. This kind of power is often met with resistance. Sounds like: • I know we're over time, but we've got to get through this agenda today. If you stay on task, we should finish soon. • You know that it's a requirement to meet with me. I have to submit records of all the coaching sessions we have, and I know that our principal considers those for evaluations. • If your lesson plans aren't submitted by 5 p.m., a note will be made in your file. • We know what is best for you.

Way to Use Power	Definition and Examples
Power-with	Power-with leads to collective action and the ability to work together. It is built on respect, mutuality, and collaborative decision-making. Leaders focus on strengths and assets rather than deficits. Using power-with can build bridges within groups and across difference. The underlying belief of using power-with is that power is infinite when shared, leadership is about service to others, and collaboration and collective efforts enable us to accomplish a mission or fulfill a vision. Sounds like: • It sounds like there are a few things we could talk about today. What would be most helpful to you? • It sounds like my question didn't land in the way I hoped it would. Is there a question you can think of that I could ask that would be more helpful? • Based on the feedback admin got last year, this semester we'll try . . . • This activity will help us collect information about our students from a number of people who know them.
Power-to	Power-to is the power to make a difference, achieve goals, and create something new, and is often combined with power-with. Power-to is generative and part of what constitutes agency. When you use power-to, you act on a belief that self-realization is a basic human right. Sounds like: • Today we're going to analyze your students' most recent writing assessments. What do you want to look for in their writing? • Take a couple of minutes to identify your hopes for this conversation. Looks like: • Identifying individual professional learning goals • Reflecting on core values and striving to work from them • Creating new thoughts that free you from imposter syndrome • Initiating a challenging conversation

How to Navigate Power Dynamics in a Coaching Conversation

Transformational Coaches source from relational power and almost always use power-with and power-to. Here are specific ways to source from relational power and to use power-with and power-to in a coaching conversation:

- Coach from compassion, curiosity, and humility. Your way of being shapes how you relate to your own sense of power.
- Be clear on decision-making—clarify things like which decisions have been made by whom, your client's ability to influence a decision, and which decisions you can make.
- Acknowledge power dynamics. This sounds like, "I recognize that because I'm a central office coach, you may perceive me as having more access to people with power. I'm curious what this brings up for you."
- Invite partnership into problem-solving. This can sound like, "I hear your frustration at having to teach this curriculum, and I'm here to support you to implement it. What are your thoughts about how we deal with this situation?"
- Stay out of fix-it mode. If you want to fix someone or think you have the answers, you'll show up as believing you have more knowledge, insight, and understanding than your client.
- Admit when you don't know something.
- Admit when you make mistakes and take responsibility for the consequences.
- Act with impeccable integrity outside of the coaching conversation. If you violate confidentiality, for example, your client may perceive your actions to be indicative of the positional power that you hold.

Back to the Conversation with Isaac

Let's return one last time to this conversation. In Table 3.5 I identify some of the ways that I coached Isaac back toward his agency, coached his will, and navigated power dynamics.

Table 3.5: Coaching Conversation with Isaac

What Happened	Agency, Will, or Power Dynamics	Comments
In the beginning, I named that I wasn't there to force Isaac to teach the curriculum but that I wanted to hear his perspective.	Power dynamics	I said this to indicate that I was sourcing from relational power and leveraging power-with.
At no point did I disagree with Isaac or engage in a debate or argument about the value of the curriculum.	Agency	Because I did not share my opinion, I created space for Isaac to explore his will and agency. I was careful not to source from positional or coercive power.
I asked Isaac about his biggest fear in teaching Perspective.	Agency	I know that often when people demonstrate what we call *resistance*, they are experiencing fear. In asking this, I created the possibility that he could acknowledge and perhaps release underlying fear. I hoped Isaac might return to a sense of empowerment that fear had blocked.
I asked Isaac if he'd be "willing to unpack this belief."	Agency Power dynamics	I gave him a choice about how to engage in the conversation and, thus, reminded him of his autonomy. I cued that I wasn't leveraging power-over.

(Continued)

What Happened	Agency, Will, or Power Dynamics	Comments
Isaac said, "It's infuriating. What can I do?"	Power dynamics	I didn't offer solutions. I didn't disagree with him. I just validated the emotions. This is a way of navigating the power dynamics. Offering solutions might have reinforced his perception of me as having positional power and authority.
I challenged Isaac on the conclusion he'd come to about Perspective—I challenged *his thinking*.	Agency	I told him he was free to disagree (reminding him of his agency), but I shared what I was hearing from him, and asked him if that was the only possible outcome—that his students wouldn't be prepared for middle school. In challenging him, I was inviting him to consider his agency to shift his thinking.
I surfaced the contradictions in Isaac's thoughts: he recognized that Perspective was rigorous, that he'd been successful as a child because he was challenged, and that he thought of himself as a teacher who wanted to deliver rigorous instruction.	Agency	When I named these contradictions, without judging him or suggesting that he change his thoughts, he didn't push back—he understood that he had the choice to decide how he felt. When he acknowledged that he didn't know how to make the curriculum accessible, he named *a skill gap*.

Table 3.5: (Continued)

What Happened	Agency, Will, or Power Dynamics	Comments
After recognizing that he had some skill gaps, I asked him if he thought he could close those gaps—if he could learn how to scaffold instruction.	Agency Power dynamics	This, again, was an invitation for Isaac to identify his agency. I didn't tell him he had to close the skill gaps; instead, I asked him whether he thought he could and whether he wanted to. I gave him choice and leveraged power-with.
Isaac said, "I mean, do kids in the suburbs even know these terms?"	Power dynamics	I evaded this question by shrugging and proceeding with the conversation. This question could have been an attempt to bait me into debate—and to test our power dynamics or to shift the conversation into something outside of our sphere of influence.
I asked Isaac many questions that pushed him to consider his skills and knowledge as an educator (e.g., "Could you teach them those concepts?").	Agency Power dynamics	My tone when asking these questions was invitational, which allowed Isaac to come to his own conclusions and then to decide whether he was willing to proceed. This was also a strategy to navigate our power dynamic, as I was leveraging power-with and sourcing from relational power.

(Continued)

What Happened	Agency, Will, or Power Dynamics	Comments
When Isaac expressed willingness to try the curriculum, I reflected that back for him to see: "I'm hearing that you're willing to try this curriculum."	Power dynamics	This helped him recognize the shift in his will—and I hadn't forced him. He needed to leave the conversation feeling like he had decided, on his own accord, to try Perspective.
Isaac revealed old resentments that contributed to his opposition to Perspective.	Power dynamics	I didn't disagree or debate his perspective or tell him that he was telling a victim story. I tapped into relational power, validated the feelings of frustration, and didn't engage in a debate over which story was correct.
I acknowledged Isaac's potential to be a leader and to contribute.	Agency	I attempted to activate his will to take action based on a sense of power. I wanted him to feel a sense of possibility and a way by which he could have more impact on children.

All We Need Is 15 Minutes

Sometimes when coaches and leaders hear about Transformational Coaching, they complain: "We don't have time for long conversations about emotions or beliefs or do all the things you describe!"

This is a victim story, told when people feel powerless, given the conditions in which they find themselves. But the excerpt you read of my conversation with Isaac took about 15 minutes.

We don't need to be therapists to acknowledge emotions, we don't need to be magicians to reignite a teacher's passion, and we don't need hours and hours to coach for transformation. We need skills. Between where we are now (unable to meet the needs of children, stuck in victim stories) and where we want to be (thriving) there is a tremendous skill gap. When we are skilled, we can accomplish a tremendous amount in a short period of time.

What if all we need to do is learn skills?

We have tremendous power over what we choose to believe. What do you choose to believe about what it'll take to be a Transformational Coach or to influence teachers or to thrive?

Pause and Process

Reflect:

- Which of the foundational abilities of Transformational Coaching do you feel like you already do well?
- Which of the foundational abilities do you feel most drawn to developing?
- What made you feel uncomfortable in this chapter? What came up around that discomfort?
- What made you feel hopeful or excited in this chapter? What came up around that hope or excitement?

Next steps:

- Listen to *Bright Morning Podcast* episode 199 about how to coach toward agency.

- Set an intention to notice how power dynamics show up in your coaching conversations over the next week or two. Before the conversations, reflect on how you can navigate power dynamics. After the conversations, reflect on what happened and how power showed up.
- Read Chapter 3 of *The PD Book*, which provides a deep dive into power. Write about how power shows up in one of your coaching relationships. Consider where you source power and whether you wield it as power-over, power-with, or power-to.

CHAPTER 4

How to Listen

This Will Change Your Life

Common misconception:	Transformational Coaches know:
Listening is hearing what someone says.	Listening is gaining insight into what someone thinks, feels, and believes.

When my teammate, Cary, was in elementary school, her superintendent spoke at an assembly, and Cary sat in the front row, demonstrating what she knew to be attentive listening. Her body was still, her eyes were fixed on the superintendent, and she nodded appropriately. At the end of his speech, the superintendent—who had noticed what he interpreted as good listening—called Cary to the stage and asked her to summarize his speech. But Cary hadn't registered a word. She had been so focused on performing listening that not a word had sunk in. After that mortifying incident, she committed to becoming a good listener.

I suspect you've had experiences like Cary—ones where you wanted to listen or thought you were listening or tried to listen, but you knew you weren't successful. Maybe the person you were speaking to said, "Are you listening to me?" I've been on both sides of that experience—I've attempted to listen and not absorbed the information, and I've expressed myself to someone else and noticed that they weren't present. On either side, once I'm aware of what's going on, I usually don't feel too good.

The contents of this chapter will change your life. Learning how to listen won't just make you better at your job, it will make you a better partner, parent, friend, sibling, child, and human. What I've learned about listening has transformed my relationships with my son and husband, with my neighbors and cousins—really with all the people I interact with. I often feel like this is a great bonus in my work—I get to practice skills that make every aspect of my life better. In contrast to the *don't-try-this-at-home* warnings that you hear with risky endeavors, I encourage you to try all of these strategies at home.

What Is Listening?

Listening is taking in information about someone's thoughts, feelings, and experiences. It's the primary way we develop social awareness and manage relationships; it's an essential skill for creating connection and meeting our core human need to belong.

When you listen deeply, you are fully present with someone. You meet them where they're at and get curious about what it's like for them to be there and how they got there. When you do this, your client will sense your care and recognize that you honor their autonomy, and their trust in you will increase.

Coaching is not a linear process—unfortunately, I can't outline five sure steps that always result in a client's growth. But the starting point is always listening. Without listening, you can't understand what they are thinking or feeling, so you can't guide them to change their behaviors, beliefs, and ways of being.

When I observe struggling coaches, what stands out is that they just aren't listening to the person in front of them. Because they aren't listening well, they can't recognize the root causes of their client's problems, they don't communicate the kind of empathy that their client needs, and they don't pick up on problematic underlying beliefs. When the coach asks a follow-up question, it doesn't land well. The client's thinking doesn't deepen, their agency isn't activated, and they may appear defensive. I recognize that the coach is trying different thinking tools and crafting careful questions, but nothing they do results in a shift in their client's thinking or feeling. The problem is that the coach isn't listening.

How do you know when you're really listening? Listening is one of those things that we think we understand, and yet there's so much complexity to the skill.

Transformational Listening

My husband described a frustrating afternoon while we were putting away groceries. He finished speaking, and I said, "Wow, that's messed up. Where's the garlic?"

"Were you even listening?" he said.

"Yes," I said, my tone defensive and annoyed. I proceeded to repeat many of the things he'd told me, proving that I'd heard him.

"I don't feel like you really listened," he said.

He was right. My mind took in his words, but I wasn't listening to the underlying messages or the feelings he was sharing. I wasn't listening deeply. I'll spare you the details of what went on in our kitchen afterward—in brief, I suggested that when he needed my full attention that he let me know, and I apologized for not being more tuned in. He acknowledged that bringing up something big while unpacking groceries at the end of the day wasn't optimal and committed to asking for focused time when he wanted to share something upsetting.

There are many different ways we can listen, including like a machine that records audio input. But a Transformational Coach listens to understand a client, not just to record the words that are spoken. We listen to gain insight into what someone thinks, feels, and believes. It's only with that

Figure 4.1: Key elements of transformational listening

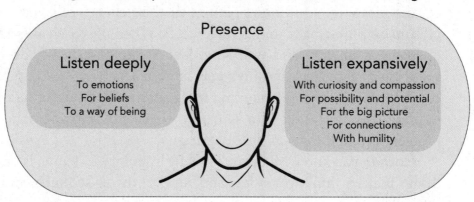

understanding that we can guide them in reflection, problem-solving, and decision-making.

There are two phrases I often use to describe the kind of listening that Transformational Coaches do: "expansive listening" and "deep listening." When we listen deeply, we're listening to what's not said, to emotions, for conscious and unconscious beliefs, and to a way of being. When we listen expansively, we listen with compassion and curiosity so that we can identify possibility and potential. When we listen expansively, we can see the big picture and the interconnectedness of all things. Presence is a requisite for deep and expansive listening.

The way that we listen will dictate what we say—our responses. When we listen with impatience and judgment, our responses will come from a place of anger. When we listen from compassion, our responses emerge from a place of love. Before we explore responding in the next chapter, there's a lot more to understand about listening. Figure 4.1 is a reminder of the key elements of Transformational listening.

Listening to Metacommunication

Communication researchers say that 65% of the messages we share are expressed through *metacommunication*; only one-third of a message is transmitted through the words we say. Metacommunication includes the messages that come through body language, eye contact, use of objects, facial expressions, tone of voice, pitch, pace, volume, and tactile (or touch) communication. We communicate through words and through metacommunication all the time. But sometimes our metacommunication is delivered below the radar, so we don't always read these nonverbal signals in others, nor are we aware that we're sending them sometimes. Listening to metacommunication is a skill to hone.

Here are some of the things I "listen to" when a client speaks:

- Where their eyes focus: whether they look up, make eye contact, gaze down, or close their eyes
- What their hands do: twist in their lap, relax on their legs, cup their face, clasp, or fidget with a pen
- Whether they lean forward, away, or hunch over
- The rate of their speech and how long they speak without stopping
- Whether they take shallow breaths, deep sighs, or loud exhales
- When they yawn repeatedly
- The tightness or relaxation of their mouth and jaw
- Furrowed eyebrows, the winces reflected in their eyes, the tension or relaxation of their forehead
- Whether their eyes moisten or fill with tears

This information provides indicators as to what a client is feeling. For example, when someone's pace is rushed, they might need uninterrupted time to process. When coaching someone who speaks without pausing, I listen to whether they are finding a pathway forward in their thinking or looping through thoughts and getting stuck. When a client responds enthusiastically to a question—perhaps their eyes light up, their face relaxes and they smile, and they gesticulate with their hands—I know my question led them somewhere helpful, perhaps into a source of energy. I'll likely ask another question or two that invites them to go deeper into that topic so that they can access those emotions more fully.

It's helpful to understand the meanings of some nonverbal cues. When I asked Jackie, a new teacher, "What came up for you when your principal gave you that feedback?" I noticed that she immediately hunched over and gripped her hands together.

But Jackie said, in something of a monotone, "It was fine. I always say I want feedback."

"What feelings came up when I asked that question?" I asked. "I noticed your body shift."

Jackie looked up at me and said, "I didn't realize it, but I guess I felt uncomfortable. Her feedback felt shaming, and I don't want to think about it. I didn't really want you to make me talk about it."

Although we want to be cautious about jumping to interpretation, many nonverbal cues are universal. For example, social scientists observe people around the world cross their arms over their chest when they feel defensive—including blind people who have never seen others taking this action. Reaching our arms overhead (imagine someone crossing a marathon line) is a cross-cultural indication of pride. Furrowed brows indicate concern or disagreement. When we feel safe and emotionally open, our shoulders relax downwards, our jaw softens, and we breathe evenly and slowly.

Nonverbal communication is a primary way that we can take in someone's emotional experience and build trust. Rafael Echeverría and Julio Olalla, ontological coaches, write "without trust, there can be no coaching" (1993). But *without listening*, there can be no trust. Therefore, without listening, there can be no coaching. I know that many of us want to be better listeners, because we want connection and belonging, so what makes this skill so challenging?

Common Obstacles to Deep Listening

The next time you notice that you're struggling to listen deeply, pause. Ask yourself, *what's going on with me, or within me, right now that might be making it hard to listen?*

While you might experience unique circumstances that make it challenging to listen, there are a number of common situations in which many of us find it hard to listen deeply and expansively. These include being distracted, prioritizing intellect and efficiency, thinking we don't have time, having an agenda, and letting our emotions get in the way. Let's unpack these obstacles.

We Are Distracted

Researchers say that 75% of the time, people are distracted or preoccupied. It might sting to read that but may also feel true. I'll admit that I am distracted and preoccupied a lot of the time. Those researchers also report that one hour after hearing something, we recall only 20% of what we heard. Furthermore, over the last few decades, the human attention span has shrunk. In the year 2000, our attention span was 12 seconds; now it's 8 seconds. Apparently, goldfish have an attention span of 9 seconds.

Yes, we can blame social media and other online platforms for our shortened attention spans. Twitter and Instagram have changed our brains. We have become habituated into dividing attention and shifting from one thing to the next. Furthermore, we don't have the time we need to process the overwhelming amount of information that's available. This makes our minds feel jumpy and disorganized.

Aside from social media, sociologists and psychologists agree that people have never been as busy, worried, or pulled in different directions as we are now. Working conditions, chronic stress, and social pressures of all kinds have contributed to our inability to listen. We have to contend with some mighty forces to listen deeply.

We've Been Conditioned to Prioritize Intellect and Efficiency

Since we were very young, the majority of us have received messages from our family, communities, and society at large that being intelligent and getting things done fast is valuable. We want to be perceived as smart, competent people who take care of problems quickly—especially when we are in a role supporting others.

Here's how this impedes listening. In my first year as a coach, Lisa began a meeting saying, "I am so behind in grading. I'm drowning in papers to grade, I still haven't finished the midterm quizzes, and I have to give another assignment this week that I can't imagine finding time to assess. I don't know what to do!"

I said, "Let's take the next 10 minutes to get organized. We can make a plan to get through all of this and get started on it today. I could help you grade after you've got a clear rubric and a plan."

This response did not reflect listening. It came from a desire to solve Lisa's problems efficiently. In contrast, I could have said, "Wow, that's a lot. I can hear you're overwhelmed in your voice and in what you're sharing." When we move quickly to solutions, we miss out on surfacing mindsets or getting to the root cause of the issues. Problem-solving can come later—there's a place and time for it—but when we jump there, we don't acknowledge our client's full humanity, which includes their emotions.

When you want to demonstrate your knowledge or prove that you are intelligent and experienced, it's harder to listen deeply: as your client is speaking, you'll think about what to say when your client stops. At least, this is what I used to do. It's an important tendency to notice and explore and probably comes from feeling insecure, uncertain about your role, wanting to help, and also from not having the coaching skills to do anything else. At least that's where it came from in me.

Furthermore, if you are a principal or in a role where people see you as responsible for dealing with problems, you might be more likely to jump to fixing mode when someone shares a challenge with you. It can feel hard to hold off on sharing what you know and trust that the other person can find solutions to their problems, but that's what can happen when you listen deeply.

We Think We Don't Have Time

When I first started coaching, I thought, *I don't have time to listen to everything this teacher wants to say—our sessions are only 50 minutes! There's so much work to do.* I worried about the clock ticking and the 43 things I wanted to talk about, and I didn't process the words my client said.

The tyranny of time can hijack your listening. Because we're so often swamped, this pressure can feel constant. How often does your mind wander to your To-Do List? When it does, perhaps even while you're reading, low-level anxiety creeps in and reduces your capacity to concentrate and learn. If this is happening right now, take a couple of deep breaths.

In a coaching conversation, the antidote for the fear of not-enough-time is to trust the process and build your coaching skills. When we don't have the abilities to do what we want to do, we can feel like we don't have enough time. As your coaching skills improve, you'll see that you need less time for a coaching session than you think. While an hour is a good amount of time, once there's trust in the relationship and you have the skills, a 15-minute coaching session is extremely powerful. With trust in the process and refined coaching skills, you always have enough time.

We've Got an Agenda

Any time we enter a conversation with an outcome we're driving toward in that session, our listening is restricted. This might be confusing, because as a coach working with educators, we always have a goal—even if it's just to improve teaching and learning. But here's what happens. You go into a coaching session with an agenda—perhaps you want your client to recognize that unless they manage their emotions, they're going to continue responding to student behavior in a way that amplifies students' stress and indirectly creates more "classroom management" issues. This might be a worthwhile agenda, but it also narrows the aperture of your attention, and you won't be as receptive to all the information you could receive. If you're listening openly and deeply, you might learn more about how your client is experiencing the situation. With that insight, you can help them shift their beliefs, behaviors, and ways of being.

When we cling to an agenda, we hear what we want to hear. When someone speaks, it passes through our filters for right and wrong, and their message becomes distorted. This is what's meant in the old saying, if you only have a hammer, everything looks like a nail.

You can navigate the paradox of having an agenda and not clinging to an outcome by first cultivating awareness of when this tension is at play. The antidote to the tendency to cling to an agenda is to hold lightly to outcome, or even to be unattached to outcome—perhaps even just for that particular session. With awareness, you can make a choice to hold lightly. You can believe that a teacher needs to meet the needs of every child, *and* you can be unattached to the outcome of that coaching session.

Sometimes, when you're least attached to outcome, that's when transformational changes happen. Perhaps this is because when you aren't gripping an agenda, you meet them where they're at, which communicates acceptance of your client. Your client may unconsciously register your openness, which allows them to vulnerably explore their behaviors, beliefs, and ways of being. This allows them to trust you, and in turn, they might be more receptive to listening *to you*—to your questions or suggestions and to taking risks.

Loosening our attachment to an agenda is scary and difficult. But it can be done. Like every other coaching skill, it just takes practice.

Our Emotions Get in the Way

There have been countless times when my husband starts describing something he's upset about and I lurch into fix-it mode. I offer my analysis, opinions, and suggestions—I've got so many brilliant ideas. Then he says, "Can't you just listen to me?" Once he even said, "I know you know how to listen because you teach this. Why can't you listen to me?"

It was a good question.

I came to understand that when my husband was upset, I felt sad and scared. I sought to relieve my discomfort, my sense of powerlessness, and my fear that he wouldn't feel better, by taking action. Although I feel very accomplished at solving problems, this behavior didn't help him or me.

As I explore the root causes of my tendency to shift into fix-it mode and as I learn to respond to uncomfortable emotions, I practice being kind to myself. Yes, I do teach this stuff, but I'm also a human in development, and I don't have to be perfect. Also, let me plug therapy again—that's what helps me get down to the roots.

Many emotions can block our ability to listen deeply to a loved one or client—the emotions take us out of the present moment, which is the only place where we can listen. I'll describe how certain emotions can get in the way by sharing my experiences. However, I know that my experiences are common, and so I suspect you'll relate.

Impatience blocks listening. Sometimes, during a coaching conversation, I've found myself thinking, *Why are you bringing this issue up again? I thought we talked about it already!* Or I feel impatient with a situation, thinking, *I'm so irritated that we even have to deal with this problem—it's not fair!* Impatience is a form of anger, and anger can mask fear or sadness. When I acknowledge my underlying emotions, I often experience relief, and I return to my commitment to expansive listening.

Stress, which is often anxiety, can also make it hard to listen. When I'm feeling stretched and tired and worried about how much I need to do, it's very hard for me to access the spaciousness of deep listening. My mind whirls and buzzes, my body feels unsettled and distracts me, and I'm not present in a conversation.

My ability to listen expansively is slammed shut when I feel judgmental. Judgment pushes me into the territory of right and wrong thinking, of superiority over others, and of separation from them; it's a form of aversion or anger. I hate feeling judgmental, but like most of us, I sometimes experience it, and then I can't listen in the way I want to listen.

Insecurity also constricts my listening. When I feel insecure, I want to prove my worth and show how much I know. Sometimes I want my client to think of me in a certain way—as helpful, smart, or capable—which leads me to listen for indicators of approval or validation. Insecurity is fear that I won't get my core human needs met—often my needs for connection, competence, and purpose. When I recognize this fear, it's alleviated.

When I feel afraid of someone, then sometimes I become defensive and focused on protecting myself. To clarify: I've never felt physically threatened by a client, but I've felt intimidated by their positional authority (when I've coached a central office leader) or I've felt afraid of the beliefs they're holding. When this has happened, I find that I'm listening for signs of danger or threat, for their disagreements or arguments, and I'm not present with my client.

These uncomfortable emotions—fear, anger, insecurity, judgment, aversion—take us out of presence. They create obstacles that block us from listening deeply and expansively.

The good news about emotions is that the comfortable emotions—love, ease, happiness, and joy—help us listen. Those emotions are the gateway to presence, which is the state from which we can best listen. When we are fully present, we become open and quiet. Then we can trust the process and ourselves, and we can receive a tremendous amount of information. We'll explore presence in the next section, but for now know that if you experience uncomfortable emotions in conversations, there are many ways to work with them.

How to Be a Good Listener

Ibrahim was one of the first principals I coached. We met each week for two hours, during which time he'd talk and talk and talk. He usually gazed out the window while he spoke, although occasionally he'd get an idea and would capture it in his laptop. Sometimes it didn't seem like he registered that I was in the room. I worried that I wasn't asking enough questions or being helpful, but at the end of our third session, he exhaled loudly, made eye contact, and said, "You are such a good coach. I don't even know what you do—but I feel much better after we meet, and I leave with many next steps."

I thought, *I haven't said a word in two hours. I'm just listening.* This was a bit of an exaggeration, because during that conversation I had said five things. These were:

1. What would be most useful for us to talk about today?
2. That sounds really difficult. Do you want to say more about that?
3. What are some other ways you could interpret that situation?
4. How did that make you feel?
5. I have a feeling we could unpack this situation and get more understanding of what's going on.

These questions reflected my deep listening—I tuned into his emotions, beliefs, and ways of being. I had also listened expansively for connections and possibility. In addition, I'd emitted a lot of sounds that affirmed that I was listening such as *hum, ah, mmm.* I had nodded a lot. I'd made sounds that indicated empathy, that communicated the sentiment of, *Oh, I'm sorry that happened.* But I still worried that I didn't say enough.

For months and months, Ibrahim talked and talked. He often said, "You're the only person I can talk to about everything," which in some ways was true. Principals are bound by confidentiality agreements, and there's often a lot they don't feel comfortable sharing with supervisors or colleagues. As a coach, bound by our confidentiality agreements, Ibrahim could share his thoughts, feelings, and dilemmas with me freely. After a while, I realized that my insecurities about coaching Ibrahim didn't impact the experience he had with me. Yes, I was a new leadership coach and, no, I'd never been a principal. But all I had to do was let him talk. It was a relief.

You can become a better listener—it's a capacity that can be developed. It can feel scary to practice deep listening at first. It can feel like you're not "doing anything," it can make you feel vulnerable, and you might question your value. And then, when you begin listening deeply and expansively, you might find that your energy is freed up and that you slip into a state of flow. After a coaching session, you might find that you're more energized than before. And you might hear clients say, "Wow, that was so helpful."

I've got a lot of suggestions for what to do before, during, and after a coaching conversation to help you be a good listener. Like any skill, these take practice, repetition, and feedback. You might find, however, that you're committed to developing these skills because they are so useful within and outside of our places of work—they'll help you create connection and belonging in all areas of your life.

What to Do Before a Conversation

There are a number of things you can do before a coaching conversation to set yourself up to listen deeply. These include clearing the inner mental and emotional clutter; remembering what it feels like to be listened to; identifying what a successful session might look, sound, and feel like; and setting an intention.

Clear the inner clutter. Meditation and journaling can help you get quiet. Tuning into what's going on inside of you can clear some of the mental and emotional clutter that surfaces during a conversation. Sometimes physical activity also really helps to clear the inner clutter.

Remember what it feels like to be listened to. Think of a person who listens to you well. Recall how their listening helps you find clarity. Write about what it feels like to be deeply heard.

Identify what a successful coaching session might look/sound/feel like. Determine what a successful session outcome might be—that your client feels relieved, heard, or clear on next steps—and then connect your listening to that outcome. Identifying that pathway can assuage your ego's inclination to take over. With all of its fears and needs and wants, your ego can get in the way of listening. You don't need to eliminate your ego to be a good coach, but you need to direct it.

Set an intention. Intention setting can help us get clear on what we want to experience. It's useful to describe what it might look and sound like for you to fulfill that intention. Here's an example of an intention with descriptors:

> I commit to listening deeply. I'll do this by paying attention to my listening so that I can hear my reactivity, judgments, fears, and urge to fix. When these arise, I'll notice them and be kind to myself. I'll use self-talk to bring myself back to listening, and I'll take a deep breath. I know that my mind may wander, and I know that I can return to presence.

What to Do During a Conversation

During a coaching conversation, strategies to be a good listener include listening to your own listening (cultivating awareness of what's going on in your mind), paying attention to your client's metacommunication, observing your own nonverbals, being quiet, and returning to presence. Let's explore these.

Listen to your listening. Our minds often drift in conversations. They might plan a response, space out and think about lunch, lapse into judgment or disagreement, or recall experiences that were similar to the speaker's. When our mind drifts, we're no longer listening. The first step in shifting this behavior is awareness—we can't change what we don't recognize we're doing. Awareness creates an opportunity for choice, so when you're listening, cultivate awareness of your mental journeys.

Pay attention to your client's metacommunication. Notice how your client speaks—to their pace, tone, pitch, and volume. For example, if you see that your client folds their arms over their chest and they have stopped making eye contact with you, these may be signs that they are feeling fear or distrust.

Observe your nonverbals. Be sure there's congruence between your words and your body language. It can help to maintain eye contact, keep your body open and relaxed, and sometimes lean forward toward your client. Especially when someone shares something vulnerable, they'll unconsciously tune into subtle cues about your attention and emotions. They'll notice a glance at a clock, squirmy feet, or a stifled yawn.

Be quiet. Practice pausing and holding silence. During those pauses, you can look down and take notes, make soft eye contact, make an affirming *hum* sound, or nod slightly to indicate that you're listening. If it feels awkward, you can say, "I'm letting what you said sink in."

Return to presence. When you notice that you're emotionally activated, bring yourself back to presence. Table 4.1 provides strategies you can use during a coaching conversation to return to presence when you realize that emotions are blocking your commitment to listen deeply.

Table 4.1: How to Return to Presence

When You Feel . . .	Tell Yourself . . .	Try This Strategy . . .
Like you want to fix someone	• *I'm afraid that I'm not doing a good job; it's okay to feel afraid.* • *What if all I need to do is listen? What if helping is that easy?* • *Give the process a chance.*	• Remember how it feels when others want to fix you. • Remind yourself you don't need to save anyone. • Recall a few things your client knows how to do well. • Assure yourself that if your client doesn't get to any of their own solutions, you can offer one or two.
Impatient	• *There is enough time.* • *Is there some sadness or fear here? Can I acknowledge it?*	• Acknowledge any fear or sadness that's present and resist the inclination to understand it or get rid of it right away. • Take a few deep breaths. • Identify one thing you appreciate about your client.

When You Feel . . .	Tell Yourself . . .	Try This Strategy . . .
Stressed or anxious	• *I'm feeling anxious. I don't need to get rid of it now; I just need to notice it.* • *There'll be time to explore my worries—I'll come back to them at 4:45 p.m.* • *Right here, right now, everything is okay.*	• Take a few deep breaths. • Feel the pull of gravity on your body. • Notice sounds, scents, or colors in your environment.
Judgmental	• *I remember what it feels like when I'm judged, and it doesn't feel good.* • *I'm not inherently better than anyone else.* • *I wonder why they've made the choices they've made.* • *Is there any fear present for me?*	• Notice how your body feels and see if you can relax one or two areas such as your shoulders or jaw. • Identify a couple of things you appreciate about your client. • Imagine your client as a five-year-old child playing.
Insecurity or fear	• *I'm safe right now.* • *After this session ends, I'll explore these feelings.* • *Fear is a normal human emotion, and there are ways to manage it.*	• Take a few deep breaths. • Feel your body in your seat and your feet on the floor. • Commit to exploring the roots of the fear. • Imagine being inside of a protective bubble where nothing can hurt you.

What to Do After a Conversation

Reflecting after a conversation will help you improve your listening skills as it's a potent time for learning and growth. In that reflection, explore the moments when you were triggered or experienced uncomfortable emotions, and celebrate the moments when you noticed yourself listening deeply.

Reflect on moments when you were triggered. It's very likely that you'll experience uncomfortable emotions that will take you out of presence during conversations. The key is to notice when they arise, make a mental note to come back and explore them later, and then do so. The more you explore your activation, the greater the likelihood that you'll get to the root causes, and the more your listening will improve. Again, at this stage it can be really helpful to have the guidance of a therapist, because usually when we're triggered there are childhood experiences at play.

Celebrate moments of listening. Be sure to notice when you listen well. First, appreciate yourself and take in how good it feels to listen deeply. Second, see if you can identify what contributed to your ability to listen deeply. Perhaps you recall that when your attention drifted, you used a self-talk phrase that brought you back, or you see that as you leaned into curiosity, you returned to presence. The purpose of reflecting is to identify what allows you to listen in the way you want to listen.

The Joy of Listening

I find listening to be an exceptionally pleasurable state. When I'm in the spacious quiet of deep listening, I feel open, present, and alive. I feel like my ego takes a nap and I don't have to do anything. In these moments, time slows, and I sense the great mystery of life. Questions and responses materialize without much effort. I leave conversations in which I've been listening deeply and expansively feeling energized. With intentionality and practice, you can have this kind of experience—or maybe you already do.

When you have these moments, be sure to let the experience sink in. Notice and appreciate the joy of listening. Doing so will enable you to continue taking the actions that created this experience (because you did create it), thereby helping you continue to be a good listener. You'll also notice the reciprocity of coaching—that by being a good listener for another person, you feel good. You feel more present and connected. Your need for purpose and perhaps even transcendence is met.

Listening requires presence. Presence is required for genuine connection. Listening brings us back to love.

Pause and Process

Reflect:

- How do you like to be listened to? Who do you know who is a deep listener? How does it feel when they listen to you?
- What do you know about yourself as a listener? What kind of feedback have you received about your listening?
- What brings you out of presence in a conversation? Which of the strategies from Table 4.1 could you use to return to presence?

Next steps:

- Listen to *Bright Morning Podcast* episode 181, "Learn from Your Client's Non-Verbals."
- Download Table 4.1, "How to Return to Presence," and staple it into your coaching notebook.
- Download "Listening to Your Own Listening" to learn what kind of a listener you are and to learn how to improve your listening.

CHAPTER 5

Fifty Questions to Ask

And Four Types to Avoid

Common misconception: Coaches drive the conversation and have the answers.

Transformational Coaches know: Whoever is doing the talking is doing the learning.

When I first started coaching, I often felt like a deer in the headlights. My client spoke, I'd process their words, and then they'd stop. I knew it was time for me to say something. I'd make eye contact and make sounds like, "Mmmm . . .," but my mind was blank.

Then I tried a new strategy: a client would begin to describe a problem, and I'd blurt out a list of suggestions. Later, as my client shared more information about the situation, I'd realize that my directive coaching had been off-target. It hadn't helped for me to interject ideas so quickly. But I didn't know what else to do. I didn't know what to say.

By the end of this chapter, you'll have read more than 50 things you can say in response to what your client says—these are compiled into a nicely formatted document that you can download from my website. The sentence stems are categorized to help you understand why you'd use one or another and to help you remember them.

This chapter digs into the *behaviors* enacted by a Transformational Coach. Having read the previous chapters, you'll recognize the beliefs and ways of being behind the behaviors I'll describe. At times I will point to them so that you see the connection, but I'll focus on telling you what to say in a coaching conversation.

What Not to Do

Let's get this over with. Coaches make common mistakes when they speak. With awareness and practice you can eliminate these mistakes from your repertoire. Common mistakes include asking fake questions (leading questions or advice disguised as questions), asking rambling questions, interrupting, and asking "Why" questions.

Fake Questions

A "fake question" is just what it sounds like—there's no real curiosity behind the words, and the speaker is trying to share an idea or manipulate the other person into thought. Leading questions are those in which you prompt or encourage an answer, and the response is suggested within the question. An example is, "Don't you think you should talk to his parent about what happened today in class?" Leading questions usually contain one right answer.

A question disguised as advice sounds like, "I'm wondering if you've considered changing the daily schedule?" In these cases, the coach may have a suggestion, but when cloaked as a question, it's manipulative. When you give people answers, even good ones, you take ownership of the problem, and you block them from their agency, which undermines the very purpose of Transformational Coaching. Asking fake questions also chips away at trust.

There are a couple of ways to address a tendency to ask fake questions. First, generate questions that begin with "What" or "How." Ask: "What might happen if you shifted your daily schedule?" Or "How could you respond to what happened in class today?" As long as you ask an open-ended question, one for which there could be many responses, you move away from fake questions. Also ask yourself: Is there something I'm really wanting to tell someone to do and I'm disguising it as a question? Am I feeling impatient or frustrated with my client and I want to direct them? Checking in on your intentions can help you determine whether you're asking fake questions.

When you notice yourself itching to give a suggestion, be transparent about offering advice. Rather than try to disguise your idea as a question, say, "I have a suggestion. . . ." Or, "I'd like to share some advice that you can take or leave" or "Some things people have done in your situation are. . . ."

Rambling Questions

Rambling questions are exactly what they sound like: "I was wondering what came up for you when J.P. stormed out of class? I mean, I'm sure you were upset, I could see that on your face, but I wondered if you were aware that you were that upset? Did you notice those feelings in your body? What were you feeling?"

We ramble when we're nervous, when we lack confidence, and when we are trying to find the perfect question. If you know you're a rambler, ask one question and then pause. Even if that question wasn't a great one, you'll have a moment to collect your thoughts and determine the next one to ask. Also, know that there is no such thing as the perfect question.

I used to be a rambler. As I noticed this tendency, I'd sometimes stop myself mid-ramble and say, "Let me pause." I'd take a breath and then ask, "What do you think would be helpful for me to ask you right now?" In asking this, I was also redistributing power in the conversation—I honored my client's agency by giving them a chance to take the reins.

Interrupting

Interrupting is dangerous behavior. No one likes being interrupted. It can feel dismissive, invalidating, and hurtful. It can create a rupture in trust. As a general rule, don't interrupt your client.

Exceptions to this rule include when a client's well-being is in jeopardy and when a client is stuck in unproductive thoughts. In those instances, skillful, intentional interrupting can be extremely powerful. I interrupt a client when there's a high level of trust and I aspire to interrupt a thought pattern that undermines my client's well-being—and that I know they are committed to breaking. Here's what this can sound like:

Teacher: I can't believe I shouted at Maggie again. I'm such a failure as a teacher, I shouldn't be in the classroom, I'm hopeless. She's always going to remember me in this way, isn't she, as the screaming teacher? I hate myself—

Coach: I want to interrupt you. You're heading down a path of self-denigration. You've told me you want to stop berating yourself. So I want you to make an intentional choice right now about what you think and say—do you want to keep going down that path?

In this situation, I'm using the *confrontational approach*, which we'll explore later in this chapter. I'm attempting to redirect the teacher's thinking. When you interrupt someone, say that you're doing so—this lets them know that you're being intentional.

You might also interrupt someone if they are complaining, ranting, or venting for a while and you hear that they aren't discovering solutions to their problems. In those instances, gently insert yourself, saying something like, "Can I suggest you pause?" Then ask, "What are you hearing in what you're saying?" Or, "I just want to check in. I'm not hearing that you're getting to clarity or next steps. Would it be helpful if I ask a question?"

With this kind of interruption, you create space. You might see your client focus their eyes on you, almost as if they've snapped out of a trance. We all tumble into unproductive thought loops. If your client trusts your intentions and they know you care about them, your interruption might bring them relief.

"Why" Questions

In general, it's best to avoid questions that begin with "Why," specifically questions that ask a client to explain why they did something. When we ask a "Why" question, we're asking someone to explain their behavior, thoughts, or feelings. "Why" questions compel a client to justify their actions and can put them on the defensive. For example, if you ask a new teacher, "Why did you decide to do this unit first?" they may unconsciously feel, or consciously think, *Oh, my coach must know this unit should come later, and I messed up.*

When you want to ask a "Why" question, rephrase it. You can say, "I'm curious about your decision-making around the order of the units you are teaching." Or, "Tell me about your choice to teach that unit first." Or, if you want to avoid as many "Why" questions as possible, even those that might be helpful, you can say, "I wonder what's going on with your students around homework. What are your thoughts?"

There are a few instances when you might ask a "Why" question. For example, when you take the confrontational approach, which we'll explore later in this chapter, you ask someone to explain themself—but this question must come from a place of love and care, and you need to be sure there's trust. When you begin a question with "Why," make sure it's an intentional choice, and then pay attention to the impact it has on your client's thinking.

Whenever Possible, Be Quiet

Most coaches talk far too much in coaching conversations. That might sting, and I'm also guilty of it, but having heard thousands of coaching conversations, I'll stand by this claim.

Why do we talk too much? Some people need a lot of time to process thoughts verbally. In addition, most of us simply like to hear ourselves talk—it can feel like a way to meet our needs for belonging and connection. There's nothing wrong with wanting or needing time to verbally process, or wanting or needing to be heard, but not when you are in coach mode. Your time with a client is for the client—and whoever is doing the talking is doing the learning.

Coaches also talk a lot because we are trying to be helpful. But when we insert ourselves, we center ourselves. Furthermore, we deny our client the opportunity to find solutions to their problems; we rob them of their agency. I'm not suggesting that you *never* tell a story about your first year as a teacher or that you shouldn't offer your hard-earned wisdom about navigating burnout. There's a time and place for that—and the skill is to identify that time and place.

Talk Less, Even Less

As a general rule, explore how you can speak less in coaching conversations. Aim for speaking for no more than a third of the conversation. If you really want to focus on this, record your conversations, listen to or transcribe them, and then count up the number of minutes that you talked. You'll only need to do this a couple of times to see that you probably talk a lot more than you think. That awareness can instigate a commitment to talking less.

When in doubt, WAIT. WAIT stands for Why Am I Talking? When you're inclined to talk—to offer an opinion or advice or ask a brilliant question or share a story—pause and tune into your intentions. Why do you want to say what you want to say? Once you are clear, then choose what to say.

Pause and Let There Be Silence

The easiest way to talk less is to allow for pauses. After your client says something, nod slightly, make soft eye contact, and then perhaps look away or jot down what they've said—and just let there be silence. At first, you may feel uncomfortable, perhaps very uncomfortable. This will pass. In most instances, the silence is more uncomfortable for you than it is for your client. In fact, they might enjoy the quiet. It might allow them to keep processing their thoughts.

After your client speaks, count the seconds—and aim for at least 10 or 15 seconds before you say anything. During that time, note what your client is doing. Are they gazing out a window? Do they sigh and drop their shoulders? Are they staring at you with an expression that seems to convey, *say something!* Each person and each conversation will be different, and some clients may feel uncomfortable with your silence. If you observe discomfort, say, "I'm just processing what you said" or "I'm letting that sink in."

Coaches often direct the conversation too early—they ask a question that takes the client into one channel of thought. This sounds like:

> **Teacher:** I don't know why homework submission rates have dropped so much in the last few weeks. I know my kids can do this work—they're all meeting expectations on daily exit tickets.
>
> **Coach:** Have you considered scheduling a daily email to arrive at 7 p.m. asking them if they've done their homework?

Offering a solution or narrowing the conversation too early can block your client's learning. Also, remember that your client knows far more about themselves and their situation than you ever can. When you hold silence, you're trusting the coaching process, and you communicate confidence in your client's ability to find solutions to their problems. After a client speaks, if you are quiet, they may resume speaking and may deepen their reflection or identify a next step. In the previous example, if the coach had paused, the teacher might have said something like, "Now that I think about it, I realize that they're in the final weeks of college applications, and they're probably overwhelmed. Maybe I need to reduce the amount I'm assigning."

As you begin practicing the pause, notice what arises—what thoughts go through your mind? How does your body feel? How quickly do you want to break the silence? These are opportunities for you to learn more about yourself. I'll confess that early on, when I noticed that I was talking much less, I felt unsettled. I felt like I should be offering brilliant questions more often. I felt a little insecure—what was my real value? Then I realized that it was both hard and easy to simply listen and hold space. I noticed that often, all I needed to do was to be fully present and trust the process.

The Hardest Coaching Skill of All

Many coaching trainings start with exploring a skill set called *active listening*. If you attend more than one PD on coaching, you might think, *oh, not this again*. But active listening is really hard to do well, so much harder than it initially seems. And it is absolutely essential in coaching. In Chapter 4, "How to Listen," I described how to listen deeply and expansively. Active listening is the bridge between those strategies and what we say when we respond to a client. It is the way we demonstrate our deep listening.

Active listening is a powerful and subtle way of communicating empathy. When active listening is done well, a client can feel like you're reading their mind, or saying exactly what they needed to hear. Active listening also allows for a client to see and hear themselves—it's the moment in a conversation when you hold up a mirror for your client to see themselves. This allows the client to build their reflective capacities and learn about themselves.

Sometimes it seems like my clients have the biggest breakthroughs when all I do is use active listening.

But so much can go wrong. Many coaches rush through parts of a conversation where active listening would be most useful because they're eager to ask the questions they planned. Sometimes active listening can sound and feel contrived—for example, when paraphrasing is done poorly, it sounds like someone is being parroted or even mocked. Active listening is worth getting right.

What Is Active Listening, and Why Use It?

Active listening is sometimes called *reflective listening*, as you often echo back what you hear. It often includes paraphrasing, which indicates that you took in your client's words and metacommunication—their body language, facial expressions, tone, pitch, pace, and volume. When you listen actively, you tap into your intuition. You might get "a feeling" about something and ask a question that opens a new channel for exploration. Active listening indicates that you've received the totality of a message, that you've listened between the lines or below the words. See the examples of active listening in Table 5.1.

Table 5.1: Active Listening

Example	Implementation
Paraphrasing	Restate what you heard, using some of the words that the speaker used and also using different words. Be sure to preserve the essential meaning. Paraphrasing confirms that you understand what the speaker was trying to convey.
Affirmations	Short phrases such as "Say more," "Hmm," or "I hear that" indicate your engagement and presence.
Requests for clarification	Ask for confirmation that you understand what was shared. This allows the client to check their own thinking; it can activate their agency, and it invites their input.

How to Use Active Listening

The key to active listening is to practice until you're fluent. Remember that active listening is communicated through words *and* metacommunication.

Active listening sentence stems:

- So . . .
- In other words . . .
- What I'm hearing, then . . . Is that correct?
- What I hear you saying is . . . Am I missing anything?
- I'm hearing many things . . .
- As I listen to you, I'm hearing . . . Is there anything else you feel I should know?
- I'm curious to hear more about . . .

Active listening metacommunication:

- Nonverbal affirmations (*Mmm, oh, ah*)
- The body's movements or stillness
- Facial expressions
- Pitch, pace, and volume of the voice

Here's an example of active listening in a coaching conversation:

Coach: Last week you shared that you were nervous about your principal's upcoming observation. Do you want to process how it went?

Client: Yeah, it was the observation for my evaluation, and I'm nervous, which I guess is really normal since I'm a first- year teacher, but also my principal is so serious and professional. She's worked in this district for 25 years, and I feel so new to it all. But I felt like the observation went well—I spent so long preparing and I felt confident. I hate waiting for her report—I thought I'd get it already, but the lesson went well and the kids were into it, and I saw my principal smile at one point. So I'm relieved.

Coach: That sounds great. It sounds like you've been accepting all the feelings and moving through them. Does that resonate?

Client: Yeah, I guess so. I was really aware that I was nervous and intimidated and also excited in some ways about the observation. I guess I was aware of my feelings. But I feel more on edge now than I thought I'd be. I hate waiting. Maybe I should ask her if I can expect to get my eval by a certain day so I'm not checking email every 10 minutes.

Coach: I hear that you're a little anxious, and it sounds like you might want to take action to relieve it. Is that right?

Client: I would like to—I mean, I would like to ask her. But I don't want to bother her. I don't know what I should expect or what's appropriate for me to do.

Coach: Hum. [Nodding and holding silence]

Client: Maybe I could ask the other fifth-grade teacher. I trust her. I'm just nervous. What if I'm not re-elected? My principal never comes in to observe me, so she got one glimpse of me as a teacher.

Coach: Those are a lot of valid concerns. . . .

In this snippet of a conversation, active listening creates space for the client to process their thinking and identify the actions they want to take. Active listening can be used in the beginning of a conversation for the purpose of connecting with a client and hearing what's on their mind, but active listening can also, and should be, used throughout a conversation.

Using active listening requires you to be fully present. Sometimes at the start of a coaching conversation, if my mind is fluttering all over with ideas for where to take the conversation, I tell myself to use active listening. During a conversation, if I get stuck and can't think of what to say, I return to active listening. This will likely provide my client with more space to understand themselves, and it'll help me return to a state of presence.

The Coaching Stances

While active listening is a coach's superpower, there's a lot more you can say. The *coaching stances* offer a way to categorize many questions and statements. John Heron, a pioneer in counseling and professional development, was the first to describe a facilitative and directive (or authoritative) stance. Within these, Heron identified six approaches: the supportive, cathartic, and catalytic approaches (within the facilitative stance) and the prescriptive, informative, and confrontational approaches (within the directive stance). Most coaching questions can be categorized into these six groups. Understanding the categories helps you make decisions about what to say. Figure 5.1 provides an overview of the coaching stances.

Facilitative and Directive Coaching

In any coaching conversation, a Transformational Coach usually takes, alternately, both facilitative and directive stances. Imagine you have an internal dial: when the dial is cranked all the way on one side, you use a facilitative stance; on the other side, you're fully directive. Coaching from both stances facilitates growth; both are useful. But most coaches rely on directive coaching and benefit from learning to turn the dial to the facilitative side more often. In general, a Transformational Coach mostly uses facilitative approaches, which are most effective at cultivating a client's agency. When we use a directive approach, we do so intentionally.

Use the facilitative stance when:

- You suspect that the client might have the answers to their problems inside themselves

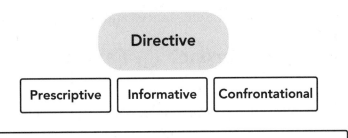
Figure 5.1: Coaching stances

Facilitative

| Supportive | Cathartic | Catalytic |

Coach:
- Elicits reflection and supports client to find answers to their problems.
- Guides client toward new behaviors, beliefs, and ways of being.
- Is positioned as a partner, facilitator, or guide.
- Metaphorically holds up a mirror and invites client to look at themselves.

Directive

| Prescriptive | Informative | Confrontational |

Coach:
- Provides information and feedback.
- Tells a client how to solve their problems.
- Directs client toward new behaviors, beliefs, and ways of being.
- Is positioned as an expert or authority.
- Metaphorically holds up a mirror and names what the client should look at.

- You know they've already received training or information about the problems they are struggling with
- The client exhibits emotions that might need to be released.

Use the facilitative stance to:

- Create psychological safety with a client
- Navigate power dynamics (the facilitative stance communicates confidence in the client's abilities to problem solve)

Use the directive stance when:

- The client has clear skill or knowledge gaps that can be easily filled or that need to be (and can be) quickly filled

What's essential is that we cultivate awareness of our tendencies and which approaches we use more often and, furthermore, that we pay close attention to the impact of whichever approach we use. Regardless of what we say, we need to observe our client's reaction—does our question or statement lead them to new insights? Does it help them tap into their agency? Does it cultivate kindness and compassion? As we practice using different approaches, we focus on impact.

We'll now explore the six stances and what it sounds like to use them.

The Supportive Approach (A Facilitative Stance)

Being supportive is not about fluffy words and pats on the back but rather about communicating authentic empathy. Take the supportive approach to provide confirmation, offer encouragement, help a client maintain focus and motivation, build self-esteem and self-confidence, highlight moments of success and progress toward goals, and encourage risk-taking.

While the supportive approach is very helpful, I've seen coaches get stuck in using it. Especially if you know you've got a "helper" personality, you might rely too heavily on this approach. However, I've also seen coaches who have a strong action-oriented inclination, or tendencies to jump to fix-it mode, who rarely use the supportive approach. Pay attention to which approaches you use most often and what impact you have on your clients.

Supportive Coaching Sounds Like
- I noticed how when you . . . the students . . . (to identify something that worked and why it worked).
- It sounds like you have a number of ideas to try. It'll be excited to see which works best.

- What did you do to make that lesson so successful? I'm interested in learning (or hearing) more about. . . .
- Your commitment is really inspiring to me. It sounds like you handled that in a very confident way.
- I noticed that you were demonstrating your core values of . . . and I know you've been intending to do that.
- I'm confident that you'll be successful.
- Hmmm. That sounds really hard.

Tips and Reminders
- When using a supportive approach, you'll likely offer thoughts and reactions more than asking questions.
- Active and reflective listening is very useful and appropriate when you intend to take a supportive approach.
- Be authentic and specific if you offer praise.
- Highlight micro-movements toward growth.
- Use nonverbals that communicate care.

The Cathartic Approach (A Facilitative Stance)

When using the cathartic approach, we ask wide-open, probing questions. Sometimes we offer what sounds like a supportive response, followed by such a question. We take the cathartic approach when we recognize that a client is experiencing emotions that are either a block to their well-being or could be a source of energy. If someone is afraid of risk or failure, if they feel incompetent, or if they are frustrated or unmotivated, the cathartic approach can be impactful.

Use the cathartic approach to help someone process and release emotions, to explore fear of failure or taking risks, to access feelings that might be a source of energy or motivation, and to release frustration or the feeling of being overwhelmed.

Cathartic Coaching Sounds Like

- What are you hearing in what you're sharing?
- I'm noticing that you're experiencing some emotions. Would it be okay to explore those for a few minutes?
- What's coming up for you right now? Would you like to talk about your feelings?
- Wow. I imagine I'd have strong feelings. What are you feeling?
- What's another way you might look at this situation?
- What would it look like if . . .?
- When has something like this happened before?
- How do you want me to listen?

Let me expand on that last question, because for me it's been a game-changer. Many years ago, I called my good friend, Lettecia. "Do you have few minutes to talk?" I asked. Lettecia is a masterful coach and exceptional listener.

"Of course," she said, "but how do you want me to listen?" There was a pause as I wondered what she meant. She explained: "Do you want to talk and I'll *just* listen? Do you want me to be your friend and agree with whatever you say? Do you want me to help you find solutions?" I felt energized by this choice.

When someone grabs you in the hallway and asks if you've got a second or when a client begins speaking and you sense that they have a lot to share, ask: how do you want me to listen? This question can help someone consider what they want from a conversation—and it'll make your life easier.

And when you're on the other side of this exchange—when you call up a friend or colleague and ask if they have a minute—you can be direct and say, "I want to talk about a challenge I'm having at work, and I'd love for you to let me rant for about five minutes so I can get it out of my system and then help me identify some things I can do. Also, a little empathy sprinkled in would be nice."

Tips and Reminders

- Active listening is helpful for the cathartic approach.
- If a discussion of emotions might be new for the other person, ask for permission to discuss feelings. You'll read a lot more about how to coach emotions in Chapters 7, 8, and 9.

The Catalytic Approach (A Facilitative Stance)

When we take the catalytic approach, we explore what's possible in the future or what we would have done if we could have gone back in time. Our questions sometimes feel like they have a unique kind of spark or charge in them—these are the questions that feel like with just a handful of words you can shift someone's mental model. They are a catalyst—they speed up the rate of change dramatically.

Take the catalytic approach to help a client reflect on their emotions, challenges, and successes; prompt self-discovery and problem-solving; and take responsibility for past and future actions.

Catalytic Coaching Sounds Like

- Tell me about a previous time when you. . . . How did you deal with that?
- What do you think would happen if . . . ?
- I hear you're really struggling with. . . . How do you intend to start?
- It sounds like you're unsatisfied with. . . . What would you do differently next time?
- You've just talked about five different things you want to work on this week. The last thing you mentioned is. . . . How important is this to you?
- How was . . . different from (or similar to) . . . ?
- How do you want your students to remember you?
- How do you want to remember this time or situation in 15 years?
- Is there a question you think I could ask you right now that would be helpful?

- Ask a lot of open-ended, probing questions.
- Incorporate a clarifying question or two to help the client get clear for themselves on what's happening.
- Your tone of voice and body language might be a little more assertive or bold when using the catalytic approach, but always communicate care and kindness.
- Nudging can be helpful, but nudge gently.
- Notice if the other person uses metaphor or symbolic language, and if so, explore those.

The Prescriptive Approach (A Directive Stance)

Transformational Coaches rarely use the prescriptive approach and should do so with caution. It's appropriate to use when a coach sees or hears something that merits a direct response because of legal, safety, or ethical guidelines that need to be followed. The prescriptive approach also may involve giving advice, but only when the client is open to hearing it; ask permission from the client before giving advice. When a client can't direct their own learning, you can also use this stance.

Take the prescriptive approach to help someone act on your guidance, understand the ethical and sometimes legal issues that need to be addressed right away, and quickly prompt a shift in behaviors.

Prescriptive Coaching Sounds Like
- I would like you to discuss this issue with your principal.
- You need to know that our district's policy is. . . .
- Have you talked to _____ about that yet? Last week you said you planned on doing so.
- Would it be okay if I share some advice that I think might help you? You're welcome to take it or leave it, of course.
- I'd like to suggest. . . .

Tips and Reminders
- Use this approach when legal, ethical, or safety issues are in play.
- Use with caution.
- If your client responds to advice with repeated "yes, but" responses, they are not open to hearing what you have to offer. Try using a facilitative stance.

The Informative Approach (A Directive Stance)

When using the informative approach, it's likely that you'll ask concrete questions, present options for the client to consider, and offer resources, tools, and explanations. Most of your coaching stems will be more declarative rather than rooted in questions (e.g. "there's a useful article on that topic by . . ." or "an effective strategy to accomplish that goal is . . ."). Most coaches play this role at some point with their clients, and many overuse it. When using the informative approach, be careful that your client doesn't become reliant on you as their source of expertise.

Take the informative approach to provide a client with resources and tools they may not have identified on their own and to be a thinking partner as they determine their next actions.

Informative Coaching Sounds Like
- There's a useful blog on that topic that I can send you.
- An effective strategy to accomplish that goal is. . . .
- You can contact _____ for that resource. . . .
- Reach out to _____. He's very effective at using those methods, and you could observe him.
- It sounds like you think that students need more scaffolding. . . . Would you like to create a graphic organizer together?
- Some teachers do ___ in this situation. You might try that and see if it works.
- I'll share some resources with you that will be useful.

- Offer a selection of resources and guide the client to make decisions. This can sound like, "Some teachers do this . . . and others do that. . . . What do you think would work best in your situation?"
- Use this approach in conjunction with facilitative approaches so your client directs their own learning.

The Confrontational Approach (A Directive Stance)

The word *confrontation* makes many people uncomfortable, because we associate it with conflict. In Transformational Coaching, confrontation is a way of *interrupting thoughts*. When you use a confrontational approach, you help a client deconstruct unhelpful mental models and shift their beliefs.

A coach is poised to use this stance when they've built a relationship with their client. It's critical that be a solid level of psychological safety for confrontational coaching to be effective; without such safety, harm can be done.

Take the confrontational approach to challenge assumptions; to stimulate awareness of behavior, beliefs, and ways of being; to help someone see the consequences of an action; and to boost confidence by affirming success. As you read the following stems, you may notice that some are the same as those in the catalytic approach. You can offer the same question from different places and with different intentions. Sometimes your tone of voice might hint at the differences, or sometimes the follow-up questions will take your intention further along.

Confrontational Coaching Sounds Like
- What do you hear yourself saying?
- Would you be willing to explore your reasoning (or assumptions) about this?
- I'd like to ask you about. . . . Is that okay?
- What's another way you might . . . ?

- What would it look like if . . . ? Is there any other way to see this situation?
- What do you think would happen if . . . ?
- What sort of an impact do you think . . . ?
- I'm noticing (some aspect of your behavior). . . . What do you think is going on?
- What criteria do you use to . . . ?
- Who do you want to be in this situation?
- How do you want others to see you in this situation?
- How did you come to that conclusion?

Tips and Reminders

- A confrontational approach invites clients to explore their assumptions and reasoning and to see situations from different perspectives through questions such as, "Would you be willing to explore . . . ?"
- Be calm, confident, and courageous to interrupt beliefs and ways of being that don't serve the organization's mission.
- Be sure that you're acting from a place of love and care. If not, the confrontational approach can backfire and become an unhealthy conflict.

It's Not About the Nail

The two-minute video *It's Not About the Nail* offers profound lessons about listening and speaking (Google it). It opens with a close-up of a woman talking about feeling a pressure—a relentless, scary pressure—and she doesn't know if it will ever stop. In an anguished voice, she says she can literally feel the pressure in her head.

A man (whom we assume is a boyfriend or husband) replies in a dry, matter-of-fact tone, "Well, you do have a nail in your head." And the camera moves to reveal a 3 inch nail embedded in the woman's forehead.

"It's not about the nail!" she says, exasperated.

Her partner raises his eyebrows. "Are you sure? Because, I mean, I'll bet if we got that out of there. . . ."

She interjects: "Stop trying to fix it!"

As the conversation continues, the woman urges her partner to stop trying to find a solution because all she wants is for him to "just listen." He insists that if he could only help her remove the nail, then everything would be solved. Relieved when he eventually concedes, the woman continues to explain her feelings: the unexplained achy pain, her lack of sleep, how all of her sweaters are snagged.

Her partner responds, his voice saturated with empathy, "That sounds . . . really hard."

Her face softens. "It is," she says, and she leans forward to kiss him, only to be propelled backward by the protruding nail.

It's About How We Communicate About Communicating

The characters in this video are depicted in stereotypical gendered ways, the implication being that men don't listen and just want to solve problems, and women are emotional, irrational, and just want to be heard—even when they've got a nail in their forehead. I'm not going to deconstruct this depiction here, but I invite you to consider these two people as representing two different communication styles that anyone can embody.

When I first saw this video, I thought, *If I was him, I'd just lean over and pull the nail out of her head. It would be a waste of time to listen to her.* I've got strong fix-it tendencies, especially when the problem seems so obvious. Then I wondered: If I pulled the nail out of her head, maybe her brains would spill out and she'd die? Maybe the nail serves a purpose that I'm not aware of? Maybe she wakes up every morning and hammers it into her head? In the video, she seems aware of the nail in her head. So what is going on?

One issue in the way that her partner responds is that he's not curious about the root causes of the situation. He sees a quick fix and is impatient with her need to share her suffering. I empathize with him—it can be hard to hear someone drone on in confusion about their pain when it seems so obvious. And yet, at the end, when he uses an active listening phrase ("That sounds . . . really hard"), her emotional defenses drop. She expresses relief at the validation.

This illuminates the second problem in the way he engages: he centers his needs to move quickly through the issue and find resolution and doesn't recognize that her process is different. This is an issue of sequence: perhaps once she's shared, then she'd be receptive to hearing his questions and exploring the root causes of the problem, or even to a suggestion to remove the nail. She needs empathy before problem-solving.

Addressing the Nail from a Transformational Coaching Stance

If the man in the video wanted to use Transformational Coaching, he'd need to activate his curiosity and re-engage his trust in the process. Here's what he could say using some of the approaches introduced in this chapter, perhaps in this order:

- I hear you're having a hard time. How do you want me to listen right now? (Cathartic)
- This sounds really hard. I'm sorry you're going through this. (Supportive)
- What's a question I could ask you that might be helpful? (Catalytic)
- I imagine if I was in this situation, I'd experience a lot of fear. Do you want to share more about the emotions that are coming up for you? (Cathartic)
- I'm curious what you think might be causing the pressure in your head? (Clarifying, active listening)
- What do you hear in what you're sharing? (Confrontational)
- What do you think the relationship is between the nail in your head and the fact that all your sweaters are snagged? (Confrontational)
- I'd like to ask you about the nail in your head. Would that be okay? (Confrontational)

- I want to suggest that you talk to J.P. He had a nail in his head last year. (Informative)
- I think you should go to the doctor, today. This could be serious. (Prescriptive)
- I'd like to pull the nail out of your head. What do you think about that? (Prescriptive)

There are many ways to respond when you think that a solution is obvious. But when someone is in distress, they need empathy. Leaping into fix-it mode, even when there's a nail sticking out of their forehead, won't alleviate the suffering in the moment, and it won't empower the person to deal with subsequent challenges. Furthermore, operating from fix-it mode is exhausting for the fixer. There are other ways to respond to problems, and anchoring in compassion is a starting place.

Tapping into humility also helps. Most of us live with nails in our heads— small and large. We stay in relationships in which we're not satisfied, we work at jobs that drain us but provide security, we avoid going to the doctor because we're afraid of what they might find, we eat food that makes us sick, and so on. It takes courage to look at what causes us pain. Before we can consider solutions, next steps, or action plans, we often need to just be heard. We need someone else to be with us in the messy place that is our suffering and our humanity.

Of course, we don't want to get stuck in that liminal zone, not as a coach nor as a client. If the man in the nail video had that conversation with his partner every day, week after week, he'd need to take a confrontational approach and say something like, "For the last three weeks, every evening, you've expressed your distress about the pressure in your head. I've listened and empathized, and you've said you were going to get professional help with it, but you haven't. This is the last time I'll listen to you because my listening isn't helping, and it might be enabling this behavior. I care about you and want you to feel good. I know you can take responsibility for your situation. When you've taken action, let me know."

A coach might say, "Almost every time we meet, you express your frustration with the administration. Would you like me to help you plan a conversation with them to discuss these concerns?" This is what it sounds like to set boundaries.

Five Coaching Survival Phrases

If you're overwhelmed by all the options I've given you for what to say, let me make this easier. Jot down the following five phrases, stick them your back pocket (or memorize them), and use them when you can't think of what to say. Although these "Survival Phrases" are particularly useful if you're a new coach, I use them all the time.

Survival Phrase 1: Tell Me More About . . . or I'm Curious About. . . .

This underused phrase is incredibly powerful. Use it heavily at the start of a conversation so that you can have a vast understanding of what's on your client's mind. Use it when your client reveals something and you feel like you need to know more to figure out what to say or to determine a meaningful direction for the conversation. Use it when your client isn't forthcoming or seems disengaged—it communicates your openness to what's going on for your client.

When you use these phrases, elicit specific information. This sounds like, Tell me more about . . .

- How you felt when . . .
- What came up for you when . . .
- What happened next
- How you interpreted that
- What you wish had happened
- What that made you want to do
- How that made you feel about yourself

Survival Phrase 2: What Would Be Most Useful for Us to Talk About Right Now?

This question activates your client's agency. It's helpful to ask at the start of a session, perhaps if your client shares a lot and you're not sure where to take the conversation. By inviting your client to prioritize their issues, you're relieved of having to make a decision that you may not have enough information to answer. Doing so also redistributes power—you communicate confidence in your client's ability to direct the conversation. Remember, your clients know themselves and their situation far better than you'll ever know—let them take the lead.

This question is also useful when your client rambles or vents. Rather than digging into the material they bring up, you hold up the metaphorical mirror and invite them to make a choice. In doing so, again, you're expressing trust in their decision-making.

You might be wondering, however, about how to honor a client's priorities for a conversation if they don't align with yours. What if they say they want to talk about a difficult incident with a student's parent? Or the administration credentialing programs they're considering? Perhaps you've prepared to debrief a lesson or have a conversation focused on equity or coach around the district's initiative of inclusive classrooms. The short answer is: there's usually time for both. You can weave your client's needs together with your plans. Here's an example of what this sounds like:

> **Teacher:** . . . And so I'm still really upset about all of that. I did not deserve to have Tyrell's mother shouting at me after the way he behaved. And then to have my principal reprimand me! That's the last time I organize a field trip.
>
> **Coach:** I hear your frustration. What would be most useful for us to talk about right now?
>
> **Teacher:** I guess I'm curious how you would have dealt with Tyrell's mother. I mean, parents can't just scream at us, right?

Coach: Okay, I'm hearing that you want to explore how to have better relationships with students' caregivers. Is that right?

Teacher: Yeah. How to get them to treat me with respect.

Coach: Okay, we can talk about cultivating mutually respectful relationships. This feels like it fits in with our district's initiative of inclusive, student-focused classrooms because it's about building relationships, so I see a direct connection with our goals. How does that sound?

Inviting a client to share what they'd like to talk about doesn't mean you surrender and avoid hard topics. It means you gain insight into what they're thinking and feeling, you take their needs into consideration, and you look for connections between their priorities with yours. Doing so can get their buy-in to the conversation.

Survival Phrase 3: So, What I'm Hearing You Say is . . . Did I Get That Right? Or, It Sounds Like . . . Is There Anything Else You Want to Add?

These are two versions of the same active listening stems. Using these demonstrates that you are listening fully and offers the client an opportunity to reflect on whether you are hearing them accurately—and to correct your understanding as needed. These stems also remind a client that they are a partner in a conversation, not a passive recipient of coaching. As such, they activate their agency. Finally, when a client expresses strong emotions, active listening can be an expression of empathy and care. Here's an example of what this sounds like:

Coach: I'm hearing that the interaction you had with Tyrell's mother raised a lot of feelings—including anger, as well as a desire to be appreciated for all that you do by parents and administrators. There's a lot here for us to explore, but first I want to check and see if I got that right?

Teacher: Yes, I guess I was feeling angry. I wouldn't have used that word, but that's accurate. I think I'm also tired because I'm just working so much. And I think I also felt hurt—I put so much into teaching, I'm always thinking about how to bring this curriculum to life, and I thought a field trip would engage kids like Tyrell who have been struggling. I just want to be respected. Is that too much to ask?

Coach: It sounds like that incident brought up a lot of feelings, desires, and dissatisfaction. And I hear your commitment to kids—that's always present when we talk. I hear that you want to meet the needs of your students. Is there anything else you want to add?

Teacher: Yes, I want to be good at what I do! I want all of my kids to be on grade level by the end of the year and ready for seventh-grade math. This is why I became a teacher.

Coach: I hear that. I hear your commitment to being a masterful teacher and to fulfilling your sense of your purpose in life. Does that resonate?

Teacher: Yeah, it does.

Coach: What would be helpful for us to dig into more deeply now?

Remember, active listening requires that you listen beyond the words that are spoken and to feelings. It requires that you have knowledge about emotions—for example, when someone says they're frustrated, you know that frustration is anger. Active listening requires that you be comfortable with acknowledging anger and that you can explore the hurt beneath the anger. It requires that you listen for strengths and possibilities and for a client's commitment to students. And active listening requires that you recognize when a client is struggling to meet their core human needs for competence, belonging, and purpose. You have to listen below the surface of what they say—below the blaming and the externalization of responsibility, to the terrain where love is possible.

Survival Phrase 4: What Do You Hear Yourself Saying?

This is one of my favorite questions to ask as it puts a client firmly in the driver's seat of their life. It invites their insight and wisdom when they experience intense emotions or need to make a decision. As you might already suspect, it requires paying attention to your tone of voice: this question needs to be delivered with a gentle tone that invites self-reflection.

When you ask this question, it's common for a client to exhale loudly or sigh, to be quiet for a moment, and perhaps to say, "That's a good question." You'll often be surprised by how insightful your client is about what's going on for them. If you ask this question and your client says, "I don't know!" then share what you hear (use active listening) and follow up with, "Does that resonate?"

When someone asks me this question, I feel like I hover above my current reality and can look down with a new perspective. I'm reminded of my ability to understand the turmoil I'm in, and the foggy confusion clears. I'm reminded of my power, and that always feels good.

Survival Phrase 5: Is There a Question That Would Be Helpful for Me to Ask You Right Now?

This is my other favorite question to ask, and also to be asked. Remember that your client is the expert on themselves and their situation, so this question invites them to step into their expertise. When you ask this question, your client will likely share both the question and their response to it. It's also a great question to ask when you feel like none of your coaching strategies are working, you've asked every question you can think of, and you keep hitting a brick wall or your client pushes back on your questions.

Here's what this can sound like:

Teacher: I've tried everything with Tyrell! I've consulted with our Special Ed teachers, I've talked to his mother so many times, I've talked to his elementary-school teachers also, and I've given him extra attention. I just don't know what else to do. In my 18 years of teaching, I've never felt so challenged by a student. And he's so far behind. I can't imagine how he can catch up and be ready for seventh-grade math. I don't know what to do!

Coach: I'm curious what you hear yourself saying.

Teacher: I guess I'm hearing that I'm really struggling. That I'm frustrated. That I'm surprised that I'm feeling challenged like this.

Coach: What else are you hearing?

Teacher: I'm hearing that I'm sad. To be honest, I'm hearing that I'm heartbroken. That I feel powerless. I love Tyrell. He's funny and sharp and a brilliant artist. I don't know what to do.

Coach: Is there a question that would be helpful for me to ask you right now?

Teacher: Maybe you could ask me what else I could do? No, that's not right. I feel like I've tried everything, so don't ask me that. Maybe you could say, "Can you accept that you've tried everything and this is really hard?" Maybe you could ask me if I could take a few deep breaths. And yes, it would probably help if I took some deep breaths. And if I accepted that I have really, really tried to help Tyrell. And if I accepted that yes, I've been teaching for a long time, and I'm still going to be stumped at times by how to help students. I guess I thought I know so much that I won't have this kind of challenge again.

Coach: How does it feel to ask yourself those questions?

Teacher: It's hard. And also a relief. I think I need to take a step back and look at this situation with a little perspective.

Coach: What else?

Teacher: I didn't realize how angry I was feeling—with everything. And how that might be affecting how I work with Tyrell. I'm just so frustrated with things in our district, and in our country, and maybe I'm feeling a little burned out on all of it. I think I overreacted about his mother. I know I snapped at Tyrell on the field trip—or I guess I should admit, I yelled at him. I probably would have done the same if a teacher had screamed at my kid.

Coach: That's a lot. What are you hearing in what you're sharing?

Teacher: I'm hearing that I need to slow down. Maybe even take a day off and get my head back on straight. I feel like I'm getting lost. This isn't who I want to be.

I hope you can see how these Survival Phrases can have a powerful impact on a client's thinking; how they achieve a Transformational Coach's goal to cultivate insight into behaviors, beliefs, and ways of being; and how they instigate a client's agency. These stems also anchor us in compassion and curiosity—and in a conviction that we can trust the process.

A Little More on What to Say and How to Say It

By the end of this chapter, you'll have more than 50 questions to ask, all of which are compiled on a document that is downloadable from my website. But there's a little more to say about what to say and how to say it.

Guidelines for Using Sentence Stems

First, you have permission to make the questions sound like you. Modify stems so that they feel authentic to the way you talk and so that they align to the relationship you have with your client. For example, I coached Miguel for four years, and I knew what kinds of phrases he used. Instead of saying, "I hear that that comment was challenging to receive," I might have said, "Damn, that sounds really hard!"

You may also need to modify stems so that they are culturally, linguistically, and generationally responsive. For example, when working with people who don't speak English as a first language, it's a good rule to avoid idioms. Or if I'm coaching someone who I perceive may not be comfortable talking about emotions, rather than saying, "What feelings came up for you in that meeting?" I might say, "What came up for you during that meeting? What were you thinking or feeling?" Pay attention to the person in front of you.

So far, you've been introduced to active listening stems, stems from the six coaching approaches, and the five Survival Phrases. As you explore the last type of stems, clarifying questions, know that these categories are fluid. For example, a clarifying question can also be a cathartic question. The stems are grouped to help us think about them in different ways, but how you classify the question has a lot to do with your intention when using it.

Finally, a reminder that your tone of voice, pitch, pace, volume, and non-verbal communication is just as important in how your question is received as the words that you say. Pay attention to who you are being every time you speak.

Clarifying Questions

When working with new clients or when a client describes a challenge, we might feel the need to ask a lot of clarifying questions such as *Why was Marco placed in your class? How long has she been the principal? Why was that curriculum selected? Were you trained in that method? How long was the training? Who trained you?* These questions may seem relevant, but we often ask too many clarifying questions. We don't need as much contextual information as we might think.

When you are tempted to ask a clarifying question, ask yourself *why* you need the information. Is your limited knowledge about the situation truly preventing you from coaching your client? If you were provided the information, whose needs would be met? Consider the following scenarios.

Scenario 1

Client: My assistant principal stormed into my room and said I was out of compliance with the accommodations I've made for Tyrell. I constantly feel like she's after me. If it's not one thing, it's another. And I know I'm in compliance!

Coach: Which code did she say you were out of compliance with?

Client: I can't even remember. She also commented on my hair and said she didn't think I was dressed professionally. But I'm the one with a background in Special Ed—she's never taught it. I know these codes.

Coach: What is her background in?

Client: I think math. She's from a small town in the Midwest. She's never taught in a big urban district like ours.

Coach: Do you think you should pull up the code and show her that you were in compliance?

Scenario 2

Client: My assistant principal stormed into my room and said I was out of compliance with the accommodations I've made for Tyrell. I constantly feel like she's after me. If it's not one thing, it's another. And I know I'm in compliance!

Coach: Wow, that sounds unsettling. What came up for you?

Client: I just felt so angry. And also nervous—she's my evaluator.

Coach: What would be helpful for us to talk about now?

Client: I think I need support on how to respond to her. Should I talk to our principal and request a change in my evaluator? I don't know. I'm new here, and I don't want to overstep. But I feel like she's singling me out and making comments that feel inappropriate.

Coach: Say more about that.

Scenario 2 is an example of Transformational Coaching in which the client is invited to direct the conversation. In Scenario 1, the coach requests information (and drives the conversation) to meet their need for context. Sometimes context is helpful. But often, coaches center their need for clarity, rather than the client's need to reflect, process, and identity the most useful direction for the conversation. When you've got only 50 (or 15) minutes, you need to use every one of those intentionally and wisely.

There are, however, instances when eliciting information or clarity is supportive.

Clarifying stems include:

- Let me see if I understand . . .
- I'd be interested in hearing more about . . .
- It would help me understand if you'd give me an example of . . .
- So, are you saying/suggesting . . . ?
- Tell me what you mean when you . . .
- Tell me how that idea is like (or different from) . . .
- To what extent is . . . ?
- I'm curious to know more about . . .
- I'm intrigued by . . .
- I'm interested in . . .
- I wonder . . .

What to Do with All of These Sentence Stems

Without intentionality in coaching conversations, you might feel like you're hurling half-cooked spaghetti onto the wall—some questions stick, but many tumble to the floor. We categorize responding strategies to be more intentional in conversations.

Once you've internalized the different kinds of coaching stems, you can ensure that your coaching is varied. When you plan for a conversation, you can select stems from the different approaches. You can have your coaching stems in your notebook during a conversation, and you can reference them if you get stuck.

You can also record a conversation, transcribe it, and code what you say. Notice if there's an approach you are uncomfortable using, or that you avoid, and make a commitment to try it. Notice if there was an approach that you relied on heavily such as the prescriptive approach or asking clarifying questions. You might notice that when you asked a Survival Phrase, your client sighed loudly, and really opened up. You may see patterns in how clients respond to different approaches. One might relish catalytic questions, while another makes their biggest growth when you take a confrontational approach.

There's no one right way in coaching—there's just what you do and what happens. Pay attention to impact. If the impact of what you say leads your client to greater insight about themselves, into exploring their beliefs and ways of being, and toward behavior change—keep doing what you're doing. If not, try something else. You've now got a whole lot of options for what that could be.

Sharing Your Stories

It's normal to want to share your experiences with clients—we often create connection and belonging through sharing our stories. But when you notice a desire to describe your first year teaching or how you survived a toxic team or your trials and tribulations decades ago as a seventh grader, pause. Ask yourself: *what purpose is served by telling this story?* You might realize you're inclined to share because you want to connect with your client or you've gleaned some wisdom or you're still processing an experience and want empathy.

Once you've identified the purpose (or intention) behind your desire to share an experience, ask yourself if it's appropriate to reveal that story in a coach-client relationship and what impact that sharing might have on your client. Your client will not be served if you become the center of the conversation—which is a possibility when you share stories. Also consider the power dynamic between you and your client—either you have more positional power or you are perceived to have it by the nature of your role as a coach. This means that your client may ascribe more value to your story and may perceive your story as holding more validity than their own experiences. Share wisely.

Don't Overlook Your Body Language

Visualize an impatient person. Imagine their body language, how they sound when they talk, and the words they use. It's easy to do that, because we know what impatience looks and sounds like. Our metacommunication—body language and tone of voice—together with our words convey a way of being, and impatience is a way of being.

Let me suggest a couple of behavioral aspirations for every time you speak to a client: first, make sure your communication reflects who you want to be, and second, strive for congruence. If you aspire to coach from a place of compassion and curiosity and if you want to communicate trust in coaching, convey those ways of being in your nonverbals and words. Ask yourself these questions during a conversation:

- How can my facial expressions communicate curiosity?
- How can my tone of voice reflect compassion?
- How can my body language indicate trust in the process?

Of course, if you don't actually *feel* curious, compassionate, or trusting, those ways of being won't be reflected in your nonverbals or words. Sometimes, however, we feel those feelings and aspire to reflect those ways of being, but we don't show up that way. Start with commitment and intentionality.

Congruence—the alignment of words and nonverbals—is the second behavior to strive for. Simply said, congruence builds trust; incongruence undermines it. For example, if someone says "It's so great to see you!" but they stand six feet away, look down at their feet, and scowl, then their body language communicates something else. Such incongruence between words and metacommunication can make us feel like someone is hiding something from us. It's unsettling.

Forget the Stems, Remember the Source

I have two therapists. They each use different modalities, and I benefit from both. One of my therapists uses active listening for about 90% of my sessions. (Yes, I analyze his therapizing and categorize the things he says.) In one session, during the writing of this book when I was very anxious about the looming deadline, I noticed that mostly he said, "That sounds really hard." Every time he said it, I felt relieved. I felt like he saw me, he heard me, he felt my pain.

Later, I thought, *Is it* really *that simple? That we just need to hear someone say "that sounds hard" when we're suffering?*

And I answered myself, *Yes, because what we need more than anything else is empathy and to know we're not alone in a difficult moment.* At least, this is what I've learned about myself: it's not the emotion (fear or sadness or anger) that's hard to be with—it's the sense that I'm alone with it that causes my suffering. When I share the state I'm in with someone who doesn't try to fix it, who listens and empathizes, I feel so much better. And I know this isn't just my personal preference—our core human need is for connection, belonging, and companionship; we can't survive physically, socially, or emotionally without others. We need empathy from each other.

I've offered more than 50 things you can say in response to what your client says. It's nice to have a lot of options to pull from, but perhaps what matters most is where the response comes from in you and whether it comes from a place of love. Perhaps you won't remember all the phrases or questions I've offered, but I know that you can remember to source your responses from a place of care and compassion. Try it, and pay attention to the impact it has on your client, and on you.

Pause and Process

Reflect:

- What are your favorite ways to be listened to? What kinds of questions do you appreciate hearing from friends, colleagues, mentors, or coaches?
- What do you want to stop doing, start doing, and continue doing around the way you respond in a coaching conversation?
- Which ideas were most challenging or uncomfortable in this chapter?
- What resonated most in this chapter?

Next steps:

- Listen to *Bright Morning Podcast* episode 182, "Less Talking, More Impact," and episode 187, "What Would be Most Helpful for Us to Talk About?"
- Download the 50 Questions tool from my website and practice the Survival Phrases with a colleague.
- Record a coaching conversation and categorize your responses.

CHAPTER 6

Listen, Think, Respond

Inside the Mind of a Transformational Coach

Common misconception: Some people just always know the "right" thing to say.	*Transformational Coaches know:* I can learn and apply thinking tools to respond effectively in any situation.

Esther and I were sitting in a coffee shop talking about coaching. "What goes on in your mind when you're coaching?" she asked. "I wish I could just crawl inside of your brain and watch what happens," she said.

This was a question I'd been trying to answer for years—a question that still compels me.

"Okay, let me think about it," I said. Esther leaned forward, her hazel eyes fixed on me. "Maybe there are three steps to what happens." I looked out the floor-to-ceiling glass windows while I described my process.

"First, I listen. I often feel a stillness come over me when I'm listening. It's quiet inside. It's almost empty. I'm taking in someone's words and their body language and something else—I don't know what to call it. Maybe their energy. Just everything about them. I let all of this information flood me. Sometimes my mind starts analyzing what they're saying, or thinking about what I'll say in response, but usually I try to stay in a quiet place as long as I can."

Esther nodded. I felt a little vulnerable describing my inner process, but we'd worked together for many years, and I trusted her.

I continued: "There's a point at which I allow my mind to start thinking, maybe when my client pauses, or stops talking. Sometimes in that moment, I don't say anything—or I say, 'I'm processing what you said,' so they don't get uncomfortable with my silence. In this thinking step, I filter through the frameworks I use to analyze a situation. I might consider whether my client is working within their sphere of control or how much agency they're experiencing or where their gaps are. I reflect on how they're relating to their emotions and whether they might need to process any feelings. I consider whether there are beliefs or ways of being that might be worth exploring. All of this thinking happens fast—it's like I rapidly click through all of these filters that illuminate what's going on." I paused and sipped my lukewarm chai.

"Okay, so there's listening and thinking," Esther said, waiting for what would come next.

"I guess then, at some point, when I need to say something, I respond. That's the third step—responding. A question or statement comes out of the thinking."

Esther had been nodding, but she stopped. "When I listen to you coach, I often wonder, *how did you know what to say?* It seems like you find the perfect thing to say. How do you decide?"

"Yeah, that's the hard part," I said. "The decision-making that happens between *thinking* and *responding*. That has to do with where we're at in the conversation, the trust I believe exists with my client, where they're at emotionally, what I sense they need, and what their goals are, among other things. For example, when someone is experiencing or expressing strong emotions, there's a questioning sequence that we need to follow. Until they have released some of the feelings they literally can't access the part of their brain that allows them to sort through problems and identify solutions. This is neuroscience, and that understanding is one of the frameworks that I quickly click through. So if I see and hear that there are strong emotions present, I start there. I'll often use active listening, because that's validating and strengthens trust. Reflecting back what I'm hearing also gives me a moment to process what I've heard, and sometimes it offers my client an invitation to dig in more deeply. There are so many decisions that go into deciding how to respond, and it happens really quickly in my mind."

"Why do you think you can do that?" Esther asked. She'd been a coach for a few years and had attended a number of my trainings. "It seems so fast and easy for you."

"I think it's practice—years and years of coaching and reflection and practice. After a while, it's easier to hear and see the patterns. It's like when you're teaching and on the first day of school a kid walks in and they remind you of another kid you taught, and you remember what helped that child feel comfortable on their first day, so you try that and it works. I guess after a while you know and remember the ways that all humans are the same and the ways that adults learn." I paused. An image came to mind.

"Maybe," I said, "you can think about it like trails in the forest that we take clients on. When I'm coaching I often ask one thing, and within just a minute or so I can tell whether walking along that trail will be useful. Let's say I ask a question to explore their sense of agency and the spheres of control comes to mind. So I say, 'I hear you're really frustrated about the changes in the master schedule. I'm wondering if that's something you feel like you can influence?' But they respond with, 'I spent all summer planning the first six units and now I'm told I'm not even teaching this course?'

"What I hear in that response is, 'I'm angry!' So this means that we need to explore emotions before the spheres of control."

"So you went back to the listening step," Esther said. "Listening to how your client responds to what you say."

"Yeah," I nodded. "You always have to listen. Always. You listen when you ask a question, you listen to yourself listening, you listen to how they respond. If you can't listen, you can't coach."

Esther was pensively looking into her coffee mug.

"I think what you're describing is presence," she said. "What you call listening is presence."

My eyes widened. "Yeah," I said, "I don't know how you can separate listening from presence. But that's true—when I'm really listening, I feel fully present. When I'm speaking, I also feel fully present. I guess that's the key—you can't coach if you aren't present. If your mind and heart aren't present with the person in front of you, then you're on autopilot."

"Okay, so your workshops need to teach the art of being present," Esther said.

I sighed. "People want sentence stems, and they want to know how to make resistant teachers do what they are told to do. They feel so much urgency. I get it, I wanted the same things when I started coaching, but yeah, many skills enable the questions we ask, including skills that facilitate presence."

Esther nodded. "Well," she said, "I would still love to be inside your mind, but you've given me clear steps."

"That's a start," I said. "And we need a place to start."

The Three Steps in a Transformational Coaching Conversation

Transformational Coaching skills can be sorted into three categories that we use somewhat sequentially: listening, thinking, and responding. Each of these three modes is a critical component of Transformational Coaching conversations. Many coaches, particularly when we're starting out, register a client speaking and leap to the responding step—we're eager to help. But in our haste, we don't engage in transformational listening (see

Chapter 4), and we may skip the thinking step entirely. Without processing and analyzing what our client shares, our questions or offerings are much less likely to help.

Furthermore, it's during the thinking step that we can be intentional about coaching behaviors, beliefs, or ways of being. We process what we've heard, determine a direction for the conversation, and select a sentence stem that will lead us in that direction. During the thinking step, we make decisions by using "thinking tools," which I'll explain shortly. Based on what we've heard and the insights we glean by using the thinking tools, we hone in on one of the Three Bs to explore further. Only then can we select a response.

When I first became aware of the potential in using this process, I would mentally pause during a coaching session and tell myself, *listen, think, respond*. This helped me focus on what a client said: I could take in their words without feeling anxious about coming up with a response; then I would think for a moment; and then, after thinking, I would offer a considered response.

As much as it is useful to tease apart these three modes that we work in, it's also true that describing listening, thinking, and responding as distinct, sequential steps is an oversimplification. Not only do we cycle through the modes over and over in a conversation, but they often overlap.

Recently I was coaching Audra, a Black female leader, who described a situation in which she felt that her older, white, male supervisor was not taking her concerns about racism seriously. When I listen to a client describe a challenge, as I take in their words and body language, I immediately organize this information—I start thinking. As Audra shared her experience, I registered the power dynamic and the racial equity issues at play. I also noticed that she seemed restrained in how she spoke to me—as if she was trying to contain her emotions, perhaps her anger. As I wondered if this was because she was afraid of being perceived as a stereotype, perhaps due to the differences in our racial identities, I recognized that my listening had morphed into analysis. My response to her was a fusion of listening, thinking, and responding: I said, "If you had no fear of what I'd think about you or how I'd react to whatever you say, how would you describe this incident?" Then I moved back into listening mode.

Although these steps overlap, it can be helpful to think of them as a template on which to build your conversations. We've already explored listening and responding. The thinking step is the most complex. In Chapters 7–15, I'll show you how to do the thinking that allows you to craft effective responses. In these chapters, we'll dig into what it means to coach behaviors, beliefs, and ways of being, and I offer the many thinking tools that support this kind coaching.

Figure 6.1 is an overview of these three critical steps in Transformational Coaching.

Figure 6.1: Three steps of a Transformational Coaching Session

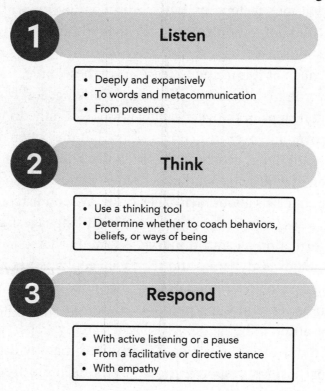

1 Listen
- Deeply and expansively
- To words and metacommunication
- From presence

2 Think
- Use a thinking tool
- Determine whether to coach behaviors, beliefs, or ways of being

3 Respond
- With active listening or a pause
- From a facilitative or directive stance
- With empathy

An Overview of the Thinking Tools

Imagine a big red toolbox full of useful coaching tools. These tools are what you need to move your client from wherever they are to the place where they can thrive and serve children. I call these *thinking tools*. After we've listened, and before we respond, we need to think. These tools, the analytical frameworks that we use in Transformational Coaching, make that thinking intentional and anchored in research-based best practices.

Thinking tools help us to process what we hear in our coaching conversations so that we can respond strategically, in a way that moves conversations forward, and that supports shifts in clients' own thinking. For example, we can use the *Spheres of Influence* tool to guide a client out of a victim mindset. Alternatively, we can select the *Exploring Beliefs* framework to help clients shift beliefs. Or we might choose the *Gaps Protocol* to identify a client's areas for growth and create a scope and sequence for their learning. Each thinking tool has a precise purpose—we select the tool we need based on our listening. Each tool helps us coach a client's behaviors, beliefs, or ways of being.

The thinking tools can also interrupt our own default mental models in helpful ways. In Chapter 11, "How to Coach Beliefs," we'll explore how beliefs are constructed, but in short, thoughts are beliefs, and all of our thoughts are constructed by life experiences and dominant culture. While our default mental models aren't necessarily good or bad, the thinking tools create space in our thinking so that we can be conscious of what those mental models are and we can make intentional decisions.

I recall one of my first years of coaching when a teacher complained in a session about students not walking quietly in the hallways. I felt annoyed—I thought that she was raising an inconsequential issue to avoid other issues and that she was focusing on controlling children's bodies. I lurched into prescriptive coaching and told her what to do. Now, when I hear those same complaints, the Gaps Protocol interrupts that thinking pattern, and I ask myself which skills the teacher might need, and may not have, to support students to meet expectations about walking in the hallways. I wonder about the values, beliefs, and assumptions that the teacher has around hallway etiquette and how those might be culturally influenced. I listen for the emotions that might be present for a teacher when describing student behavior and their relationship to that behavior. This interruption in my thinking allows me to coach a teacher on their ways of being and beliefs and respond in a helpful way that addresses behaviors as well.

Frameworks are incredibly valuable. They organize complexity and help us make sense of it. They can push our understandings and help us create new connections among ideas. That said, no framework can ever be absolute (because humans are dynamic and endlessly complex). As you learn about the frameworks, and as you begin to use them, watch for fragile elements, places where they don't support the weight of a situation or where they obscure nuance. As you explore the frameworks, appreciate their sturdiness and usefulness, but also notice when they don't hold up. Take these moments as opportunities for learning.

Table 6.1 provides an overview of the knowledge and skills required to coach in each Transformational Coaching domain and identifies the

Table 6.1: An Overview of How to Coach the Three Bs

Domain	Knowledge	Skills	Thinking Tools/ Frameworks
Being	*Understand . . .* • What emotions are and how to navigate them • When emotions need attention • The value of coaching emotions • The role of identity	*Guide clients . . .* • To acknowledge, accept, and release emotions • To identify who they want to be and align to that aspiration • To recognize their strengths and spheres of influence	• Core Human Needs • ACE Emotions • Identifying Strengths • Spheres of Influence • Core Values • The Wheel of Power

Table 6.1: (Continued)

Domain	Knowledge	Skills	Thinking Tools/ Frameworks
Beliefs	*Understand . . .* • When beliefs are at play • The difference between beliefs that harm and help • How beliefs are constructed • The neuroscience, psychology, and sociology of belief change	*Guide clients . . .* • To recognize when a belief might be harmful • To shift and deconstruct a story and to create new stories • To understand how their beliefs were constructed and to construct new beliefs	• Exploring Beliefs • Ladder of Inference • Equity Lens • The Wheel of Power
Behavior	*Understand . . .* • Adult learning principles • The impact of organizational systems • The Lens of Inquiry and how an inquiry process can be used to identify pathways to solutions • The Lens of Change Management and how to facilitate change processes	*Do . . .* • Conduct classroom observations and debriefs • Categorize and prioritize learning needs • Scaffold and chunk learning • Guide clients to acquire new skills and masterfully enact them	• Adult Learning Principles • The Gaps Protocol • Systems Thinking Lens • Change Management Lens • Inquiry Lens

best tools for each one. You can refer to this table as you learn to use the frameworks. As you look at it now, here's an example of how to read this table:

- Domain: *In order to coach a way of being . . .*
- Knowledge: *You need to understand what emotions are and how to navigate them . . .*
- Skill: *You need to be able to guide clients to acknowledge, accept, and release emotions . . .*
- Framework: *The Core Human Needs framework can guide this process.*

Every Conversation Counts

Every conversation is an opportunity to create a more just and equitable world. Conversations are the places where connection happens, so every single conversation with a client is an opportunity to cultivate compassion and curiosity, activate agency, and transform behaviors, beliefs, and ways of being.

A Transformational Coach knows they can make every conversation count and commits to doing so. When we select a thinking tool, we're holding this vision in mind—we know that our choices can propel us toward this vision, and so we select intentionally. When we craft our responses, we consider how they will create more kindness and compassion in the world.

When you know that every conversation can help create a world in which we thrive, you'll feel a thrilling sense of possibility at the outset of a conversation. You'll notice shifts in your behaviors, beliefs, and ways of being—you'll feel absorbed, focused, and engaged, like you're in a flow state. Anchoring in a belief of hope and possibility means that your conversations are more likely to have a transformational impact.

Pause and Process

Reflect:

- Of the knowledge and skills listed in this table, which do you feel you are competent in or have some familiarity with? Which feel entirely unknown?
- How do you imagine your work changing if you were to be able to skillfully employ the knowledge, skills, and tools outlined in this table?
- What would it feel like if every conversation you had felt like it contributed to creating a better world? Can you imagine this?

Next steps:

- Listen to *Bright Morning Podcast* episode 22, "Coaching Across Lines of Difference with Adam Morales," to hear an example of a coaching conversation where listening, thinking, and responding are demonstrated.
- Continue developing your vision of who you want to be as a coach.
- When you're in conversations, see if you can differentiate between listening, thinking, and responding. During the "thinking" step, see if you can identify the frameworks, thoughts, and beliefs you use to make sense of what you hear. Get to know your default settings.

CHAPTER 7

What You Need to Know About Emotions

And Why You Don't Need to Be a Therapist

Common misconception: Emotions don't belong in the workplace.	*Transformational Coaches know:* If humans are present, emotions are present. And they can be a tremendous source of energy, insight, and wisdom.

It wasn't until I was in my mid-30s that I started to learn about emotions. Like many of you, as a child, I didn't go to schools where social and emotional learning was taught intentionally. And, like many of you, I internalized societal messages about emotions—that they made us weak and led to craziness; that thinking and doing were far more valuable than drowning in a puddle of feelings. *Who has time for emotions?* I thought. *There are bills to be paid, books to read, papers to grade.* In addition, I worried that if I unlatched the door to my feelings, I'd be sucked into a vortex from which I would never return.

When I started coaching, I observed countless ways in which clients were upended by their emotions. I heard teachers describe being crushed by a student's rudeness or afraid of a child's parent. I saw principals who were unable to facilitate team meetings or discussions about student data because they became defensive when teachers asked questions. I heard the ways in which teacher leaders blocked their own aspirations because of the fear and self-doubt they experienced. *If they could only manage their emotions better,* I thought, *they'd be so much more effective.* I began reading about emotional intelligence because I wanted to be a better coach. What I learned helped me professionally. I acquired knowledge and skills to guide my clients in working with their feelings. But equally important, my desire to help my clients was the impetus for a journey into my own relationship to emotions, which has been illuminating and liberating.

To be human means to experience emotions.

We can't choose whether or not to have emotions, but we do have a choice about how we engage with them.

If we see emotions as a part of our humanity and if we understand them as allies and wise teachers, we can build individual and community resilience. On the other hand, when we get stuck in emotions, we can get lost. When we suppress and deny them, we can become depleted. We cannot create thriving and equitable schools without feeling our feelings and learning from them. We cannot create healthy, resilient communities without learning how to be present with each other, in helpful ways, when we experience emotions. Emotions can be a portal to freedom.

A Transformational Coach coaches emotions. We recognize when they are present for clients, we create space for them, and we explore them. We recognize them in ourselves, we feel them fully, and we listen to what they want to teach us. Emotions manifest in our ways of being, they inform our beliefs, and they show up in our behaviors. Similarly, emotions shape our clients' ways of being, beliefs, and behaviors. You can't be a Transformational Coach without coaching emotions because emotions are an essential part of who we are and how we move through the world. This commitment distinguishes Transformational Coaching from most other coaching approaches used in schools.

You do not have to be a therapist to coach emotions. You *do* have to believe in the value of emotions, and you have to learn some skills. To coach emotions effectively, you can't believe that emotions should not be addressed in a professional setting, that emotions are a waste of time, and that talking about emotions will distract us from having important conversations about student performance or accountability or equity. Those are false beliefs propagated by dominant culture to separate us from ourselves and from each other. If you hold any variation of these beliefs, you must work to release them if you want to be a Transformational Coach. By coaching emotions, we take a radical stand to honor the complexity of the human experience. In doing so, we access tremendous energy, insight, and wisdom.

In this chapter, I'll provide the foundational knowledge required to coach emotions. You'll also want to refer to Chapter 2, "A Transformational Coach's Ways of Being," which presents an overview of emotional intelligence, as well as to the introduction, which defines core human needs. Chapter 8 dives deep into how to coach emotions, and in Chapter 9, "How to Coach Resistance and Resilience," we'll dig into how to respond to resistance and coach toward resilience—two additional facets of working with emotions.

As you read this chapter, notice the feelings that arise. Notice if you feel resistant, frustrated, intrigued, surprised, relieved, uncomfortable, or hopeful—and notice what triggers each emotion. Notice what you can learn simply by cultivating awareness of your emotions.

But I'm Not a Therapist . . .

What does it mean to "coach emotions"? Who is qualified to coach emotions? What does a therapist do that a coach doesn't do? Let's start with these important questions.

What Does It Mean to Coach Emotions?

In the most basic terms, coaching emotions means we consider emotions as valid as any other kind of data and respond to them accordingly. A Transformational Coach recognizes when a client is experiencing or expressing emotions. With that awareness, we ask ourselves if it might be beneficial for the client to explore the emotions that are present for them, and if so, we skillfully open that line of inquiry with the client. We may also follow a client's lead if they initiate reflection on emotions. And we always normalize emotions when they are present.

A Transformational Coach has skills to facilitate reflecting on, processing, feeling, and releasing emotions. We acknowledge, accept, and embrace emotions as a source of energy and wisdom. We know that by working skillfully with emotions, we can create the conditions in which every child can thrive.

What's the Difference Between a Coach and a Therapist?

The best way to understand this difference is through experience. I hope you've had the opportunity to work with a coach and a therapist, and have experienced these complementary methods of support firsthand. If you haven't yet, here are the main differences.

A therapist:

- Diagnoses and assesses a client's mental health
- Supports a client to explore the past to understand the present
- Helps a client understand how their early life and conditioning contributes to the choices they make
- Helps a client develop skills to process past issues, manage emotions, and make intentional choices

A coach:

- Helps a client explore the impact of emotions on their current professional experiences

- Supports a client to understand emotions and build basic skills to engage with emotions
- Acknowledges that the past affects the present and encourages a client to get professional support to explore their past
- Provides information or resources on mental health

Let me exaggerate what the difference between what a therapist and a coach might sound like in a conversation. Imagine a teacher says, "I can't believe my principal called me out like that in front of everyone. I felt so ashamed I thought I was going to die!"

If this teacher were sitting in a therapist's office, the therapist might say any of the following:

- That sounds really hard.
- Which feelings came up?
- What's the belief you're holding about yourself?
- Does his behavior remind you of anyone else's in your life?
- What part of you felt hurt? How old is that part? What is that part afraid of?
- You've shared that your father shamed you in front of your siblings. I wonder if that old pain was activated.

If this teacher were sitting in her classroom, with her coach, the coach might say any of the following:

- That sounds really hard.
- Which feelings came up?
- Do you want to explore those feelings?
- What is the story you're telling about yourself?
- How does it feel to share this with me?
- What actions do you want to take?
- Do you want to consider talking to your principal about his behavior? Would you like my help to figure out what you might say?

A therapist probes the psychological origins of how we respond to events; a coach acknowledges emotions, invites the client to explore them as they present now, but does not dig into the roots of those reactions. A therapist supports you to explore your psyche, childhood, and emotional patterns, and is focused on how the past affects the present; a coach guides you to make changes in your behaviors and is focused on how the present creates the future.

When I present workshops on coaching, I often hear, "But I'm not a therapist." I appreciate this sentiment when it comes from concern for a client's well-being and from a place of humility. Unless a coach has studied psychology and been trained as a therapist, it's unethical and dangerous for us to open doors that we're ill-equipped to walk through. When we coach, we inevitably hear clients express limiting beliefs that stem from their childhood wounds and traumas. We can acknowledge what's been shared and recognize our own limitations so that we don't cause harm.

On the other hand, sometimes coaches protest, "But I'm not a therapist . . ." because they don't want to deal with emotions. If you are reluctant to coach emotions, explore whether your reluctance comes from lack of skill and knowledge, from a belief about the value of addressing emotions, or perhaps from fear or discomfort about what might arise for you. If the idea of coaching emotions generates doubt in you, explore that doubt—it's a feeling that's trying to tell you something. And remember that if you're committed to enacting Transformational Coaching, you need to learn how to coach emotions.

A final distinction between the way a Transformational Coach works with emotions and what happens in therapy relates to context. As educators, we are ultimately committed to every child, every day—our clients are a core part of this vision, and we care for them, *and* we have a greater calling than the individual in front of us. In contrast, therapy centers on the individual. Many therapeutic approaches allow the client to direct their own healing. This means your therapist might occasionally point to something for you to explore, but if you don't want to go there, you don't have to. In contrast, there are times when a Transformational Coach might take a directive approach with a client and, for example, might present student data that illustrates educational inequities and then might take a confrontational stance to unearth the teacher's beliefs. This difference in context between coaching and therapy requires different approaches: A person generally goes to a therapist for their own personal healing, but a teacher works with a coach so that they can be more effective at serving students.

Why Is It So Hard to Deal with Emotions?

Note which of the following statements ring true to you:

- Emotions are a pain in the butt.
- Emotions are an obstacle to creating equitable schools.
- Deal with feelings in therapy or with a best friend. Not at work.
- Leave your emotions at the door—don't bring them into school.
- If a man cries, he's weak.
- If a woman cries, she's not fit to lead.

Our beliefs about emotions can make it hard to deal with them. But we've been socialized and conditioned into many of these beliefs, which means we can release them if we want. Many of these beliefs have made us afraid of emotions—and this is not by chance. For thousands of years, systems of oppression have cultivated beliefs that reject emotions and disconnect us from ourselves as a means of domination. These ideas have been disseminated through culture so thoroughly that many of us no longer see that they are just beliefs—we engage with them as truths. It's easier to release beliefs that no longer serve if you can see their origins.

Contextualizing Resistance to Emotions

Patriarchy, colonialism, white supremacy, and exploitative capitalism are institutionalized ideologies that generate and reinforce systems of inferiority and superiority. Within these systems, cis-gendered males are superior to women and trans and nonbinary people; white / Northern European/ light-skinned bodies are superior to Black and Brown bodies; and those who possess economic wealth are superior to those without wealth. A massive set of beliefs has been propagated to enforce this hierarchy—including beliefs about emotions.

An effective system of oppression creates and disseminates values that become invisible to those who are subjugated. Such a system must operate in every home, organization, and relationship—and ideally, it must operate "naturally," without needing military enforcement. The oppressed must adopt these values, norms, and codes, and act on them as if they are natural. The oppressed must internalize the rules of the oppressors and believe them.

When it comes to emotions, the system of oppression we call patriarchy has effectively taught us to that boys shouldn't cry, that men should be stoic, that women can't show anger, that we shouldn't be afraid, and that girls should smile. When we buy into these norms, we regulate ourselves and unconsciously uphold systems of oppression.

Patriarchy has maintained its power in part because it vilifies the full human range of emotions. When we reject and suppress emotions, we are severed from what it means to be human.

The oppressive systems of colonialism and capitalism uphold the patriarchal repression of emotion. Men hold the political, economic, and social power in these systems in which women (and those who are not cis-gendered male), and everything in women's domains, including children and emotions, is deemed inferior. Within these systems, norms around emotions are created—norms that define socially and culturally acceptable parameters for emotional experiences.

These parameters become clearer when we consider the emotions we expect to see expressed by people around us. What kind of emotional expression is acceptable from Black women? From Black men? From Asian men? From white women? From white men? What do we think and feel when someone from one of those groups expresses emotions in a way that is outside of what we consider acceptable? For example, part of the stereotype of

Blackness is that Black people will be emotional. However, dominant culture places limits to how emotional Black people are allowed to be, which emotions are okay to express, and when and where it's acceptable to express strong emotions. If Black people violate those social norms on expressing emotions, the repercussions can be severe.

Intersectional bigotry affects how we perceive other people's emotions. If a Black woman at work advocates for her position assertively, she may be seen as being pushy or angry. If a white woman does the same, she might be admired for "leaning in." Heteronormative white men are perhaps given the narrowest range of acceptable emotional expression: they are expected to be stoic and emotionless—unless they are expressing anger.

All of these norms mean one thing: we aren't allowed to authentically experience or express emotions. Emotions are mediated and regulated by exploitative capitalism, colonialism, misogyny, and racism. This has harmed all people in all economic classes of all races and ethnicities. It can feel hard to coach emotions because of the beliefs and behaviors into which we've been socialized.

So who or what is irrational? The teacher who can't stop crying because she's exhausted from working 60-hour weeks, because she's heard one too many stories of trauma from her students and their mothers, and because she believes her self-worth and value as a human is tied to how much she can give to her students, because her test scores (that were published in the newspaper) say that her kids are underperforming and her school is in the red and she's anxious it will be closed? Or the economic system that funds schools based on property taxes and a federal taxation system that prioritizes purchasing drones over books? Or the lack of social services and support systems for students and their mothers who have experienced multiple traumas?

Accepting and embracing emotions is an act of political resistance. To do so is to reject systems of oppression that intentionally, by design, seek to dehumanize and subjugate us—that seek to sever the relationships we have with our bodies, minds, hearts, and spirits; and that seek to undermine empathy and divide communities. When you coach emotions, you consider data that is as valid as any other kind of data. You recognize the wisdom of tears, the truth of rage, the guidance of fear. When you coach emotions, you facilitate individual and collective liberation. You open up the conversation to include all kinds of information.

What is this information? Let's shift gears and get into the essentials of emotions.

What You Need to Know About Emotions

A great deal of fear about emotions comes from not understanding what they are or how we can work with them. This section provides a primer on emotions, which I hope will boost your confidence in coaching emotions—as well as deepen your understanding of your own.

Basic Terminology

The language and concepts we use to talk about emotions shape our understanding of them. Here are some of basic terms that are relevant to coaching emotions:

- *The brain* is the big organ in our skulls. It controls many body functions. It receives sensory information including sights, sounds, smells, and taste. The brain is like the hardware in our system.
- *The mind* is separate from, yet inseparable from, the brain. Our thoughts, emotions, attitudes, and memories arise from the mind. The mind is like the software in our system. The mind uses the brain, and the brain responds to the mind.
- *Neuroplasticity* is the ability to create new thoughts. For a long time, it was believed that our brains don't change; neuroscientists now know that we can change our brains—we can create new thoughts, and as a result our brains change. This is important because new thoughts create new feelings, and thus neuroplasticity makes way for a changing emotional landscape.

- *The nervous system* includes the brain, the spinal cord, and a complex network of nerves. It sends messages back and forth between the brain and the body. If the nervous system gets dysregulated from chronic stress or trauma, it may not function effectively, which can lead to anxiety, depression, and a range of physical symptoms. A nervous system can be regulated with structures and tools.
- *An emotion* is a biochemical reaction that begins as a sensation in the body and is created unconsciously in response to external stimuli. Emotions result in visible and noticeable physical changes such as increased heart rate, changes in breathing, and temperature changes. Emotions are raw data.
- *A feeling* is a mental process that's generated in response to an emotion. Feelings are social, cultural, and individual interpretations of emotions. Feelings are stories.

You might often hear the words *emotion* and *feeling* used synonymously. That's okay—they point to the same experience. I find it helpful to understand the difference between the tingling sensation in my fingers when someone cuts me off in traffic (the emotion of fear) and the feeling I have as a result, which shows up as thoughts—*I'm not safe on the freeway; what's wrong with people?*—which I call anxiety and anger. In this book, I've attempted to use the terms with fidelity to their definitions.

This distinction is also helpful in understanding how we experience emotions and trauma. We'll dig into trauma later in this chapter, but the key idea is that when our bodies experience an emotion, if we let that emotion be fully felt, it lasts around 90 seconds and then "moves through us." Often this means that the *emotion* doesn't become a *feeling*, laden with all the stories we tell about it (*I'm not safe; I can't trust people*)—and doesn't become a limiting thought or belief.

Perhaps you've seen young children playing and experiencing waves of emotions one after another such as crying one minute and laughing another—that's a healthy experience of emotions. But when we experience fear, for example, and we aren't able to let it course through our body and we feel shame at having felt fear, our experience becomes a tangled knot of emotion and thoughts and feelings. That knot can be activated later by a seemingly minor incident, and when we respond out of proportion to the incident, the expression becomes problematic.

When you're coaching, this terminology and the concepts I just outlined for you are helpful in making decisions about what to say or do with a client, as well as for helping your client build emotional literacy. Here's an example. Marco was a new teacher I coached who struggled with classroom management. After a few months of diligently implementing a program with his second graders, he reported that his class now felt focused, calm, and responsive. "I never thought that could happen," he said.

This could have been an opportunity to validate Marco and help him recognize his accomplishment. But it was also an opportunity to enforce the emergence of new neural pathways. "What's it like to tell me this now?" I asked Marco. "How are you feeling?"

Marco smiled. "It feels so good," he said, the lines around his eyes creasing and reflecting his happiness.

"What are you noticing about how your body feels?" I asked.

"I've got a lightness in my chest that I haven't felt in school," he said, "and I feel like I can breathe easier."

"What's the story you're telling about how you manage your class?" I asked.

"I guess I'm telling myself that I can do it. That it's not impossible. That I'm capable."

"How does that story make you feel?" I asked.

"Really good. Joyful. Proud," he said.

I want you to see in this brief anecdote how simple it can be to coach emotions, as well as how cultivating awareness of pleasant emotions can be an integral part of coaching all emotions. I also want you to see the link between emotions, feelings, and stories, and to hear what it sounds like to guide someone to build new neural pathways. As I coached Marco, I was acting on my knowledge of the connection among emotions, feelings, and the mind: I didn't need to offer Marco definitions of those terms to coach him around his emotions, but I used that knowledge to spend a few productive minutes coaching emotions in a way that was likely to impact how Marco experienced future challenges.

"Positive" and "Negative" Emotions

Emotions are not positive or negative: they are biochemical reactions that arise in the body in response to stimuli. In other words, they are just what happens when you're having a human experience. Some emotions, of course, are more comfortable than others (joy often feels good in the body), and so we want to experience them more often. But as soon as we label emotions as "good" or "bad," we generate an aversion to certain emotions and an attachment to others.

One of the results of labeling our emotions in this way is that when, for example, anger shows up, we feel afraid or ashamed of our anger, and we don't get to truly experience it or learn from it. In this way, the emotion of anger generates a feeling of shame, which leads to another feeling, and so on. We can get stuck in a cycle, rather than moving through and processing the thoughts and physical sensations that arise.

All of our emotions have lessons to teach us. For example, fear tells us to pay attention to threats to our physical and emotional well-being. There are times when it's really important to feel afraid—fear protects our vulnerable bodies—and so we never want to get rid of all fear. Many people have a false notion that to be courageous, you have to conquer your fear. In fact, to be courageous, you must accept, honor, and know your fear. A healthy relationship with fear is exactly what allows you to be courageous—to practice wise discernment about what is really dangerous and where you can take risks.

If you'd like, talk about emotions as "pleasant" and "unpleasant" or "comfortable" and "uncomfortable"; try to avoid judgmental labels such as good or bad.

It's All About How You Respond to Emotions

There is a critical distinction to make when we talk about emotions, and that is the difference between *having* an emotion and *acting on* an emotion. There's nothing wrong with fear. If you notice that fear arises in you when a student gets angry, throws his textbook across the classroom, and curses at you—that's okay. Responding to your fear by screaming, "Get out! You're acting like an animal!" is not okay.

Anger can be a wise teacher, often showing up in response to a boundary being crossed. Anger tells us, "Whoa! Something happened that wasn't okay." Anger can help us clarify how to take care of ourselves, it can guide us to action to correct injustices, and it can anchor us in our core values.

Anger can also manifest as what's called a "secondary emotion," as a mask for sadness, shame, or fear. Many of us have a hard time with the vulnerable emotions of sadness, shame, and fear. To cope with that vulnerability, we generate anger. Think for a moment about how your body feels when it's angry—you'll probably recall feeling significant energy. In contrast, remember how fear or sadness feels in your body: perhaps you remember a feeling of constriction or depletion, maybe the impulse to get under the covers and close your eyes. Our mind turns the emotion of sadness into the feeling of anger as a mechanism of self-preservation. The problem is that when it does this, sadness doesn't actually get to be felt or known. We lose out on learning, the emotion gets bottled up, and the thoughts get tangled.

Sometimes, when someone experiences anger, they respond by doing or saying hurtful things, what we call aggression. Aggression is throwing a plate across the room, belittling someone, shutting down and not speaking, ghosting someone, complaining relentlessly, or being hypercritical, resentful, or bitter. Aggression is a response to suffering, and that response—*not the anger*—is the problem. People respond to anger in harmful ways when they don't have the tools to work with strong emotions. They're attempting to discharge uncomfortable feelings, but the impact of their actions is destructive—to others and to themselves. We are responsible for how we engage with our emotions and work with our needs. We need to understand that there's nothing wrong with experiencing emotions; what's problematic is acting on them in harmful ways.

The good news—there's so much good news about emotions—is that we can learn the skills to respond to strong emotions productively. We can learn to regulate our nervous system, to anticipate what will activate (or trigger) us, and to recognize when intense emotions arise. Critically, we can learn to respond to emotions in ways that allow us to release them, learn from them, and deepen our connections to ourselves and others. We can learn that it is in experiencing the intensity of the uncomfortable emotions—in allowing your body to be wracked with grief or shaken with despair or crying until you feel dehydrated—that we open up to the intensity of emotion at the other end of the continuum of emotions. Experiencing the full continuum of emotions creates the expansiveness within our bodies that makes space for us to experience and express that which we all crave: ease, joy, satisfaction, pleasure, connection, love, delight, awe, wonder, and bliss.

Stressed, Tired, and Overwhelmed

When I ask teachers how they feel, sadly, the most common responses are "stressed," "tired," and "overwhelmed." For many years, I also used these three descriptors regularly. But if you look at Appendix B, "The Core Emotions," you won't find those words. According to the people who study emotions, *stressed*, *overwhelmed*, and *tired* are symptoms that emerge from emotions; they signify an *emotional state*, not an emotion. Likewise, "fine" and "okay" also reflect emotional states—they aren't emotions. When you feel "fine" or "stressed" or when your client tells you that's how they feel, follow up with kind curiosity: "Tell me more about that" or "Do you want to explore 'overwhelmed'?" Usually, "stressed," "tired," and "overwhelmed" are a combination of sadness and fear, sometimes with a sprinkling of anger.

About 10 years into teaching, I experienced a difficult period. I felt frequently frustrated by my students, I was set off by little things that had never bothered me before, I couldn't find the joy I'd previously felt in the classroom, and I often felt pessimistic about the impact I could have on children. I would get home from school and lie on the couch and watch TV, which was out of character for me. After some months, I signed up for a 6 a.m. exercise boot camp that helped me shift out of the depression, and I started making changes in my work life. Thinking back to this time, I wish I'd found a therapist to help me get to the roots of the sadness and fear I was experiencing. My burnout was situational—and also a manifestation of a lot of unprocessed emotions.

The research is alarming. It's estimated that some 10% of teachers suffer from depression, which is higher than the suspected national average of 6.7% (Wulsin, Alterman, Bushnell, Li, and Shen, 2014). When teachers face a lot of stress and get little support to manage it, they may respond in maladaptive ways. In addition to their internal responses, they may create climates of stress in their classroom that are harmful to students: teachers who are under-supported spend less time engaging with children and are less attentive to their relationships with students (Jeon, Buettner, and Snyder, 2014).

As a former teacher who has experienced cycles of depression, this is painful to read. I feel sad when I think that I may have negatively impacted my students; I also feel sad for myself for the phases when I felt hopeless, irritated, and lonely. I knew then that I wasn't being who I wanted to be, but I didn't know what to do. I wish I'd had a Transformational Coach to help me recognize what was going on for me emotionally, to help me find ways to process my feelings, and to tell me that I deserved healing and support and that a therapist could help.

Burnout

Many of us use the term *burnt out* to describe a physical and emotional state that's overwhelming. It's helpful to know what burnout is so that when you feel it or when you hear a client use the term, you'll have a sense of what's going on.

Burnout is a state of physical, emotional, and mental exhaustion caused by excessive and prolonged stress. It can include depression and anxiety and is characterized by apathy, fatigue, frustration, sadness, and dissatisfaction. The term was originally coined by a psychologist to describe the consequences of severe stress coupled with the high ideals in the "helping" professions—and so it makes sense that so many educators experience burnout.

Many people who feel burnt out are experiencing depression. This is important to know: when someone says they're "burnt out," coaches often respond by suggesting they take time off of work, but time alone will not necessarily resolve the situation. If there's more going on than simple exhaustion (and there usually is), those root causes need attention. Furthermore, while a teacher might feel like most of their problems are related to work, it's likely that there are underlying issues or tendencies that deserve exploration that contribute to the burnout.

What are those underlying issues, you might be wondering? Some experts say that burnout is a result of having unhealthy expectations of yourself and not setting boundaries. This was true for me. As a result of childhood experiences, I'd unconsciously adopted a belief that my worthiness was contingent upon caring for others—and that my value was in working and working and working in service to others. Because my worthiness was tied to how much I gave, and in schools there's never-ending need, I could never win. I could never satisfy my inner need to feel worthy. I knew my limits, but I ignored them until I was completely depleted. I learned to avoid the edge of the cliff by doing things like the 6 a.m. bootcamp or taking a short vacation or saying no to a few requests, but the effort simply to manage my burnout was exhausting, and the root causes—those core beliefs and early life experiences—weren't addressed.

I'm sharing this for a couple reasons: first, because I suspect that a good number of you might relate to my experience; second, to nudge you, again, toward therapy. As I've already shared, it's only been since I committed to therapy that I have truly felt like I'm thriving.

Depression and Anxiety

If you find yourself feeling "overwhelmed" a great deal, this can be a sign of depression. And if you find yourself feeling "stressed" a lot of the time, this can be a sign of anxiety. It's also helpful to understand that many psychologists now consider depression and anxiety to commonly be experienced together.

It's important to know the signs of depression and when to get help or encourage someone else to get help. Common indicators of depression include changes in sleep, appetite, concentration, energy levels, daily behaviors, and self-esteem; excessive crying, agitation, and irritability; and social isolation, loss of interest in or pleasure in activities that used to bring you joy, and a persistent state of hopelessness, guilt, anxiety, sadness, or apathy. On my website you can find a resource to self-assess for depression and anxiety.

A few important things to know about depression and anxiety: these "disorders" are far more common than we often imagine, and some psychologists now say they are a predictable response to the stresses and traumas we experience in life.

Finally, know that if you experience depression and anxiety, there are many ways to relieve the symptoms and feel a whole lot better. Yes, it can feel hard to muster the energy to seek out the help you deserve, and time and money can be barriers, but know there is hope.

What Do You Do When You're Coaching Someone Who You Think Is Depressed?

All this basic information about emotions and emotional suffering will help you understand how best to support your clients. If I hear a teacher tell me week after week that they're struggling to get up and come to school every day, that they no longer feel excited about teaching, and that they feel hopeless about their ability to serve children, I hear indicators that might suggest depression. If I've been using strategies to coach emotions and cultivate resilience and if those strategies are not making a dent in the teacher's experience, I need to say something about what I'm perceiving. Here's what I say to a client to invite them to get help:

> I really care about you, and it seems like you're in a lot of distress. I want to make sure you get the care you need—you deserve care. I'm not a therapist and don't have that skill set, and I'm wondering if you feel it would be helpful to talk to a mental health professional.

If the client agrees to seek help, sometimes I encourage them to make an appointment right then and there. I sit with them while they go online or call their healthcare provider to take the first step, because sometimes that first step is the hardest. I follow up to see if they are getting help, and I reiterate, over and over, that there's nothing "wrong" with them—that the majority of us experience periods of stress and grief and that we all deserve caring, skilled support.

Coaching emotions means you repeatedly normalize emotions and normalize the need and desire to get support in navigating them.

Trauma-Informed Coaching

Tony was a mid-career principal in his 30s who had received accolades for his strong and determined leadership—and also a great deal of criticism. His supervisor was concerned by the number of teacher and parent complaints about him, and she had observed him speaking to staff and children in a way she characterized as "intimidating." Much to his annoyance, he was put on an improvement plan, which mandated leadership coaching. Initially, he was reluctant to engage in coaching with me, but I trusted the process and worked on building a relationship with him.

About six months into our work, Tony was required to conduct a survey intended to gather feedback from his staff. On a rainy Thursday evening, Tony and I sat down in his office to look at the results. I watched Tony's facial expressions as he read dozens of statements in which teachers described feeling afraid of him, feeling like he was always angry or upset at them, feeling like they could never say or do the right thing. Tony closed his eyes and dropped the papers. He sat very still. Then his breathing accelerated. And then tears began to stream down his face.

"I've become my father," he said over and over, his eyes closed, his chest heaving. "He was a monster. I was terrified of him," he gasped. "They're saying the exact same things that I felt about my father, the same words," Tony said as he pushed his chair away from the table, folded himself over his body, and began to rock back and forth.

"What's happening? What's happening?" he asked. Sweat poured down his face.

I had a flash of fear, but I've been around a lot of adults and children who became dysregulated, and I moved through my fear.

"Tony," I said, my voice calm and commanding, "can we take some slow breaths together?" I breathed audibly, and Tony joined me.

"My chest feels like it's going to explode," he said.

"You're safe. I'm here, and we'll get help if you don't feel better soon. Can you take another breath with me? Let's see if we can breathe in to five. I'll count." Tony breathed with me again.

"Now slowly exhale to the count of seven," I said. We breathed together.

"What's happening?" Tony said as he opened his eyes and looked at me. His breathing had slowed a little. He looked terrified.

"We'll figure that out, but first, can you tell me what color my shirt is?"

Tony answered correctly. His eyes were glazed, and he was still perspiring heavily.

"Okay, can you name three things you see in this room?"

"Chair, desk, pen," Tony said, his eyes darting around the space.

"Great." I said. "Can you tell me three things you can hear right now?"

"I can hear . . . ," Tony paused and closed his eyes. "I can hear my heart. I can hear my breath. I can hear the train going by."

I could see that Tony was starting to calm. His hands had relaxed into his lap. I continued to invite him to identify sights, sounds, and things he could touch and to bring his awareness to his breath. Once the intensity subsided, Tony began crying again.

"My father was a violent alcoholic," he said, "and I've never talked about this, not with anyone. I'm sorry. I'm sorry I'm doing this. You're my coach. This isn't why you're here. This is so unprofessional. I'm sorry."

"Tony," I said, "you deserve care and healing."

"I'm so sorry. I shouldn't have told you this." Tony stood and began putting on his jacket.

"Sit down," I said, more forcefully than I'd intended. "I don't have to leave, and I don't think it would be wise for you to drive in the rain until you're a little more settled. You did nothing wrong."

Tony sat. I called his partner and suggested she pick him up. While we waited, Tony spoke a little more about his father—and I repeated that he deserved healing and care. "I am honored that you're sharing this with me, Tony, and you deserve the guidance of a skilled professional."

"I know I need therapy," he said at the end of the evening.

"Has anything like this happened before?" I asked, not sure what "this" was, but suspecting that Tony had had a panic attack.

"A long time ago," Tony said. "But I'm anxious all the time. I don't sleep, I have stomach issues, I get migraines."

Once again, I said that he deserved care.

When we met the following week, Tony proudly told me that he'd had his first appointment with a therapist. He said he was embarrassed that he'd had what his therapist called a panic attack, but he also expressed gratitude that I hadn't been alarmed and that I'd been able to help him settle.

In the weeks following that evening, I questioned my response—had I done the right thing? What should I have said?

Tony had experienced a trauma response, and, unfortunately, trauma is so widespread that it's irresponsible for coaches not to have a basic understanding of what it is and how to respond. Since that session with Tony, I've been with other clients who have had a trauma response (also in moments that I didn't anticipate), and I'm grateful for all that I've learned that's enabled me to be responsive, helpful, and kind.

In recent years there's been a lot of new information about trauma and guidance on how to work with it. While I'll provide a brief overview here, I strongly encourage you to continue learning about how trauma affects individuals, communities, and our society at large, and how to heal from it. You'll be able to support teachers, and you might also find a lot of personal healing. My favorite resource on trauma is Dr. Gabor Maté's 2022 massive tome, *The Myth of Normal: Trauma, Illness & Healing in a Toxic Culture*. You could familiarize yourself with Dr. Maté's approach through a podcast or a YouTube video. He's the world's expert right now on trauma, and his work is accessible, compassionate, and hopeful.

What Is Trauma?

Trauma is not what happens *to us*—it's not an external event. Trauma is what happens *inside of us* when what happens *to* us overwhelms our ability to adapt or cope—it's what happens as a result of a stressful experience that leaves us feeling helpless, frightened, overwhelmed, or profoundly unsafe. Often trauma is what happens when we don't have anyone to work out the difficult experiences with—it's the loneliness compounded with the events.

A simple working definition of trauma is anything that is *too much, too soon, or too fast* for our nervous system to handle. Children are particularly susceptible to "too much, too soon, or too fast" for obvious developmental reasons. As a result of experiences that are too much or that happen too soon or too fast, some people develop a range of symptoms that are called Post-Traumatic Stress Disorder (PTSD). Traumatic events such as war, accidents, and sexual assault can generate these symptoms, which can include flashbacks, physical sensations, or strong emotional reactions that emerge without warning.

Any experience in which someone feels overwhelmed and disempowered, especially for long periods, can lead to PTSD symptoms. This includes being a person of color in a racist society, being unhoused, being a queer child and not experiencing identity safety, being bullied, and so on. What makes an experience traumatic is being unable to control the circumstances that led to harm. As a result, we're left with a feeling of being unsafe with others, in the world, or in our own skin. The impact of trauma, whether it develops into PTSD or not, can simply be a decreased ability to feel satisfaction or emotional or physical pleasure.

Traumatic stress can also result from experiencing or witnessing a traumatic event or learning that the event occurred to a family member or close friend. And it can result from repeated or extreme exposure to the others' trauma—such as for first responders, emergency-care physicians, and educators who work in communities where there's a lot of trauma. Sometimes this is called *vicarious trauma*, but it is trauma nonetheless.

The following facts can help illuminate the scope and significance of trauma in our communities:

- Some 64% of adults in the United States report childhood experiences that can be classified as traumatic. The CDC's web page on Adverse Childhood Experiences is a helpful place to start to learn more (https://www.cdc.gov/violenceprevention/aces/index.html).
- Trauma can be intergenerational, unless resolved.
- When someone experiences trauma, their nervous system can get easily "stuck on high" (hypervigilant, anxious, irritated) or "stuck on low" (depressed, numb, lethargic). It can also oscillate between high and low.
- Trauma affects our brain, cells, neural pathways, hormonal system, nervous system, and immune system—and all of these impacts can be reversed.
- Systems of oppression perpetuate trauma. Individual and collective trauma is created and exacerbated by systems of oppression.
- People who are targeted by systemic oppression (people of color, women, poor people, disabled people, queer people, and so on) live inside of traumatic conditions every day and face a greater likelihood of experiencing trauma.

Given how prevalent trauma is in our world and how many of the students in our schools suffer from trauma, it behooves us to learn about how to respond to trauma.

How Do People Recover from Trauma?

Dr. Maté explains that healing is not about getting rid of the pain; it's about learning to live with the pain. I find this incredibly hopeful as I know that humans are masters at learning. Furthermore, I understand Dr. Maté's insight as an invitation to not just "live with" pain but to transform our pain into something of beauty. So much creative expression (music, poetry, movies, dance) is the result of humans exploring and processing their pain. Perhaps healing is about transmuting pain into something we can relate to differently, and perhaps about sharing in a way that helps others through their suffering.

There's more good news. Because trauma affects us physiologically, socially, and emotionally, one of the primary ways we recover is through relationships. When we feel cared for by others (perhaps by a therapist, close friend, or partner), our bodies produce oxytocin, which is the hormone that calms our nervous system. When this happens, we are more likely to feel safe enough to talk and make sense of our experiences. This allows us to integrate those experiences, learn from them, and get distance from them. When that happens, we live with the pain rather than in unpredictable reaction to the pain.

The overwhelming majority of trauma happens in relationship to other people, so rediscovering trust through safe, stable, nurturing relationships teaches us to regulate emotions, release trauma in the body, and form new mental habits. Competent, skilled trauma-informed therapists can facilitate this process, but it's also essential for those who have experienced trauma to form trusting relationships with others in their personal and professional lives. While coaches should not venture into the terrain of mental health professionals, we are ideally positioned *to contribute* to someone's healing through creating safe, trusting spaces for reflection and growth, spaces that are predictable, consistent, and compassionate.

Relationships are not all that's needed to heal from trauma—the nervous system also needs support to learn to regulate. Many modalities help us do this, including exercise, meditation, yoga, breathing, being in nature, and therapies such as Eye Movement Desensitization and Reprocessing (EMDR), biofeedback, somatic experiencing, and psychedelic-assisted therapy. Every year, there's more hopeful research indicating that we can heal from trauma.

One of the reasons why I deeply appreciate Dr. Maté's work is that he addresses the systemic role of trauma. In the movie *The Wisdom of Trauma* (2021), Maté says, "So much of what we call abnormality in this culture is actually normal responses to an abnormal culture. The abnormality does not reside in the pathology of individuals, but in the very culture that drives people into suffering and dysfunction."

The flip side is understanding that the collective can play a role in healing. Here's where coaches and leaders come in. Imagine what might be possible if we could create organizational cultures that acknowledge suffering and trauma and that create the conditions in which individual and collective healing can occur. This is what's possible when we coach emotions.

What Is Trauma-Sensitive, or Trauma-Informed, Coaching?

The U.S. National Center for Trauma-Informed Care (2016) defines trauma-sensitive practices as follows:

- You *realize* the widespread impact of trauma and understand potential paths for recovery.
- You *recognize* the signs and symptoms of trauma in clients and others in a system.
- You *respond* by integrating knowledge about trauma into policies.
- You *seek to actively avoid* re-traumatizing clients.

Echo (echotraining.org) is an organization committed to educating families, communities, and professionals about trauma and resilience. In Table 7.1 you'll see an excerpt from their resource on *what is* and *isn't* trauma-informed care. As you read this list, note to what degree your work as a Transformational Coach is already aligned with trauma-informed care.

Table 7.1: Trauma-Informed Care

Trauma-Informed Care	Not Trauma-Informed Care
Power with a client	Power over a client
Observing	Judging
People need safety first	People need fixing first
Multiple viewpoints	Right and wrong
Empowerment/collaboration	Compliance/obedience
Transparency and predictability	Need-to-know basis for info
Whole person and history	Presenting issue
Empathy-based	Fear-based
Respect	Shame/blame
Goal is to connect	Goal is to do things the "right way"
Choice	Prescriptive
Consider lived experience	Consider only research and evidence
Enlightened witness	Expert

In the "Not Trauma-Informed Care" column, we see many of the hallmarks of the compliance-based, transactional institutions that dominate our world. Coaching or professional development that replicates the status quo in those institutions doesn't create transformation. When traumatized people are asked to work within a context that activates their trauma, not only are they not going to perform optimally, they'll likely show up as resistant (which we'll explore in Chapter 9).

How to Coach in a Trauma-Informed Way

Trauma-informed coaching requires that coaches learn about trauma, its causes, its indicators, and its effects. There are a few reasons why you should know about trauma. First, you may be among the majority of adults who have experienced trauma. If so, you deserve healing. If you don't have awareness of how your trauma impacts you or shows up, you might also inadvertently and unconsciously impact others. To responsibly coach others, which includes not getting triggered by things your clients say or do and not projecting your own stuff onto them, you need to know yourself and your trauma and receive the care you deserve.

The second reason why you should know about trauma is to recognize how trauma and chronic stress can present in coaching. For example, if you see a teacher belittling a student (and you are rightfully horrified), you will understand that you may be hearing trauma speaking—that, for example, it's possible that as a child the teacher experienced an abusive adult. This knowledge may allow you to recognize when a client may need to seek additional support. Trauma may also show up as resistance, passivity, or self-sabotaging behaviors. Resistance, for example, is an expression of fear. Resistance can be a client's way of saying, "I don't trust you yet." Taking a trauma-informed approach, you'll be less likely to be activated by your client's behavior, and it may be easier for you to work from a place of compassion. A client's unprocessed trauma will show up in a coaching session because until it's healed, it shows up in all areas of their life. This awareness will help you respond not to your clients' surface behaviors but to the root causes.

Incorporating trauma-informed practices into your coaching and leadership is not only critical for those who have experienced trauma, it will support everyone you work with. Transformational Coaching offers an inclusive, trauma-informed model.

Here are some additional, specific trauma-informed practices to incorporate into your coaching:

- If you don't meet in your client's room, attend to the physical space in which you meet: make sure the room isn't too small or cluttered, provide a place where your client can sit near an exit if they want, make sure the room isn't too hot or cold, be sure there aren't strong smells (trauma survivors often have heightened sense of smell), and make sure the client can be heard when they speak.

- Ask a client if they'd prefer to have the door to the room open when you meet with them.
- Never touch a client without permission: don't pat them on the back or reach out and take their hand if they're crying or hug them without getting consent.
- Be considerate about the amount of space between your bodies. Leave an arm's length space between you, and if you move closer, ask if that's okay.
- Be aware of how much eye contact you make with a client and whether they seem to need more or less. Some people who have experienced trauma are very sensitive to eye contact, especially in a relationship where there's a power differential.
- Be cautious about directing a client's awareness to their body when they're distressed—sometimes cultivating awareness of the somatic experience of uncomfortable emotions is helpful, but for people who have experienced trauma, tuning into physical sensations can also be activating. If you direct attention to the body, ask, "Is this okay?"
- Create as much predictability and consistency as possible. Do this by sending agendas ahead of time, closing a session by identifying a few things you'll talk about next time, being clear on agreements before you do an observation, and doing what you say you'll do.
- Provide opportunities for choice. Remember that feeling powerless is at the core of the experience of trauma. Coach toward agency and offer choices.
- Cultivate trust. Start and end on time, never speak about a client behind their back, ensure congruence between your metacommunication and your words, and so on.

You don't need to know if a client has experienced trauma to incorporate these strategies, and you don't need to talk about trauma with your client. These are basic good practices that can support all learners and that will especially support those who have experienced trauma.

In addition, it's helpful to know the basics on how to guide someone if they become highly emotionally activated or have a panic attack. Panic attacks are intense surges of fear, characterized by shaking, sweating, numbness, dizziness, chest pain, heart palpitations, stomach distress, shortness of breath, chills or hot flashes, and/or fear of "going crazy" or dying. The tricky thing is that these symptoms are also signs of cardiac distress. If someone loses consciousness, check for breathing and pulse, and get help—from 911 and/or other staff who may have first-aid skills if you don't. In other situations, you may also recognize that these symptoms arise due to whatever is going on, as when Tony had a panic attack.

The following strategies are easy to remember and simple enough to use if you're working with someone experiencing intense fear:

- Ask if they've had a panic attack before and if they think they're having one. If they say yes, ask if they know what might help them.
- Remain calm, speak calmly, and assure your client that they are safe. Say that what they are feeling is scary but that it will pass. Speak in clear, firm, short sentences. Be patient. Don't tell them to "calm down," and don't say that "everything is okay." Let them know that you'll get help if necessary, but don't jump to call 911.
- Breathe slowly and audibly—in through the nose and out through the mouth or nose, and make the exhale longer than the inhale. Invite your client to breathe with you if they'd like.
- Once your client has settled a little bit, invite them to name the colors on your clothes or in the room and then to identify sounds, smells, and other sights in the space you're in. This brings the senses back online in the present moment.

While the specific strategies I've shared with you are invaluable, know that whenever you coach someone back to their agency, you help them heal from trauma. Trauma is what happens when you feel you are powerless. Every time you give a client an opportunity to step back into their power, you help them heal.

When Someone Tells You They've Experienced Trauma

Coaches can be exceptional listeners. I can't tell you how many times a client has said, "I can't believe I just told you that." Sometimes I feel honored, and sometimes I feel concerned. Some people who experience trauma struggle to set appropriate boundaries, and they can share more than what's appropriate in an attempt to receive the care they need. Because I don't have the training and skills to help them heal, there's a risk that I could exacerbate the wounds.

If someone tells you that they're working with a therapist on trauma, thank them for sharing. Don't probe or ask for details. You can let them know that if there are strategies that they use for emotional regulation that would be helpful for you to know about, and reinforce in coaching, they're welcome to share those. If someone reveals too much information about their psyche, childhood, or mental health, you can say something like, "I'm honored that you'd share that with me. I want to remind you that, as a coach, I don't have the knowledge or skills to support you in working in those other areas. I'm grateful to know what you're working on, and I'll keep that in mind, and I also want to be sure that you've got the kind of skilled support you deserve for healing." If you know you might be hesitant to communicate this type of message to a client, perhaps because you fear making things awkward, I promise you that doing so will save you both from much bigger challenges in the future.

Whether in working with clients who reveal their trauma, or with anyone, you probably can't say often enough, "You deserve healing. You deserve skilled support to help you work through what you've experienced. You deserve a life of ease and joy." We all do. We are all working through stuff. We all deserve care and we all deserve to thrive. These simple messages are a way of coaching emotions. Normalize, normalize, normalize.

When Did You Stop Dancing?

Angeles Arrien, an anthropologist and teacher, writes that in some traditional societies, when someone feels depressed and goes to a healer, they are asked: When did you stop dancing? When did you stop singing? When did you stop being enchanted by stories? When did you stop finding comfort in the sweet territory of silence?

These four questions compel us to consider the individual in relationship to community and the role of creativity, joy, awe, wonder, and contemplation in our well-being. Our Western medical model is limited and narrow, just like our educational model. Talk therapy can help relieve some symptoms of distress, but it's limited; pharmaceuticals may help some people manage some of the symptoms of anxiety and depression, but they are also limited (and can have unpleasant side effects).

For those of us who coach tired teachers or who might be tired leaders, these questions invoke the need for holistic remedies. They remind us that, until we reclaim communal practices that address the mind, body, heart and spirit, we might struggle—individually and collectively.

What would happen if you began a coaching session with three minutes of meditation, breathing, or journaling? Or took a walk while you talked? What if you invited your client to tell you stories about themselves? Or read a poem to end a coaching session? What if, regardless of your title or what you're supposed to coach someone on—be that technology, English Language Development, chemistry, or classroom management—you always coached clients back to resilience? We'll explore how to do this in Chapter 9.

A Transformational Coach always starts with themselves; we have to attend to our emotions first. So what do the four questions mean to you? Do you dance or sing or let yourself be enchanted by stories? Do you spend time in silence?

When I attend to all aspects of myself, I'm at my best as a coach and leader. After a long weekend in the redwoods, a deep early morning meditation, or a therapy session, I feel energized and fully present. Even if I'm grieving or anxious about something, I can be with those emotions. It has taken me decades to prioritize my own need for silence, dancing, contemplation, awe, and healthy connection with others, but doing so now is liberating. And I know I'm better able to serve others because I do.

Pause and Process

Reflect:

- What did you notice about your thoughts and feelings as you read this chapter? What did you notice about how your body felt?
- What did this chapter make you want to learn more about?
- What's one thing you'll do differently as a coach as a result of reading this chapter?

Next steps:

- Listen to *Bright Morning Podcast* episodes 127, 128, and 129, in which I coach anger, sadness, and joy.
- Download the free tool on my website that you can use with clients to self-assess anxiety and depression. Add this to your coaching notebook, or wherever you keep coaching resources.
- Assess your coaching space. Are there changes you can make in order to make it more welcoming to all clients, especially those who have experienced trauma?
- Identify one thing you can do in the coming week to prioritize your well-being—and do it.

CHAPTER 8

How to Coach Emotions
Without Making Things Weird

Common misconception:	*Transformational Coaches know:*
Spending time on an adult's emotions means less time focusing on kids.	Clients can release strong emotions in minutes when guided through a few steps.

Imagine it's February. It's been a month since you came back from winter break, it's still a month before spring break, and as you reflect on your work with teachers, you realize why you are feeling drained. All week, your meetings with teachers have surfaced strong emotions. Yesterday a first-year teacher told you about issues in her life outside of school—with her partner and her finances—that are making it hard for her to concentrate. This morning you did a midyear check-in with a veteran teacher. "I'm so disappointed in myself," he said. "I promised myself that this year I wouldn't get so behind in grading. And now it feels impossible to catch up. I do this year after year. I'm so angry at myself. And the end result is that I'm failing kids. I don't give them timely feedback, and I can't adjust lessons to address the skill gaps that I see when I grade their work. My inability to manage my time and my procrastination is hurting children. I am just sick of myself. I shouldn't be teaching. I'm doing more harm than good. And I'm so tired of saying these same things to you month after month."

Coaching emotions can be intense, but it doesn't have to be draining. In fact, with knowledge and skills, coaching emotions can be satisfying, even joyful. The first thing you need in order to coach emotions is the knowledge presented in Chapter 7, "What You Need to Know to About Emotions," as well as the overview shared in Chapter 2, "A Transformational Coach's Ways of Being." Any additional learning that you do about emotions will benefit your coaching tremendously, and at the end of this chapter, I offer additional resources. In addition to knowledge, coaching emotions requires skill. This chapter shifts into the skills of coaching emotions.

Address Core Human Needs

Why do we experience emotions? One reason—a primary reason—is because emotions help us meet our basic needs. Those include needs for things like safety, food, and shelter, but they also include the need for community, love, joy, celebration, purpose, and so on. Our emotions guide us: Shame, for example, is a powerful emotion that attempts to guide us into socially acceptable behavior. It occurs when we fear that we've crossed a social boundary. For example, in one of my first years teaching, I yelled at a student. I shouted at him, across the classroom, in front of his 19 peers—I said, "Shut up, Raul!" As soon as those words came out of my mouth, I was mortified. I felt shame pulse through my body. I wanted to bolt from the room and quit my job. I apologized immediately and attempted to repair the harm with Raul. I never screamed at a student again. I learned from that intense experience of shame.

Social scientists say that emotions are fundamentally constructive—they play an evolutionary role for our species. Through this lens, I understand how the shame I experienced was useful. It helped me become a better teacher and create the conditions in which children could learn.

Many of our emotions arise to help us get our core human needs met. I discussed these in the introduction, but as a reminder, our core human needs are belonging and connectedness, autonomy, competence, self-esteem, trust, and purpose and meaning. We are motivated by the desire to meet these core human needs; we struggle (or experience uncomfortable emotions) when one or more aren't met. When your clients seem resistant, they might sense that one of their core needs is in danger of being undermined, or they may be struggling to get a core need met.

Working from an understanding of core human needs has transformed the way I relate to myself and to all people. This framework roots me in compassion and curiosity and helps me identify immediate actions to address unskillful behavior. Here's what attending to the core human needs sounds like in a coaching conversation:

Teacher: I got my evaluation back yesterday, and I'm so upset. I couldn't sleep last night thinking about my principal's comments on the lesson he observed. It was one thing after another that I did wrong. And the thing is—I don't disagree with a lot of his feedback. I feel like that lesson wasn't good. I feel like no matter how hard I work, I can't seem to get it right. He made a comment about an interaction I had with Jayla where I responded to her question in a way that was sharp—that hurt, because it was true. I felt so frustrated in that moment, and the fact that he observed that . . . I mean, I felt embarrassed. I didn't get into teaching to be mean to kids or to teach lessons like that.

Coach: I hear sadness and that your need to feel competent wasn't met. That's normal; everyone wants to feel good at what they're doing. It also sounds like your need to feel like your life has purpose isn't being met—you're not feeling like you're being the teacher you aspire to be.

When I say something like this in a coaching conversation, clients relax. As I validate their experience and contextualize it within these core human needs, they begin to accept their emotions—which is the first step in processing them. They see how their emotions might be serving them, guiding them, and they become more curious.

Why the Framework of Core Human Needs Is a Paradigm Shift

The beliefs that many of us hold about "bad" behavior are a reflection of the beliefs propagated by dominant culture. "Pathological" or "bad" behavior often includes expressions of anger, shutting down emotionally, and withdrawal (depression). How we label these behaviors matters tremendously; what we believe about their causes is equally important. Remember that beliefs shape our actions, so if we want to take different actions (in a coaching conversation, for example), we need to be conscious of the beliefs from which we're operating. When we're conscious, we have choice—we can be intentional about dropping beliefs that may not align with our values.

Many of the beliefs held by Western dominant culture about the expression of emotions and mental health don't serve us. Until recently, modern psychology and psychiatry focused on psychopathological problems and the origins of those problems. The important thing to understand is that the roots of the way we think about emotions come from a focus on pathology. Therefore, when a teacher sobs uncontrollably, our default assumption may be, "There's something wrong with her."

In the 1950s, the psychologist Abraham Maslow introduced "positive psychology" and a "hierarchy of needs" to explain what motivates people. Physiological and safety needs were foundational, he said, followed by love and belonging, esteem, and self-actualization. Maslow was interested in human potential, in how we fulfill potential, and in people's strengths and assets. Maslow initiated a revolution in thinking about human behavior and motivation, a massive shift from looking at what's wrong with people to what's right, or what could be right.

The shift from deficit models toward asset models has enormous implications. In sum:

- Traditional psychology sees "maladaptive behavior" and asks: What's wrong with this person? Why are they doing this? What happened in their childhood that explains this behavior?
- Positive psychology sees behavior through a needs framework and asks: Which human need is not being met for this person? How is the behavior they're engaging in an attempt to meet one of those needs? How might they be able to get those needs met in a different way?

There's value in some traditional approaches to psychology. Our childhoods play a role in forming our personalities and behavior and in shaping our psyche. Psychologists and therapists can be very helpful in guiding us into insights about our past, processing the accompanying emotions, and creating new behaviors. But coaches are not therapists, and our clients don't come to us for therapy. It's unethical and irresponsible for us to probe into someone's childhood. It makes sense that coaches operate from a different framework.

Understanding the core human needs allows Transformational Coaches to coach the whole person. Our clients show up to coaching sessions with emotions and often express them. When we see maladaptive behaviors or the expression of emotions, we need tools to respond. When we use the core human needs, we move out of judgment and blame; we can activate our empathy, and we are likely to see the full human in front of us.

Using the core human needs is profoundly humanistic, compassionate, and actionable. As you explore the concept, you might try it on yourself. Next time you're feeling a strong emotion, ask yourself which of your core human needs are being met, or not met, in that moment. Ask yourself how you might be able to meet that need just a little bit more.

When to Use the Core Human Needs:

- When you sense fear and want to explore what might be at risk for the client.
- When you perceive resistance in a client.
- To cultivate deeper awareness of emotions.

How to Use the Core Human Needs:

- Use them as a way to access empathy for your client.
- Introduce the concept to your client and invite them to reflect on which of their needs might be at play when they experience fear.
- Use them to normalize emotions.
- Consider them to make decisions about how to coach—each need can be considered an end goal. For example, you can coach someone toward connection and belonging by working on their social and emotional skills, or toward competence, by addressing skill and knowledge gaps.

Use ACE Emotions

Even after I'd built a solid set of coaching skills, I could still feel rattled when a client showed up to a session experiencing intense uncomfortable emotions. There was Stephanie (and many other new teachers), who cried so much during coaching sessions that I couldn't figure out how to get to her lesson plans or student engagement or anything related to kids. There was Meylin, who never felt satisfied with anything she did and criticized herself mercilessly. There was Carlos who was often furious with his administrators; when he talked, his face often got red, his hands shook, and he cursed profusely. I'd sit in front of these teachers, observing their distress and wanting to comfort them and help them feel better but not sure how to do that—or even if that was my job.

ACE is an acronym for a three-part process that allows you to guide someone to explore and release strong emotions. This thinking tool, which I call ACE Emotions, is informed by what I've learned from Buddhist psychology, particularly from meditation teachers Tara Brach and Jack Kornfield. ACE stands for:

- Acknowledge and accept emotions.
- Cultivate compassion for yourself and others.
- Expand the story.

Although emotions—both our own and those of others—can feel scary, engaging with them is a skill set we can learn. As you acquire these skills, you'll notice your coaching and leadership improve. It's also likely that you'll feel better—clearer, more connected to yourself and others, and more confident.

The ACE Emotions process can be best understood by experiencing it for yourself. To get started, recall a recent experience when you felt activated by uncomfortable emotions. Don't pick a moment when you felt extremely triggered, but one when you felt moderately upset. Jot down a few sentences about what happened. As I describe the components of ACE Emotions, I'll bring you back to this experience and guide you to process it so that you can appreciate its impact.

Acknowledge and Accept Emotions

Sometimes when we experience challenging emotions, it can be hard to recognize precisely which emotions we're feeling—all we know is that we feel bad. Recognizing which emotions are present is a skill, an ability to rise above the intensity for a second and say, "Oh, I'm feeling really angry." When we can do that and when we have words to label the experience, we feel better. We are also more likely to use our emotions to inform the choices we make.

There are two steps to navigating strong emotions: acknowledgment and acceptance. This is really hard to do. Sometimes, we don't recognize that we're experiencing an emotion, or we don't have the language to label it. So how do you know when you're experiencing an emotion? For some of us, emotions register as physical sensations—we know we're angry when our face flushes, our hands tremble, or our stomach tightens. For others, we recognize emotions as thoughts—our anger courses through our minds as statements: *I can't believe he did that! That was unfair! How dare he talk to me that way!* Most people experience emotions as both physical sensations and thought patterns, as I discussed in Chapter 7.

Another reason it can be hard to accept our emotions is our feelings about our feelings. For example, when we recognize that we're experiencing an intense emotion and we label it as anger, we might then add secondary emotions: *I shouldn't be angry at him—if I'm angry at him, he's not going to want to talk to me, and I don't want to push him away, and maybe I did something to make him angry.* Those thoughts generate a new emotional tornado of shame, fear, and doubt.

Cultivating awareness about our emotions is an empowering skill and starts with naming. As soon as you can label an overwhelming emotional experience, you create a distance from it—almost as if you're airlifted out of the drama. You can look down and say, *Ah! That's fear!* One of our big fears about our most intense emotions is that they'll trap us forever. Becoming aware of an emotion and naming it can relieve us of this worry and can remind us that we are not our fear. Once we name an emotion, we can accept that it is present. Here's what I tell myself to facilitate acceptance: *I'm experiencing fear. It's temporary. It's okay for fear to be here right now. It wants me to know something, and I can learn from it. I am not my fear, and I can make space for it.* A resource like Appendix B, "The Core Emotions," is invaluable in helping us develop the vocabulary to name emotions.

There's a critical difference between experiencing an emotion and expressing an emotion, as I discussed in Chapter 7. We will *experience* emotions over and over again—experiencing emotions is always okay. The way we *express* emotions, however, can cause harm for ourselves and other people. Remember, there's nothing wrong with feeling angry—anger is a powerful teacher that can help us connect to sadness or galvanize us into action. But if we unskillfully express our anger as aggression, it can hurt people.

Let's practice acknowledging and accepting emotions. Go back to the incident I asked you to recall in which you were triggered.

- In the moment, did you recognize that you were experiencing a strong emotion? If so, what were the cues? Bodily sensations? Thoughts?
- What emotions were you feeling? Use the Core Emotions thinking tool (Appendix B) to find those words.
- Can you accept that you experienced those emotions? Do you sense any discomfort about the fact that you experienced them? (Not how you expressed the emotion—just about the existence of it.)
- What can you tell yourself now to accept that you experienced those emotions?
- How does it feel to reflect on this incident that you're recalling? Can you name the emotions that are arising for you right now in this reflection? Can you accept that you're experiencing them?

As a coach, you can help a client to acknowledge and accept challenging emotions as the first step in the ACE Emotions process. This first step of the process can also be a good time to recommend that our clients seek additional support if it seems necessary. Struggling to accept an emotion can mean that we need more time to process it, make meaning of it, and understand what it's trying to tell us. Every emotion contains wisdom. Sometimes we can access this wisdom quickly and easily; sometimes we need the support of an expert in working with emotions, such as a therapist.

A good indicator that you could benefit from skilled guidance in exploring emotions is the re-appearance of the same (or similar) emotions in similar situations. For example, if you recognize that you are often emotionally activated by what you experience as dismissive or disrespectful behaviors by someone in an authority position (your principal cuts you off when you're talking and brushes off your concerns) or you find yourself doubting yourself a lot and questioning your value, these might be indicators that there's healing for you to do around interpersonal relationships, self-worth, and more.

The great majority of us are walking around with unhealed wounds; these will continue showing up and trying to get our attention until we tend to them. When we ignore them, they fester and ache, like blisters. We can keep trudging along, changing the Band-Aids as our feet bleed, and learn to bear the pain, or we can stop, care for ourselves, and heal.

After we explore the next two stages of the ACE Emotions process, I'll show you what using it as a thinking tool in a coaching conversation sounds like.

Cultivate Compassion for Yourself and Others

Let's go back to the incident you've been reflecting on in which you were triggered. I want you to imagine now that an archetypal kind, nurturing grandma wraps you in her embrace. Still holding you, the loving grandma says, "Oh, sweetie. I'm sorry that you're suffering. I'm sorry you're feeling sad/angry/scared/ashamed. I'm here, let me hold you. It's really hard to be a human." Imagine your body sinking into her lap; imagine yourself relaxing completely.

You're welcome to modify those words so that you can receive them in the way that you want to be spoken to by someone who sees the best in you, who loves you, and who accepts you and all your human foibles. We all need and deserve to experience this kind of love.

If you're like me and you tend toward self-doubt, at this point your mind starts saying, "But I might have said things I regret, and maybe I shouldn't have lost it. . . ." Know that the grandma loves you and accepts you. She may agree that your actions were problematic, she also may suggest that you work on your behavior—and she still loves you. Give yourself a moment to feel her arms encircling you.

Compassion for yourself (and others) means that you see and believe in the part of humans that is good and kind and that can change. Compassion doesn't mean that you agree with problematic behavior or condone it; in fact, compassion includes holding yourself (or others) accountable for behavior.

Rather, compassion is an expansive state in which you see everything: someone's potential, the context they're in, the impact their behaviors have, and their essential humanity.

It's really hard for many of us to access this way of being. We've been conditioned to separate ourselves from others and to judge—these ways of being are lauded in our world today. We are taught that being hard and judgmental makes us safe, but deep inside of us, we know this isn't true. We know we are all connected and dependent on each other—and this truth is both terrifying and liberating. We ache for connection, to love and be loved, and we struggle with meeting that need.

Before you can feel compassion for another, you have to feel compassion for yourself. Sometimes, we think we accept others, forgive their messes, and see the best in them. But then when we make the mistakes that we've forgiven others for, our cruel inner critic berates us and tells us we're hopeless. For many of us, loving and accepting ourselves is a big project. If cultivating self-compassion feels overwhelming, think of it as a skill to build—and you can learn, right? Consider seeking the support of a therapist to help you acquire the skills of self-compassion, practice them every day, and you'll make significant growth in a relatively short period of time.

I know you might be thinking, *But what about coaching? How do I help Stephanie stop crying so we can talk about lesson plans?* A core concept of Transformational Coaching is that you have to start with yourself. You have to work on your own stuff to effectively coach others. When we practice the "C" in ACE, we must also offer ourselves compassion. Then and only then can it expand into a place of true compassion for others.

Recall that moment when you were triggered. What could you have said to yourself to activate compassion for yourself and perhaps for anyone else involved in the situation? Here are some options:

- This was a hard moment. How could I offer myself a little kindness?
- If my best friend was in this situation, what would I say to them?
- I'm doing the best I can. And I can learn and grow.

- What else might have been going on for me and/or the other person that's contributing to this experience?
- How might the other person be experiencing this? How might they feel?

You'll know when you're effectively activating your compassion because you'll sense a softening. Perhaps you'll notice this in your body—maybe your breathing slows or you sigh a couple of times or your shoulders drop. Maybe new thoughts float through your mind: *Oh, I'm sad. I messed up, and I want to repair that relationship,* or *I can see that I've got some unresolved stuff to work through—maybe it's finally time for me to dig into all of that.* You'll sense relief, perhaps the beginning of a way forward; you might sense gentleness or kindness or even love. When you do, acknowledge that you're feeling compassion (or love), and accept it.

When we find that we're unable to access compassion for ourselves or others, we probably need to return to the first step of ACE—acknowledging and accepting emotions. When we don't accept our emotions, we can feel blocked in moving through this second step, and the next one.

Expand the Story

Our thoughts trigger emotions. When my husband, Stacey, doesn't wipe the counter in the morning after he makes his coffee (as I've asked him to 100,000 times), I can tell myself this story: *He doesn't care about me. He doesn't think my need for a clean countertop is worthy of his consideration.* This thought generates anger, sadness, and fear that I will never get my need for a clean kitchen met and, by catastrophic extension, that our relationship is bad, I shouldn't have married him, I've wasted all of my life with someone who doesn't respect me, and, of course, it's really the fault of the patriarchy that invalidates women's experiences, and it's all hopeless.

Do you see how much suffering that story caused me? I can get trapped in that story for hours. Or I can tell another story. I can tell an expanded story, or a story that provides me with a pathway toward freedom. Here are some alternate stories I can tell about Stacey's inability to wipe up the coffee grouds:

- Stacey loves me. His not wiping the coffee grinds has nothing to do with me.
- Stacey is able to wipe up the schmutz—he just forgets; he can learn.
- I can learn how to effectively communicate my need for a clean kitchen, and Stacey can meet this need.
- It's just coffee.

When I tell myself those stories, I feel love, hope, care, and agency. My therapist encourages me to say, "Stacey, when you don't wipe the counter, my need to feel seen isn't met, and I feel sad. Do you have ideas for what might work for both of us?" But I haven't yet been able to say those words with a straight face. However, I have said, "Could you figure out a way to remember to wipe the counter in the morning?" And that's worked pretty well. Ultimately, I get to pick the story I tell.

I'm beginning this section with an example that I hope you can relate to. Of course, our thoughts and the stories we tell are impacted by the contexts that we're in—and power dynamics are an often invisible but constantly present part of our contexts. So yes, this is where things get more complicated. And while we need to honor the complexity of power dynamics and our emotions and all of it, the unequivocal truth is that we get to pick our thoughts—the stories we tell and choose to hold onto. That's the ultimate freedom.

Go back to that incident in which you were triggered. Recall the emotions that arose and the compassion you activated for yourself and others. Now, can you identify the story that you were telling in the moment when the strong emotion arose? Getting clear on the story you defaulted to is the first step of expanding the story you are telling. Sometimes, this may be a "victim story," a story in which you are powerless and someone or something else creates your suffering. You'll know you're telling a victim story if you hear yourself saying things like, "I felt like she didn't listen to me" or

"She never says anything I'm doing well" or "The district . . ." or "What can I do? Every year it's another thing."

The next step is to acknowledge the emotions that the thought generates. Make the connection between the story and the emotions.

Then ask yourself if there's any other way to see what happened. Is there *any other story* you might be able to tell? Brainstorm as many alternate stories as possible. If this is hard for you to do, it's likely that you've still got to feel some of the feelings—you might benefit from re-engaging in the process of acknowledging and accepting the emotions.

You can pick the story you tell. You have choice.

Another option is to not tell any story at all. Pema Chödrön, a Buddhist teacher, says, "Feel the feelings; drop the story." I find this challenging—I love stories. But when I face the coffee my husband spilled on the counter and I tell myself, *Oh, there's coffee on the counter*—this is an observation, not a story—and I continue about my morning business, I feel spacious. It's just coffee. This observation doesn't prevent me from asking Stacey to remember to wipe the counters, but it prevents annoyance from surging and doesn't send me spiraling into rage at the patriarchy.

So when the district issues a new mandate, or a student rolls her eyes for the 30th time in one day, or you are told there's an emergency staff meeting after school, remember, you have options. You can expand the story, or, if you want, you can drop the story, feel the feelings, and activate your agency.

ACE Emotions in Action

Here's what it sounds like to use ACE Emotions in a coaching conversation.

Coach: Stephanie, I can see that you're feeling some strong emotions today. [Passes over the Kleenex box.]

Stephanie: [Blows her nose and wipes the tears from her face.] I'm just exhausted and I can't do anything right and I don't know if I'll make it through this year. Teaching is so much harder than I thought it would be! If Talia looks at me again with that side-eye thing she does or Zoli mocks me, I think I'll lose it. Why am I falling apart like this? Everyone else in my cohort seems like they're doing great. I'm the only one crying for hours after school. What's wrong with me?

Coach: I think it would help to take a few moments to unpack what's going on for you. Does that sound okay? [Stephanie nods.] What emotions are you experiencing right now?

Stephanie: I'm so stressed and overwhelmed, and I just can't do this anymore!

Coach: Let's see if we can name these emotions. It'll help. [Gives Stephanie the Core Emotions.] Skim through this and see if you can find words that reflect what you're feeling.

Stephanie: [Reads document.] Okay, this is helpful. I am feeling scared and disappointed and ashamed and annoyed. Anxious. Humiliated. Miserable. Pessimistic. So much.

Coach: Right, you're feeling a whole lot of intense emotions. That's what overwhelm is. [Stephanie sighs loudly.] What are you feeling right now?

Stephanie: I guess it helps to see that yeah, it's a lot.

Coach: So are you feeling relief?

Stephanie: I think so.

Coach: Okay. How does it feel to recognize that you're experiencing all of these emotions?

Stephanie: It helps. Because teaching is so hard.

Coach: So you're accepting that all of these emotions are present for you.

Stephanie:	Yeah.
Coach:	You're accepting that there's nothing wrong with experiencing them.
Stephanie:	[Sighs loudly.] I guess so.
Coach:	Stephanie, if your best friend was going through what you are going through right now as a new teacher, what would you say to her?
Stephanie:	I'd say, "I'm so sorry. I know this is super hard, but you'll make it through. I know you, and I know how strong you are. This will get better, and you need to remember why you became a teacher in the first place." I'd say, "I love you! Let's schedule a spa date. I'm here for you."
Coach:	Can you say that to yourself, right now?
Stephanie:	I was worried that's where you were going with this.
Coach:	Say more.
Stephanie:	Because I have double standards. If it was my best friend, I'd be there for her. But I expect more from myself.
Coach:	Okay, I hear that. What's the story you're telling about yourself right now, as a new teacher?
Stephanie:	What do you mean?
Coach:	What do you believe about yourself right now, as a new teacher?
Stephanie:	I'm failing and disappointing myself and my students. I shouldn't have become a teacher.
Coach:	Okay, if that's the story you believe, what's possible?
Stephanie:	I guess not much. I guess it means I should quit.
Coach:	Is there any other story you could tell about what's going on for you right now?

Stephanie: I guess I could say I'm a new teacher, and it's going to take some time to learn how to do this. I guess I could say I had certain expectations because I've always been an A student and so I thought this would be easier. So I could say, well, I've met a learning edge.

Coach: What might be possible if you told that story?

Stephanie: I'd probably feel a little better. I wouldn't be so hard on myself. I mean, this is what I tell my students—to have a growth mindset and all.

Coach: What else might be possible?

Stephanie: I might make it through the year. I really want to. I might not feel so angry at Talia. I might take a spa day.

Coach: Okay, how does it feel, right now, to think about telling that story?

Stephanie: I feel a little more relieved. I also feel nervous—what if I can't do it?

Coach: Sure. Can you accept that you feel nervous?

Stephanie: [Sighs.] I guess so.

Coach: Nervousness—or fear—is normal, especially when you're starting something new that feels hard.

Stephanie: If I told the story that it's my first year and maybe I won't be good at everything from day one, I think I'd feel energized, actually. It would motivate me to keep learning and meeting with you.

Coach: Well, you get to pick the story you tell.

I've had this conversation—and very similar ones—with more new teachers than I can count, and I've had parallel conversations with veteran teachers who are weary in the face of change. The ACE Emotions tool provides a structure that supports change in the face of big emotion because it gives us ways to move through the emotion—and often quickly—toward whatever is next.

When to Use Ace Emotions:

- When a client is distressed and the way they're presenting is either an obstacle or an opportunity for deeper self-knowledge.
- To help a client deepen awareness of and savor comfortable, pleasant emotions.

How to Use Ace Emotions:

- Begin with using the steps sequentially—starting with "A." If you face pushback when you try to cultivate compassion or expand the story, return to acknowledging and accepting emotions. If you can't get any traction with the "C" or "E," return to "A."

Coach into the Spheres of Influence

One way to expand the story is to use the Spheres of Influence, a tool within the tool of ACE Emotions.

Take a moment to identify a few things you've complained about recently. Now determine which ones are within your control or influence and reflect: How much of your energy or attention goes to the things that are outside of your control? Coming back to the areas that are within your control or influence, how important does it feel to make changes? What does this reflection bring up for you and make you want to do?

The concept of the Spheres of Influence is simple: we can classify challenges or complaints into three buckets. These buckets—what we can control, what we can influence, and what we can't control—offer a clarity that is impossible to deny. Using the spheres in a coaching conversation can powerfully intervene in someone's thinking and can provide a catalyst for action.

Here's what it can sound like to use the spheres in a coaching conversation:

Teacher: I know that I'm supposed to be integrating more cooperative learning structures into my lessons, but how can I do that when things are so chaotic? Just yesterday, there was an unscheduled fire drill, J.D. came to class acting like a clown again, I got a long email from a parent asking me to do a dozen things for them, and how can we be expected to teach in this heat? Every year they say we'll get AC, and we never do. Also, have you heard that the district is going to be dropping into classrooms unannounced to see if we're using the new Smartboards?

Coach: That's a lot. Of the challenges you're raising. Which ones are within your sphere of influence?

Teacher: Well, I can't do anything about the heat or what the district decides. I guess I could influence J.D. when he comes into my room.

Coach: Anything else?

Teacher: I don't know. It just feels like there are so many things acting against me.

Coach: I hear that. You have a choice where your energy goes. If you can identify anything that you might be able to influence, you might feel better.

Here's what's important to know about the concept of the spheres:

- Our thoughts are the only things that are really within our control.
- There's a lot we can't exert any control over.
- There's a lot that's within our influence—which means we have tremendous agency in our lives.

The Tyranny of Thoughts

So much of our suffering is created by our thoughts. The good news is that what we think is within our control. Researchers say we have 68,000 thoughts per day (and that yesterday, we had 98% of those same thoughts). Our thoughts aren't bad, necessarily, and having them comes with being human. But we suffer when we're unaware of our thoughts, when we think we *are* our thoughts, and when we are carried away by an endless stream of thoughts that don't serve us or that make us feel powerless or afraid or alone.

For example, let's say I'm coaching a teacher, and I have the thought, *This teacher doesn't trust me, she thinks I'm judging her, and she doesn't want to work with me.* In response to this thought, my blood pressure and heart rate increase, cortisol and adrenaline are released, and I experience the emotion of fear. I may not be conscious that I'm experiencing fear—I might just notice that I'm slightly distracted or the doubtful chatter in my mind might get louder. My thoughts have created my suffering.

The Buddha explained that what we think about creates our reality, the experience of our body, and our life—where attention goes, energy flows. Neuroscience tells us that neurons that fire together wire together. So if your mind regularly tells you that your client doesn't trust you, you create an emotional experience of fear for yourself, and this neural pathway becomes strong and well-traveled. Our thoughts create our suffering.

The Buddha also taught that we can suffer much less, or even not at all. Cultivating mindfulness is one way to end suffering. Through mindfulness, we can learn to notice our thoughts, recognize that they are just thoughts, and choose thoughts that help us be free. We can learn that we don't have to fixate on our thoughts—or the emotions that come up in response to them—because we aren't our thoughts or our emotions. Through meditation, we learn to observe thoughts and emotions and see them coming and going without getting hooked into them and without believing them to be true.

What we think—or how we relate to our thoughts—is within our control. That said, it takes dedication to cultivate awareness of thoughts. Our thinking patterns are so habitual and entrenched that we need daily practice to see what's going on in our mind, to recognize that we have a choice in what we think, and to take different actions.

Spheres of Influence Can Interrupt Thought Patterns

When you hear someone expressing thoughts that leave them feeling powerless, bringing in the concept of the spheres can act like a knife cutting through those thought patterns. Inviting someone to recognize their thoughts, and giving them the option of shifting their energy, can allow someone to make changes in their behaviors, beliefs, and ways of being. This concept has been around for a long time, perhaps even back to the time of the Buddha. It continues to offer wisdom and clarity—and relief.

As with all of the thinking tools, the more you use the Spheres of Influence for yourself, the better you'll understand it and be able to use it with clients. You can use the spheres on a daily basis—perhaps in the morning, in anticipation of what's on your schedule as you set an intention for the day, or in the evening, in reflection about your day, or when you notice yourself thinking thoughts that feel draining. In that moment, you can ask yourself, *What's within my control or influence? Where's my energy going?* And see what happens.

When to Use the Spheres of Influence:

- To help a client expand the story they're telling
- When you hear that your client is telling themselves disempowering stories
- When you recognize that their energy is being drained by what they can't control
- When you want to offer your client an opportunity to make a choice about their thoughts and actions

How to Use the Spheres of Influence:

- When a teacher vents, you might say, "I'm hearing that you're frustrated about many things. Of the things you just mentioned, which ones are within your control or influence?"
- Give your client a copy of the graphic (Figure 8.1), and say, "I'd like to share a concept with you. It's called the Spheres of Influence. It suggests that we can sort things based on what we can and can't control. This can help us figure out how we can deal with the frustrating things we can experience. How do you see that this concept might be helpful?"

Figure 8.1: Spheres of Influence

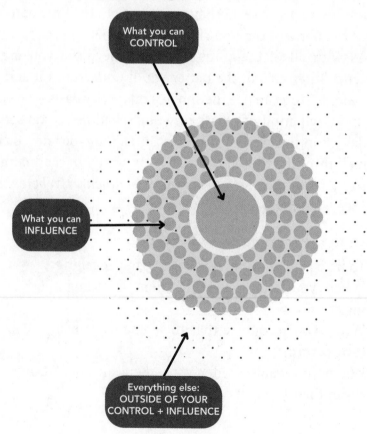

- Once you've explained the concept, when you hear your client complaining about things, it's easier to say, "I'm hearing that you're talking about things that seem outside of your control. If I've got that wrong, tell me. But I'm wondering if you'd like to shift into talking about things that are within your influence?"
- You can also say, "There are always going to be many things outside of our control. When we focus on those, we're likely to feel depleted. One thing that's within our control is where we direct our energy. When we use energy on things within our sphere of influence or control, we feel better."
- Try saying: "I hear that you're frustrated about things that are outside of your control. Do you want to talk more about those, or would you like to talk about the things that you can influence?"

Use Strength-Based Coaching

If you feel like you have a tendency to focus on the negative and on all the things that could go wrong, blame the three-pound organ in your skull. Biological evolution takes a while, and our brains and nervous systems are only a little more developed than those of lizards. Like reptile brains, human brains constantly scan for danger, which means we have a built-in negativity bias. This makes us fearful creatures. The good news, however, is that our brains can change—we can train our minds to notice different things and create new neural pathways, and as a result we can feel better.

Strength-based coaching is what it sounds like: an approach to adult learning in which we consciously pay attention to what's going well and in which we hone our own ability, and our client's, to see possibility. When we practice strength-based coaching, we hold an expansive view and take in both someone's areas for growth and their strengths. Strength-based coaching often makes both coach and client feel better, but its purpose and greatest impact go beyond good feelings. When we identify strengths, we identify potential and ways to move forward.

As you read the following conversation between a coach and a novice teacher, imagine yourself as the teacher:

Coach: How do you think that lesson went yesterday?

Teacher: It was a disaster. I was so embarrassed that you were there and saw that. You must think I'm hopeless.

Coach: I want to hear more about what didn't go well in a moment, but before we get to that, I am curious if there was *anything* that felt okay?

Teacher: I guess I didn't start crying or screaming at my kids.

Coach: Okay, is that something you've done before?

Teacher: No, I would never do that. I was being facetious.

Coach: [Smiles in acknowledgment, then speaks seriously.] So I'm hearing that yesterday you were frustrated or disappointed, that you were feeling really bad, but you were able to manage your emotions and react in a way that you wanted.

Teacher: I guess so.

Coach: Is that something you value? That you didn't cry or scream at your students?

Teacher: Of course it is! If I start yelling at children, I shouldn't be teaching.

Coach: On a scale of 1–10, how successful do you feel like that lesson yesterday was, with 10 being extremely successful?

Teacher: A 1! It was terrible. I didn't get through it, my demo was unclear, and it was a total failure.

Coach: When did you realize it wasn't going well?

Teacher: Just after we started. The hook didn't go as I wanted, the kids didn't seem engaged, and the directions I gave for the first activity were confusing.

Coach: Okay, so it was a 1—and I promise we'll talk about how you can improve. But in spite of realizing early on that it wasn't going well, you showed up being the teacher you aspire to be—calm, self-regulating.

Teacher: Yeah, that's true.

Coach: What does it feel like to recognize that?

Teacher: I mean, that's important. I guess it's a relief.

Coach: Say more.

Teacher: I want kids to feel safe in my class. I'm the grown-up. I can't lose it just because a lesson doesn't go well. It's not their fault.

Coach: So again, I hear that you were really living into some important values about who you are as a teacher.

Teacher: I guess so.

Coach: So the lesson flopped. Do you think that after we talk about it, and perhaps if you did some practice, you'd be able to do it better?

Teacher: Yes.

Coach: Why do you think that's so?

Teacher: I guess because I know I can learn. I'm not hopeless.

Coach: And what makes you think that?

Teacher: Because I've learned other things in my life.

Coach: Have you ever failed at something before? Or done something that flopped?

Teacher: Of course I have.

Coach: So you have the ability to learn—and I'd agree with that; I've seen you improve already this year. And even under stress, you live into your values and regulate your emotions. How does it feel to hear me say this?

Teacher: I feel relieved. It feels good. I wasn't thinking about all of that.

Coach:	I'll add to this and say I think it's courageous of you to recognize that the lesson didn't meet your hopes—to hold a vision for yourself of the kind of instruction you want to deliver. Sometimes that recognition can deepen a commitment to improvement.
Teacher:	Yeah, I guess I feel like I can't get any worse, and I want to do better.
Coach:	So you're not feeling shame—you feel like you can improve.
Teacher:	That's true. I'm embarrassed, but I believe I can learn.
Coach:	How do you feel now?
Teacher:	Strangely energized.

This transcript is based on a conversation that I had with my coach during a rough year. It wasn't just that she helped me recognize strengths that I hadn't valued before but that she also was able to see more about me than just the terrible lesson she'd witnessed the day before.

After this conversation, I felt like I could really trust my coach. Beyond simply feeling seen, there may have been a biochemical component to this trust: because I'd felt seen and accepted by my coach during our conversation, my body would have released oxytocin. This hormone makes us feel connected to others—it's called the "bonding hormone." When we use a strength-based approach and when we help our clients see their strengths, we orchestrate our biochemistry to facilitate connection and trust.

Looking for strengths and surfacing them isn't about putting on rose-colored glasses. It doesn't mean we make excuses for our clients or pretend they don't have areas for growth. We can acknowledge strengths and also give hard feedback. In fact, it's easier to receive hard feedback when you recognize your own strengths—and when you know that your coach does too.

Strength-based coaching challenges our dominant culture's focus on deficits. When we shift attention to what's going right and to our clients' assets, we shift our way of being and our behavior. Again, this isn't about denying problems or areas for growth—it's about seeing everything, noticing potential, and exploring what's possible when we identify and amplify the skills, orientations, and contributions of our clients.

When to Use Strength-Based Coaching:

- When you're using ACE Emotions and coaching someone to expand the story they're telling about themselves.
- When you're using ACE Emotions and coaching someone toward self-compassion.
- When you're building a relationship with someone. Everyone wants their potential to be seen. Surfacing strengths is a powerful way to build trust and connection.
- When someone feels defeated or discouraged. Helping someone remember what they can do well offers them catharsis and serves as a catalyst to shift them back to a place of empowerment.
- When you want your client to explore transferable skills; many core skills that we need to be successful in life in general transfer to work in schools.

How to Use Strength-Based Coaching:

- Look for strengths in what someone does, how they think, and who they are being.
- Make sure that the strengths you identify are accurate, that there's evidence for your assertions, and that you are being genuine.
- Invite your client to identify their own strengths. It can be powerful for you to name strengths, and even more powerful for them to name their own. We want and need to be recognized by others, but ultimately we crave our own approval and praise even more.
- Guide your client to integrate the insights into their strengths into the story they're telling about themselves.
- Identify and celebrate your own strengths. This makes it easier to see other people's strengths.

Additional Considerations When Coaching Emotions

What follows are additional things to know and things to do when coaching emotions. These tips, reminders, and considerations, together with suggestions I offer for continued learning, complement the strategies already described.

Things to Know

Understand the difference between venting and releasing emotions. Venting can feel like a release initially, but it can also strengthen neural pathways that we don't want to strengthen—especially those in which someone describes feeling like a victim. Sometimes we vent because we want and need empathy; sometimes we vent because we're stuck. Venting sounds like going around and around, over the same content, with the venter positioned as the victim.

If a client is venting for a long period of time, you can interrupt them and invite them to redirect. This could sound like, "I hear that you're really frustrated with your principal. I'm curious whether you'd like to explore the emotions that you're experiencing or talk about the actions you could take to raise your concerns with him?" Or you could say, "I'm hearing you tell a victim story. Is that one you're consciously choosing to tell? Do you want to shift your experience of this situation?"

Learn about triggers. Often, when we have an intense emotional reaction, an old wound is being activated. We can call this unhealed wound a trigger, and we can see it an opportunity for healing. Remember the phrase "Triggers are friends to follow." When someone expresses strong emotions such as fear, anger, sadness, or shame, a part of themselves that needs healing might be showing up. There are many ways to respond to our triggers, but we must start with kindness toward ourselves. When you notice you're triggered, you can say something to yourself like, "Oh, something is coming up. There's old pain here that deserves attention." This is critical, because many people become even more self-critical when they notice they're being triggered. They feel angry at themselves for their response, when what's needed is self-compassion.

Remember that we are not our emotions. Emotions come and go; they're like weather patterns, and they don't define who we are. We can be curious and welcoming and also not get attached or clingy with them. We can feel them and learn from them and let them pass. Remind your clients of this truth—kindly and gently.

Accept that the past influences the present. The unresolved "stuff" from our lives shows up in all of our relationships, often without our awareness. Our relationships in early childhood with our primary caregivers have a tremendous impact on how we relate to others—especially when there's a power differential such as between a teacher and a coach, or a teacher and a principal.

Stay alert to how relationship dynamics might be a reflection of old stuff. When you suspect that old stuff might be at play for a client, you can say something like, "You know, our relationships in early childhood with our primary caregivers have a tremendous impact on how we relate to others— especially when there's a power differential. It might be helpful for you to reflect on whether your feelings about your principal have any origins in other times in your life." Point to the possibility, but don't invite your client to unpack that with you. Add something like, "Exploring this with someone you trust, maybe a therapist, could be helpful."

Understand the difference between guilt and shame. Shame is "I am bad," a statement about how someone feels about themselves, a statement of a way of being. When you hear someone say, "I feel so ashamed," explore the story they're telling about themselves—you'll often hear a note of unworthiness and a fixed mindset. Guilt, on the other hand, is "I did something I regret," which is a statement about a behavior. Guilt can be an entry point to making behavioral change and an indicator of a growth mindset. That said, shame does serve a purpose and can morph into guilt. As a new teacher, I felt tremendous shame over yelling at a student. That shame shifted into guilt as I reflected on my actions, and this guilt motivated me to cultivate self-awareness—I learned to pay attention to my feelings of frustration with students.

Understand the concept of projection. Projection is a concept in psychology in which we displace our feelings onto another person. When we project, we're unconsciously taking our own unresolved stuff and projecting it onto another person. For example, let's say I'm frustrated with a client, but I perceive her as being frustrated with me—I think, *Why is she so annoyed with me?* It's as if I am an LCD projector and my internal stuff is being displayed on her, so I see it as her and not me. Projection can reveal unconscious beliefs and unfelt emotions that we need to deal with. Coaches do this with clients; teachers do this with students. It's a way we try to discharge uncomfortable emotions. But as you might see, it makes things messy. When you have strong reactions to clients, or others, explore whether you're projecting something onto them.

Things to Do

Continuously build your own emotional intelligence. This is firmly within your sphere of influence. The more you recognize when you experience emotions, the better you'll be able to show up for others. This can't be emphasized enough: your emotional intelligence is central to your potential as a coach and leader and, likely, to your ability to thrive in all areas of life.

Recognize and respond to triggers. When you recognize that a client is triggered, coach them into curiosity about what's arising. This sounds like, "I'm hearing that you felt some strong emotions when your student rolled her eyes at you. It sounds like you were emotionally activated. Would you be interested in exploring what was coming up for you?"

When you are activated by something a client says or does, note in the moment what incident or stimuli generated the emotions, and commit to exploring those at an appropriate time. Honor that commitment by digging into the roots of the activating experience to find your own unhealed wounds and to attend to them.

Explore your reactions to other people's emotions. Stay calm when your client expresses strong emotions. If they express deep sadness, fear, or even anger, just be with them. You don't need to fix them or make them feel better. You can offer a tissue box or just set it on the table in reach. You just need to be present with your client and use strategies to help them recognize, accept, and explore their emotions. And if you are unsettled by other people's emotions, that's probably your past showing up in the present—remember that you deserve to explore childhood experiences with your own emotions.

Honor the need for emotions to be felt in the body in order to be released. Sometimes you can guide a client through this experience by inviting them to bring awareness to the physical sensations associated with an emotion. This sounds like, "Where are you feeling this emotion in your body? Can you describe what it feels like—what temperature it is; the level of intensity; whether it's prickly, tingly, hot, cold, etc.?"

A coaching session may not be a safe or appropriate place for clients to explore intense fear, anger, or sadness. When powerful feelings come up, you can name this: "I can see that you're experiencing a lot of grief over what happened this weekend. I want to encourage you to find a place where you can feel safe enough to let those emotions be felt—to cry or scream or do whatever your body needs to release them. Do you have a place and perhaps a person who can support you in that?" At the least, you can help a client understand that emotions need to be felt in the body in order to be truly released.

Teach clients to describe their emotions. There's an important difference between describing emotions and describing thoughts. Let's say you ask a client, "How did it feel to get that feedback on a lesson you worked so hard on?" And your client says, "It just made me think about how many times my principal has come into my classroom and not said anything and I've asked for feedback so many times. That feedback came out of the blue." Your client is not describing feelings—they're describing *thoughts*. This is an important distinction as we develop awareness of emotions and how they manifest in our physical experiences and behaviors. Describing emotions is a part of developing emotional intelligence. You might follow up with, "How did you feel when you had that thought?"

Learn about cognitive distortions: It can be useful to understand that there are common ways of thinking that create suffering. These cognitive distortions include black-and-white thinking, over-generalizing, catastrophizing, and having unrealistic expectations. We can interrupt cognitive distortions by replacing them with different thoughts. For example, if you are a catastrophizer, you likely imagine worst-case scenarios all the time, and you warn others about those scenarios. But you can try a new way of thinking: *Things rarely go as badly as I fear. In fact, most things have turned out to be fine.* Recognizing distorted thinking patterns is the first step on the path to lessening their intensity, but know that substituting thoughts is unlikely to completely transform those habitual thinking patterns. You can find more about cognitive distortions in *The Onward Workbook.*

Coach the underlying emotions, not the symptoms. There are ways to categorize responses to uncomfortable emotions—these could be considered personality types or behavioral patterns. For example, it's likely that as a coach, you'll work with perfectionists, disempowered teachers, despairing teachers, and teachers whom you might consider to be arrogant. Sometimes I've wanted a handbook for how to respond to each of these kinds of teachers—for instance, I've wanted to know which sentence stems might be most useful with the highly self-critical, perfectionist first-year teacher.

However, at the root of the ways these teachers show up we find common emotions. When we learn how to attune to the underlying emotions and to coach someone through exploring them, we relieve ourselves of the need for personality-specific strategies. Listen for the emotions that might be generating behavior, invite your client to identify those emotions, consider which of the core human needs might be unmet, and use the strategies for coaching emotions.

Learn to hear, sense, see, and feel fear. Fear is often at the root of the great majority of uncomfortable feelings, behaviors that don't align with who we want to be in the world, or behaviors that create suffering for others. There is so much fear in humans and in the world. Fear is not a "bad" emotion—we don't want to get rid of it all. It serves a very important purpose, and we want to learn from it. But fear often leaps into the driver's seat and stays there for a very long time. And it's not a skilled driver. Fear has tunnel vision—it tries to keep us safe, keep us safe, keep us safe. Sometimes it's not even clear what our fear is keeping us safe from, and often it's keeping us safe from things that happened decades ago, things that are no longer a danger.

When you're coaching, ask yourself where fear is present. You can also ask this question when a client is distressed. This can sound like, "What are you afraid of? And if that happens, what's the next fear?" Or, "What's your biggest fear?" Or you can ask, "Where is fear present for you?" Or, "Is fear driving the car right now?" Normalize the experience of fear. And help your client bring awareness to the impact of their fear—how does it affect them and others?

Finally, learn to hear, sense, see, and feel *your own fear*. Make friends with it. Do the work you need to do to get it buckled into the back seat. Fear is skilled at disguising itself: learn how to recognize when fear is trying to convince you that it's something else, like passion, ambition, commitment, or urgency.

Suggestions for Continued Learning

My exploration of the modalities and ideas offered in the following resources has shaped my own personal growth and informed the way I coach others. I recommend them all as part of your own continued learning:

- *For a general introduction to psychology and emotional well-being:* Dr. Nicole LaPera's *How to Do the Work* is a fantastic, easy-to-read overview of all things mental health related.
- *On trauma:* Dr. Gabor Maté's *The Myth of Normal* is the most accessible book I've read on the topic. I also appreciate how thoroughly he

contextualizes trauma within a sociopolitical framework. This book has radically transformed the way I understand myself and others.

- *Parts work:* Dr. Richard Schwartz's theory, which he calls Internal Family Systems, is an easy-to-comprehend, powerful way to understand ourselves. His book *No Bad Parts* is a great starting point, and he's also been a guest on many podcasts.

- *Attachment theory:* Developmental psychologists propose that we develop attachment styles as a result of the relationships we had with our primary caregivers when we were very young. Each of us forms one of these four styles (anxious, avoidant, disorganized, and secure) or a combination of them, and this attachment profile shapes how we relate to people now—to our friends, partners, bosses, colleagues, and clients. The good news is that attachment styles aren't fixed. We can learn how to shift how we relate to people, usually through working with a therapist. Understanding this theory has been invaluable in helping me understand myself and others. There isn't a book I can recommend on this topic (the ones I've found are written for mental health professionals), but you can Google "attachment theory" and find lots of resources.

In my fantasy world, every school and organization would have both Transformational Coaches and expert therapists available for educators. The coaches would have refined abilities in supporting people with their emotions and would also recognize when to refer a client to a therapist. In a coaching session, a teacher might say, "I'm so disappointed in myself. I promised myself that this year I wouldn't get so behind in grading. And now it feels impossible to catch up. I do this year after year. I'm so angry at myself. And the end result is that I'm failing kids. I don't give them timely feedback, and I can't adjust lessons to address the skill gaps that I see when I grade their work. My inability to manage my time and my procrastination is hurting children. I am just sick of myself. I shouldn't be teaching. I'm doing more harm than good. And I'm so tired of saying these same things to you month after month."

The coach could say, "I hear your sadness and frustration. And yes, I've heard you express these thoughts and feelings before. I'm thinking it might be helpful to schedule some sessions with our therapist and explore the roots of these behaviors. I have a feeling they might go deep, and you deserve that healing. What do you think?"

In this fantasy world, working with a therapist would be normalized, and the teacher could get the support they need to address the psychological origins of the behavior. At the same time, the coach could offer to support this teacher to strengthen systems and routines for grading and, perhaps, to evaluate the assessments themselves.

I'd wager that most of the time when a client is stuck or is experiencing uncomfortable emotions, the source of that discomfort lies in their childhood. I often think, *you deserve to explore that in therapy*—but I don't say it as often as I might if high-quality therapy were more available. Few communities have affordable access to enough skilled mental health professionals, and in many communities there's still a stigma around working with a therapist. It's not ideal that coaches, who aren't trained deeply in working with the psyche, are often the only resource available to support educators' personal growth—and it's also the reality many people live today.

The good news is that you can learn the skills to coach emotions, and the even better news is that you'll likely benefit personally from doing so. In the process, you'll gain insight into your own emotions, and you'll acquire new skills to engage with and learn from them. I'm a perfect example of someone who teaches what she needs to learn—in the process of teaching others about their emotions and how to engage with them, I've learned so much about my own. For this, I'm deeply grateful.

Pause and Process

Reflect:

- If you had a coach right now, which of the strategies described in this chapter would you want your coach to use in your next session? Why?
- Which of the strategies described in this chapter feel most accessible for you to use in coaching clients? Which feel like they'd be a stretch?
- Recall a conversation in which a client presented with strong emotions. Which of the strategies in this chapter do you think might have helped them?
- What have you learned about yourself in this chapter? About your own emotions?
- If you don't already work with a therapist, what might need to be true for you to find one?

Next steps:

- Listen to *Bright Morning Podcast* episode 162, in which I coach emotions in just 12 minutes, and episode 200, which is a demonstration of using the core human needs in a coaching conversation.
- Download the Spheres of Influence, the Core Human Needs, and the Core Emotions tools from my website. Make copies of them so that you can give them to clients if/when necessary.
- Download "Head, Heart, Hands: A Tool for Finding Strengths" from my website and use it to explore your client's strengths, and your own.
- For the next week or two, make a note of every time you're emotionally activated and what caused you to feel activated. See if you notice patterns. Explore what's below the emotions that arise and what wants to be known and healed.

CHAPTER 9

How to Coach Resistance and Resilience

It's Easier—and Harder—Than You Think

Common misconception: Resistance is inevitable.	*Transformational Coaches know:* Resistance is optional.

One February afternoon I was scheduled to meet with Sandra, a seventh-grade English teacher. I had analyzed the latest benchmark assessments, and I was prepared to show her how she'd once again failed her Black boys. I knew I was right, I knew she would resist the truth, and I swore her resistance would be futile. As I approached her classroom, which had big windows facing the hallway, I saw her flip off the lights and duck down behind her desk. I didn't bother knocking or confronting her about her passive-aggressive behavior—I made a U-turn in the hallway and stormed into the principal's office.

"What do you expect me to do?" I demanded. "I can't coach these teachers! They're acting like seventh graders!" Looking back, I am clear that it wasn't Sandra's behavior that was the problem. The truth was that I hadn't actually intended to "coach" Sandra that afternoon. The truth was that I had wanted to use the data I'd collected to shame her.

This was during a time, early in my career as a coach, when I had concluded that two-thirds of the teachers in my middle school were resistant to examining their own behaviors and beliefs. Furthermore, I was convinced that our students were suffering and struggling because of the teachers' resistance. The evidence was in what teachers said, which included statements like:

- Our kids can't do this! This curriculum is way too hard for them.
- Well, you know how their parents are. . . . What do you expect from them?
- I'm not going to teach this "student-centered" BS. These kids need structure and order.
- If we had a real discipline system, we wouldn't have these problems.
- This is the way I've always taught and it's worked. Why should I do anything different now?

The resistance was evident when teachers walked out of the PD sessions I facilitated or arrived late, in their incessant pushback against trying alternative instructional strategies, in their refusal to teach new curriculum, and in the way they spread rumors about administrators and rallied behind my back to file union grievances. I was on a mission to eliminate the plague of resistance, and nothing would stop me.

Until everything did.

Depleted and demoralized, I turned to my own coach, Leslie. "No one can learn from you if you think that they suck," she reminded me. I came to see that I was guilty of some of the same kinds of behaviors that I abhorred in others—such as shaming or manipulation—and I realized I needed to rethink how I was coaching. I started by changing the only thing I could control—the stories I was telling. Changing my stories shifted my beliefs and attitudes, and my behaviors followed. As I began thinking and doing different things, I saw different results. I began to see resistance for what it truly was, and I began to employ strategies that addressed the dynamics at the core of what I'd deemed resistance.

Now, when I recall that afternoon when I was supposed to meet with Sandra, I recognize that the truth was that I did not know how to coach Sandra or any of the other "resistant teachers." I didn't have the tools or the training. The truth was that I was sad and scared and angry, and I didn't know how to process and release those emotions. *I created the resistance I experienced* through how I showed up with teachers who were also sad and scared and angry and lacking necessary tools or training. What I know now is that resistance arises when we feel confused, lonely, isolated, fearful, and ill-equipped in the face of challenge.

Resistance arises when resilience is depleted. This could be resistance to change or to looking at one's behaviors, beliefs, and ways of being. Encountering resistance in a client (or in ourselves) signals us that we need to reconnect with our inner reserves, agency, strength, trust, courage, compassion, and curiosity. The antidote for resistance is to boost resilience.

If thriving lays along a continuum, then resistance (which appears as fear, constriction, judgment, and aversion) anchors one end; resilience (which looks like growth, connection, expansion, and openness) lies at the other. Someone who experiences and expresses resistance is not thriving. When we encounter resistance as Transformational Coaches, we do what we can to build our client's resilience and help them restore their well-being. Figure 9.1 is a representation of this simple concept to help you remember it.

Coaching resistance requires that you draw from many Transformational Coaching strategies: you *must* coach the Three Bs to address resistance, and you must be supremely conscious of how you show up. At its core, the ability to coach resistance is the ability to respond to sadness, fear, and anger; it's

Figure 9.1: From resistance to resilience

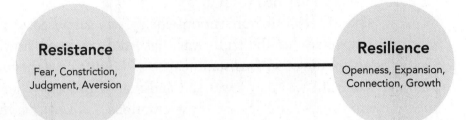

the ability to help someone shift from a contracted way of being to an open and hopeful way of being.

This chapter will teach you how to respond to resistance and cultivate resilience. The content rests on what was presented in previous chapters—if you jumped to this chapter because you're desperately seeking solutions for dealing with resistant teachers (which is what I would have once done), go ahead and read it. And then read the rest of the book.

What Is Resistance?

If you want to coach resistance, the first and foundational step is to adopt an expansive definition of what *resistance* means. Only by expanding your beliefs can you embody the ways of being and behaviors required to do so effectively. So what does a Transformational Coach know about resistance? Resistance is:

- Your response to someone's fear
- A label you place on someone's behaviors
- A dynamic between you and another person
- An indicator that someone's core human needs aren't being met
- An indicator that someone feels their core values are in danger
- An indicator of your own fear
- An opportunity for healing and connection
- An opportunity to cultivate resilience (in yourself and in another)

Which Behaviors Do We Label as "Resistance"?

One year, my principal purchased a new literacy program to be implemented schoolwide. I responded by researching the curriculum's impact in other districts and presenting that data to the principal in an effort to change her mind. I didn't change her mind, but I implemented only a fraction of the program in my classroom. Over the course of the year, I continuously gathered data to prove that the new curriculum wasn't working. I'd bet my principal felt I was resistant.

Another year, I worked in a school that adopted a severe approach to student behavior. I refused to enact the strategies, which included sending children to the "isolation room." One afternoon, I walked into the front office and saw a 12-year-old girl screaming and crying, handcuffed to a chair, and surrounded by four massive male police officers. Later that day, I threatened to call the local news outlets, the American Civil Liberties Union (ACLU), and human rights lawyers. "This is cruel and unusual punishment," I said to the principal. "You espouse a commitment to equity and yet you're enabling the school-to-prison pipeline."

Recall a time when you might have been perceived as resistant. What did you say or do that might have been labeled as resistance?

The behaviors we label as "resistant" aren't necessarily *good* or *bad*. They include arguing, refusing to engage, passive-aggressive behaviors, rejecting offers of support, withdrawing, declarations that "everything is fine!" and compliance. These behaviors can also be classified as fighting, fleeing, freezing, or appeasing.

There are times when resistance is righteous and necessary—I think we'd all agree that the Civil Rights activists in the 1950s and '60s were entirely justified in resisting racial segregation. Gandhi's anti-colonial leadership was admirable. I'm grateful for my indigenous ancestors who resisted the Spanish invasion of Central America. Resistance to change, or to the status quo, is not always a problem.

So when is "resistance" a "problem?" And for whom is it a problem? And what do we do about resistance when behaviors (such as walking out of a PD session on developing positive relationships with students or on restorative justice) negatively impact children?

Getting Curious About Resistance

Let's look at other people's resistance (or what we perceive as resistance). The only effective way into this exploration is through curiosity. When you sense resistance in another, ask yourself these questions:

- What might this person be feeling?
- Where is fear present? Where might it be in the other person?
- What am I feeling? Is there fear present for me?
- Might the other person be experiencing sadness? Shame, anger, or despair?
- What is the impact of this person's behaviors on themselves?
- What is the impact of this person's behaviors on their students, school, team, organization, or community?
- How can I tap into my humility and be present with this person from a place of compassion?

Read those questions a second time—slowly. What comes up for you as you consider them? What do you sense might be possible if these questions guided you when you encountered resistance? Are you feeling any resistance to these reflective questions?

Notice your feelings. Whatever is arising is okay. See if your feelings have anything they want to tell you right now.

Getting Curious About Fear

Reflecting on the questions to ask in the face of resistance, new coaches often notice fear arising. Our fear says: *These are good questions, and yes they expand my mental model, but what do I do when I encounter resistance? What if I can't do it right? What if I get too angry? What if start shaking and crying? What if it turns out I'm not a good enough person to do this work? Or any meaningful work? What if no one loves me? What if I die alone feeling unfulfilled?*

Fear is a powerful force. It serves an important role, and we don't want to get rid of it, but do you see how it constricts us? How it shrinks possibility?

Here's what I say to my fear: *I hear you, fear. I know you're trying to protect me from being alone, from feeling powerless, from not feeling safe. I hear you. Let's keep exploring your resistance, and let's also explore our strength. Let me know when you want to check in again—I'm listening. And let's see what else we discover on this journey.*

When I let my fear (or any emotion) know that I hear it and see it but that I'm in charge, it often settles and returns to its place in the back seat. Then I return to my place in the driver's seat. When my fear doesn't settle, when it still tries to give directions, I am likely working with old fear (usually from childhood) that deserves attention. Calcified, stagnant fear blocks our thinking. It wants to be cleared. When my fear doesn't settle, I turn to the modalities and people who help me heal. Yes, courage and perseverance are required to clear these blocks, but it's usually less challenging than I anticipate to get back in the driver's seat.

Who is the "I" in the driver's seat, you might wonder? Dr. Richard Schwartz, who developed a therapeutic approach called Internal Family Systems, (IFS), calls this *the Self*—your core or essence, who you are beneath the thoughts, feelings, and roles, the wise, calm center of who you are. Everyone has this Self: it can't be damaged or destroyed by life experiences or trauma, and you can access it through ways of being, including compassion, curiosity, courage, and connectedness.

The more you can connect to your Self—through processes including reflection, meditation, contemplation, creative expression, and therapy—the easier it becomes to relate to your fear and other people's fear. That brings us back to one of the core beliefs of Transformational Coaching: the injunction to start with yourself.

Getting Curious About Sandra's Resistance

Sandra was one of the most challenging teachers I've coached, not because of who she was but because of my own inexperience and emotional activation. In Table 9.1, in the first column, you'll read questions to reflect on resistance. If I'd used these questions on the day when I was supposed

Table 9.1: Reflecting on Resistance

Reflection Question	My Insights
What might the client be feeling?	Sandra might be feeling afraid of me. She might have seen the results, and she might be feeling worried about what I'll say and what our principal thinks. I don't think she likes meeting with me—I know she feels like she has no choice. I guess she might be feeling powerless—her need for autonomy is in jeopardy.
Where is fear present? Where might it be in the client? Where is it in me?	I can imagine that Sandra is afraid of these results. Maybe she's afraid of how she's perceived by students, parents, staff, and me. I'm afraid that I won't know how to have this conversation. I'm afraid that Sandra will get defensive, and then I'll get frustrated. I'm afraid that I'll feel confused and murky. I'm afraid that I made a mistake taking this job. That I'm a bad coach. That I'll never make a difference here. That people don't like me. That I won't be able to meaningfully contribute to the world, and my grandparents will be disappointed in me.
Might the client be experiencing sadness? Shame, anger, or despair?	It's very possible that Sandra feels sad. And maybe some shame too. She's a Black woman, and I wonder what she feels when she looks at the test results and sees that her Black students are failing. She might be experiencing strong feelings. I'm a little afraid of her feelings. They could be big and deep. I'm afraid I wouldn't know how to help her with her feelings.

Reflection Question	My Insights
What is the impact of the client's behaviors on themself?	I don't really know. She often seems checked out—she assigns long written exercises during class, and then she sits at her desks and does paperwork. She doesn't seem to enjoy teaching. She always wears a cap pulled down over her eyes. She rarely smiles.
What is the impact of the client's behaviors on their students, school, team, organization, or community?	Sandra's students, and especially her Black students, are failing at disproportionate rates to other seventh graders. On student surveys, large numbers of students report not feeling safe or comfortable with her. I've witnessed her mocking students' names and publicly shaming them. She sends more Black girls to the office than any other teacher. In our team, Sandra's doesn't bring student work to share and discuss, she arrives in the middle of the meeting and says something urgent came up, and she often reviews meeting agendas and insists we talk about other topics.
Is there love present here? In the client? In myself?	I feel disconnected from love when I think about working with Sandra. I don't know if there's love present for her, and I haven't bothered to look. I feel so much anger at her that I can't access love. I do feel love for her students. When I go into her class and see what students are experiencing, I feel like my heart will break. When I imagine seeing my son in her class, I feel rage and terror; if he has a teacher like Sandra I don't know what I'll do. The students in her class are other people's babies. I feel so much responsibility to them and their parents. Until now I haven't thought about love at all.

(Continued)

Table 9.1: (Continued)

Reflection Question	My Insights
How can I connect to love?	First I have to decide I want to connect to love. I feel so much anger and fear that empathy feels inaccessible. Perhaps I can start by feeling the anger and fear and then slowly exploring what Sandra might be experiencing. Maybe I can try to engage her in some conversations (if it's not too late) about her experiences. I haven't really tried to build a relationship with her—I was irritated by her from the first day. I imagine she sensed this. Maybe I need to ask if we can start over. Maybe I need to apologize. Maybe I need to forgive myself for my lack of skill. Maybe I need to process some of my fears around my son's entrance into the school system. Maybe I need to process some of my anger at how I was treated as a child in school. Maybe I need to get some training in how to coach. Maybe I need to explore my aversion to Sandra. Maybe I need to decide that my worthiness as a human isn't contingent upon the impact I have in this school.

to coach Sandra on her benchmark results, I might have arrived at the insights in the second column. These insights might have allowed my beliefs to shift enough so that I could have showed up differently in our coaching session.

Can you imagine how different my work with Sandra could have been if I'd slowed down, reflected on resistance, and felt some of my feelings? I worked with Sandra many years ago, and she's one person whom I often wish I could go back and apologize to, now that I've forgiven myself for who I was and what I didn't know.

Curiosity is a mind-expanding state that can lead to heart expansion. It's one of the dispositions of a Transformational Coach for this reason.

Addressing resistance is not easy, because it's not technical. Without curiosity, compassion, humility, courage, and trust, you'll likely be unable to respond to resistance, and you might even cause harm.

Resistance Is Often an Expression of Fear

When people act in ways that we label resistant, fear is often an underlying factor. We may fear diminished autonomy, worry we're not competent or that we don't belong, or be afraid that we don't have purpose. These are fears that our core human needs are in jeopardy or are being undermined. When I reflect on the times I felt resistant, I was afraid of all of these things.

Resistance often arises in the face of change—to new initiatives, new administrators, or new curriculum. Humans are wired to love predictability and routine. When change brings instability, our resistance is often less a reaction to the changes themselves and more a response to the fear that arises in connection to the changes. People are not resistant to change; people feel afraid when things change. This dynamic is compounded by the fact that so many change initiatives are poorly led and so many educators have residual fear from past experiences with change. Finally, it's worth understanding that change is even more challenging for people who have experienced trauma (as discussed in Chapter 7, "What You Need to Know About Emotions").

Fear can also arise when it feels like our core values are being threatened. When I worked at the school where the 12-year-old girl was handcuffed to a chair, I identified justice as one of my core values. You can imagine the dissonance: I lived every day with a commitment to justice, and yet I worked at a school where a terrible injustice was committed. Living in alignment with our core values is key to living with integrity and a sense purpose, and my fear arose from this misalignment: How could I be who I wanted to be and witness children being treated this way?

To make matters more complicated, Sandra was the teacher who sent the girl to the office—because the student was "repeatedly rolling her eyes" at

Sandra. So when I coached Sandra, I was confronted by what felt like an unbridgeable difference in core values. I was angry at her; I wanted to have nothing to do with her.

Judgment Is Fear in Disguise

Feeling judgmental about what someone says or does is often an indicator of our own fear. Negative judgment is something that happens in our minds—it's a set of thoughts that push someone away, enforce an us/them mentality, and activate hierarchy and superiority. Judgment has a quality rejection: "My way of doing something is better than theirs and so I'm better than them." Sometimes we judge others to protect ourselves or affirm our own choices. At its essence, judgment is a reflection of fear and creates separation.

During the time I worked with Sandra, I was aware of how judgmental I felt about her. And yet, it felt justified—I knew that 12-year-olds shouldn't be handcuffed to chairs! This was confusing because I also knew I didn't want to be a judgmental person. Since then I've come to understand the difference between judging someone and having an opinion or holding a value—I know it now as the difference between judgment and discernment.

When you practice wise discernment, you don't believe that you are inherently superior to another. You hold a wide perspective, recognize that someone's opinions have emerged from their life experiences and socialization, and see the detrimental impact from holding those opinions. This is different from judging them and thinking, "What an ignorant jerk she is."

If I'd operated from discernment, I might have been able to engage Sandra in meaningful conversation. I might have recognized her humanity and been curious about what led her to take the actions she took, I might have been open to multiple truths, and I might have been able to hold an opinion and not be firmly attached to it. A discerning mind gives you an eagle's perspective—you soar above a situation, recognize all that is, take everything in, and make intentional choices. You accept that you are not the judge and jury and that there's more going on than what you perceive. You also know that discernment isn't synonymous with moral relativism—you can still assess the impact of someone's behaviors and consider the power dynamics at play, and you can say, "The impact of sending a 12-year-old girl to the office for rolling her eyes is too damaging. Let's practice other ways of responding to student behavior. And let's also explore what comes up for you when a child rolls her eyes."

Resistance Is Optional

Imagine holding up your hand, like you're commanding someone to stop. If nothing presses against your hand, is there any resistance? You can only experience resistance if someone pushes back. Similarly, if your hand isn't up, there will be no opposing force. It takes two to create resistance.

Resistance is an experience that you create in response to someone else's experience. Resistance is what arises when you encounter someone else's strong emotions and that activates your own. You *think* someone is resistant, but the experience of resistance arises because of the story you tell about their expression of an emotion—because you raise your hand. It's instinctive, reactive. You raise your hand to block someone else when you experience fear and you don't know what to do.

You can greatly reduce, or even eliminate, the experience of resistance. The skill is to learn not to raise your hand. You'll still encounter fear, sadness, and anger—your own and other people's—but you'll be able to work directly with it when you see it for what it is.

Let me offer an example of an interaction that looks and sounds like resistance; then I'll show you what it can look and sound like for that seeming resistance to dissolve.

A Tale of Two Realities

Mike was struggling with classroom management, and the reasons seemed obvious to me. Some were technical, but many pointed to deeper reasons related to his relationship with students. I wanted to start, however, with offering a suggestion for a simple fix, or so I thought: "When students talk over you when you're giving instructions," I said, "stop talking and wait until—" But I couldn't finish my sentence; Mike cut me off.

"I'm sick of hearing these suggestions," Mike said. "You're not the first one to tell me to do this—you know that, right? This is patronizing. I've been teaching for eight years, but it's only these kids who treat me like this." Mike crossed his arms over his chest and then continued. "At my last school, in the suburbs, they didn't talk over me. These kids don't know how to respect authority. You need to do something about them, not tell me to do something different."

Mike's face was red. He was a tall, middle-aged white man.

Take a moment to visualize this situation. What would you have felt? How would you have responded?

You'll now read two scenarios. The first, "Fighting Resistance," is what could have happened had I put my hand up, had I used the same strategies as when I coached Sandra. In the second scenario, "Addressing Fear," you'll read what actually transpired after Mike said, "I'm sick of hearing these suggestions."

Fighting Resistance

If I hadn't learned about resistance, Mike's words would have activated me. *Oh yeah?* I would have thought, gearing up for a fight. *I know I'm right, and he's a racist pig, and he's treating me like crap, and I'm going to win this battle. Your resistance is futile, Mike.*

Here's how the conversation could have proceeded, if I'd fought what I perceived as his resistance:

Elena: "It sounds like you're unwilling to do anything different, right?"

Mike:	"What do you mean by that? What are you insinuating?"
Elena:	"You're the teacher, Mike. It's your responsibility to change what you're doing. And your comment about 'these kids'— what do you mean by that?"
Mike:	"I'm supposed to change because they are disrespectful brats? This is why teachers don't stay at this school! Admin blames teachers for everything and doesn't enforce rules and coddles parents. I thought you were a coach. Why aren't you coaching me on English since that's what I teach?"
Elena:	"I am a coach, but we can't work on your English instruction if kids won't listen to you."
Mike:	"Which is exactly why we need to enforce rules about respect. They need to behave like civilized people."
Elena:	"When you talk about Black and Brown kids like that, it's racist."
Mike:	"Now you're calling me a racist? I'm done with coaching. In fact, I'm going to file a grievance with the union because this is a hostile work environment."

I would have left the room shaking, afraid of what might happen, furious at Mike, angry at my principal for hiring him, and frustrated with the superintendent who didn't take a strong equity stance. Later I would probably also realize that I was disappointed in myself—I would have wished I'd known what else I could have said, wished I could have said something that he could have heard.

But the worst thing about this scenario is that nothing would have changed for kids. Had I fought his resistance, Mike would still be an ineffective, biased teacher. But by the time I had the real session with Mike, I had acquired a lot of skills and the conversation was more productive.

Addressing Fear

Here's what our conversation actually sounded like:

I took in the scene, Mike's words, his red face, his arms crossed over his chest. I took a deep breath and exhaled slowly. "Mike," I said calmly, "I can hear that you're experiencing intense emotions." I was fully aware that saying these words to a male teacher felt awkward—and yet I said them anyway. I strove to make the tone of my voice sound authentic and confident. Mike's facial expression didn't change, which I took as a positive sign that my words hadn't intensified his irritation.

I continued: "What would be helpful for us to talk about right now?" I genuinely wanted to know where he was interested in taking the conversation. It sounded like he was feeling disempowered—when someone blames others for what's going on and asks others to take care of the situation, they are expressing the fear that comes with lack of agency.

Mike answered my question with this: "I told you. You—or admin—should do something about their behavior. It's not my fault that they are disrespectful."

I wondered: *What need is Mike not getting met right now? Perhaps a need for competence, autonomy, or connectedness?*

"Okay, I want to be sure I'm understanding you right," I said. "Are you feeling like you need help? Are you feeling anxious about your ability to deliver instruction?"

Mike's face took on a puzzled expression. "Why are you asking me about my feelings?" he asked. "I was clear: do something about the students."

I nodded. "I'm glad you asked why I'm asking about your feelings. You are having them, right?" I waited until he nodded. "Yeah, I mean I can see that you're experiencing emotions—which is normal. Humans experience feelings. And I can see that they're uncomfortable for you, right?" I waited.

Mike shrugged and said, "Look, this isn't about my feelings. I can deal with them. This is about student behavior." His pace had slowed just a little; the register of his tone of voice had dropped.

I pressed on in addressing his feelings. "Mike," I said, my voice still commanding authority. I knew he'd be comforted by that—it was a way I could convey that he'd be okay. I registered that underneath his anger and sense of disempowerment, he was afraid. I continued: "It's okay to ask for help. It's okay to feel stuck. I'm hearing that you want to be an effective English teacher here—for these kids, for *our* kids—and that you're not sure how to do that."

Mike stared at me with a blank expression. Blank was better than enraged, I thought.

"Does that feel accurate?" I asked. "That you want to be an effective teacher here?"

"I *am* an effective teacher," Mike said. "They just won't be quiet!"

"Yeah," I said. "It must be really frustrating to remember being in another school and feeling effective there and not having that experience here."

"It's *not me*," Mike said. "It's the kids."

I responded: "I hear that you think it's the kids, Mike, I do. Wherever the problem is, it's frustrating. And sad. And disappointing. I'm just acknowledging those emotions. Those are uncomfortable. And when they flood our system, the part of our brain that can think clearly is diminished."

"So now you're saying that my brain is diminished?" Mike said.

I smiled, in a way that I hoped wasn't mocking but instead brought a little levity. "No, Mike. I'm expressing empathy for you—those are uncomfortable feelings—and I'm sharing neuroscience about what happens in our systems when we experience those feelings."

I paused. "I want to help you figure this out, Mike. I know, from personal experience, how hard it can feel when you can't do what you showed up to do—and I know you're here because you want to teach our students English."

What you can't hear in these written words is my tone of voice. You can't see my body language. You can't gauge my intentions. It's essential that there's congruity between who you are being in a conversation like this and how your communication is expressed. I felt true empathy for

Mike. He was suffering. He became a teacher because he wanted to serve children. And since he'd come to our school, he went to bed every night not having lived up to that internal commitment and desire. He was frustrated and angry and had used all of his resources to figure out what to do, and he still felt ineffective. He felt vulnerable and scared. And he was taking those emotions out on his students—which wasn't fair. But I felt empathy for him.

Mike exhaled and uncrossed his arms. He rested his hands on the table in front of us. "So what am I supposed to do?" he asked. "I just don't know what to do."

"I know," I said. "And not knowing is really scary. I hate it when I don't know what to do." I paused. We sat in silence for 15 or 20 seconds.

"I don't want to scream at them, because I know that's not cool," Mike said, "but it feels like if I just stop talking and wait for them, I'm giving them all the power."

"Right," I said. "So that's scary too! Can you see all the fear? I mean, just seeing it can feel like a relief."

"I wish you'd stop talking about my feelings and help me figure out what to do," Mike said.

I laughed. "Okay, so now I hear that you're getting frustrated with me because you feel like I'm not responding to what you're asking for. Got it. I hear you—you want to move to action, right?"

"Yes, that's right."

"One last question about feelings, and then I promise I'll shift gears, okay?" I waited until Mike nodded. "How do you *want to feel* in your classroom?"

Mike exhaled again, this time loud and long. "I just want to feel like I'm doing a good job. I want to feel like kids are learning. I want them to respect me. I want to feel appreciated. I want to not have to fight for attention every day. I want to feel calm and in control. I want to feel like I know what to do when they get off-task, like I don't have to come to you to get ideas."

"Okay," I said, "You want to feel calm and competent and effective." Mike nodded. "Okay, so when kids talk over you, I want you to stop. . . ."

The conversation I just described, up until this point, took about eight minutes. We spent the rest of the session exploring and practicing how to get students' attention. I also shared strategies with Mike for how to recognize his emotions when they came up in the moment and how to navigate them and respond to them in a way that didn't create further discord for anyone. I helped Mike anchor in his purpose for being a teacher. I helped Mike connect with his own agency and power. I raised a question about the role that Mike's identity markers played in how he experienced his students. I suggested we come back to talking about that next time. On my way out, Mike said, "I'm sorry I can be so difficult. Thanks for being patient with me." I told him I appreciated his honesty.

I left Mike's classroom feeling energized, hopeful, and efficacious as a coach. When I visited Mike's classroom a week later, he was using the strategies we'd talked about, and there were longer and longer stretches when he was giving instructions and students were attentive. Two weeks later, we had a conversation about Mike's racial identity and the assumptions he held about his students because of their identity markers. A Transformational Coach doesn't avoid those direct conversations—we sequence them in a way that enables them to be effective.

Takeaways from Two Conversations

In both of these scenarios, the first fictional, the second one real, Mike was the same person. The only difference was the coaching strategies I used. In the second scenario, I drew on my knowledge of emotions and core human needs, I activated my compassion and curiosity, and I trusted the coaching process. I experienced his resistance as a response to unpleasant emotions and unmet needs. I saw his resistance as his way of saying: "Help me. I am suffering. I don't know what to do."

This is a formula I've used over and over and over—it's why I don't experience resistance. When I see resistance for what it is—*fear*—then I see many options for how to respond.

Here are the key ideas I want you to take away from this example of how to respond to resistance:

- Don't take what your client says or does personally—their emotions are not about you. They're about unmet needs. How you respond to their behavior is entirely within your sphere of control.
- To counter the "kids need to change now" feelings, you need to be able and committed to scaffold the interventions in a realistic sequence.
- Reflect on your behavior, beliefs, or ways of being. Your response to whatever your client does can be reactive, based on problematic beliefs, or misdirected. You bring your needs and emotions to the situation, you create a dynamic, and you can exacerbate the situation. Commit to your learning and healing.
- Communicate empathy over and over. What you perceive as resistance is someone's suffering. This doesn't mean their actions are justified. Activating empathy helps you find a place from which you can see their suffering and respond with patience and kindness.
- Get their buy-in. Look and listen for the entry points, where the conversation can matter to them and how the conversation can meet their needs.
- Stay in relationship with your client. Remember that behaviors change when beliefs change, and beliefs change when behaviors change. But change doesn't happen when there isn't trust.
- Be persistent. Just because someone responds to something you say in a way that makes you feel like they're pushing back, don't give up—if it's the right thing to be persistent about.
- Keep your eyes on the prize: to have a positive impact on the experience and outcomes of kids. Staying in relationship with the person in front of you is the best way to do that—often, to stay in relationship, you'll need to be acutely aware of your own emotions and needs.

- Stay grounded in who you want to be—that's what's most in your control. Draw on courage to stay aligned to your vision for yourself.
- Acknowledge, accept, and attend to emotions, and then talk about instruction, implicit bias, equity, and meeting the needs of our students. You can do both.

Just as I provided some social context for Sandra's behavior, I want to name some of the social context that contributed to Mike's behavior. Mike was suffering—and his students were suffering—because he couldn't fully experience and express his emotions. I would have been thrilled if Mike had sobbed and wailed. His fear and sadness manifested instead as anger, and that was hurting other people. I assumed that Mike didn't allow himself to experience sadness or fear or to cry because he had internalized beliefs that men don't cry. Our patriarchal culture is very clear that men don't cry or express vulnerability or weakness—that is what women and children do, not heterosexual men. Mike had been socialized into this norm since birth, and he was suffering.

We have all been socially and culturally conditioned into so many of our behaviors, beliefs, and ways of being. As we make that conditioning visible and see it for what it is—usually a means of controlling people and diminishing our humanity—we can make different choices. The coaching model I'm inviting you to practice is transformational because of this comprehensiveness.

Perhaps you've been reading this, nodding in sections, and also having doubts and thinking, *But what about Mrs. . . . ?* What about that one teacher who you can't imagine would ever be receptive to this kind of coaching?

Can Someone Be Uncoachable?

Maggie was in her final year of teaching, after spending 35 years in Oakland public schools. She was literally counting down the days until retirement when her high school adopted a new literacy program. She didn't want to implement the curriculum, she didn't want to meet for coaching, and she wasn't receptive to any of my dozens of refined coaching strategies. She was also caring for her elderly, ailing mother and supporting her daughter and newborn grandchild, and these obligations required her to leave as soon as the bell rang every day. After yet another canceled session, I said, "Maggie, I need to be direct. It seems like you don't want to engage in coaching with me. Is that right?"

She sighed. "No, and you know it's not you. I just don't want coaching. It doesn't make sense. I'm done."

"Got it," I said, "I appreciate your honesty. So you're saying you're not coachable, right?" Maggie nodded. "Okay, because coaching has been mandated for all ninth-grade teachers, and you're refusing, I'll need you to let your principal know about your choice, okay?"

"He's going to be pissed off," Maggie said.

"Probably. But I'll let you tell him. Can you do this by tomorrow at 4 p.m.? He'll need to make a decision about how I spend the time that was allocated for you."

Maggie nodded. She did tell her principal, who became angry—at her and at me. He wanted to know why I couldn't make her engage in coaching.

"She's not coachable," I said. "She refused. Do what you need to do, but I can't make her engage in coaching."

When someone consciously turns away from an opportunity to learn or grow and declines coaching, they are uncoachable. A client can label themselves "uncoachable," but you should be cautious about doing so. This isn't just an issue of semantics; it's about you honoring another person's choice—even if you disagree, even if you see that they are negatively impacting children. "Uncoachable" has a permanent, fixed ring to it.

Maggie was a clear-cut case of someone not being open to coaching. She had limited capacity and no incentive. But was Sandra *uncoachable*? Over and over, her behaviors indicated that she wasn't receptive to engaging in a learning and growth process—at least not that year and not with me. So perhaps a more interesting (and difficult) question to ask is whether

I was the right coach for Sandra. Maybe if I'd had more skills to respond to my fear, I wouldn't have been as triggered. Maybe if I'd had more experience, I could have anchored in curiosity, compassion, humility, courage, and trust—and Sandra would have been coachable. Maybe our different racial identities were at play and Sandra would have been receptive to working with a Black coach.

I grapple with two truths. The first truth is that, as meditation teacher Ruth King says, "Nothing is perfect, permanent, or personal." The second truth is that we create our realities. Sandra's rejection of me was and wasn't personal. If I was Sandra, I would not have wanted to be coached by me. I could have shown up very differently in that relationship, and our experience together might have been very different. When I take responsibility for what I've done and who I've been, I am empowered. I can also activate self-compassion and acknowledge the many reasons why I showed up in the way I did—I forgive myself. To be human means to grapple with paradox: it is and it isn't personal; I create my reality, and there are other factors at play. As coaches and humans we must hold multiple truths.

Alternatives to "Uncoachable"

If you have reflected on your own coaching practices, explored how your emotions might be affecting a coaching relationship, recognized your contribution to creating resistance, and used every strategy I've shared with you and you are still unable to enroll someone in the coaching process—then consider the following:

- What are the identity differences between you and your client? Could they be at play in your ability to cultivate trust?
- What are the school or district's expectations for your client to engage in coaching? What is their understanding of those expectations? Is coaching optional in the school or district? Is there anything to clarify with your client around what coaching is, how it works, or what's expected?

- Finally, ask your client, "I want to clarify: I'm hearing that you don't want to engage in coaching with me. Is that correct? Is there anything else you want to share about your willingness to be coached?"

Here's how you can describe someone whom you perceive as being uncoachable:

- They're not willing to engage in coaching, right now.
- They're not willing to be coached by me, right now.
- They don't have the capacity to engage in deep reflection and learning, right now.

It might feel personal to think that you aren't the right person. This is due to fear arising. Alternatively, it could be liberating—what if someone else could be successful with that teacher? Similarly, what if we held the space for the thought that this person might be open to coaching in the future? This is an example of seeing a situation through a lens of fear or love.

Implications for the Organization

When someone is not willing to engage in coaching, there are implications for the larger systems. It is the responsibility of a school/organization to message a value about continued learning and growth. I'd argue that every school and organization needs to be a learning organization—there's no way we can stop learning given the ongoing challenges in the world. Everyone needs to engage in continuous learning so we can have the impact we want to have. Therefore, continued learning should be an expectation for any adult working in any school or as part of the larger school system.

It's the responsibility of the organization's leaders to message this, as well as to create the conditions in which people learn, to provide high-quality professional development for all staff, to ensure that those who provide that PD are well-trained, and to hold people accountable for learning. It should not be optional for staff to learn—and staff should have access to transformative learning experiences.

Here's what this could sound like if a teacher decides they don't want coaching:

Teacher: As I told the coach, I do not want coaching.

Principal: In this school, coaching is the primary vehicle for growth and learning. We know we can't meet the needs of our students unless we continue to develop our skills. Am I hearing you that you are unwilling to do this learning?

Teacher: Coaching is great, but my classes are going fine. I don't need to grow my skills.

Principal: Okay, thanks for being clear. Given that you're unwilling to learn, we're faced with an irreconcilable conflict, which means that you might not be a good fit for this school.

When an individual's choice undermines a school's ability to accomplish its mission, the leaders must take action. I should add that I am very aware that such a situation might be more complicated than it is in the previous script. There are many variables that can result in someone not being receptive to coaching, and in some cases we first work with teachers to mitigate the effects of these variables, especially because we're facing a shortage of teachers. I also acknowledge that when it is time to terminate a teacher's employment, we might have to engage in significant, labor-intensive procedures. It's imperative that school leaders work to avoid hiring educators who might become unwilling to learn and that organizational conditions are created that enable learning to happen.

How to Respond to Resistance

I hope that as your understanding of resistance expands, you are recognizing that Transformational Coaching can prevent resistance and address underlying issues when they surface. The specific strategies that follow are described in depth in other parts of this book. I hope this list serves to remind you of the most impactful responses to resistance. What follows is a sequence of steps, and the sequence is important.

Step 1: Look Inward

- *Explore your fear:* Which fears arise when you experience someone's resistance? What are those fears protecting you from? What might fear want to tell you? Which of your core human needs are at play? Are you afraid of not fulfilling those needs? How does your fear manifest in behavior—does it make you fight, freeze, flee, or appease? Can you accept your fear? Can you ask your fear if it would be willing to move into the back seat so that it's not driving your behaviors?
- *Follow your triggers:* When you become emotionally activated (which will happen at some point), remember the saying, triggers are friends to follow. The stimulus that was activating is an indicator that you've got some stuff to explore and heal from.

Step 2: Ground in Curiosity and Compassion

- *Activate empathy:* What do you think is going on for your client? Imagine you're in their shoes. What do you think they're feeling? How do you imagine they experience you? What do you think they want and need from you?
- *Consider core human needs:* Which of your client's core human needs do you think might be at play? How might their resistant behavior indicate a need for connection, autonomy, or competence?

Step 3: Take Action

- *Stay in relationship:* Use a lot of active listening. Be mindful of your body language and tone of voice. Give your client choice and permission—remember that they're likely feeling disempowered, so coach toward agency.

- *Acknowledge the state of the relationship:*
  - "I'm sensing that you don't trust me. I'm wondering if you'd be willing to share what your experience has been like with me. I would like to repair any trust that's been breached and welcome your feedback."
  - "I want to apologize. I recognize that when we started working together, I said and did some things that may have generated distrust. I regret how I began this coaching relationship and would like to know what you need from me to try a do-over."
  - "What does this coaching relationship feel like for you? Is there any way you'd like it to feel different?"
- *State your commitment to the relationship:*
  - "I care about you, and I want to explore how to best serve you and our community. I'm committed to helping you thrive."
  - "I take responsibility for getting off on the wrong foot together, I'm grateful for your honest feedback, and I want to see what's possible. How does this land with you?"
- *Use the confrontational approach (see Chapter 5):*
  - "I'm not sure how to understand what's happening. You cancel meetings, don't bring the work that you agreed you'd bring, and respond to my questions with one or two words. It seems like you don't want coaching. Can you help me understand what's going on for you?"
- *Use ACE Emotions (see Chapter 8):*
  - "I'm perceiving some reluctance to working with me. Would you be willing to explore this? What are you feeling?"
  - "Tell me if this feels off, but it seems like you might be experiencing some apprehensions or fear around coaching. Is that right?"
- *Cultivate resilience:* See the suggestions in the following section to help someone move out of fear and back to agency, curiosity, and compassion.

Step 4: Anchor in Who You Want to Be

- *Explore the two truths:* Don't take your client's behavior personally (it isn't personal), and identify your role in the dynamic (you contribute to it). The resistance you're experiencing is something you've created by raising an opposing force.
- *Activate your will:* Why are you a coach? What legacy do you want to leave? How do you want people to remember you in 5 or 10 years? How do you want to remember yourself—and how you engaged with a specific client—in 20 years?
- *Be persistent:* Don't lose hope in your ability to learn and grow. Practice coaching conversations, get feedback from a trusted colleague, and remember that you can acquire the skills to have these conversations. Then, keep showing up for the conversations, taking responsibility for your part, listening to your client, and allowing your heart to open. Let love fuel your courage and persistence.

But Do I Really Have to Do This? Why Me?

Even if you're doing everything I've suggested, it can be tiring to work with someone whose actions are too often driven by fear. I was a pretty experienced coach during the two (long) years I worked with Mildred, a veteran kindergarten teacher. I didn't experience the challenges of working with Mildred as resistance—I knew that she lived with a tremendous amount of fear and unprocessed trauma—but that didn't change how hard she was to work with. I had to muster all my patience, equanimity, and acceptance for every session. Even then, I often felt like we weren't getting anywhere, and Mildred's behaviors, beliefs, and ways of being had undeniable negative impact on children. *Why me?* I'd ask myself. *This is a waste of time.*

But I kept coaching Mildred, and she kept showing up for our sessions. Here's what I told myself: *Elena, you've got your foot in the door. I know that it keeps slamming on your toe and it hurts, but you're the only one right now with a foot in the door.*

It can feel uncomfortable to say or do the things that help us respond to resistance. I feel squirmy when I have to tell someone that I messed up, that I got off on the wrong foot with them. I am uneasy when I recognize that I let my fear drive the car. When I recognize that I am activated, I accept that I need to do my work to heal the wounds at the root of these reactions. Then I get up and step back into the path that I've selected for myself—the path of Transformational Coaching. As long as the door is open, even just an inch or two, I'll keep walking through it.

This is what I did with Mildred—I kept showing up, even though I felt ineffective, even though I was afraid. And little by little, Mildred changed. She slowly came to trust me and to engage in conversations in a more meaningful way. There was no miraculous transformation of her teaching, and eventually the principal found a way to move her into a role where she wasn't working directly with kids. But that transition was a lot smoother than it might have been, I'm sure of it, had I not been coaching Mildred at that time.

Here's another thing I tell myself when I'm in situations that feel frustrating, pointless, or like a waste of time: *The story isn't over yet, Elena. You don't know what impact this might have on someone. Trust the process; trust the universe.* This reminder is humbling and offers relief from the magnitude of the responsibility I often feel. And I know it's true.

But What About Boundaries with Toxic People?

You can be curious and compassionate and humble and also extract yourself from toxic people and situations. It's unhealthy to be around someone else's fear when it transforms into anger and is expressed as aggression. You don't need to tolerate behavior that is hostile, manipulative, dishonest, blaming, shaming, or selfish. It's extremely important for Transformational Coaches to have boundaries.

Maintaining boundaries with clients is easier when you realize that the problem is *their behaviors*—not *who they are*. There's a difference between saying someone "is a liar," and saying, "they say things that aren't true." Behaviors can be changed, and they don't define us as people. It might also be helpful to see toxicity as a coping mechanism. Aggression, for example, can be a form of protection, keeping a person safe by keeping others who might hurt them at a distance; in other words, a person's core human need for connection and belonging won't be met by behaving aggressively. You can have compassion for someone, and recognize their suffering, and also not want to be around them.

So what do you do if you are assigned to coach a teacher who is relentlessly hostile? And you've tried everything to build a relationship with them? Talk to your supervisor. Be very clear about the situation and precise about your needs. Your well-being matters.

How to Cultivate Resilience

Resistance, you'll remember, indicates that a person's reserves of resilience are depleted. My book *Onward*, and the accompanying *Onward Workbook*, offers a comprehensive, research-based methodology for cultivating resilience. What follows are brief descriptions of strategies to boost resilience. If you've read *Onward*, then these will serve as a reminder; if you haven't read it, consider picking it up next.

You can incorporate any of the following strategies into coaching conversations (and many of them are described in other parts of this book), or you can use them as activities to engage in with clients, occasionally or regularly.

Understand Emotions

While some schools today include social-emotional learning (SEL) for children, most adults didn't receive any instruction in SEL as kids. In the same way that you'd feel comfortable describing strategies for front-loading information or classroom management techniques, for example, you can teach your client about emotions. When the need arises, it's appropriate for you to take an instructive stance and teach your client about emotions. You can do this without sounding patronizing, or awkward, or crossing lines. There are a few key strategies to start with:

- Help someone learn to recognize when emotions and feelings are arising—to recognize the physiological and cognitive indicators.
- Share the Core Human Needs and explain the role that they play in generating emotions.
- Help them expand their vocabulary to name their emotions—use the Core Emotions (Appendix B).

If you do nothing beyond these three activities, you will have a significant impact.

Cultivate Compassion

Compassion toward ourselves and others is essential for our well-being, and it's a quality that we can practice and strengthen. When we access compassion, we feel better. Cultivating compassion is the second component of the ACE Emotions framework, but here are reminders of strategies to weave into conversations:

- *Offer self-talk strategies:* "I'm doing the best I can" or "This is a hard situation, and I'm doing everything I can."
- *Explore self-compassion:* "What would you say to your best friend if they were in this situation?"
- *Invite empathy for others, including students, parents, colleagues:* "If you were walking in their shoes, what would you notice and experience? What would you feel?"
- *Invite forgiveness:* "What would need to be true for you to be able to forgive yourself?"

Re-ignite Curiosity

Curiosity brings us back into a sense of agency and openness. These are a few ways to invite someone back into a place of curiosity:

- Ask questions that begin with "I wonder ..." or "What might be possible if ... ?" or "What if it could be easy?"
- Invite consideration of broader perspectives and reframing of the situation. This can sound like, "Is there any other way to see this?" (This is part of the "E" of ACE Emotions—expanding the story.)
- Share the Zen parable about the farmer (from Chapter 2, "A Transformational Coach's Ways of Being"). This can be an anchor text to refer to when your client feels challenged.

We need to feel some level of safety and trust in order to access curiosity—so if your client doesn't seem receptive to curiosity, work to strengthen the relationship.

Take Care of Yourself

There are many ways that we can take care of ourselves—and doing so is key to restoring ourselves to a place of physical and emotional equilibrium. Here are a few strategies to offer clients:

- *Do a self-care check-in:* Ask about how your client is sleeping, whether they're eating enough nutritious food, and whether they're getting any movement for their body. Ask if there are any tiny things they might be able to do to boost these physical self-care practices—go to sleep 10 minutes earlier, sit in the sun for 5 minutes, eat a handful of blueberries.
- *Invite presence:* Incorporate mindfulness practices such as breathing exercises into coaching sessions. Introduce self-talk strategies such as, "right here, right now, everything is okay."

- *Encourage "savoring":* This has three components: Noticing a moment that feels good, bringing awareness to how the body feels (it helps to close the eyes and register the temperature of the air, the sensations in the body, any surrounding sounds), and then noticing the emotions that are present. This is a way to take in the good, which is a form of self-care.

Activate Optimism and Agency

Agency is the feeling that we can make changes in our life, that we can act on a sense of empowerment. When we feel optimistic, we are far more likely to access our agency. The following strategies are invaluable in supporting optimism and agency:

- *Cultivate awareness of bright spots:* Bright spots are anything that brings a sense of relief, satisfaction, connection, joy, or other pleasant emotion. We experience many of these every day, but we often miss them. Invite your client to jot down the bright spots they experience, perhaps to share them with you on a regular interval or to share them with another person. The more awareness we can bring to these moments, the more resilience we'll have.
- *Reflect on growth:* Engage your client in a process of identifying their growth over time—perhaps from early days of teaching or further back if they're a new teacher (perhaps to their time as a student). Guide them to see how they've grown and developed helpful coping skills or perhaps how they've abandoned coping skills that didn't work as well. Help them identify any skills or coping strategies that might transfer into their current situation and that they could draw on.
- *Explore affirmations or mantras:* There's a saying that where our attention goes, our energy flows. When we say to ourselves, "I can get through this," our energy to accomplish a challenge follows. Help your client identify the words that might be most helpful or meaningful to them in a given situation.

Deepen Connectedness

Our resilience reserves become depleted when we're disconnected from ourselves, others, and something bigger. There are many strategies described in *Onward* for fostering connection, and I trust that you have some ideas about how to do this. Here are a few that might not immediately come to mind:

- *Explore gratitude:* There is a mountain of research indicating that practicing gratitude reduces the risk of depression, increases satisfaction in relationships, and boosts our well-being. If you're doubtful about the benefits of a daily gratitude practice (as I once was), you might appreciate reviewing the research. My favorite gratitude practice is this: At the end of the day, write down three good things from the day and what role you had in making those three things happen. This exercise deepens gratitude and also our sense of agency—the feeling that we can make good things happen. I often invite clients to do this and to share their three things with me when we meet.
- *Offer gratitude to others:* Invite your client to write a letter to someone they appreciate (a colleague, leader, or even a student) and then challenge them to read it aloud to that person. This is one of the gratitude practices that Dr. Seligman found to be most impactful on an individual and a relationship.
- *Practice kindness to others:* Invite your client to engage in a week of kindness toward others. Encourage them to engage in small, simple kindnesses each day (such as smiling at a parent at pickup, asking a colleague about their day, appreciating a student) and then to report back about their experience.
- *Explore awe:* Awe expands our thinking and allows us to access expansive states and profound emotions. Invite your client to reflect on awe, to be alert to moments of awe each day, and to consider how to experience

awe more often. On this topic, I love Dacher Keltner's book, *Awe*, and the resources at the Greater Good Science Center's website.

- *Explore the "shadow"*: When we feel disconnected from ourselves, we've often rejected parts of our being that we don't like. These parts can show up as emotions, needs, or desires. It's not easy to explore what psychologists call the "shadow"—that's where feelings like anger, resentment, shame, and dependency can be found—but when we ignore or suppress those human experiences, we feel disconnected from our whole selves.

Just as we need to sleep every night to replenish our energy, we need to regularly restore resilience. Cultivating resilience is a practice—the more we explore and use a range of strategies to refill our reserves, the more impact we'll see. You'll also find that some of these strategies work better for some people than others. And you'll find that some strategies work for a little while, and then their impact diminishes. This is predictable—we need different things at different times. The key is to explore these routes for boosting resilience and pay attention to the impact. Try different strategies, practice them, and see what happens.

A Warning: Beware of Toxic Positivity

When you tell someone you're feeling sad and they smile (perhaps inauthentically) and reply, "Everything happens for a reason!" or "This too shall pass," they are exposing you to toxic positivity. Their responses serve to deny your uncomfortable emotions—they communicate that sadness should be repressed or suppressed. A negation of our humanity, toxic positivity often appears as a coping mechanism when we lack other ways to deal with discomfort around our own or other people's emotions. Even when the intention behind it is to be helpful, toxic positivity's impact is harmful.

Toxic positivity and its cousin, spiritual bypassing, have been used by those in power to dismiss the suffering of marginalized people. In these situations, the concept of resilience has been misused. I was once asked to speak at a school where a horrible racist incident had occurred. District leaders had identified the community's response as problematic—people were angry and sad—and the superintendent wanted me to tell students and teachers to be more resilient, to "look for the bright spots and be here now." I saw the problem as the superintendent's response—the message I heard from her was "get over it, it wasn't that bad, we need to move on." I said I could speak about honoring and accepting emotions—and that I'd invite anger, sadness, and fear. I told the superintendent that without acknowledging the pain and giving space for folks to express their grief, more harm would be done and that I couldn't play a role in that. I was uninvited.

Only after our clients have felt their feelings and accepted them can we invite them to reframe an experience and explore the stories they're telling about a situation—only then might a client be able to say, "I know this moment is really hard, and I know it will pass, because nothing is permanent." When we coach toward resilience, we acknowledge and accept challenging emotions. We offer them a place at the table—then we listen to them and work to learn from them.

Witness and Behold

For me, being witnessed has been the most powerful catalyst for growth. When my compassionate therapists hold space for me to experience my emotions and explore memories, thoughts, and feelings, I am restored to my wholeness and agency. Within a secular context, witnessing enables communion with my Self; it feels holy.

Even within the parameters of the role of instructional coach, principal, or department head, you can witness others. You can hold space for someone to share their fear, their hopes, and their desires to live into their vision for themselves. You can hear their need for connection and belonging, their aspirations for growth and competence, and their longing for love.

What does witnessing entail? Let's start with what it sounds like:

- Say more . . .
- What else?
- What do you hear yourself saying?
- What would be a question that I can ask you right now that might be helpful?
- What's coming up for you right now?
- I'm hearing sadness. Does that resonate?

These sentence stems should be familiar—they're in any Transformational Coach's basic tool set. They are transformational when they create a container to witness someone.

Witnessing is presence, deep listening, receiving someone's experience, and walking in their shoes. Witnessing means you accept someone as they are, recognize the complexity of who they have become, and hear and see their potential. You ask open questions. You invite your client to find their own answers. You invite them back into their agency. When you bear witness, you behold someone in their full humanity.

When you witness, every conversation becomes an opportunity for healing—for yourself and your client. Healing is reciprocal, because our brains fire neurons that mirror each other. When your client feels seen and heard in a conversation, you will "catch" those emotions. The empathy and care you offer a resistant teacher will rebound and nourish parts of you that are fearful and constricted. This might sound metaphysical, but it's neuroscience. If you have doubts about what I'm suggesting, it's okay: your doubt is welcome; you might also experiment with buckling your doubt into the back seat and seeing what it feels like to witness your clients.

As resistance dissolves and relationships solidify and resilience rises, be sure to pause and appreciate the process. When we recognize growth and change that's underway, we build motivation to continue. We increase confidence in ourselves. We deepen our trust in the process.

Remember that the journey of growth is the destination—and that the journey, with all its messiness and twists and turns, is one to behold. Yes, there may be steep climbs and moments when the views are obscured, but you will arrive at places where you can pause. In those moments, as you reflect on where you've been—and the journey itself—you'll likely access feelings of connectedness, competence, confidence, trust, agency, meaning, and awe. By letting yourself bask in these feelings, you'll refill your reserves of resilience.

Pause and Process

Reflect:

- What are your top two or three learnings from this chapter?
- Which feelings arose for you while reading this chapter? What did those feelings want to tell you?
- Which of the strategies for responding to resistance feel most accessible to you? Which do you feel you could start doing?
- Which of the strategies for boosting resilience might be most helpful to you, right now? Which ones could you incorporate into your life?

Next steps:

- Listen to *Bright Morning Podcast* episode 205 to hear a demonstration of coaching a resistant teacher.
- Over the next week, pay attention to when fear arises within you. See if you can get curious about that fear. See what you learn from getting curious.
- Read *Onward* and begin using *The Onward Workbook*.

CHAPTER 10

How to Coach Ways of Being

Coach the Person, Not the Problem

<table>
<tr>
<td>

Common misconception:

My clients are who they are.

</td>
<td>

Transformational Coaches know:

My clients have tremendous control over who they are and how they show up.

</td>
</tr>
</table>

Our ways of being are shaped by our identity and our core values, and they are often expressed as emotions. When we coach a way of being, we work at the foundation of who someone is and how they show up. As you read the anecdotes in this chapter, you might think, *I'd love to be coached around my way of being.* You might also think, *It seems hard to coach someone in this way! We don't talk like this in schools.* And you'd be right.

The conversations you'll read in this chapter are rare in the context of professional development. But just because they don't happen doesn't mean they can't—*or shouldn't.* If we had conversations about ways of being,

I'd wager that we'd have far less turnover in schools, we'd have far more effective teachers and leaders, and we'd do a better job of serving children.

So what does it mean to coach around a way of being? It means you do the following:

- *Guide a client into awareness* of who they are being—of how they show up through their actions, through what they say, and through the feelings they express.
- *Help a client explore what contributes* to who they are being—how their emotions, identity experiences, and values intertwine to form a way of being.
- *Support a client into a vision* for who they want to be. In this process, you are neutral—you don't have an opinion about who they should be.
- *Help a client accept and embrace* who they are—if they've determined that their way of being reflects their values and who they want to be, and is in service of students and the community they serve.
- *Help a client identify behaviors* they want to start, stop, or continue that help them be who they want to be.
- *Hold your client's vision for themselves as a north star* to continuously orient toward. When you notice that your client veers from their vision, you raise that observation and invite reflection on the gap between who they say they want to be and how they are showing up.

The good news is that you can learn to have conversations in which you coach ways of being. Even if you think, *But I'm a technology coach . . .* , I want you to know that you can coach ways of being—you can talk about integrating technology *and* you can talk about who someone is being. If you feel like you can't move toward such conversations, consider exploring your agency and spheres of influence. And if you're worried about your ability to enact this kind of coaching, remember that this is a skill set that you can acquire.

Coaching ways of being might not be as hard as it initially seems because it feels good—both to you, as the coach, and to your client. This is because coaching ways of being creates authentic connection between people, surfaces what's most important to us, and often feels like a relief. Coaching ways of being helps us meet our core human needs more effectively than other kinds of coaching—both for the coach and for the client—and this boosts our motivation to learn how to effectively enact this skillset.

A Transformational Coach starts with themselves—when we're learning something new, we start with reflecting on our relationship to the novel ideas. Before proceeding, take a moment to consider these questions:

- Who are you being, right now, as a coach or leader?
- How does this way of being show up in your behaviors? How do you see that way of being manifesting in your relationships at work?
- What do you think contributes to who you are being and how you are showing up?
- Are you being who you want to be? In which ways are you aligned to your vision for yourself? In which ways are you falling short of embodying that vision?
- Are there any shifts you could make in your behaviors that would allow you to be who you want to be?
- How does it feel to reflect on who you are being right now? What do those emotions want to tell you?

As you read the following section, in which you'll read a conversation I had with a principal around her way of being, consider how I supported my client to work through many of these questions.

The Complexity of a Way of Being

Adi was distressed. Teachers were pushing back on her initiative to support reading in the third grade, which focused on outcomes for Black and Brown students. "I know it's partly because I'm the third principal they've had in three years, but our reading scores are dismal," she explained. I'd observed Adi leading several staff meetings and PD sessions, and although she was a novice principal, I was impressed with her facilitation skills and ability to be responsive to teacher concerns.

"Tell me more about what you're experiencing," I said. Adi paced around her office while I sat in a comfortable desk chair.

"I feel like they're questioning my values and commitments. I feel like they don't see me for who I am. I'm a Black woman. I grew up a mile away from here. I'm the mother of Black boys. This is who I am, and I feel like they want me to be a different person."

In every coaching conversation, after a client says something, a coach has to select a path—one of many possible paths—to proceed down. In this moment, I decided to offer Adi more space to explore how her identity, and her identity experiences, contributed to her way of being. The centrality and importance of her identity deserved exploration, but I also wanted to give Adi the option of traveling this path—I wanted to honor her agency.

"Adi," I said, "I'm hearing that your identity is central to how you're showing up as a leader. Is this something you'd like to unpack some more?"

"Do you think that would help me figure out how to respond to their insistence that we focus on classroom management this year and postpone reading till next year?"

"Yes," I said. I could see that Adi was experiencing strong emotions, I suspected that exploring those emotions might help her figure out her next steps, and I knew that as she gained clarity about who she was being she'd feel more confident.

"Okay," she said. "So I'm a Black mother from Oakland, and that's who I am." Adi's voice had an irritated tone, which I assumed was because she was stating the obvious. We'd talked about her identity before. But I didn't think she was annoyed with me; I suspected she was frustrated with the situation.

"My intention in supporting you in this reflection is so that you get clear on what's going on," I said. "So how do you think these identity experiences influence how you are showing up now?"

Adi paused in front of the window that looked onto the playground. It was late in the day, and most students had left campus, but a small group who were in the after-school program were playing basketball. Adi sighed and turned to me. "I often feel like I care so much deeper than everyone else. I feel like my chest is open and my heart is visible. When I look at those test scores, I feel like I'm seeing my brothers when they were in third grade; I'm seeing my sons. It's personal."

I nodded and exhaled loudly. We were quiet for probably 20 seconds. "Tell me more about what it feels like to have this experience," I said.

"Elena, it's hard," Adi said. "It's so damn hard." I nodded.

"Tell me more," I said.

"I don't know—do other principals or teachers wake up at night and lie there thinking about how much work there is to do and how many kids' lives are at stake?"

"So you're feeling a tremendous responsibility," I said.

"Yes, it's huge! It's overwhelming!" Adi's jaw clenched, and she crossed her arms over her chest.

I reached into my bag and pulled out the copy of The Core Emotions that I always carry. I handed the document to Adi, who had seen it before, and said, "What are you feeling right now?"

Adi skimmed the lists. I could see her eyes stop on one word and then another. "I'm feeling so much sadness," she said. Her tone of voice didn't waver; her facial expression remained unreadable. "So much sadness I feel like I could drown in it."

"Thank you for sharing that," I said slowly. "That sounds so painful." I exhaled, loudly, again.

"I'm also feeling angry," she said.

"That's helpful to recognize. Say more about the anger."

"Are you sure? I mean, you know what I'll say. You know why I'm angry," Adi said.

"I do know why you're angry," I said. We'd had many conversations about why our schools were inequitable, about racism and systemic oppression. "Why don't you tell me about the anger—not what you're angry at? What does it feel like? What does it want you to know?"

"My anger wants me to know I've got work to do—it wants me to get out of bed. It wants me to know I've got to speak up for kids. It wants me to stay focused on third-grade reading scores." Adi had resumed pacing. I was glad to see that she was moving—the body needs to process and release intense emotions like the ones that Adi was present with in that moment.

"Seems like there's a lot to appreciate about your anger," I said. "It can be a motivator."

Adi nodded. "It's also intense," she said. "Sometimes I feel like I'll explode from it. And sometimes I want a break from it."

"I hear that. And that sounds scary." I paused and took a long deep breath. "Will it listen if you ask it to motivate you?" I asked.

"I've never tried. I don't know," Adi said.

I waited so that Adi could absorb that idea. Then I continued. "Sometimes anger shows up to get us mobilized. It helps us prioritize and act on what's most important. It sounds like it's doing that for you." Adi nodded. "And sometimes," I said, "it can also mask other feelings."

"What do you mean?" Adi said.

"Anger can sometimes mask sadness or fear. You've mentioned sadness. Is there also fear present for you?"

"There's always fear," Adi said. "Fear that I won't do right by kids, fear that I am not using my positional authority to create the kind of change that children deserve, fear that I'm not good enough, fear that my sons won't get a fair shake at life. So much fear."

I nodded and breathed audibly. I observed my own fear and sadness arise, as well as my compassion for Adi. I also noticed that I was feeling nervous about whether I could figure out the next coaching move—Adi had never been this vulnerable with me, and I felt responsible for ensuring that this conversation went somewhere productive. I silently acknowledged my fears and reminded myself to trust the process.

"It's courageous of you, Adi, to acknowledge all of these feelings. I appreciate you for trusting me with sharing what's going on. This is a lot."

Adi turned away and looked out the window again. I wasn't sure how she'd received my words. "Do you think I can do this job?" she asked, and I heard a catch in her voice suggesting that tears were forming.

"I really don't know if I can answer that question," I said. "I think the question might be, do you want to do this job? Or maybe, what does it mean to do this job?" I paused. "Or maybe the question is, do *you* think you can do this job?" I stopped talking, noticing that I was stacking questions. "What do you think you're asking?" I said.

"You're right," she said. "You can't answer my question because what I'm asking is can a Black woman, from this community, who has her heart open and who has a vision for student success do this work?"

I nodded in agreement. I couldn't answer that question. "If you answered that question, right now," I said, "what would the answer provide for you?"

"I guess I want a yes or a no. And if the answer is yes, great. I'll press on. And if it's no, then, I don't know what I'll do."

"That's a hard spot. You want to know the future. We all like certainty." I saw the hint of smile forming on Adi's face. "Adi, I'm curious about something. I can't think of a way to ask this question in a more 'coachy' way, so I'm just going to ask the way it's coming to me. Do you feel like your identity is a hindrance to your ability to be successful as a principal? Or is it an asset? Is it a problem or a contribution?"

"Well," Adi said, after taking this in, "things aren't black and white, as you always tell me," she smiled. "So I guess I see it as both. I mean, it's not 'a problem,' but it makes my work harder sometimes. I feel things on a personal level. Sometimes it feels like a burden. And it's also a help—a contribution. I know I have much more understanding and empathy, and maybe more skin in this game, and I'm grateful for the way I see the world. I'm grateful that my life has given me this path and that I can serve my community in this way." Adi stopped and made eye contact with me, which was something I'd noticed she rarely did. I held her gaze for a moment.

"Adi, what do you hear in what you're saying right now?"

She sighed and looked at a poster on the wall. "I'm hearing that this job is hard, and I want to do it, and I am who I am. And the truth is—I like who I am. I like my dedication and conviction that third graders need to be on grade level, and I like my conviction that we can make this happen."

"So are you being who you want to be right now?" I asked.

"Yes," Adi said, her voice authoritative, "I am." She looked at me again, her eyes clear and confident.

"Can you do this job?" I asked.

"I want to," she said. "And that's the most important question. Right now, I want to. Right now, I'm going to do everything I can to do it well. And that means staying focused on reading and showing up in the way I know I need to show up for teachers—and that includes with conviction. And it also means I need to have patience with them, and I need to hold clear expectations, and I need to make sure they're getting coaching and good PD. But yes, I can do this job."

"Adi, is there an animal or a bird or a mythical creature that symbolizes who you are or who you want to be as a leader?"

Adi thought for a moment. "Well, the first thing that came to mind is a tardigrade—a water bear. My fourth graders were obsessed with them."

My facial expression must have revealed that I didn't know what a tardigrade or a water bear was because Adi explained: "They're bugs that can survive extreme conditions, and they live everywhere and nothing kills them." I winced. I'd intended to ask her to put a photo of this creature up on her office wall.

"But I think I'd rather go with something regal and beautiful," Adi said as she brushed back her hair and smiled. "Maybe a cheetah or an eagle."

"Give it some thought. See if you can come up with something that symbolizes how you want to show up every day." Adi nodded. We sat quietly for a moment.

"This work is hard, Adi," I said. "It's hard. And I think there's space for you to be you. I see how your identity markers make your work extra hard and also how they make you extra skilled for this job and how they might also make it extra rewarding. And you don't *have to* do it. This is your choice."

Adi sighed, loudly. "Keep reminding me of that," she said. "This is my choice to lead this school."

"In our work, with me," I said, "there's always space for you to be who you are and to bring all the feelings and thoughts and all of it."

"I think sometimes what I need more than anything is just to be able to pour it all out and say that this work is freaking hard," Adi said.

"Yeah, that's a totally normal human need," I said. "How are you feeling now?"

"Tired," Adi said, "I didn't sleep much last night. I also feel a little lighter, like I can breathe a little more easily."

"I'm glad," I said.

In this conversation with Adi, I hadn't anticipated that we'd unpack her ways of being, and I wasn't following a formula to do so. But as soon as she started talking, I heard that what was central to her distress, and what she deserved an opportunity to explore, was her way of being. I helped Adi unpack what contributed to how she was showing up as a principal, in this case, her identity experiences; I helped Adi deepen her awareness of who she was being; I guided Adi to recognize the complexity of the emotions entwined with how she was showing up and to accept those emotions; and I invited Adi to sharpen her vision for herself for who she wanted to be.

A week later, Adi told me she'd decided she wanted to be a goose. "They're graceful, and they glide on air currents. And they take turns leading. So maybe I'll be here for a while, and then maybe someone else will lead. Plus, I like that they migrate because I love to travel."

Pulling Back the Curtain

In my podcast episodes where I coach someone, I "pull back the curtain" to describe my thought processes and decision-making during the conversation. In this conversation with Adi, I:

- Guided her into awareness of who she was being
- Facilitated an exploration of what contributed to her way of being
- Invited her to consider whether she wanted to shift any aspect of her way of being
- Helped her accept and embrace who she was
- Supported her to articulate a vision for herself

Throughout the conversation, I thought about how I could help Adi more deeply connect to her agency, in part by acknowledging her emotions.

In addition to coaching Adi toward agency through her emotions, I also drew on what I know about coaching identity and identity experiences. Doing this isn't easy—coaching identity requires knowledge about how identity experiences manifest; comfort in talking about race, class, gender, and identity differences, among other topics; and the skills to facilitate equity conversations. We explored how to do this in Chapters 12 and 13; for now it's important to recognize that coaching a way of being requires knowledge and skills around coaching for equity.

In addition to coaching emotions and identity, I listened for how Adi was living her core values. I heard that she was being who she wanted to be, even though she was experiencing pushback. I also heard opportunities for her to more fully claim who she was being, which was why I invited her to select a symbol to represent her vision for her way of being. This element—how we live our values—is connected to our sense of our identity. It's what we'll explore next.

Coaching Core Values

We all have core values that we aspire to live from. However, sometimes our actions and decisions do not reflect our core values. This can happen when we're not clear on what our values are or when we're conflicted about enacting them. Clarity on our values and what it looks like to live them becomes a compass for behaviors.

Core values is a central concept for Transformational Coaches and a pretty easy thinking tool to use. When using this tool, a coach helps someone identify their core values, makes space for the client to articulate how they can demonstrate those values, and guides the client, over and over, back to living in alignment with the values. When someone lives and works from their core values, they have far more access to emotions such as courage, confidence, perseverance, calm, clarity, and satisfaction. When we coach someone into their core values, we coach them into ways of being.

What Are Core Values?

Based on what you read about Adi, I wonder if you'd be surprised to hear that her core values at the time that I coached her were community, responsibility, and perseverance. In the portion of the conversation I shared, I think you can find evidence of those values and how Adi grappled with honoring them.

What are your core values? If you aren't aware of them, there's an activity on my website to help you identify them (it's also in *The Onward Workbook*). You might also just consider what comes to mind in response to these questions:

- What do you value most?
- Which behaviors and values in others do you most appreciate?

- How do you aspire to consistently show up in the world?
- What bothers you most in others? What value might be reflected in that behavior?

Examples of values include compassion, responsibility, humor, forgiveness, gratitude, hard work, justice, love, and community. You'll likely find that your core values are umbrellas for other values—one can encompass many others. You may feel, for example, that your core value of joy represents your other values of community, creativity, and self-expression. Or you might be like my son who says he has only one value: love.

Our values orient us, drive us, and anchor us, and we experience integrity when we act in alignment with them. When we act in ways that do not align with our values, we physically feel bad. This is why when you are asked to do something you don't believe in, you might say, "It makes me feel sick to my stomach to have to do this." Interestingly, psycho-neuroimmunologists find that our immune systems are strengthened or depleted by the degree of integrity with which we live our lives. When an inner voice says *This isn't me*—listen closely.

When we aren't living in alignment with our values, we can experience what feels like an identity crisis. This is why we listen for breakdowns between who our clients think they are ("I'm a compassionate person!") and how they show up (shouting at children, dismissing parent concerns, snapping at colleagues). Any time you hear a client say, "This isn't who I am," know that they are experiencing a breakdown in how they live their values.

When supporting clients to live and work in alignment with their values, it's helpful to understand that our core values can be *aspirational* or *lived*. For example, I might proclaim my core value to be community, but on most days I might be alone. I might say, my value is community, and I enact that by creating healthy opportunities for others to convene. Or my value of community might indicate my desire to be part of a community. Acknowledging the discrepancy between ways I hold a value *as an aspiration* and the way I live it might allow me to make valuable changes in my behaviors.

As you begin to reach for the core values thinking tool in your coaching conversations, you may find that you often end up talking about beliefs. Values and beliefs are closely related. Core values can be enduring beliefs from our families of origin or religious traditions. This is neither good nor bad, but we can help people we work with to be clear on whether they truly want to hold a value or whether they're hanging on to it simply because it's an inheritance. For example, perhaps you were given the value of hard work as a child. Maybe now as an adult, you recognize that you've lived that value by working to exhaustion and putting the needs of others ahead of your own. Perhaps it's time to release that value. The key is awareness: until you are conscious of your values, old ones can operate without consent.

How to Coach Core Values

When I coach a new client, I ask them to engage in the core values exercise that's on my website, often during the first session. After clients identify their three core values, I ask how they're feeling. Usually, they say things like, "I feel clearer—this felt good." It's a relief to remember what matters most. However, this awareness can also raise uncomfortable feelings if someone recognizes that they haven't been living into their values. They might sigh and say, "I really value creativity, but I feel like I haven't done anything creative in years."

After I hold space for a client to acknowledge any feelings that arise from engaging in the activity, I ask some of these questions:

- Tell me a story about a time at work when your actions reflected one of these values. What did that look like? How did it feel?
- Tell me about a decision you've recently made that reflects a core value.

After they respond, I'll ask some of these questions:

- Tell me about a time when you didn't demonstrate one of your core values but, in retrospect, you wish you had. What do you think prevented you from enacting it? If you could go back in time and do it over, what would you do differently?
- Tell me how your calendar reflects your core values.

How we spend money and spend time (and who we spend time with) often reflects the degree to which we're living into core values. It can be uncomfortable to see discrepancies between our aspirational values and our lived values. As a coach, when we help a client recognize that gap—there are gaps for most of us—and we can acknowledge and normalize the feelings of sadness, disappointment, frustration, and fear that might arise from this recognition. And then we can coach toward closing that gap.

In the first conversation with a client about their core values, I might also ask these questions:

- Tell me about your process for determining those core values. What insights did you get into yourself in your exploration of your values?
- How do you feel when you recognize that you're enacting a core value? How do you register those emotions? Do you notice sensations in your body or specific thoughts?
- How can I help you live into your core values?

Maybe you're wondering if you should share your values with your clients. Most of the time, clients just want to be heard—they're less interested in you than you think they are. So I usually only share my values if my client asks me. Remember that every second you're talking is a second when your client isn't talking—and whoever is doing the talking is doing the learning. If your client continues to ask you questions about yourself, then answer to the degree that you're comfortable. Some people build trust in others through knowing information about them.

Once I know a client's core values, I write them on the first page of the notebook I use for them and commit them to memory. Then I listen for how my client lives their core values. When a client isn't aligned with their values, they might blame other people or disparage themselves, and in that blame and disparagement I hear that they aren't being who they want to be. For example, a teacher I was coaching said, "Sixth period was out of control today. I was already having a bad day because I didn't sleep last night. We didn't get through anything."

I said, "Sounds like a rough day—I know that when I don't sleep everything is so much harder. I also know that one of your core values is responsibility. How do you feel like you lived into that value today?"

Coaching core values can sound like:

- Tell me how the way you've been spending your time reflects, or doesn't reflect, your values.
- I'm hearing you describe a day that went really well. Which of your core values do you recognize that you were enacting?
- I know that one of your core values is kindness. I just observed you shout at a student. How do you make sense of this breakdown between who you want to be and your actions?
- What are the opportunities next week for you to live into your values? Can you anticipate a specific situation when you'll have an opportunity to intentionally enact one of them?
- I hear that you were really triggered by her behavior. Do you think any of your core values felt violated?
- I know that one of your core values is _____. I'm hearing you express a belief that seems like a conflict with that value. I'm curious whether you see that?

Identifying values is relatively quick. Giving them the time, energy, and space to bring them to life takes time and effort. We are habitual creatures, and we get pulled into behaviors that may not be aligned with our values.

A simple first step is to post values where they can be seen—on an office wall, notebook, or phone. You can do this with your own values and encourage your clients to do the same. Then talk about them with friends, colleagues, coaches—with anyone. The purpose is to remember to use core values as a filter to make decisions about the actions we take; the goal is alignment between someone's vision for who they want to be and the behaviors they take every day.

Just as it is for our clients, it can be painful to recognize when you're living out of alignment with your values or to notice your values changing. Sometimes, before you are aware of it, a value begins to shift. This can lead to confusion or frustration: just beneath the surface of your awareness, you're changing, but you're still being an older version of yourself—acting on outdated values. The moments when you recognize the discrepancies between who you are being and who you want to be are opportunities for growth.

Core values can change, so it's useful to revisit the core values exercise and reflection process every 6 to 12 months. For about a decade, my core values were compassion, community, and justice. Then, one year, I realized that my ultimate commitment is to *liberation* of the mind, heart, body, and spirit—liberation of the individual and the collective. I define liberation as the experience of self-realization or self-actualization, as the ability of an individual and a community to express their full potential. Justice, the value that I aligned with for so many years, is a necessary prerequisite for liberation, but it's not, I came to see, my end goal.

Contemplating the relationship between justice and liberation led me to recognize a connection between liberation and *transcendence*—and to see that transcendence is my ultimate aspiration. Transcendence is a philosophical and spiritual concept that means to go beyond. But beyond what? My commitment to transcendence means that I'm curious about what this all could mean—I'm drawn to the unknown. It means that I want to write books for educators that take us beyond what we assume to be possible; it means that I engage with creativity as a portal to something else; it means that I explore personal relationships outside of conventional roles and labels; it means that I move toward the paradox of seeking that which is unknowable.

As I write this book, I try to align with three core values: liberation, transcendence, and compassion.

What I hope you read is that the process of exploring core values led me into a meaningful reflection. It also spurred me to make concrete changes to my daily life and schedule. Recently, I was scheduling a therapy appointment— therapy for me is an essential pathway toward self-awareness and understanding and therefore to liberation and transcendence. The time my therapist had available conflicted with a meeting I had scheduled. A couple years ago, I would have skipped therapy that week because I wouldn't have wanted to change what was already scheduled; this time I accepted the appointment and changed my previously scheduled meeting. It felt good to make a values-aligned decision and to make it without inner turmoil.

When to bring core values into a coaching session:

- When a client is making a decision
- When a client is distressed or conflicted
- When a client feels successful about something—to invite reflection on how they lived their values
- To facilitate deeper insight into who someone is, who they want to be, and who they are being

How to use core values with a client:

- Introduce them at the start of a coaching relationship.
- Use them to guide your client to align their behaviors and beliefs to their aspirational values.
- Invite your client to reflect on how they're living their values.

Coaching Personality Traits

Adi often described herself as a "Type A." She'd use this label to explain why she was so hard on herself or to justify her "perfectionism." When we first met, she also told me that she was "high strung," and that's why during our sessions she preferred to pace her office and give me her desk chair. "This is just who I am," she'd say. "It's my personality."

I was interested in personality types and how typing systems provided quick insights into who someone was, or at least how they saw themselves. But I found that Adi thought about her personality as fixed ("this is just who I am") and avoided acknowledging strong emotions, like fear, by writing them off as personality traits. The two biggest dangers in working with personality typing systems are considering them to be fixed and allowing them to obscure emotions. With these warnings in mind, we can use an understanding of personality to powerful effect.

What Is Personality?

Personality is a way to describe who we are, which is the compilation of our thoughts, feelings, and behaviors. Our genetic makeup plays a role in our personalities, as do our life experiences and environmental factors, and then there's also the great mystery of our innate dispositions and inclinations that can't be directly attributed to nature or nurture. Personality is developed in childhood and can change over a lifetime, although it usually remains relatively consistent in adulthood.

Attempts to classify personality abound. The Myers-Briggs Type Index can offer insights, as can the Enneagram, a psycho-spiritual personality typing system. However, I recommend these and all systems with the qualification that they are incomplete. Because typing systems are too simplistic to account for the complexity of being a human, they can obscure psychological needs that deserve attention.

Adi recognized sometime after we started working together that the anxiety she experienced was negatively impacting her life. "I thought this was just who I am," she said. "I've always been called a Type A. I didn't think it was anxiety." The notion of a "Type A" personality (competitive, organized, high strung, workaholic, high achieving) has been debunked by psychologists who identify these traits as maladaptive behaviors or indicators of unhealed parts of ourselves. But talking about psychological wounds, healing, and well-being can feel harder in a professional setting than introducing the concept of personality typing. In this way, personality typing can be an entry point to coaching ways of being.

How to Use Personality Typing in Coaching

Psychologists generally agree on five basic personality traits: openness to experience, conscientiousness, extraversion, agreeableness, and neuroticism. Everyone falls along a continuum on each trait. For example, extraversion is considered the level of energy with which someone interacts with the outside world and other people. This includes someone's general energy, enthusiasm, sociability, and assertiveness. Someone can be more extraverted or more introverted.

As both a coach and a facilitator of learning spaces, I consider extraversion more than any other aspect of personality. It's said that extraverts talk so that they can think, and intraverts think so that they can talk. When I design learning experiences, I'm thoughtful about varying engagement structures so that I meet the needs of different people. Likewise, when I coach, it's helpful for me to consider someone's introversion/extraversion tendency to help them reflect on how they work with their energy, given that energy is a resource we all need to think about renewing.

In recent years, as I've come to understand our psychological makeup more, I've shifted away from using personality typing as much as I once did. However, I still find that any personality taxonomy is an entry point into conversation and deeper knowing of ourselves and others. As long as we remember that we can change and that every system is inherently limited, that no type is better than another, and that we are not defined by our type, we can use any of the personality typing systems that exist for insight and growth.

If you want to invite your client to take a personality test or share their results with you, the opportunity lies in the reflection you facilitate. Here are some questions to get that conversation started:

- How does this personality test, or the results, help you understand yourself?
- Given your results, what are the implications for you in your role?
- What do you see as areas for growth, given your results?
- What does this personality test not explain about who you are? What additional questions come up about yourself?
- What would you like me to do, or do differently as your coach, given what you've learned about yourself from this personality test?

Whether it's a personality type, an astrological chart, a scientific theory, or a specific ideology, we all use systems to make sense of the baffling experience of being human. As a coach, your job is to see the world as your client sees it so that you can help them navigate it and expand their perspective. While any given system might provide insight into who people are, the greatest value will be in what your clients say about the results and how those results help them think about themselves.

Coach the Person, Not the Problem

When Adi began describing the pushback she was getting from teachers, I could have coached her to respond to their behavior. I could have begun with any of the following:

- Tell me more about how you rolled out the initiative.
- What do you think teachers heard and felt when you described the initiative?
- What do teachers know about why Black and Brown kids' reading scores are often lower than those of kids from other racial groups? Might you think about providing some PD on systemic oppression?

- Sometimes teachers push back when they've experienced a lot of change. What could you do to assuage their fear?
- Have you thought about trying . . . ?

These questions wouldn't have been wrong, but the focus would have been on the situation, on the problem. In contrast, I centered Adi's way of being. By honing in on a way of being, we start in the sphere where our client has the most influence or even control. Furthermore, when we coach the person and not the problem, we express trust in our client's ability to solve their problems. In doing so, we honor their agency. Maybe for Adi the "problem" was teacher pushback, but the solution would emerge when she could anchor in who she wanted to be and then act from that place.

When we work from who we want to be, we are compelled toward a vision. In contrast, when we work to address a problem, we are reacting to what is. When we are reactive, when we're just responding to problems over and over, and our energy is finite. Problems are draining. When we work towards a vision, we're compelled by a new reality. We have a lot more energy available when we're inspired by what we can create. Coaching the person and not their problems allows a client to reconnect with their power, and when we guide an empowered client to align their intentions and behaviors to the needs of children, we're transforming the world.

There's a final reason why I encourage you to coach the person—and that's because by doing so you'll meet your own core human need for connection. Often my favorite coaching sessions are those in which I'm coaching someone around their way of being. Those conversations get into the nooks and crannies of what it means to be human, and they're deeply satisfying for both me and my client.

Many years after coaching Adi, I ran into her at a conference. We were both so happy to see each other and our catch-up began right where we'd left off—in an exploration of who she was being and who she had become. Her present-day circumstances (and problems) didn't feel relevant; I didn't need her to fill me in on the details. I know that Adi appreciated the conversation, and I left feeling energized, connected, and purposeful, as well as feeling a sense of competence.

Coaching is a reciprocal experience—sometimes I feel like I get just as much from a conversation as my clients do. When they thank me, I thank them back. I really mean it—I feel honored to be part of their process, I am grateful for their trust, and my need for meaning is more than met.

Pause and Process

Reflect:

- Were there parts of this chapter that you disagreed with? If so, imagine a conversation in which you coach yourself around that disagreement.
- How does the kind of coaching described in this chapter compare to the kind of coaching you've been doing?
- What's one thing you'd like to try doing as a coach based on what you read in this chapter?

Next steps:

- Listen to *Bright Morning Podcast* episode 28 in which I coached an assistant principal on her core values.
- Download "Coaching a Client on Their Core Values" from my website.
- During coaching conversations over the next week or two, jot down every time you hear a client share a problem that you're tempted to coach, and reflect on how you can shift to coach the person.
- Download and complete "A Cloze Script for the Legacy Question" from my website. This activity will provide you with a concrete example of how to evoke an aspirational way of being in a coaching conversation.

CHAPTER 11

How to Coach Beliefs

Change the Story, Change the Reality

Common misconception:	*Transformational Coaches know:*
I need to call out problematic beliefs wherever I see them.	It takes time and trust to change beliefs, and it's my job to invest in both.

Diana had taught at Eastside Elementary for almost 30 years when I began coaching her. She also lived in the community and had sent her sons to local schools, and her husband was a police officer in the city. When our district adopted a new approach to teaching English Language Development (ELD), she was eager for support and responded to my offer of coaching. Diana was of Lakota and Black descent. Her fifth graders were predominantly Black, although increasingly she taught English Learners from Mexico and Central America. She was committed to meeting those students' needs.

Diana's classroom was traditional in some senses—spelling tests on Fridays, monthly book report assignments, and seasonal decor. But she also created science units that had students collecting and analyzing water from local creeks, history units in which students interviewed older community members, and art projects in which students worked with found objects. Her rapport with students seemed warm and caring; parents respected her and advocated for their children to be in her class.

I was surprised, then, when I observed her teaching for the first time one fall afternoon, that she handed packets of coloring pages to a small group of students. The class was working in stations so that Diana could pull a group of English Learners with whom she was using the new instructional strategies. This was what I was present to observe and offer feedback on, but I was distracted by the group of fifth graders who colored. As Michaela opened the stapled packet, I saw her glance over at the group who were engaged in a cooperative math project, sigh, and drop her head.

"Would you rather be at that station?" I asked her as I grabbed an extra chair to sit on.

"Of course," she said, "coloring is for kindergarteners."

"Well, you'll do that activity at some point, right?" I asked.

She shook her head and sighed again. "We don't get to do that kind of math. We get worksheets." Michaela registered my look of confusion. "We're the dummy group," she said in a tone that implied how obvious it was. "We color, and then we do adding and minusing, and then we write the spelling words over and over. That's what the Apples do in station time." The other four students at her table nodded.

"Each of our groups has a name," said Israel. "We're the Apples. They're the Peaches," he pointed at the group at the math station.

"Peaches think they're better than us," Michaela said as she looked down and her shoulders slumped over.

"My brother was an Apple too. We're in the same group all year." He began carefully coloring within the lines of a cityscape. "I like doing art, so it's okay. I'm going to give this one to my grandma 'cause she puts them up on the wall."

Michaela shrugged. "I think it's boring," she said. "I wish I was from Guatemala so I could be with Mrs. D."

"Do Apples ever get to work with Mrs. D?" I'd seen the rotation schedule, which suggested each group got time with her.

"Sometimes," Michaela said. "But we just show her our packets, and she talks to us about things like how we have to study hard in school and not get in trouble and not take drugs." A flash of anger crossed Michaela's face.

"Mrs. D's nice," Israel said. The other students nodded. "She was my dad's teacher when he was in third grade."

Michaela laughed. "That's how come she's always saying to you, 'Don't follow in your daddy's footsteps.'" Israel's brows furrowed.

Diana looked over at me at this point, perhaps wondering if I was going to make it to observe her group. "I got to get over there," I said to the Apples. "I'm sorry that this is boring for you, Michaela."

I tried focusing on how Diana incorporated the ELD strategies, but I couldn't stop replaying what I'd seen and heard with the Apples. I felt like I'd stumbled on the brazen tracking of students, that I'd witnessed what happens when a teacher's low expectations of students drive her behaviors. Sitting behind a few learners at the ELD station, I wondered what beliefs were driving this seemingly inequitable classroom structure. Whatever they were, I thought, these beliefs impacted not only the Apples but also the rest of her students who were surely aware of the status of different groups in the classroom. I thought about the broader cultural tensions between the Black community and the Mexican and Central American immigrant community. It seemed like Diana's choices could exacerbate those broader social divisions.

As I left her room, I felt a wave of sadness—I'd had the impression that Diana was a model teacher. I wanted to just stay in my lane and coach her through ELD standards like enunciating, frontloading vocabulary, and avoiding idioms. Diana had been in the district for 20 years longer than I had and was decades older than I was. But Michaela's resigned expression kept coming to mind, and I knew I'd need to raise my observations with Diana; I hoped I could help her explore the roots of her beliefs and shift them.

Where do I start? I wondered as I walked across the playground to my car.

Research conducted on patients receiving medical treatment concludes unequivocally that the more that patients trust the doctor, the better their outcome will be. This is the most important variable—more than the doctor's years of experience or the particular treatments or medications. Prognosis is determined by evaluating the patient's confidence in the doctor's skills and care. Some elements of this analogy transfer to coaching: your client must trust you if you're going to help them change, and this is never truer than when you are coaching beliefs.

To effectively coach beliefs, you need to do the following:

- Build, maintain, and repair trust with a client.
- Understand what beliefs are, how they develop, and the neuroscience of working with beliefs.
- Recognize when beliefs are driving behavior problematically.
- Guide a client into seeing their beliefs and the impact they have on themselves and others.
- Guide a client to deconstruct beliefs and construct new beliefs.

As we explore these skill and knowledge sets, I'll return to the story about Diana and the Apples, and I hope you'll see again how behaviors, beliefs, and ways of being are entwined. But first, let's take a look at what beliefs are and how we can recognize problematic ones.

Recognizing Beliefs

The first step in working with beliefs is noticing when they are present. Here are some common stories, which reflect underlying beliefs, that I've heard teachers tell—and that I sometimes told myself when I was a teacher:

- If I could just close my door and do what I know how to do, I could stay in this field.
- I'm not going to put a ton of effort into learning this curriculum. In two years, there'll be a new fad, and we'll be told to drop this curriculum and teach something new.
- There's a limit to what I can do given all that these kids are dealing with in their homes and communities.
- I can't do anything without parents questioning and challenging me. They feel entitled to tell me how to teach.

Can you identify stories you told as a teacher, or that you're telling now, about your situation? Consider stories that empower you—that move you toward your values and the legacy you want to leave—and stories that drain you and make you feel disempowered. Sometimes we can identify our stories by completing these statements:

If only . . . (name something that you want to be different)
then . . . (name what you'd be able to do or feel).

For example, I used to tell this story: If only this district had stable, competent leadership, then we'd be able to make huge strides in meeting the needs of children. This story I told myself was my belief at the time.

What Is a Belief?

A belief is an opinion, a thought, or a story. It's the words in our mind that make meaning about the things that happen. People need beliefs; if we aren't able to make meaning from our experience, life is very hard. What's key is becoming aware of the impact that the beliefs we hold have on ourselves and on others.

I use *story* and *belief* synonymously. It's easy to identify a belief when someone uses the phrase "I think . . ." or "Well, I just believe . . ." or even "I know that . . ." When you hear clients use these phrases, note that you're hearing a belief. When I bring up a client's beliefs, I often use the language of stories. I might ask, "What is the story you are telling yourself?" or "How does that story shape your understanding of . . . ?"

Beliefs Create Behaviors

All of our actions are born from beliefs. When I taught middle school, I started most days by welcoming my students at the door and greeting them by name. I did this because I believed that my relationship with students was foundational to their learning, and I believed that connecting with them as they entered the room strengthened our relationship. Beliefs can shape behaviors for better or for worse. When I was a central office administrator, I had to attend meetings that I believed were irrelevant and purposeless. During those meetings, my mind wandered or I multitasked. My distracted, disengaged behavior reflected my beliefs.

Take a moment to identify some beliefs that shape your behaviors. It can be easier to identify and work with beliefs—your own and others'—if you refrain from judging them. Identifying the causal relationship between your beliefs and behaviors may be easier if you can approach them with an open curiosity.

When I observed Diana give the Apples the coloring sheet, I suspected she was acting on beliefs about student deficits that needed unpacking. I also noted that some decisions she made, such as working with English Learners in small groups and taking kids to collect water from local creeks, seemed to indicate a contradictory belief that her students had a lot of potential. Human beings are a tangle of contradictions. Sometimes the pathway to freedom appears from recognizing and accepting these contradictions, aligning our beliefs, or releasing some beliefs that no longer serve us or others.

Unpacking Helpful and Harmful Stories

The stories we tell can serve our well-being, or they can undermine us; they can enable us to serve others, or they can hamper our willingness and ability to do so. When we coach others on their beliefs well, we extend an invitation for transformation. Trust increases the likelihood that our clients will accept such an invitation—but trust is not enough. To choose to shift beliefs, people need to explore and come to an understanding about the impact of their beliefs.

When we talk about the impact of the stories we tell ourselves, we consider *the impact on ourselves* and *on others*. Sometimes we might notice a contradiction—we might recognize that the stories we tell inadvertently harm ourselves. When we explore stories, we must make space for all of them, including the contradictions. As clients begin sharing their stories and as they recognize their inner conflict, you may find yourself thinking, *What's wrong with you!? Don't you see that you're a big pile of contradictions?* Remember that you, too, are probably a pile of contradictions. Then get curious about what's going on inside of them (and inside yourself).

Impact on Emotions

Impact can be evaluated on a number of levels, but it's often useful to start with the innermost level—the emotional terrain. As you read the following statements, notice how they make you feel. See if you can read and respond to them quickly, as if you were flipping TV channels. Don't linger on a statement or its corresponding emotion. Read, pause for a second or two, notice the feeling, and then go to the next one.

- I will never find someone who loves me.
- I'm not good at anything.

- I've made so many mistakes in my life.
- I have friends who care about me.
- I'm good at what I do.
- I trust the timing of my life.
- I am loved.

I hope that you were able to see how thoughts have a quick, immediate, and sometimes intense impact on your emotions. (If you feel any kind of heaviness right now, stand up and stretch or jump or take some long, deep breaths.) In fact, our beliefs give rise to our emotions and our sense of what's possible. If I hold a belief that I'm not worthy of love, then I have limited what is possible: I may not be receptive to love and care, and I may not recognize love when it's present. If I hold a belief that I can find a job in which I can thrive, I make space for such an outcome: I'll be more inclined to figure out what kind of job that might be, to look for such a job, and to recognize it when I see it.

Think of a belief related to your work that feels alive for you right now. It could be something like, *I believe I can help a lot of students in this role* or *I can feel fulfilled in this job* or *I'm not working from my core values in this position*. Now ask yourself: What's possible if this is the belief I hold? See if you can engage in this reflection without judging yourself for the belief.

When we recognize that we hold a particular belief—and what is or is not possible when we hold it—we can make intentional choices around the belief. We can find the motivation to shift beliefs that aren't serving us, and we can root more deeply in the beliefs that are. Affirmations, or mantras, are statements of belief. People repeat mantras to help ground themselves in a belief. When our minds default into a fearful, disempowered state, mantras pull us back. This is why some people repeat mantras or affirmations as part of a daily morning practice, write them on sticky notes and leave them around their office, or perhaps tattoo them on their body, as I've done—inked on my right forearm is my reminder to *Be here now*. This mantra brings me back to the belief that presence and awareness is a first step to making intentional choices, choices that allow me to live the kind of life I want to live.

Beliefs are not inherently good or bad. They can help us thrive, or they can undermine our well-being and the well-being of others. The next step after recognizing beliefs we hold is to determine the impact that our stories have on us, as well as on the people around us.

The Stories Diana Told

The day after I observed Diana's ELD small group instruction, I sat down with her at her kidney-shaped table to debrief. When I asked Diana about the students in the Apples group, she shook her head. "The odds are stacked against them," she explained. "And the stack is so high. I know their parents, their siblings, the streets they live on. I know the challenges they're facing. I'm just being realistic."

I'd heard stories like this before, and I knew this story served as a defense for Diana, blocking feelings of sadness, fear, and anger. As Diana told herself that she was prioritizing other students' learning needs because of what the students in the Apples were facing, she was setting herself up to not be disappointed by what she imagined would be their future.

"I used to be less naïve," Diana told me. "I used to think I could save them all. But after 30 years, one sobers up."

I tucked these statements away as I packed up that day, knowing that I had work to do. If I coached Diana solely on her instructional practices, we wouldn't be able to get to the underlying mental models from which she made decisions. I also knew that I needed to do more than just coach Diana on her ways of being. To support Diana to be who she wanted to be, I needed to guide her to surface and name the beliefs that drove her decision-making and to see how those conflicted with who she wanted to be. Then I would have to help her to shift those beliefs.

One afternoon when Diana and I were meeting, Michaela came into the class to get homework she'd forgotten. "You know, that little girl could be something," Diana said after Michaela left. She shook her head. "She's forgetful, but she's sharp."

"What's the story you really want to tell about Michaela?" I asked.

"I want to say she's got potential," Diana replied.

"If that was the belief you held about her, what might be possible?" I asked.

"Elena, I don't have low expectations for her," Diana said. "I'm just realistic."

"Okay, but imagine with me. If you believed that she had potential, what might be possible? What actions might you take?"

Diana sighed. "I suppose I'd be more curious about her. Maybe pay attention to what she does well and what she likes."

"Say more. What else?"

"I guess I'd give her more challenging work."

"What about station time?"

"I guess I would give more thought to what her group does during station time."

I nodded and paused.

"Diana, what's the story you're currently telling about Michaela? The story that drives your actions?"

"It's a realistic story. It's that there's not much I can do to help her have a good life. It's that she's not going to make it." Diana's voice caught, and she pinched her lips.

"That's a painful story to tell," I said.

"It's just realistic," Diana said.

"Yes, you've said that a number of times. And I want to challenge you. This is a belief you're operating from. What's the impact of that belief on Michaela and the Apples?"

Diana was silent for what felt like a long time. Finally, she looked at me and said, "I'm contributing to this fate that I see for them. That's the impact." Her tone was monotone and low.

"Is this the story you want to keep telling?" I asked.

"No, but the other stories feel hard."

"Say more."

"I'm tired of the heartbreak. I'm tired of seeing my old students on the streets, selling drugs, having babies at 16."

I nodded. "That's really hard. And it takes a toll."

"Do you know how many funerals I've been to of former students?" Diana leaned back and locked her arms over her chest.

I shook my head.

Diana broke eye contact. "Listen, Elena. I know I'm heartbroken and cynical."

I took a deep breath. "Those feelings deserve attention, Diana." I took in Diana's facial expressions, attempting to interpret how she was receiving my coaching at this moment. "And you know, it *is* possible to process them and release some of the intensity." Diana looked at me for a moment and then looked away again. "I'm not telling you what to think or do," I continued. "I am just hoping to help you reconnect to the part of you that is hopeful—that sees who Michaela could be."

"I feel like I'm out of ideas for how to teach the Apples."

"I could help you with that, if you want."

"I'm tired of seeing myself fail," Diana said.

"That's a limiting belief to hold," I said. "That's hard."

"I feel like I've been failing for 30 years," Diana said.

"That's also really painful." I paused. "Diana, what do you want to believe?"

"That I don't give up on kids."

"You get to choose what you believe." I paused for a few long seconds. "It seems like you've been working from a belief in which you are powerless. And you're recognizing the impact that's had on you and your kids." I took a slow breath. "So again, what do you want to believe?"

"I need to pray on this," Diana said. "I hear what you're saying." She exhaled loudly, shook her head, and said she wanted to wrap up our meeting.

When we met the following week, Diana opened our session saying that she'd given a lot of thought to our conversation, and she'd decided she wanted to have different beliefs about the Apples. "I don't want to talk about this today," she said, "but you should know that I'm willing to change."

I smiled. "When do you think you want to talk about it?" I asked.

"I don't know. But in the meantime, you can help me figure out what the Apples can do so that they don't bother the class while we're in station time but so they are doing something that's not coloring."

"Sounds good," I said.

Naming the Stories

I recognized Diana's story about the inevitability of Michaela's fate because I'd heard it before. In fact, many of the stories we tell that hold us back from being the educators and humans we want to be fall into a few common categories.

The Drama Triangle: Victim, Villain, and Hero Stories

In the 1960s, psychologist Stephen Karpman outlined the *Drama Triangle* to help understand patterns of relationships under stress (Figure 11.1). This model posits that when we experience emotional distress or conflict, either with another person or internally, we take on the role of victim, villain, or hero (also referred to as rescuer).

In the victim role, we feel helpless, hopeless, ashamed, powerless, and misunderstood. We avoid responsibility and making decisions, and we seek a hero to validate our feelings and solve our problems. We complain and blame others. We feel unsupported and act from self-pity. When we're in the victim role, we often blame villains for our situation.

In the role of villain, or persecutor, we are critical and judgmental. We blame others, use guilt to control, and feel like being right is the most important thing. We feel superior to others, have unreasonable expectations, and intimidate and bully others.

In the role of hero or rescuer, we are martyrs, enablers, or people-pleasers. We feel responsible for others and their problems, we sacrifice ourselves for the sake of others, we rescue others so that we feel capable, and we feel guilty when other people's problems can't be solved. In the hero

Figure 11.1: The Drama Triangle

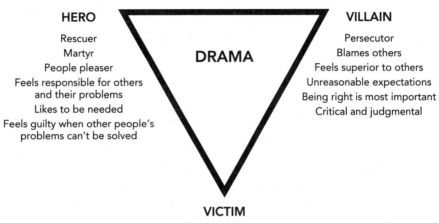

based on Stephen Karpman's work

HERO
Rescuer
Martyr
People pleaser
Feels responsible for others
and their problems
Likes to be needed
Feels guilty when other people's
problems can't be solved

DRAMA

VILLAIN
Persecutor
Blames others
Feels superior to others
Unreasonable expectations
Being right is most important
Critical and judgmental

VICTIM
Feels powerless and misunderstood
Avoids taking responsibility and making a decision
Complains and blames others / villains
Feels helpless, hopeless, and ashamed
Seeks a hero

role, we don't recognize other people's capacity to solve their own problems. We like to be needed, but by putting others ahead of our needs, we end up feeling exhausted and resentful.

Perhaps, as you read these descriptions, you've recognized a role that you tend to play, or maybe you noticed that you play all three roles well. Context can influence which role we slip into: Perhaps at work, you're more likely to take on the hero role with those you coach—until an unwelcome change is made in your work assignment. Then you shift into the victim role, blaming admin for your distress. Then when you get home, you become the villain when you see that, once again, your husband didn't load the dishwasher correctly.

When I'm coaching and I hear someone struggling, I listen for where they are on the Drama Triangle—because the role they play writes the story they tell. I'd estimate that most of the teachers I've coached tell victim stories when distressed. Leaders, on the other hand, tell villain or hero stories. And coaches are prone to victim and hero stories.

Recall what you've learned so far about Diana and the stories she told. In which role had she cast herself on the Drama Triangle? What narrative characterized the stories she told? In my conversations with Diana, I found that she, like so many teachers, tended to tell victim stories: that there was nothing she could do; she was powerless in the face of the realities in which her students lived and the fate she'd decided was theirs.

Imagine that you have an electronic device inside your mind that blasts an alert when someone you're coaching lapses into a victim story. A Transformational Coach constantly listens for indicators of victim consciousness. Once this ability is strong in you, you'll be able to offer strategies to invite someone to shift out of victim mode and into their own agency. Awareness always comes first: you need to know when someone is in victim consciousness to interrupt it.

The best way to recognize when you're in the presence of a victim story is to know it in yourself. As you begin recognizing when you tell victim stories, you'll more readily hear when other people do. Start by recalling a recent time when you felt frustrated or distressed. Where were you on the Drama Triangle? How do you know that's where you were?

River or Rut Stories

Another way of thinking about the stories we tell (or the beliefs we hold) comes from leadership coach Robert Hargrove, who distinguishes between "river" and "rut" stories. Rut stories, Hargrove explains, are those in which we get stuck and feel powerless; they cut us off from other people and our potential. River stories allow us to feel open, connected, and optimistic; they reflect a commitment to growth, learning, and perseverance. When we're anywhere on the Drama Triangle, we're probably telling a rut story.

This metaphor of rivers and ruts can help you tune into the beliefs that a client holds. Do those beliefs feel like they're keeping your client from living into their values, being who they want to be, or impacting the world as they aspire to? Or do their beliefs enable them to flow with their life's purpose, their dreams, and their desires? Sometimes I start evaluating beliefs by listening for whether I'm hearing a river or a rut story; then if I hear a rut story, I consider where the storyteller might be on the Drama Triangle.

How We Exit the Drama Triangle

To get out of the Drama Triangle and away from the stories that undermine us, we need to shift our beliefs. This process often begins by taking responsibility for the impact of our beliefs—and by feeling the emotions that swirl around both the beliefs and our recognition of the impacts. That's what we'll explore in the rest of this chapter, but first I want you to know that it *is* possible to get out of rut stories and out of the roles we play on the triangle.

Furthermore, not only can we exit the Drama Triangle, we can transform the role we played. There's a positive correlate to the Drama Triangle—the Empowerment Dynamic, created by executive coach David Emerald Womeldorff, which helps us imagine what is possible. In this model, victims can become *creators* who own our power to make choices and respond to our situation. Heroes become *coaches* who facilitate others' growth. Villains transform into *challengers*, who provoke or evoke action. This framework of empowerment suggests new stories to tell when we're stuck on one side of the triangle.

Exploring Beliefs

Table 11.1, the Exploring Beliefs Framework, lays out the steps and components of exploring beliefs with a client. Know that when you're coaching someone and exploring their beliefs, you don't necessarily need to ask all of the questions associated with each step—sometimes a few is enough.

Table 11.1: Exploring Beliefs Framework

Step	Facilitative Questions to Ask Client	Directive Questions to Ask Client
Cultivate Curiosity	<ul><li>What's the story you're telling?</li><li>Is it empowering or disempowering?</li><li>Does it help or harm you or others?</li><li>How does this story make you feel?</li><li>How could you release some of the emotions attached to this story?</li><li>What's possible if you tell this story?</li><li>Is this story true? How do you know if it's true?</li></ul>	<ul><li>It sounds like you're telling a victim story. Does that resonate for you?</li><li>If you tell a victim story, what's possible in this situation?</li><li>I'm hearing a lot of grief and anger in what you're sharing. Would you be willing to feel those feelings so you can release them?</li><li>You're harming yourself with this story you're telling. Are you consciously choosing this?</li></ul>
Activate Possibility	<ul><li>What would be possible if you abandoned this story?</li><li>Who would you be without the story?</li><li>How would you feel without the story?</li></ul>	<ul><li>I know you're committed to living into your values. Are you able to do that if you hold this story?</li><li>If you hold this story, are you able to meet the needs of every child, every day?</li><li>Are you willing to tell a different story?</li></ul>
Create	<ul><li>What's another story you could tell?</li><li>How would that story make you feel?</li><li>What might be possible if you told that story?</li></ul>	<ul><li>What would it feel like to tell the story that you can meet the needs of your students?</li><li>What would it be like to tell a story in which you have agency?</li><li>What would it take for you to be willing to tell the story that you can be successful in this role?</li></ul>

Cultivate Curiosity

In the curiosity step, your purpose is to motivate your client to explore their beliefs. When you take the facilitative stance, you give your client a great deal of agency to move into an exploration, and you create that agency through attempting to cultivate a sense of hopefulness and clarity. Take the directive stance only if you are sure that a great deal of trust exists between you and your client, as directive questions can be received as confrontational (see Chapter 5, "Fifty Questions to Ask").

When you are working in the curiosity step, you may need to shift into strategies to coach ways of being, particularly around emotions, as strong feelings of sadness, fear, anger, or shame can arise. If your client isn't able to access their curiosity, it's because one of these difficult emotions is in the way, and/or they don't trust you.

As you ask the questions to help your client get curious and explore their beliefs, pay close attention to your client's body language and facial expressions—you are constantly evaluating their trust in you. If you notice anything that gives you pause, you can say something like, "I want to check in on how that question I just asked landed. How did you receive it?" Or you could say, "Let me clarify that my intention behind these questions is to help you feel more empowered and aligned with who you want to be. If any of my questions don't feel good, feel free to let me know."

Activate Possibility

In this step, you communicate hope and optimism. Your tone and energy should reflect these orientations as you remind your client that there is another way to think, another set of beliefs from which to source action. You are trying, again, to compel someone to consider shifting a story, and you are indicating that you know such a shift is possible. In essence, you are coaching possibility. Whenever you ask a client to imagine there is another way, you must believe it to be true—so ask yourself whether you truly do. What do you believe about people's ability to change beliefs?

As with the previous step, resistance to this step may indicate that your client has emotions that need to be released, and/or that they don't trust you. Be sure that you're not trying to activate possibility with toxic positivity—make sure you're not denying your client's need to experience and process negative emotions. Resist the temptation to force false optimism.

Create New Stories

When you coach your client to create new stories, you slow down. You communicate patience with the process as you gently nudge your client to write new stories. Sometimes, a client struggles to create a new story because difficult emotions block their creativity or because they haven't had much practice writing stories that serve them and support their work. If they are unable to generate alternate beliefs, you can offer suggestions. This can sound like:

- How would it feel if you told the story that Michaela *does* have a chance?
- What if Michaela does graduate from high school and gets a job she likes and ends up having a life in which she's satisfied and content? If you knew that was her future, what story would you tell about her?
- Try this: *I believe that Michaela can be successful in school and can have a meaningful, healthy life.* What would it feel like to tell that story?

It's okay for you to plant an idea in your clients' minds, as long as you are not attached to the idea. They need to be able to reject the stories you offer and land on their own, or stay in disempowerment if they choose. Remember, you always coach toward agency and honor your clients' sovereignty—even if their choice is to stay in victim consciousness. However, if you are a principal or positional leader, this doesn't mean you resign yourself to having someone on staff who is stuck in a victim story and who doesn't serve students well. You can accept that someone chooses to tell disempowering stories and that they are not a good fit for the vision you are implementing at your site.

When you coach toward new beliefs, you help someone identify concrete data points that can be the basis for their new story. We'll explore this more in the next chapter, but the core idea is that all of our beliefs are built on a selection of data. Diana believed that Michaela's fate would be dismal because she had seen many former students end up in tragic places. Diana also cited unemployment statistics and high-school graduation rates for the community, and these data points also led her to believe that Michaela would not be successful in life.

A few weeks after Diana told me she was willing to have different beliefs about the Apples and after we'd planned some small group activities for students during station time, I opened up a conversation about her beliefs.

"Diana, would you be willing to reflect on Michaela's strengths?"

"I was going to tell you that on Tuesday, during independent reading, Michaela was reading a chapter book. I hadn't noticed her reading it before, and she was almost halfway through. I was doubtful that she understood it—I thought it was too difficult for her—but she gave me a very accurate summary. I told her I was proud of her."

"Wow, that's amazing. What else did you notice or wonder?"

"When she was reading, she was completely focused. Sometimes I think she gets distracted easily, but her head was buried in that book. To tell you the truth, I feel a little embarrassed to admit that I was surprised. I wonder how I'd never noticed her reading chapter books before."

"What do you think that's about? That you hadn't noticed?"

"I guess I just haven't paid that much attention to her. Maybe because we were talking about her and I realized that sometimes I only think about how to keep her quiet and I just haven't really paid attention to what she does in terms of her academic skills. That sounds horrible when I say it." Diana turned away from me.

I exhaled loudly. "That's a painful realization." I paused. "What else did you notice about Michaela?"

"When I asked her about the book, at first she seemed reluctant to talk to me about it—as if she didn't trust why I was asking her, but then when I asked her which character she liked most, she became excited." Diana laughed. "That little girl could be something if she only focused."

"How does it feel to recognize her potential?" I asked.

"That's what we all want to see, as teachers," Diana said. "A spark for learning. Maybe it's there in Michaela and I haven't seen it."

"Okay, so her comprehension is higher than you'd evaluated, and she's passionate about reading, and maybe she's got a spark for learning. I'm curious what else you've noticed about her since that day when you saw her reading?"

"Yesterday, she was still off-task during math. She was building airplanes with the manipulatives that she was supposed to be using for multiplication." Diana sighed and smiled slightly. "But I guess I also noticed that she was being creative. She was distracting her group, but I think that was because she'd finished the activity quickly."

"Hum, that's interesting," I said. "What else?"

"I've always thought she was bossy," Diana said. "But I was watching her when everyone was getting in line after recess, and she was shouting at some other students—but she was telling them to get in line, that recess was over. I guess I saw that her bossiness could be leadership."

"Wow, that's a big shift in perception," I paused. "I'm curious—you've noticed her leadership tendencies, interest in reading, creativity, and spark. What conclusion are you coming to about Michaela now?"

"There's something there. If she could be more responsible and mature, she could probably be a better student."

"So your belief is that what's blocking her from being successful is irresponsibility and immaturity?"

"Yes," Diana said.

"Would this statement be true: If Michaela became more responsible and mature, then she could be a successful student because she is creative, bright, confident, and a strong reader?"

"Well, yes. When you say it like that, it makes me think that maybe I'm not valuing what she's got going for her. She's only 10, after all. I wasn't very mature when I was 10."

"Okay, so what belief do you want to hold about Michaela?"

Diana looked down at her hands as she rubbed them together. She thought for what felt like a long time. "I would like to believe," Diana began, but I cut her off.

"Diana, let me make a suggestion. See how it feels if you say, 'I believe . . .' Try it."

"Okay, I believe that Michaela can graduate from high school and get a decent job."

"What else?" I said.

"I believe Michaela can make good choices and have a life that's different from the one her older sisters have. I believe Michaela is a child who has great potential." Diana sighed loudly.

I let her words sink in. "What does it feel like to say that?" I asked.

"It's good. And it's scary. This is what I want to believe, Elena. I'm not a cynical person. It feels good to think that could be how I feel about Michaela."

"If you held that belief, how would it affect the way you relate to Michaela or teach her?"

"Oh," Diana smiled. "I think I'd be very different. I'd definitely push her reading—there's another chapter book I think she'd like. I'd assign her to be a group leader and create a plan with her so that she can remember her homework. I'd be more patient with her, and I'd work with her to regulate herself when she gets frustrated."

"Those are a lot of great ideas. And they seem like things you know how to do given your experience."

"Of course I do," Diana said. "I don't know why I haven't done some of those things with Michaela."

"Because you didn't believe Michaela can be successful in school," I said.

Diana turned away from me. I was beginning to recognize when she'd had enough and needed to process alone. "Let's continue this conversation next time," I said. "I want to suggest we end a little early and you can think about how to put some of those ideas into action with Michaela." Diana nodded in agreement.

Trust the Process

Beliefs take time to change. It's one thing to recognize that you're telling an unhelpful story, and to desire change—it's another thing to tell a new story and to act on it. I'd estimate it took Diana a month or so to shift into a new phase of beliefs, a phase in which she was willing to try out some new beliefs, and then a couple more months for her behaviors to really shift.

Putting a new belief into action will likely require a lot of little changes in behaviors over a period of time, as new neural pathways form. Because our thoughts have likely traveled the old pathways for a while, we need many opportunities to move along new pathways—and to try out corresponding behaviors—before those new routes become routine. Fortunately, there's a lot of information now about how to promote neuroplasticity (the brain's ability to form new neural networks). As we incorporate those practices, we'll find we can change our minds much faster than we once thought.

As you're coaching a client around belief change, pay attention to the emotions that surface *in you*. You may notice impatience arise—which is a form of anger. You may also notice sadness and fear. Be sure to explore those feelings and dig into their origins. Anchoring in humility can also help you during this phase. Remember that you, too, have been stuck in a rut story at some point and that it's a hard place to be. Trust the process—coaching works—and continue building your skills and knowledge so that you can show up fully present for your client.

In my sessions with Diana, I was well aware of the grief she carried about what she'd witnessed in her decades of teaching. But every time I offered her an opportunity to explore those emotions, she pushed back. She'd say things like, "I know I've got some feelings, but I'm not ready to go there." I would thank her for her honesty and tell her that I trusted that when the time was right, she'd explore those feelings.

At the very end of a coaching session in the middle of winter, at exactly 4:59 p.m., Diana said, "Michaela reminds me so much of a little girl I taught in my second year teaching. She was beautiful and bright. I think I even identified with her, like she was a lot like I was at that age. I tutored her after school because she'd moved around a lot and was behind in math. She made so much growth and went off to middle school at grade level. I was really proud. Three years later, she died of a drug overdose." Diana stopped. The tears pooled in her eyes. "That haunts me," Diana said as she stood and picked up her large purse. She stood at the door to the conference room we were using and looked at me.

"You've been holding that for a long time," I said. "Releasing it can't be any harder than what you've been carrying."

"Maybe," Diana said. "And I don't think it's fair to Michaela." Diana turned and closed the door.

As Diana was telling me about the student she'd lost, my own sadness had surged—the grief I held about former students who hadn't lived the lives I hoped they'd live. Doubt had surged in me too—fears that I wasn't being a good coach, that I couldn't help Diana and Michaela.

Trust the process, I told myself. *Trust the coaching, trust Diana, trust in the great mystery of life.*

The following week, Diana canceled our session. The week after that, she began our meeting telling me that she had done some deep "soul searching" and had spent many hours with her pastor. "I cried like I haven't cried since I was a child," she told me. "I let out 30 years of pain, and I prayed, and I let myself remember all my students who have passed on." Diana sighed loudly. "I'm going to change the names of the Apples—that's the name I've given that group of students for a long time. I'll let them pick a new name, because I'm also about to start giving them harder work. They're not going to color anymore."

"I'm really happy to hear all of this, Diana. You look more relaxed or something," I said.

Diana smiled. "I feel younger. I feel like I have new energy."

"I'm so glad," I replied.

"I just had a new student join our class. She's from Guatemala, and she speaks no English or Spanish—only her native language. I was thinking maybe Michaela could be her buddy. Michaela could learn a few strategies to teach English, and I think she'd love to feel like a teacher. Can we talk about this idea?" Diana said.

"Of course. I love it," I replied.

Beliefs can feel like the hardest of the Three Bs to coach, because they can trigger us. But beliefs can also feel like the most rewarding of the Three Bs to coach, because when you see clients shifting their beliefs, the positive impact is so clearly evident. The best way to build your skill in coaching other people's beliefs is to work on surfacing, naming, and shifting your own beliefs. As you understand this process from within, you'll be far more skilled in facilitating it with others. And you'll have a whole lot of empathy and patience for your clients.

Pause and Process

Reflect:

- How have your beliefs about beliefs changed from reading this chapter?
- What feels most challenging to you about coaching beliefs?
- What's a belief about yourself that you'd like to shift? How might you go about that process?

Next steps:

- Listen to *Bright Morning Podcast* episodes 201–205 to hear me bring this content to life, including in a coaching demonstration.
- Download the "Exploring Beliefs Framework" from my website and staple it into your coaching notebook, or keep it somewhere accessible.
- Take note of each time you experience frustration this week. Name the belief—or story—you are telling about the situation. Use Table 11.1 to identify a question to ask yourself to explore your belief(s).

CHAPTER 12

What You Need to Know About Equity

And Why We Must Start with Race

Common misconception: I might need to address inequities at some point.	*Transformational Coaches know:* Every conversation is an equity conversation.

I coached Noah as part of his training to become a principal. After teaching English in high school for eight years, he'd joined a leadership pipeline program that his district was running in an attempt to keep effective teachers with leadership aspirations in the community. Noah is a white man of Ashkenazi Jewish descent from a suburban middle-class background who was in his mid-30s when I coached him.

One of our primary activities was to observe teachers and to plan and practice debrief conversations. The first time we went into a classroom together—an eighth-grade history class taught by a white, female, first-year teacher—I was curious what Noah would notice. I wanted to understand the lens he looked through when observing instruction, so prior to the observation I didn't make any suggestions for what to pay attention to. "Let's just see what we each see," I said.

We observed for 45 minutes, and Noah took pages and pages of notes. While in the classroom, his facial expression was blank. As soon as we walked out, Noah looked at me with a huge smile. "She's doing so much better than I thought," he said. "I'd heard she was struggling. She sends a lot of kids to the office, but I was impressed."

"Tell me more," I said as we walked to a table outside.

"She was organized—I've heard she can be a little scattered—but her materials were prepared, and that packet she gave out was great. I was impressed that she included QR codes for the video clips she showed. She got through the entire lesson, and that's something you don't see new teachers do very often. She was also calm and patient, and I thought she was affirming with students. I'm really looking forward to debriefing with her. I feel like I can offer her feedback that'll boost her up a little."

I was surprised to hear Noah's analysis and conclusions. The summary of my notes included these bullet points: no evidence that students learned anything, disengaged students, and lack of rigor; the teacher only called on white girls, ignored off-task behavior, and didn't respond to the Latino student in the front row who said, "this class is boring as fuck," or to the Black student who said to her neighbor, "Why's this white lady teaching us about slavery?"

What I'd observed was, unfortunately, typical of what I see from unprepared white teachers with low cultural competency who haven't learned much about teaching students of color. The teacher simply had a lot of gaps. What I learned about Noah was that his equity lens was nonexistent, and I suspected that his identity as a white man influenced how he saw the teacher and what was happening in her classroom.

Let me expand on my observations and share some of the assumptions I was making about what I saw in the classroom:

There was little rigor because the teacher has low expectations of students, likely because they are predominantly students of color.

The teacher called on the white girls because she has developed more of a relationship with them, likely because of racial and gender affinity; the teacher feels she can predict their response to her questions and therefore will feel affirmed as a teacher.

The teacher ignored the comments by the Black and Latino students because she's uncomfortable with what she perceives as conflict with students of color and she doesn't know how to build the kinds of relationships with them that would allow her to effectively respond or redirect their behavior.

If I coached this teacher, I'd test my assumptions by asking probing questions to understand her thoughts and decision-making.

Here were some of the wonderings I had around Noah's response to the teacher:

He wanted to "boost her up." Would he have said the same thing about a new male teacher who was older than him? Was Noah unconsciously identifying with the teacher because of their racial affinity and perhaps feeling protective of her for that reason?

What stood out to Noah was her organization. Does this reflect an unconscious belief that students of color need order above other experiences (like rigor) to be successful? That low-level instruction keeps them subdued and controlled?

Noah thought the teacher was "calm and patient." I thought she avoided redirecting behavior and addressing conflict. Does this reflect a difference in how we perceive and respond to the behavior of students of color based on our racial identities?

Noah seemed entirely focused on the teacher moves, but not on the impact on students. Would he have been more attuned to student experiences if he'd shared more identity markers with them?

What I observed in this classroom were many of the hallmarks of educational inequity—low expectations for intellectual engagement or behavior, favoring students with shared identity markers, avoiding conflict with students of color, and avoiding issues that students raised about race and identity. What I heard in Noah's response was not only a lack of awareness about the inequity in the classroom but a lack of awareness of the ways his own identity markers impacted what he saw and how he planned to respond.

Noah didn't see inequities, and so he couldn't interrupt them. He also didn't recognize how his lack of awareness would ultimately exacerbate those inequities if they weren't interrupted.

Why Focus on Racial Equity

To coach for equity, we've got to acquire a basic understanding of identity, power, privilege, racism, and white supremacy. In the same way that the majority of us have never really learned about what emotions are or how to work with them, we also need foundational learning about these complex topics. Even if you already have an equity lens, this knowledge will help you name racial inequities when you see them and feel more confident about interrupting them.

As we learn to coach for equity, we need to start with focusing on race, and then we can learn to understand and interrupt other forms of oppression. Race is a social construct that has no bearings in science. The concept of race, and then racial superiority and then white supremacy, was created to justify the genocide of indigenous peoples, the enslavement of millions of Africans, and an exploitative economic system. Notions of white supremacy were developed hand in hand with the expansion of colonization and capitalism (Kendi, 2016). Racism, as we know it today, wouldn't exist without white supremacy. Racism is based on the ideology that "white people" are superior. When I use the term *white supremacy*, I mean the mindset and belief system of white superiority that has become institutionalized in policy.

For centuries, in the United States and other colonized countries, whiteness granted individuals freedom, allowing them to vote, own property, run for office, live in the suburbs, get a loan, attend certain schools and universities, drink from certain water fountains, sit in the front of the bus, and learn to read. Today, an individual's race is what might get them a job interview (or not), what might allow them to feel safe when camping in a rural area, what might get them pulled over for speeding (or for no reason at all) or thrown in jail, or what might provoke a police officer to shoot an unarmed teenager—and then to be acquitted of that murder. In the United States today, race is the ultimate determinant of a person's livelihood, health, financial success, home ownership, and even life expectancy. In Oakland, California, where I live, a Black man has a life expectancy of 71 years—whereas a white man can expect to live some 87 years (Bohan, 2009).

Almost every corner of this world we live in has been polluted by white supremacy. It manifests in our institutions, systems, and actions, and in our mindsets. White supremacy shows up in our schools and classrooms every day—in public and private classrooms, in classrooms taught by white people and people of color, and in homogeneous and diverse classrooms. It is a dangerous force, in part because it is often invisible. Furthermore, white supremacy has been harmful to people of color and people of European descent; everyone will benefit from dismantling white supremacy.

Beyond a professional commitment, we all need to learn more about white supremacy and racism—racism affects people all over this planet—whether or not you live or work around people of color. We need to understand what this means, how it affects everyone, and how this came to be.

Depending on our identity markers and life experiences, we also have different things to learn. As a person of color, learning about the impact that white supremacy has had on my life has given me an intellectual framework to talk about racism and has made me feel more empowered. I've acquired language to describe what I've experienced and seen in schools for decades. This learning has also opened my eyes to moments when I contributed to perpetuating white supremacy—when, because I'd internalized the messages of white supremacy or because I wasn't aware of what I was doing, I was complicit in oppressing others. This has been (and continues to be) a painful experience—but one that is ultimately liberating. As I know better, I do better.

Learning about white supremacy and racism will be a lifelong commitment for all of us. There's no finish line because humanity and our understanding of it continue to evolve. We may need to take a sabbatical from learning—cognitive understanding needs to be balanced with psycho-social/spiritual healing or else we risk physical and emotional exhaustion and malaise—and then we need to keep on learning, keep on reading and listening, and keep on deepening our understanding. People of color live racism and white supremacy every day and may feel like we have less to learn and need more breaks—at least this is true for me.

In this chapter, I'll guide you to explore your identity, and I'll define white supremacy and explain how it's affected our country and education system. I'll also define racism. I go into much greater detail on all of this, and much more, in my book *Coaching for Equity*. I've tried to keep this chapter succinct and hope that it can be used as a shared text for discussion. Portions of it can be offered to your clients—such as the section "What Is Racism?" If I'd had this chapter when I coached Noah, I would have suggested that he read it. As we coach for equity, creating shared knowledge and language is invaluable, and it makes it a lot easier.

Power, Privilege, and Identity

Figure 12.1 shows the Wheel of Power and Privilege, which presents an essential concept for understanding the intersection of identity and power. It includes some of the most commonly addressed cultural identifiers and the degree of power and privilege associated with each identifier.

As you review the wheel, notice that the outer part of the circle includes a broad range of identifying markers—race, skin color, sexuality, ability, and so on. As you read inward, you'll see more specific descriptors for each of those categories. The outer rings on the wheel are descriptors for more marginalized groups, whereas the innermost circle represents the most powerful and privileged groups—those with the most proximity to dominant culture and power.

Figure 12.1: The Wheel of Power and Privilege

Adapted from sources including the Canadian Council for Refugees and Sylvia Duckworth.

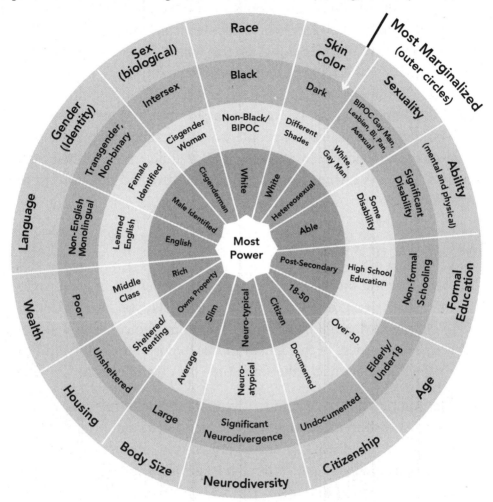

Take a moment to identify where you locate yourself on the wheel. In doing so, you'll likely appreciate the complexity of identity. Take a moment to consider the students you serve—where might they locate themselves? Perhaps consider specific students (maybe one who is "easy" and one who is "challenging"), and consider where they might locate themselves. What insights, questions, and feelings come up for you as you consider all of this?

This list of identifiers on the wheel isn't exhaustive. You could also consider family status, religion, or incarceration status, among other possibilities. Whatever the category, the question is whether the identity markers or experience places you closer to or further from power and privilege. Not every identity experience belongs on this wheel. For example, a teacher once told me that central to her identity was that she was "a scrapbooker." She wanted to know why an identity like that wasn't on here. I said that I thought she was talking about an interest or passion but that, either way, in dominant culture and institutions, people who are scrapbookers don't have more or less access to power. In contrast, a Sikh child in the United States who wears a turban is further from dominant culture and therefore from privilege and power.

Exploring Identity

You see the world through your experiences, which are in great part a result of your identity markers, and the more awareness you have of that lens, the more empowered you'll be to make conscious choices. You'll also need to have acute awareness of this lens in order to coach for equity and to coach across lines of difference. Take some time for this reflection:

1. List your most prominent identity markers including your race, ethnicity, socio-economic status, religion, gender, sexual orientation, spoken languages, nationality, political affiliations, physical abilities, citizenship status, income, educational background, and age.
2. Reflect on these questions:
   - Which of these identity markers do you prioritize when sharing about yourself?
   - Which ones do you think others typically notice about you?
   - Which ones do you tend to not think about?
   - Name your top three identity markers. Which specific life experiences made those so prominent?

- Do your closest friends share aspects of your identity? How so?
- How do your identity experiences shape how you show up in your work?

When coaching for equity, you can offer clients these questions and the Wheel of Power and Privilege to invite reflection.

In the next chapter, we'll explore coaching others around identity and how to coach across lines of difference. But, as always, we begin with ourselves, and to understand identity and identity experiences, we need more context—beginning with historical context.

What Is Racism?

Let's start with a foundational concept: Racism wouldn't exist without white supremacy. *White supremacy* is the ideology that white people are superior. This ideology began with the transatlantic slave trade and has been institutionalized for more than 500 years in the United States and in white settler societies including in Canada, Australia and New Zealand, and South Africa. It manifests in a myriad of forms and affects the lives of everyone in the world in innumerable ways. In many countries, white supremacy manifests in the legal system, in who owns property, in what we see on our screens, in who has access to higher-paying jobs and good medical care, in who and what we find beautiful, in who lives where, in the words that we use, in which schools receive more funds, in how teachers "manage" students, and in much more. You can't understand racism without understanding white supremacy, so let's deconstruct it.

The creation of a system of white supremacy is inextricably linked with colonization. In the last 500 years, colonization has been rooted in the notion that people of European origin had the right to dominate other lands and cultures because, as white people, they were more "civilized." Beginning in the 1500s, European colonizers destroyed cultural practices of indigenous people in the Americas, Africa, Australia and New Zealand, and parts of Asia and the South Pacific, compelling indigenous people to adopt European religions and languages and provide their labor—for free. Over time, many of the colonized internalized the beliefs and practices of the colonizer, and the brutality of the system became obscured.

In the United States, we too rarely remember that we are on stolen lands, lands that were taken through blankets intentionally infected with smallpox, through broken treaties, through forced marches across the country, and through violence, trauma, and genocide. History has been sanitized, and the brutality of colonialism has been erased. This perpetuates the power of white supremacy.

Remember Resistance

Here's something else that those in power have not wanted us to know or remember: People have *always* resisted oppression and dehumanization and white supremacy. From the moment that Columbus set foot on the island of Cuba, the Taínos resisted, as did the indigenous inhabitants of Jamaica and Mexico and Peru and Florida and across the Americas. Similarly, Africans fought back when they were captured in their villages, as they were forcibly marched to the west coast of Africa, when they were on ships on the Atlantic, and in the field and the house, and in more ways than we'll ever be able to catalog.

In modern history, resistance has taken myriad forms and has been unceasing. Some of this history we know, some we don't—as the African proverb reminds us, until the lions have their own historians, the history of the hunt will always glorify the hunter. It has served white supremacy to repress stories of resistance. But you don't have to look very far to find the stories of those who resisted and refused to internalize messages of inferiority. You can find them in some history books, in memoirs, and in oral histories—in the stories of train porters and strawberry pickers and churchgoers. Resistance to colonialism continues to this day. We can, and must, look to those who have resisted and are resisting for inspiration and courage.

Defining Racism

Just to be sure we're clear on one fact: *There are no race-based biological differences among human beings.* There is no gene or cluster of genes common to all Black people or all white people. Classifying people into "races" has no scientific basis. *Race is a social construct.* What is factual: A small group of men of European descent who sought wealth and power created the categorization of people into races as a way to elevate their superiority. This categorization is based on the amount of melanin in skin to make possible the dehumanization, enslavement, and exploitation of Africans. Race is not real; whiteness is a creation. Racism, however, is very real.

I've had more than one person I'm coaching ask me, "Do you think I'm racist?" For so long, our image of a racist has been of a cross-burning, cloaked Klansman or of a skinhead with a swastika tattooed on his forehead. By defining racism in these ways, a lot of us have been relieved from taking responsibility for the racism that we consciously and unconsciously act on. Defining racism, and a racist person, is essential to transforming schools and building a more just society.

While there's debate about how to best define racism, there's also general agreement about the following:

- Racism is a system of oppression that emerges from beliefs that one race is superior to another based on biological characteristics.
- The only racist system that has ever existed is one based on the ideology of white supremacy; this system is designed to benefit and privilege whiteness by every economic and social measure.
- Racism is prejudice plus power: In the United States (and in many places in the world), institutional power is held by white people.
- A racist is someone who consciously or unconsciously upholds a system and culture of white supremacy.

Two additional ways to define racism—racism as a policy and practice and racism as a toxic pollutant—will help to deepen our understanding.

Racism as a Policy and Practice

The dominant narrative about racism has long been that racist *ideas* produced racist *policies*. A *racist idea* is believing that African or Black people are inferior, uncivilized, fit for hard labor, and so on; a *racist policy* is slavery or segregation. According to this interpretation of history, beliefs about racial difference preceded slavery. White people feared African people and looked down on them and essentially said: "Enslaving you is justified because you're almost an animal."

In his book *Stamped from the Beginning*, Ibram X. Kendi turns this notion on its head. Kendi makes a brilliant 600-page case for how America's history of race relations began, not with the racist ideas but with the racially discriminatory policies. These policies, he explains, led to racist ideas, which led to ignorance and hate. Sequencing racism in this way is essential to how we understand and dismantle it. Kendi continues this exploration in his moving *How to Be an Anti-Racist* (2019). In this book, he proposes that we stop thinking of "racist" as a pejorative and start thinking of it as a simple description. Either you are racist or you're anti-racist, Kendi argues; you are either upholding white supremacy or actively participating in taking it apart. He urges us to focus exclusively on policy, arguing that the solution to racism will start with policies, not ideas.

Educational outcomes for Black and Brown children would be different if there were anti-racist policies in schools around office referrals, testing for learning differences, and curriculum choices. Different educational policies would make a tremendous difference in the lives of Black and Brown kids in school.

But we need more than policy to dismantle racism in our schools. When I reflect on the way teachers spoke to my Black son, how their perception of his defiance distorted the relationship they built with him, and how that impacted his sense of belonging and psychological safety, I know that we must address the thoughts, feelings, and beliefs that shape the experience and outcomes for children of color. We need to recognize how racism has affected our hearts, minds, bodies, and relationships as well as the social fabric of our communities, and we need to attend to this harm and heal from it. As Patrisse Cullors, one of the founders of Black Lives Matter, says, "We can't policy our way out of racism" (Cullors, 2017).

Racism as a Toxic Pollutant

In *Why Are All the Black Kids Sitting Together in the Cafeteria?* Dr. Beverly Tatum offers a useful analogy. Racism, she explains, "is like smog in the air. Sometimes it is so thick it is visible, other times it is less apparent, but always, day in and day out, we are breathing it in . . . if we live in a smoggy place, how can we avoid breathing the air?" (1999, p.6).

Tatum's analogy helps to see the toxicity of racism—and its pervasiveness. Our parents and grandparents breathed in these poisons, and we've been doing so since we were born. Our physical, emotional, and social bodies are toxic with the poison of racism. And by "we" I mean all of us. Some people of color unwittingly internalize notions of white supremacy despite that doing so contributes to our own marginalization. Everyone learns explicit and implicit stereotyped messages in families, schools, and communities. We learn these stereotypes, and we act on them consciously and unconsciously.

But we have choices. When the air is smoggy, we can wear a mask, and we can use air purifiers. Just as we have choices about the toxins we breathe, we have choices about exposure to mental and emotional toxins. We can also work for clearer air. It may not be our fault that we live in a toxic world, but we can and should call attention to it. We have a choice about where we live, what we breathe, and how we respond to the toxins in our world.

Racism is embedded into structures including schools, government, social programs, and the legal system. Our individual mindsets and behaviors will never be truly rid of the toxicity of racism if we're in poisonous environments. If we intend to permanently rid our individual systems of the toxins of racism, we'll need to transform the racist structures that surround us. Ultimately, we'll only be healthy, whole, and free if we dismantle the systems in which white supremacy is lodged.

We've been indoctrinated into a belief that racism is just the way things are, and it can be liberating to remember that human beings have not always been racist. Yes, human beings have a tendency to sort each other into categories, but sorting by skin color and phenotypical features is a relatively modern practice. Unless we remember that racism was created by people, it can seem inevitable—but that's just not true. If we recognize racism as a construct, we can dismantle it and create something new.

How Racism Manifests in Schools

Education in the United States has never been a right included in the Constitution, and from the beginning, our education system sorted people by race, gender, and class. Remember that the United States was not founded on principles of equity and justice—"We the People" only included *some* people. Access to opportunity has never been equitable or fair. This is a difficult history we're contending with—and it's why our work can feel fundamentally conflicting and contradictory at its core. And we're not alone in this conflict—it's one confronting educators all over our world.

Grappling with this history raises the question of purpose. What do we see as the purpose of education? What is our ultimate goal as educators? The solution to educational inequity is not to help students navigate a dysfunctional system that was never designed for them. *We can't use the same structures and systems if we want different results.* And yet, changing those systems will take time. What can we do right now for our kids who are forced to endure "cells and bells," order and control, and standardized tests?

To create something new, we'll need to deconstruct the systems we've been indoctrinated into—we'll need to unearth the mental models that we've worked from and question everything. As we construct a vision of education for liberation, and as we learn skills to provide our students with a more equitable education tomorrow, we must do our own learning. We can start by identifying the ways that racism manifests in schools and classrooms. Table 12.1 outlines a handful of indicators of white supremacy

Table 12.1: The Manifestation of White Supremacy

In Our Society, the Ideology of White Supremacy Manifests in:	In Schools, the Ideology of White Supremacy Surfaces in:
Institutions, systems, and policies including: • Social, political, economic, legal, financial systems • Slavery, colonialism, Jim Crow segregation, and redlining	• Discipline policies • The school calendar • Graduation criteria • Curriculum • Textbooks that center the experience of white people and erase the brutality of white supremacy • Tracking • Uniforms • The strict regulation of children's bodies
Cognition, attitude, and emotional responses including: • Prejudice • Values of dominant culture • Implicit or unconscious bias • Deficit thinking • Internalized oppression • Stereotyping • "White fragility"	• These kids can't. . . . • They need me to save them. • I'm afraid of those kids. • I need to not be like other immigrants. • Asians are just good at math. • Respect looks like a child making eye contact with an adult. • Those parents don't value education. • I feel like I'm being attacked when I get feedback on my communication.
Behaviors and actions including: • Genocide and violence • Bigotry and discrimination • Microaggressions	• The criminalization of student behavior • Insisting that only English be spoken • Incorrectly pronouncing names; giving students nicknames
Outcomes including: • Racism • Inequality, inequities, and disproportionality • White privilege	• School-to-prison pipeline • Graduation rates • College admissions • Access to opportunities

in schools. This is not intended to be a comprehensive description, but a resource to get us thinking. In my book *Coaching for Equity*, I include an Equity Rubric that is a more expansive resource to describe what equity is, and isn't, in schools.

Racial disparities are evident across several categories of education data: access to opportunities; criminalization of student behavior; and outcomes, including test scores, grades, and graduation rates. What follows is not intended to be a comprehensive list of the inequities we can find in school but rather data points to provoke reflection and further inquiry. Although Black and Latine students are more likely to receive lower grades, score lower on standardized tests, and drop out of high school, and are less likely to enter and complete college than their white counterparts, the data on student achievement is problematic. For that reason, I've chosen to provide data on access to opportunities and the criminalization of student behavior as a way to gain greater understanding of the indicators of racial inequities in school.

Access to Opportunities

Students of color often have access to fewer opportunities than their white counterparts.

- Students of color are less likely to have qualified teachers—teachers who have been prepared to teach (Goldhaber et al., 2015).
- Black, Latine, and Native American youth have less access to honors and advanced placement (AP) classes than white youth. They are less likely to enroll in advanced science and math classes, which can reduce their chances of being admitted to a four-year college, many of which require completion of at least one high-level math class for admission (Klopfenstein, 2004).
- Black and Latine students are less likely to be identified as gifted and talented. Black and Latine third-grade students are half as likely as whites to participate in gifted and talented programs. In contrast, children of color are more likely to be identified as requiring special education services by teachers (Grissom and Redding, 2016).

Criminalization of Student Behavior

Educators frequently notice misbehavior among Black and Brown students while ignoring the same behavior in white students. Black and Brown students are seen as troublemakers and disciplined more harshly than their white counterparts who are granted leniency.

- Black and Brown students are more likely to attend schools with a greater police presence, increasing the odds that they will enter the criminal justice system. The presence of law enforcement on school campuses also increases the risk of such students being exposed to police violence (Javdani, 2019).
- Black preschool students are more likely to be suspended than students of other races and are more likely to be suspended for minor disruptions and misbehaviors including wetting their pants, kicking off their shoes, and crying. Black students make up just 18% of children in preschool but represent nearly half of preschool children suspended (Smith and Harper, 2015).
- At five years old, Black boys are perceived as being threatening. A 2016 study showed that white people associated Black boys as young as five years old with adjectives such as "violent," "dangerous," "hostile," and "aggressive" (Todd, 2016).
- Black students are three times more likely to be suspended or expelled than their white peers (U.S. Department of Education Office for Civil Rights, 2014). This is even more pronounced in 13 states in the U.S. South, where 55% of the 1.2 million suspensions involving Black students nationwide occurred (Smith and Harper, 2015).
- Black girls are more likely than all other female students and some groups of boys to be suspended or expelled (U.S. Department of Education Office for Civil Rights, 2014).
- Overt and unconscious biases against Black and Brown children lead to high suspension rates and excessive absences, to not reading at grade level by third grade and falling behind academically, to the "achievement gap," and to dropping out of school (Bowman, 2018).

What Is to Be Done?

Racism hurts and dehumanizes everyone. Most obviously, racism marginalizes the experiences and identities of people of color. But white people also suffer from being a part of a racist system. In being grouped as "white," many white people have lost a connection to their ethnic group. And because white identity is based on not being something—*not* being Black or Brown, *not* being a person of color—white people can experience identity insecurity and confusion.

Furthermore, white people participate in a system in which they gain advantages that, as individuals, they may not have earned—this can generate feelings of guilt and shame. I believe that many white people recognize the damage done to their integrity and morality by participating in and benefiting from white supremacy. They recognize that they cannot be whole until the injustices of the past and present are reckoned with and until they no longer reap unearned privileges as a result of the classification systems of past and present white supremacists.

White supremacy has maintained its power by integrating itself into the fabric of our culture, into our hearts and minds, and into all institutions, and by doing so, it has become invisible. White supremacy feels normal; we experience it as the "natural" way of things. To dismantle systems of oppression, including white supremacy, we need to see those systems for what they are—to see what they're made of and how they are made and to see that they are constructed by people. We can extend this understanding to other systems of oppression: patriarchy is a construct; heterosexuality is a construct.

Things that have been constructed can be deconstructed. In learning about racism and how it was constructed, we'll see how we've all been hurt and how we've harmed others, and we'll see how we can transform our minds, relationships, schools, and world. Finally, learning about racism is healing, and healing can lead to liberation.

To heal, you must recognize the wounds in yourself—the ways in which you've been hurt by racism and white supremacy and the ways you've hurt others. As you unlearn stereotyped racial messages you've internalized about yourself and others, you'll step deeper into a healing process. Learning about racism will, inevitably, be painful. But it will be worth it.

A Note for White People

People of color are often asked to explain race and racism—sometimes we're willing to do just that (often we have to), but it can become tiring. Fortunately, there are an increasing number of excellent resources available to help you learn about race, racism, and white supremacy. Know that people of color appreciate that you are learning, and also know that we're not going to give you awards for doing so. Do this learning for your own healing and liberation, for your community and your children, and for the global majority.

This chapter might have been hard to read. I hope you will now take a break from reading to tend to your body, heart, mind, and spirit. How could you replenish the reserves of energy that it took to read this chapter? What helps you reconnect with your courage? With joy? With hope? Who could you reach out to and talk to and be with?

A Note for People of Color

Most of this chapter is excerpted from *Coaching for Equity*. When I wrote it, in 2019, it felt very hard to write. I experienced intense waves of rage and grief as I worked on it. I imagine it might have been hard to read. I hope that you will now take a break from reading to tend to your body, heart, mind, and spirit. How could you replenish the reserves of energy that it took to read this chapter? What helps you reconnect with your sense of power? With joy? With hope? Who could you reach out to and talk to and be with? How might you tap into the strength of your ancestors?

If we were sitting next to each other right now, know that I'd ask if I could hold your hand, and if you said yes, I'd do so. I wouldn't say anything; I wouldn't make eye contact. I'd just hold your hand and think, *I'm here with you. I'm here with you in this storm of emotion.* And in that moment, that would be what I could offer. My presence. For whatever it's worth: I'm here with you.

Pause and Process

Reflect:

- Which emotions came up for you in this chapter? How did you engage with those feelings?
- At which points in this chapter did you experience cognitive dissonance (a conflict between what you hold to be true and new information)?
- How do you think your identity markers (including your race) affected how you read this chapter? What do you think it was like for someone of a different race to read this chapter?

Next steps:

- Listen to *Bright Morning Podcast* series "What to Say When You Hear Something Racist," starting with episode 108.
- Read *Coaching for Equity*.
- Download "The Equity Rubric" from my website. Complete the rubric for yourself. Consider what the results make you want to do next to grow your competency in this area.

CHAPTER 13

How to Coach for Equity

On Building Bridges

Common misconception:	*Transformational Coaches know:*
Coaching for equity creates division and strife.	Coaching for equity creates connection, belonging, meaning, purpose, and love.

When Margaret, a teacher I coached said, "What do you expect? These parents don't care about their kids," I was flabbergasted. I was a new coach, and I'd never heard a teacher express disparaging beliefs about parents so shamelessly. Margaret had proclaimed this as truth, as doctrine, her voice laden with disdain. And she was a woman of color. I couldn't find words to respond. I went to an experienced colleague and asked how she would have responded. She came up with a dozen things I could have said.

A week later, another teacher said, "The reason that our Black male students aren't successful is because they don't have role models. What can we do about that?" I went back to my colleague and asked her for another list of responses.

These were not isolated comments. An eighth-grade reading intervention teacher pushed back against my coaching. "I can't teach these kids," she said, her voice thick with hostility. "Why don't you coach their elementary-school teachers? They're the ones who need coaching. It's not my fault they're so far behind."

A math teacher said, "I don't send them to the 'time-out chair'; I send them to 'isolation,' because *these kids* get that reference. They know about prisons, so I make it simple for them to understand my discipline system."

"She'll end up pregnant at 15," said the science teacher. "That's how those Mexicans are. I'm not wasting my time teaching her chemistry."

And another (young female) teacher said, "Can you come to the conference I have to have with Abdul's dad? I'm afraid to be alone with him. Middle Eastern men have no boundaries."

I collected lists of things I could say in response to each situation. And yet each time I heard something that was overtly or unconsciously racist (or sexist, classist, ableist, or homophobic—I've heard it all), I felt at a loss for how to respond. I felt that I was obligated, as a coach and as a human being, to open a conversation, explore the underlying thinking, and stay in relationship with whoever made these comments. Even though I kept adding to my list of responses, I often didn't have sentence stems to use for whatever specific situation happened that day.

These racist statements expressed *beliefs*, and we can figure out how to act in response when we remember that *a belief is just a strongly held opinion*. A belief is not the truth—even if it feels like it is. To respond to these statements I was hearing from teachers, I needed to understand how beliefs were created and how they could be shifted. I also needed to understand how to build trust with others and coach emotions and how to trust the process and respond to my own strong emotions.

To coach for equity, you'll draw on everything you've learned in this book—including how to listen, how to navigate power, how to ask effective questions, how to guide someone through their own experience of uncomfortable emotions, and how to recognize when inequities are at play. In addition, you need the following:

- Knowledge of how beliefs change
- Strategies to guide someone to shift their beliefs
- Skills to work with your own strong emotions when they arise around equity issues and those of others
- Clarity on what it means to coach for equity, and conviction to do so

Who, What, When, Where, and Why Coach for Equity

This chapter focuses on *how* to coach for equity, but before we get to strategies, I want to be sure we're on the same page about who can coach for equity, what it means to coach for equity, when and where to coach for equity, and perhaps, most importantly, why to coach for equity. Then we'll get to the how.

What Does It Mean to Coach for Equity?

I'm always looking though an equity lens, and never more so than when I'm in a coaching conversation. This means that during conversations, I consider the following:

- *My identity and my client's:* How might the differences in our identity markers impact this conversation? What role might our differences play in what my client shares or in what I say?
- *The problem:* How does my client see the situation they're in, or the challenges they're facing, in relationship to equity, identity experiences, and systemic oppression? What's their awareness of how equity issues contribute to the challenges they're facing? Whose needs are centered in my client's perception of the challenges they're trying to address?

- *My client's field of awareness:* Where, within my client's consciousness, are the needs and experiences of marginalized people? How aware is my client of the ways in which systems, oppression impact their students, the community my client serves, and my clients themselves?
- *My client's skill set around engaging in equity issues:* How much has my client built their own cultural competency? Where are they on their equity journey in terms of building skills? What kinds of emotions arise when they explore equity issues, and how do they respond to those emotions?

To coach for equity, you need to be asking these questions—and to ask these questions, you need knowledge about equity and how inequities manifest in schools and in society at large. Next, you need skills to coach someone to explore their behaviors, beliefs, and ways of being in relationship to these issues. Implicit in these actions is a commitment to equity and a willingness to be uncomfortable, to take risks, to challenge dominant culture. The only way to do all of that is to have a healthy and strong relationship with your own emotions—to know how to work with them to fuel your commitments.

Why Coach for Equity?

I'm grateful to have taught middle school for more than a decade for many reasons, including how unapologetically children of that age question *why* something needs to be learned or done. My middle schoolers trained me to lead with purpose.

So why coach for equity? Humans are innately compassionate, caring creatures who don't like seeing other people suffer. We want peace, equality, fairness, and justice; we depend on love and attachment; and our core human need is for connection and belonging *with all living things.* Researchers have found that the most common source of awe is *moral beauty*—other people's courage, strength, or kindness (Keltner, 2023). The awe we feel in response to other people's actions is something we aspire to demonstrate as well. In other words, when we can be our truest selves, we embody equity.

When our core human needs are not met, we adapt—and sometimes we adapt in ways that harm ourselves and others. In helping people to live in alignment with their core values, we are coaching for equity. Coaching for equity creates connection, belonging, meaning, purpose, and love. We coach for equity because it's who we are.

Who Can Coach for Equity, and When and Where Can That Happen?

Anyone can "coach" for equity, anywhere. To coach is to facilitate reflection on behaviors, beliefs, and ways of being. You can "coach" your child, your sibling, your neighbor, and so on. Within a professional setting, there's even more of an assumption (in most places) that a group of people have convened to get something done and that they may need to learn new skills in the process. So you can coach a colleague, a direct report, a student, and perhaps even a supervisor when equity issues arise. You don't need the title "coach" to coach. Yes, it can feel momentarily awkward to say to your best friend, "Hey, can we rewind our conversation for a second and talk about a phrase when you were describing the cleaning lady at church? I want to understand what you mean by that." And we can navigate the discomfort and have a meaningful and important conversation. Coaching for equity is not strictly about what happens within the parameters of a defined teacher-coach relationship.

Cultivating Identity Awareness

One of the first things that we all need to know is how our identity markers affect the experiences we have, the way we see the world, and the actions we take. This is true for coaches, leaders, and teachers. We began to explore this in the context of self-awareness in Chapter 12, "What You Need to Know

About Equity." Cultivating an identity awareness is also a starting point when coaching others.

How and When to Coach Identity Awareness

Within the first few sessions of working with a new client, I engage them in a conversation about their sociopolitical identity. I often ask many of the questions from the section in Chapter 12 called "Exploring Identity," and I introduce the Wheel of Power and Privilege. My purpose in doing this is to understand how my client sees themself in the world, to explore their level of awareness of identity issues, and to introduce shared language and concepts. After this preliminary conversation, they aren't surprised when I bring up identity.

Increasing identity awareness requires many coaching approaches. In my initial conversations with clients about their identities, I'll often use phrases like, "Say more" or "I'm curious about that . . ." My intention is to learn about them and help them understand that so much of the way we operate in the world is a result of our conditioning and socialization. In later conversations, I draw on other strategies to delve more deeply into issues of identity. Here's an example of what this sounds like:

Coach: How do you think your experiences as a white man, growing up in a middle-class suburb in the Midwest, impacted how you respond to Luis's behavior?

Teacher: I don't know. I just feel disrespected by him all the time.

Coach: How was respect expressed in your home or community?

Teacher: We didn't talk back. We smiled and greeted our teachers at the door in the morning. Luis barges past me and won't do anything I ask.

Coach: It sounds like your socialization leads you to think that others should adhere to those same behaviors.

Teacher: But I don't think it's a Mexican cultural thing to disrespect your elders. Do you?

Coach: No, I don't.

Teacher: So I don't think this is an issue of us having different cultural backgrounds.

Coach: What do you think this is about?

Teacher: Probably just that he's a typical disrespectful seventh grader.

Coach: Do you think he'd respond the same way if you were Mexican? If you were a woman?

Teacher: I don't know. That's a good question. I guess I'd hope not.

Coach: Say more about that.

Teacher: I hope he'd respect one of his own. Maybe if I was a woman he'd be more polite.

Coach: So you think there's something about your shared gender that contributes to what's going on?

Teacher: Maybe. I might be more triggered by young men who are disrespectful.

Coach: Do you think you feel triggered equally by young white men as you do by young men of color?

Teacher: I don't know. I guess it's easier for me to understand white people's behavior because it's familiar.

Coach: That makes sense. And so perhaps part of what's going on here is that you don't know how to interpret Luis's behaviors and so you're afraid of him.

Teacher: I wouldn't say it's fear.

Coach: What would you say is the emotion?

Teacher: Disrespect.

Coach: So is anger the emotion?

I'm going to truncate this conversation right there, even though you might be on the edge of your seat wondering where this conversation will go. I hope you noticed the way I drew on strategies to coach emotions, beliefs, and identity issues. I hope you're continuing to gain an appreciation for how robust Transformational Coaching is and the conversations we can have in using this model.

Coaching Across Lines of Difference

Another important element of coaching for equity is an awareness of difference between you and your clients. You'll coach teachers who don't share your race or ethnicity, class background, gender, sexual orientation, age group, and more. Anytime I'm coaching, I'm aware of the way these differences and similarities in our identity markers affect what I say, what I observe, and how my client responds. That awareness directs the decisions I make.

The first step in coaching across lines of difference is exploring what comes up for you around differences. Reflect on the following questions:

- Consider the identity markers on the Wheel of Power and Privilege. Which groups do you find more challenging to coach or feel less comfortable with? How do you think those feelings have impacted how you've coached?
- Consider your preferences in clients. Do you prefer to coach people who share your identity markers? If so, which markers feel most important— gender, age, religion, race, class background? Something else?
- Consider clients whom you've struggled to coach. Do you see any patterns in the identity markers that they share?

With understanding, you can make conscious choices more frequently. You can also anticipate when you might be activated or uncomfortable coaching someone and prepare for those conversations by reflecting or talking to a trusted colleague or coach.

Normalizing the fact that discomfort might come up for you and your client can make it easier to raise what can otherwise become an elephant in the room. Sometimes the best way to approach the differences is to name them and invite your client to share their feelings about them. I often do this in the beginning of a coaching relationship in conjunction with talking about identity markers. This can sound like:

- I'm curious what comes up for you, given the differences in our identity markers.
- How do you think the differences in our identity experiences might show up in our coaching work?
- What's most important for me, as your coach, to understand about your identity experiences?
- Do you have any questions for me about my identity markers?

When we first start working together, I also give my client permission to name our differences if they arise in coaching. This sounds like:

> If there's ever a point when you feel that the differences in our identities are creating misunderstanding or discomfort, I want you to know that I'd be grateful if you named that. You can say something like, "I feel like our differences are at play now" and we'll explore what's going on.

If you're a white coach working with clients of color, you can say:

> I want you to know that I'm working on developing my racial awareness. And as white person, I know I've got a lot to learn. If anything comes up that you feel has to do with the difference in our racial identities, or my identity, you're welcome to let me know.

Of course, you can also modify the previous statement so that it's relevant to your identity markers. Whenever there's a power differential (and when your identity markers afford you more power and privilege), it's worth letting your client know that you're aware of that and that you're working on your own stuff—which is your responsibility if you're committed to Transformational Coaching. At the same time, be cautious not to center yourself or your needs—just name the differences and acknowledge that they might show up.

I was once assigned to coach a principal who was a Black man from Oakland who was several decades older than me. I was assigned to coach him because he was a struggling leader. This was an uncomfortable premise to start with as I've never been a principal. He was amicable and receptive to coaching, but in one of our first sessions I said, "I want to acknowledge that I've never been a principal, I didn't grow up in Oakland, and you're a Black man leading a school that's entirely Black. What comes up for you given the differences between us?"

His eyes widened and his shoulders dropped. "Thank you for saying that," he said. "I'm glad to hear you name that, and right now I don't need to share anything else."

When you invite feedback and reflection, be sure that you're not communicating that your client has a responsibility to educate you on their identity experiences or correct you when you make mistakes. This is especially important if your identity markers are reflective of dominant culture and therefore closer to power and privilege. While people who have had marginalized experiences may choose to teach us, it's not their responsibility. When coaching across lines of difference, do your own work and learning, let your client know that you're aware of differences, and address issues when they arise.

Why Calling People Out Doesn't Work

I'm often asked, "Why can't we just call people out on their racist beliefs?" I flinch when I hear the phrase *call someone out*, because it suggests wielding power over someone and, possibly, shaming them; it's what we do when we don't know what else to do, when we're not prepared, and when we haven't processed our own emotions. I know this because I've done it—I've called people out and confronted them with their racism. *Calling people out doesn't work.* Shame is not an effective tool for transformation. It will not help us create a kind, compassionate, equitable world.

When we experience cognitive dissonance (a conflict between what we hold to be true and new information), we are likely to experience fear, which causes our brain and mind to respond protectively in an attempt to preserve our psychological sense of self. So, if someone feels like you're attacking their beliefs, they'll armor up to protect those beliefs—especially if the beliefs are tied up with their sense of self and identity. This is science; we can either fight it or work with it.

Our Brain

You can blame the amygdala for many problems we face. The *amygdala* is an ancient part of our brain structure that is always on the alert for threats. At the first sign of danger, the amygdala triggers biochemical messages through our bodies, telling us to panic—to fight, freeze, or flee. Our bodies flood with hormones, and our mind is consumed with thoughts of survival. Unless we regulate our biochemical and cognitive response, the rational part of our brain shuts down.

Here's where this gets interesting and relevant to coaching for equity: our mind perceives a threat to our identity the same way it perceives a threat to our physical existence. If we feel someone thinks that we might not be a good person or that we might be racist, we experience that as a threat to our identity. This perception triggers a biochemical response in our bodies that makes us feel defensive, that makes us check out and disconnect, or that paralyzes us. If you tell me that I've perpetuated dehumanizing stereotypes about Muslims, my body will react as if you're about to physically attack me—because I believe that I am a good person and you're attacking my sense of self. My body will prepare to fight back, and my prefrontal cortex (where rational thinking happens) slows down.

As we understand and accept the social, biological, and psychological factors involved in having conversations about beliefs, we can prioritize coaching strategies. The neuroscience affirms that it's imperative to build a relationship with a client and create psychological safety—this is not an optional stage in coaching. The research also validates the need to attend to emotions. We need to know how to respond to tears and anger and how to support clients to respond to their anxiety when it surges—to use breathing strategies, for example, to regulate their body's response to fear.

We also need to know that our brain and mind can change. We can learn how to de-escalate our neurological responses to our perception of danger—especially when that danger is a perception that we're being told we're not a good person. We can learn to recognize when a situation doesn't merit fighting, fleeing, or freezing. Our brains can develop new neural pathways that allow us to have productive and powerful conversations about race and systemic oppression.

Our Moral Identity

An individual's identity is a collection of their values, personality, upbringing, communities, cultures, sociopolitical identities, religion, experiences, families, and education. We all have multiple identities that make us feel like who we are. You'll need an understanding of the psychological concept of identity to coach others toward equity.

As we go through life, we want others to acknowledge our multiple identities. If we feel like others aren't seeing us for who we are, we can feel threatened and stressed. We might get defensive or fish for affirmations and center our own needs. For example, I believe I am a good person who is most of the time concerned about and kind to others. I want you to believe this about me without a doubt. If a reader was to comment on my omission of equity issues for people who are disabled, I may experience that as a threat to my moral identity. I might counter that my cousin is an international disability rights lawyer and activist; that my brother had disabilities; that, as a teacher, I always made accommodations for kids with disabilities; and so on. I'll present a ton of evidence that shows that I'm a good person. Wanting others to think that we're good people isn't a bad thing—but in my efforts to protect my moral identity, I might not listen to what someone else says, and I might not learn.

Professor Dolly Chugh (2019) proposes that we stop thinking of ourselves as people who are good or bad, racist or anti-racist, ethical or unethical, and that we think of ourselves as "good-ish" people. A good-ish person, Chugh says, is someone who is trying to be better. The truth is that we all do harmful things, but it's hard to see it in ourselves because we cling to an illusion that we are ethical and unbiased. What could be possible if we embraced the notion of being *a good-ish person*? If we committed to being good-ish people as often as possible?

The Lengths We'll Go to Protect Our Beliefs

Once we have a belief (about ourselves or others), our mind does two things: it searches for information to confirm that belief (which is called *confirmation bias*), and then it protects that belief from harm. For example, let's say I'm a vegan, and I believe that eating animals makes me a bad person. I will search for, interpret, favor, and recall information that affirms my belief. My belief may get stronger in the face of other information, and I may be resistant to changing this belief because it would threaten my sense of identity.

Confirmation bias makes it hard for us to be open to a wide array of data—whether about diet or what we think low-income students of color are able to do. Imagine a teacher who thinks she's a good person, who knows she cares about kids, and who came to teach in Oakland because of a desire to help kids. Despite this belief, she creates low-rigor lessons for her ninth-grade students and gives them a pass when they want to sleep in class. When a student mutters something about treating them like a kindergartner, her confirmation bias dismisses the comment, and when she sees high-level work the students produce in another class, she assumes that someone has helped them. This teacher with conformation bias will do anything to protect her belief that she's a good person doing all she can and that she's seeing all that her students can do. When this teacher is presented with information that doesn't match with what she believes, her brain instinctively protects those beliefs in what's called the *backfire effect*—it will reject the new information, and the belief gets stronger.

When we try to use facts to sway someone's opinion, we get nowhere.

This isn't a dismal situation we're in, however. There's hope. Humans are *prone* to choosing information and data that support our worldview, but we also crave community and belonging above all. That means when the conditions are right, we'll be open to other perspectives if they bring us into closer connection with others. We can change the wiring of our brains, change our beliefs, and take in new information *when we don't feel like our core identity will be crushed under the new information*. When we experience psychological safety, we can take in new data without our brain responding like it's being attacked; when we see how our core identity can be preserved, we can be receptive to new information. And then beliefs and behaviors can change.

When you call someone out for being racist, their core identity of being a good person is threatened. This is why they'll appear resistant. When coaching beliefs, we need to accept our neurobiological responses to feeling threatened and our cognitive responses to feeling attacked. This doesn't mean we can't change our responses and unlearn problematic racist practices—it means we must know how to coach emotions.

How to Change Beliefs

Six conditions allow beliefs to change. Sometimes all of these conditions need to be in place for a belief to change; other times a belief can change if just a few conditions are in place. Beliefs change when:

1. We feel safe enough.
2. We understand how the belief was created.
3. We encounter new information.
4. Alternate beliefs exist.
5. Our core identity is preserved.
6. We see benefits to changing a belief.

Beliefs Change When We Feel Safe Enough

You can't coach beliefs unless you are also able to coach someone's way of being. That's because beliefs are entwined with emotions. Letting go of beliefs entails loss, and so it brings up fear and sometimes sadness and anger as well. Regardless of which beliefs we're releasing, we deserve the support and guidance of someone who is kind, humble, and hopeful—someone who's both tuned into our needs and who encourages us to forge on through the discomfort. If a coach is judgmental, a client will be reluctant (or resistant) to unpack mental models and flawed beliefs. Feeling safe is an essential emotional condition that allows us to examine and shift beliefs.

When I reflect on beliefs that I've let go of, especially distorted beliefs about other people, I'm flooded with feelings—including shame. Shame is a feeling that we experience as *I'm wrong. I'm bad.* Experiencing shame can be intensely painful, but if we can talk about it, we can release it. A coach, therapist, or good friend can help us forgive ourselves and gain insight into what we did or believed that led to shame. This doesn't happen, however, if we don't feel safe enough with another person.

Beliefs Change When We Understand How a Belief Was Created

Ms. Russo insisted that her students speak only English when they were in her art class. "You *must* learn English!" she'd instruct her sixth graders, many of whom were recent immigrants. She would send kids to the office for speaking Spanish to each other. "This is America!" she told me. In her early 60s, Ms. Russo had taught in the same school for almost 30 years. Kids were scared of her and hated art.

One day I asked Ms. Russo about her family's background. Her grandparents had come from Italy, she told me. Did she speak any Italian? No. She explained that when her family immigrated, they'd faced discrimination. "My grandparents decided not to speak to their children in Italian because they wanted them to have a better life," she explained. Her parents, aunts, and uncles had emphasized that English was the best language in the world, a currency to access jobs.

"That helps me understand why you have such a strong belief that our children should speak English," I said.

"Yes, I suppose so," she said as if she'd never made that connection.

I asked about her relationship with her grandparents. "They knew very little English, so I could hardly communicate with them," she said. I explained that our students also had grandparents and family members who only spoke Spanish—and that having relationships with family was important. She sighed and said, "I wish I'd been able to talk to my grandmother. She was kind and sweet. I missed out."

"I'm wondering if you'd be willing to unpack your beliefs about your students only speaking in English in class?" I asked. She agreed.

Ms. Russo was scary—I was even a little afraid of her. She was cantankerous. We had a short, intense conversation about her beliefs around English. When our conversation ended, I couldn't tell how she was thinking or whether any of her thoughts had shifted.

A week later, she asked me to observe one of her art classes—the class with the large group of newcomers. At the beginning of the class, she said, "Students, I need to apologize. I have been wrong in telling you to only speak English. You may speak in Spanish to each other as long as it's an appropriate time to talk. Elena, please translate that for me so I can be sure all of the students understand."

I was shocked. I translated and registered the surprise on the faces of some of the children. "You can go now," Ms. Russo said to me.

We often experience a belief as an untouchable, monolithic truth. But a belief is a strongly held opinion, and it can change when we understand where it originated. Ms. Russo's belief about speaking English shifted as she recognized the source of her own beliefs about speaking English—and as she recognized that there were limitations and drawbacks to that belief.

The Ladder of Inference

It's empowering to recognize that our beliefs are built on specific information, often on data that is incomplete or even problematic. The Ladder of Inference, created by Chris Argyris, provides a framework for helping us see how our beliefs are formed and why we do what we do. This model describes how we unconsciously climb up a mental pathway of increasing abstraction that can produce misguided beliefs (Senge, 1994, p. 243). You can download a graphic of this framework from my website.

As we go through our days, we experience a tremendous amount of data. Because we can't process it all, our mind selects certain data that fits with what we already know and understand—when we do this, we begin to climb the ladder. Now we have some filtered data with which we make meaning. Meaning is often based on our own cultural backgrounds and experiences and/or the culture of the organization in which we are working. From that rung, we ascend again, making assumptions and coming to conclusions. And then, almost at the top of the ladder, we form a belief, which, in turn, shapes the actions we take.

Here's an example. Angela wanted to implement stations with her first-grade students—something she'd been hesitant to try but was enticed into by the prospect of working with small reading groups. While with a group, she noticed the boys across the room at a math station messing around. She noticed this, in part, because it's exactly what she was worried about (Angela already thought that many of her first-grade boys were too wiggly and distracted). The boys were building towers with the math manipulatives and talking loudly. She ascended the ladder as she *interpreted* this to mean that they were off task. Ascending the ladder again, Angela *assumed* that they were disrupting the learning of other students and that they wouldn't meet the day's objectives. She *concluded* that they just couldn't handle the freedom of being in stations, and then, almost at the top of the ladder, she *arrived at a belief* that the only thing that works with first-grade students is whole-group instruction. She decided to scrap plans for stations and return to the way she'd taught—this was the action she took. The next time Angela noticed boys talking loudly, she'd focus on the pieces of data that reinforced her beliefs, starting the climb right back up the ladder again. This is how her belief that *boys can't work collaboratively* was formed; this is how her classroom became teacher-centered; and this is why she reacted punitively when boys seemed distracted.

Our biases come in at every rung of the ladder. If we're unaware that we've been breathing the smoggy air of racism all our lives, we'll select data that matches the biased beliefs we've absorbed. We will look at the data around us, and our eyes will bypass the boys who are focused and quiet. We'll take one data point—one boy whom we perceive as being off-task—and generalize it to mean that boys can't handle group work, and then we add layers of problematic interpretation and, finally, end up with a problematic belief.

There are a few ways we can use the Ladder of Inference. First, it reminds us that all beliefs emerge from data we encounter. When I'm confronted by actions such as Ms. Russo's prohibition against speaking in Spanish, the ladder reminds me to surface data points at the roots of her belief. The ladder also reminds me that new beliefs are constructed when we see, understand, and take in data points that are different from those we've previously focused on. If Angela believes that boys can't handle group work, her beliefs will be challenged and might shift if she sees her own male students and others being successful in group work. The Ladder of Inference directs me to help clients broaden the data set from which someone is making assumptions, to guide them to see more data, and then to explore different ways to interpret that data.

With Ms. Russo, I used the ladder to construct questions that helped her reinterpret her students' desire to speak Spanish and to come to different conclusions. When I asked Ms. Russo about her family background and their attitudes about language and English, I intended to help her see how she'd arrived at her belief that only English should be spoken. As she did this, she recognized the limitations in her own beliefs, and she uncovered a willingness to shift her practices.

We can use the ladder with a client to help them see how they've arrived at beliefs and to help them create new beliefs. You can literally put the graphic in front of them (download it from my website) and describe the process we go through and then ask them if they'd be interested in unpacking their beliefs. Inviting your clients into an exercise like this communicates your confidence in their intellect and willingness. You don't need to hide all your cards or strategies or tools—engage your clients as colleagues, and begin with an assumption that they want to learn, grow, and refine their teaching practices.

The Ladder of Inference Questioning Strategies

The following questions parallel the rungs of the ladder. You can begin on any rung, or you may want or need to start with those at the bottom, at the level of data, and work your way up.

Actions:

- Can you identify the belief you hold that led to that behavior?
- What might be the consequences—intended and unintended—of acting out of this belief?
- What's possible if you act from this belief? What might be possible if you weren't holding this belief?

Beliefs:

- Which experiences might have led you to hold that belief?
- Which assumptions (or conclusions) might be holding up that belief?
- How might believing [X] affect the actions you take?
- Are there any other beliefs you might hold based on the meaning you've made and the assumptions you've drawn?

Conclusions:

- I hear that you've drawn a conclusion about [belief]. Can you identify the assumptions on which that's built?
- How do you think your culture and background have led you to the conclusion you've drawn?

Assumptions:

- Can you name the assumptions you're making?
- Can you identify any of the roots of that assumption? Where do you think it came from? Which experiences?
- Are there other assumptions you might be able to come to based on this meaning?

Meaning:

- I'm hearing that you made meaning about [an experience you had/something you heard/something you saw]. Can you tell me about the meaning you made?
- How do you think your cultural and personal background affected the meaning that you made [of that experience/what you saw/heard]?
- I hear that those specific data points caught your attention. What was the meaning that you made of them?
- I hear that you saw [X], and the meaning you made was [paraphrase]. Does that seem accurate?
- Is there any other meaning you could make from this data?

Data:

- I hear that you saw/heard/experienced [X]. I want to make sure I heard this right—you're saying you saw/heard/experienced [paraphrase].
- Can you identify the data that you selected from the entire experience? If you imagine that your mind is a video camera recording everything, can you name the specific data points that you latched on to?

Sometimes, when using the Ladder of Inference, I've seen beliefs crumble in front of my eyes, and sometimes I've seen beliefs become unstable and fall apart over time. The Ladder helps us to distance ourselves from our beliefs just a little bit—just enough so that we can muster the courage and will to examine them. But the Ladder is an intervention *at the level of cognition*—it must be used in conjunction with strategies to address the emotional experiences of holding strongly to beliefs.

Beliefs Change When We Encounter New Information

Beliefs change when we're confronted with data that doesn't fit what we believe—when we experience what's called *cognitive dissonance*—and when that confrontation happens within a trusting relationship.

Stephanie was a new teacher I coached (whom I write about extensively in *Coaching for Equity*) who struggled when she began teaching in

Oakland. She was a white woman who had never lived in a diverse community, and I quickly realized that she didn't know much about her students. Recall that the Ladder of Inference explains how beliefs are formed when we select data and attach meaning to it. I came up with a list of things she could do to learn more about them, including walking around the neighborhood, shopping in the stores her students' families shopped in, doing home visits, listening to parents, reading about immigration to California, visiting the Oakland Library's history room, reading memoirs by Black and Brown authors, reading about teaching Black and Brown kids, and more. Stephanie was eager to engage in these activities, and as she acquired knowledge—especially firsthand knowledge about the community she served—she had more data from which to create beliefs. Sometimes, we just need more information to change beliefs and behaviors.

There are many ways that coaches can help clients obtain new information. In addition to the approach I took with Stephanie, we can gather data through surveys, capture video of teachers and students, share observations, model instructional practices, and observe effective teachers. This is how coaching activities help change beliefs. What's critical is that as we engage clients in activities we help them process and take stock of the new information they're acquiring, we help them see how their beliefs are shifting, and we help them try out new behaviors.

Beliefs Change When Our Core Identity Is Preserved

Human beings are psychologically wired for self-preservation. We don't put ourselves—or our sense of self—in harm's way.

Stephanie thought of herself as a good person who helped others—many of us in education think of ourselves this way. During coaching sessions, Stephanie often cried a great deal because she was afraid that I would think or say that she was a bad person because she didn't understand her students, because she didn't share their identity markers, and because she feared that all of this meant she was racist—which in her mind implied that she was evil. Stephanie's tears were a response to her amygdala being hijacked by thoughts that she would be exposed and shamed for being racist. Those tears became a barrier to the conversation, and they were a human response to fear. She wouldn't have become less afraid if I'd called her out on her racism or told her to stop being so fragile. I had to accept her thoughts and her feelings and work with them. This is why a Transformational Coach has to coach ways of being and address emotions, as well as coach beliefs.

Defining racism as I do in Chapter 12 was essential to help Stephanie preserve a sense of self. It allowed me to suggest that she could be a good person who acted in racist ways.

You can't just smash someone's identity, or ask them to shatter it, and then leave them in pieces. Coaches help clients to cultivate a new or expanded identity by coaching a way of being and inviting a teacher to reflect on who they want to be. We're wired to crave learning, and when we can do so without abandoning our core identity, we leap toward opportunities for growth.

Beliefs Change When We See the Benefits of Changing a Belief

For a while, I despaired about the school district I worked in. I often told Leslie, my coach, "This district is so messed up. It's toxic and dysfunctional at its very core."

The first time I said this, she said, "Is that the truth or is it a belief?" Her question unnerved me—I thought I'd been sharing an objective truth.

After yet another rant about the hopelessness of my district, Leslie said, "What do you gain from holding this belief?" In the moment, I responded defensively. I was confused by the question. I thought about it for a few weeks and realized that the belief allowed me to feel superior to others, it protected me from disappointment, and it allowed me to make excuses about the ways I behaved. I often went to meetings that felt like a tremendous waste of my time, where I was critical of the way the meeting was run, and of the leaders, and yet I didn't offer solutions. And then I'd complain to Leslie about these meetings.

One day, Leslie asked, "What would it be like if you went to one of those meetings open to the possibility that it could be useful?"

I admitted, "I guess I might feel better. Less tired. More engaged." I trusted her, but I didn't want to let go of my belief in the dysfunction of my district. It let me off the hook for being truly emotionally invested in my work; it kept me from disappointment and hurt.

Leslie dangled the possibility of an alternate belief in front of me. "What if," she said, "you believed that it was possible for one of those meetings to be meaningful and useful?" She helped me see how tempting this belief could be to try on—just for one meeting. She helped me see how the new belief might align with my values. She pushed me to accept that I could be courageous and face disappointment and hurt again. She helped me connect to my integrity and my longing for hope.

I went to one of these meetings intent on being open to possibility and committed to dropping my belief that the district was deeply dysfunctional—just for that one meeting. This new belief felt like a costume—stiff and unfamiliar. And yet, I was curious about what might happen if I wore it. What happened in that meeting was that I felt a little bit better—during and after—and I had a meaningful conversation with a colleague. I expressed my ideas more clearly than I had before, and others were receptive to them. My belief shifted—perhaps just an inch away from "this district is dysfunctional at its core," but it did shift.

Beliefs provide us with a sense of security. They help us understand ourselves and the world around us. Giving up a belief can mean we lose a sense of security, so to change a belief, we need to see how changing a belief might make our lives better. We become open to change when we recognize how a belief has limited our ability to feel efficacious, to experience joy, to form relationships with others, or to do what we want to do—be that to pursue a dream job or to ensure that all of our students graduate. Although we're often fearful, when offered a glimpse of what might be possible, we'll take the risks to question our beliefs or behaviors.

Transformational Coaches invite our clients to see how changing a belief can help them manifest their vision of themselves as a teacher, feel better emotionally, and see different outcomes for their students.

Beliefs Change When We Recognize Alternate Beliefs

Our willingness to release beliefs is increased when we see a new belief to adopt. I let go of my belief that my district was "so dysfunctional" when I could substitute the belief that "there are pockets of possibility and hope in this district."

For the first couple of years that George was a teacher, he struggled to teach kids who had learning differences. "Let's not put kids with Individualized Education Programs (IEPs) in my class," he told colleagues, "because I suck at teaching them." With the support of his coach, George realized that he held a belief that he couldn't teach kids with IEPs. When they explored the impact of this belief, George recognized that it kept him from serving every child—which felt misaligned to his values. He also didn't like feeling that he had a limited skill set. He wanted to rid himself of his belief that he couldn't teach kids with IEPs, but he didn't know what that meant or what would take its place. He came up with this: "I don't have the skills to be effective with students with IEPs, but I can learn them because I want to be effective with all students."

Adopting a growth mindset helps us identify alternate beliefs while we rid ourselves of the old. Angela, or any teacher who believes that kids can only learn if she's teaching the whole class at the same time, could say, "I believe that I can learn how to teach students in different ways" or "I believe that students want to be successful when working in stations." A teacher might decide that she no longer wants to believe that eye-rolling is a sign of disrespect because she's getting in trouble for sending so many students to the office. So, she might tell herself, "I don't know what eye-rolling means right now, and I'm willing to stay open to find out." This statement of belief serves as a scaffold as she releases an old belief and adopts a new one.

Implications for Action

These six conditions in which beliefs change direct us to actions. Table 13.1 summarizes these conditions and the actions we can take.

Table 13.1: Implications for Action

Beliefs Change When:	Implications for a Coach
We feel safe enough.	• Build trust. • Cultivate a growth mindset. • Coach emotions and ways of being. • Communicate confidence in the process and conviction that it's worth the discomfort.
We understand how the belief originated.	• Use the Ladder of Inference to help a client understand how beliefs are constructed. • Engage in conversations to excavate beliefs.
We encounter new information.	• Gather and share data, surveys, and video. • Read texts. • Listen to others.
Our core identity is preserved.	• Coach to affirm a more expansive sense of self—coach a way of being. • Help the client connect with their purpose as an educator and anchor in their core values.
We see the benefits of changing a belief.	• Find a meaningful entry point to explore beliefs. • Help the client anchor in their purpose and legacy. • Raise awareness about the negative and unintended consequences of holding the belief. • Help the client see how releasing an emotion could feel liberating.
We recognize alternate beliefs.	• Scaffold the learning. • Offer alternate beliefs. • Help a client see a wider set of data.

What to Say When You Hear Something Racist: A Cheat Sheet

The sentence stems and questions in Table 13.2 will help you consider what to say when you hear a client express something that's racist. As you build your coaching skills, this table can serve as a cheat sheet and a starting point for deeper conversations. As you read the responses, highlight or underline phrases that you'd like to remember and that you can imagine using. If you say them aloud as you read, you'll be more likely to remember them.

For an expanded framework to respond to racism, check out the *Bright Morning Podcast* series called "What to Say When You Hear Something Racist." It's applicable inside and outside of schools, and it guides you through a three-step decision-making process.

How you respond to problematic statements such as those in the first column is informed by your purpose. If you are a positional leader, you will, in addition to offering opportunities to unlearn white supremacy and to create equitable classrooms, need to respond to racist comments directly and communicate your organization's commitment to equity. You might say something like this:

> What you've just said is racist. Let's talk about how you can continue to learn about what you just expressed, because our school is committed to dismantling racism.

Or you might say something like this:

> The beliefs you expressed don't align to our mission. If you're willing to explore them and how they are harmful, then I'd love for you to continue being a member of our community. If you're open to it, you can start working with our coach to learn right away.

Of course, positional leaders should also use coaching strategies with those they supervise to help them grow, so it's also entirely appropriate to use any of the responses to racist comments in Table 13.2.

Table 13.2: Responses to Racist Comments

What Is Said	Possible Coaching Responses
What do you expect? These parents don't care about their kids.	• Tell me more about how you came to hold that belief. • What does "caring" look like to you? • Would you be open to learning more about their parents? • It must be confusing to see parents who don't seem to care about their kids. Is this an assumption you'd like to unpack?
There's no way all these kids can master all of the standards.	• How do you benefit from that belief? What would be possible if you let it go? • What would have to be different for you to be able to say, "I know these kids can master all the standards"?
I can't do this. I just can't teach these kids.	• If I could wave a magic wand and make that belief disappear, how would you act? How would you be? • If you believe that you can't teach these kids, what actions are available for you to take? What do you want to do?
The reason that our Black male students aren't successful is because they don't have role models. What can we do about that?	• What do you think our Black male students need? • I wonder if that's what our Black male students—and their families—think. Would you be willing to learn what they think? • What's within your sphere of influence? What can you do to have a positive impact on our Black male students? • What do you think we could do to hire more Black males who could be role models?

(Continued)

Table 13.2: (Continued)

What Is Said	Possible Coaching Responses
I can't teach these kids. Why don't you coach their elementary-school teachers? They're the ones who need coaching. It's not my fault they're so far behind.	• It sounds like you're feeling sad that our students are so far behind. And that's not your fault. What do you want to do to help them get on grade level? • I agree that all teachers need and deserve coaching, including elementary-school teachers. Which aspects of your teaching practice do you want to work on? • It sounds like you're feeling frustrated by the limits of your own abilities. What is it exactly that you feel like you can't do?
I don't send them to the "time-out chair"; I send them to "isolation," because these kids get that reference. They know about prisons, so I make it easier for them to understand my discipline system.	• That language makes it seem like your classroom is a prison, and I doubt that's what you are intending to communicate. What are your intentions? • It sounds like you've struggled to get kids to understand your approach to classroom management. Can we start there—with your management systems and approach—and then identify the language that's best to communicate it? • I don't think you're trying to prepare your students to be good inmates, right? What is your vision for your students? What do you hope they'll be doing when they're 23 years old?
She'll end up pregnant at 15. That's how those Mexicans are. I'm not wasting my time teaching her chemistry.	• I hear that you're uncertain about what will happen to that student—and every student in our school takes chemistry in eighth grade. So, let's figure out how you can be successful with her. • How did you arrive at this belief about Mexicans? Which experiences led you to believe this? • Who deserves to learn chemistry?

What Is Said	Possible Coaching Responses
Can you come to the conference I have to have with his dad? I'm afraid to be alone with him. Middle Eastern men have no boundaries.	• What are your fears about what could happen? • What do you think has led you to hold this belief about Middle Eastern men? • I'm willing to be there with you, and I can hear that you're still learning about our community, but you're also expressing some dehumanizing stereotypes about Middle Eastern men. Would you be willing to explore where those came from?
This is America. They should just speak English.	• I'm hearing fear. Can you help me understand what that's about? • Where did this belief come from? • What might happen if they spoke Spanish in class? What's the worst-case scenario?
If we don't strictly enforce rules, they'll be out of control. These kids need tight structures and routines.	• What else do you think our students need to be successful in school—aside from routines and structure? • I think I'm hearing concern and care for our students. Is that right? Can we explore what they need to feel loved and cared for in our community? • Are you willing to explore where your fears about our students are coming from? • I'm aware that you don't share the racial or cultural background of our students, and I think it would be helpful if we explored how your identity shapes the way you see and understand our students. Would you be up for that?

(Continued)

Table 13.2: (Continued)

What Is Said	Possible Coaching Responses
I'm letting her draw today because she's had such a hard week, and if I push her, then she has a meltdown and disrupts everyone's learning.	• Giving her permission to opt out of learning communicates a belief about what she's capable of doing. If your goal is that she learns, can we explore other options for how to help her manage her frustrations? • I wonder what her mother would want her daughter to be doing in class. Would it be helpful if we met with her mom and asked her this and also asked her for insights into how to work with her child? • I hear your commitment to every child learning and that you're not sure what to do with one student. I hear that you've identified a learning area for yourself. Let's explore that.
He always sits alone, in the back of the classroom, because that's the only way he can stay focused and quiet.	• How do you want him to remember you, as his teacher? • How does this decision align with your core values? • What do you know about what he likes to do or what he's capable of doing? • It sounds like you're holding some beliefs about what he needs in order to be successful. Let's unpack those beliefs. • I wonder how he feels being isolated. I wonder what he tells his father about your class. • I've observed him in other classes and have seen him working well with groups. Would you be willing to explore what's happening in those other classes that enables him to be successful? Could we observe him in those classes and talk to those teachers about what they do?

How to Navigate All the Emotions

The hardest thing about coaching for equity is navigating the storm of feelings that will come up—your own and other people's. People of color will likely experience stormier conditions. This is an unfair truth, a condition of living in a racist world. That doesn't mean we don't deserve to address our emotions or get support. We can acknowledge that we've got extra work—the task of learning how to coach well *and* the need to attend to our emotions.

In earlier chapters, I've given you a lot of suggestions for how to engage with your emotions, so let this just be a reminder:

- Feel the feelings—feel them in your body. This can be hard for many of us, so think of it as a skill to build and know that you have to feel to heal.
- When you're triggered, remember that you're at a trailhead of pain, and there's an opportunity to get to the old wounds that deserve healing.
- Therapists can be invaluable in helping us learn how to feel our feelings and heal our wounds. You don't have to go it alone.
- Other people's feelings will be *so much easier* to deal with if you're actively addressing your own.
- Breathing really helps to regulate the nervous system. This is another practice to develop.
- Gather your people. Find community where you can talk about feelings and race and equity and liberation. Remember that our primary core human need is for belonging and connection, and when we're doing work that requires courage, we need community even more.
- Finally, anchor in your "why." When the uncomfortable emotions arise, remember why you're doing whatever you're doing—be that reflecting on your identity experiences, holding compassionate and confrontational conversations about equity, or taking responsibility for an

unintended consequence that hurt someone. If you can remember that you're traversing a storm of difficult emotions for a purpose, the journey will be easier.

Coaching for equity is perhaps the most refined expression of Transformational Coaching. It takes skill to coach for equity, and mastery takes practice—lots and lots of practice. I hope that this chapter has given you an appreciation for what's possible when we coach for equity, for the skills that are required, and for the need for ongoing, high-quality, effective PD on coaching. This book introduces key knowledge and skills, but to internalize this content, you need practice and feedback. Let this be a call to action to rally your colleagues into practice sessions, to find a community of coaches who want to role-play conversations, or to attend a Bright Morning workshop.

Pause and Process

Reflect:

- What insights did this chapter give you into your behaviors, beliefs, and ways of being as they relate to coaching for equity?
- Which strategies feel accessible to you, and which feel like a reach to implement?
- What feelings came up for you when reading this chapter?
- What's your first next step to develop your skills in coaching for equity?

Next steps:

- Listen to *Bright Morning Podcast* episode 85 and engage in the exercises and prompts I provide to find your personal "why" for coaching for equity.

- Download the Ladder of Inference from my website to remind you of the rungs on the ladder.
- Attend a Bright Morning Coaching for Equity workshop. If you are committed to equity and you are in a school or district where you can't use funds to buy my book, *Coaching for Equity*, or to attend one of my Coaching for Equity workshops, reach out to us at info@brightmorningteam.com.

CHAPTER 14

How to Coach Behaviors

It's Time to Close the Gaps

Common misconception: Gaps between current and desired abilities are deficits and liabilities.	*Transformational Coaches know:* Gaps between current and desired abilities are opportunities for growth that occur whenever we try to do something new.

The goal of any coaching approach is to see changes in behaviors. Because sustained, transformative change in practice is not possible without shifts in beliefs and ways of being, most of this book focuses on the deep work of coaching those areas. But there are times that we do coach behaviors directly, most frequently around observations.

I'll focus this chapter on my work with Olivia, a first-year teacher I coached as part of a program to clear her teaching credential. A white woman in her mid-20s, Olivia had grown up in San Francisco in an upper-middle-class family. She had hoped to teach lower elementary but accepted a position as a fifth-grade teacher because she liked the principal. She became a teacher because she wanted to do something meaningful.

In our first coaching session, Olivia asked when I would observe her. It was only the second week of school, and I'd planned on meeting with her a few more times before suggesting an observation, so I asked her to tell me more about what she wanted.

"I think if you came in," Olivia said, "you might see things that I don't." I agreed, but I wanted to hear more.

"Is there anything specific you'd want me to pay attention to?" I asked.

Olivia thought for a moment. "Everything," she said.

"Everything is a lot," I responded.

"There are so many things I'm supposed to get good at. The evaluation tool is massive, and we've got our school's initiatives around higher-order thinking skills, and I really want to be a culturally competent teacher, and I don't want to make mistakes in the beginning." Olivia paused and looked away. "Things aren't going badly," she said, "I feel like I'm doing okay, but I want feedback."

"Okay," I said, "I hear your commitment to teaching, and I appreciate your desire to learn. Usually when I do observations, we agree on something specific for me to look at, and we might select an observation tool ahead of time. But it sounds like what you might be wanting is sort of baseline data."

"Yes!" Olivia interrupted. "I want you to do a pre-assessment. I feel like that'll give me more clarity about what to focus on, and then you can do a mid-semester assessment and a final. Like I do with my kids."

I hesitated. A coach doesn't evaluate—there's a time for assessment, but it's more effective when done by a person such as a principal, and coaching is a more powerful container when the judgment implicit in evaluation is removed. And yet, I heard Olivia's desire to know if she was on the right track. "Okay," I said, "let's try this and see what happens. I'll collect observational data—what you say and do, what kids say and do—and we'll use that to debrief."

Olivia had been making eye contact, but she dropped her gaze and looked down at her hands. "This isn't something you'll share with my principal, right?"

"No. As I said in our first session, everything we talk about is confidential," I said. "I don't share my notes or observations with anyone else. But I'm glad you asked. I want you to feel comfortable with this. Is there anything else you want to ask or say?"

"Will you tell me if you think I'm a dud?" Olivia said with the hint of a smile. "If I'm hopeless as a teacher?"

"Nope," I said, smiling. "That's not my job. My job is to hold up a mirror for you to see yourself and help you make decisions about what to do."

"But what if I can't see what you see?" Olivia said.

"That's a wise wondering," I said. "And that's possible. And if or when that happens, I'll tell you what I see."

"That's good to hear. I want you to know that I'm not fragile," Olivia said. "I can take feedback."

I nodded.

"Okay, so when can you come?" she asked.

How to Do a Classroom Observation

When I walked into Olivia's classroom after morning recess, students had just settled onto the rug, and Olivia was pulling up a chair. As we agreed, she introduced me to the class.

"Students, like I told you in morning circle," Olivia said, "Ms. Elena is here to observe. She's my teacher, so she's going to be telling me how I'm doing. If she talks to you, that's okay. But otherwise try to ignore her." I waved and leaned against a side wall, perching my computer on a short bookshelf.

Olivia had told me that she was starting a new literacy unit she'd designed called "Know and Show Yourself." It was based on state standards, intended as a way to get to know her students, and she hoped it would be engaging. When she revealed the paperback in her hands, I smiled. *The House on Mango Street*, by Sandra Cisneros, was a book I'd taught and loved.

I took notes on a simple, time-stamped, three-column document: what the teacher said and did, what students said and did, and my notes and wonderings. My notes were mostly questions. For example, when Olivia revealed the book, one student loudly said, "We read this last year!" I captured that in the student behavior column and noted, "I wonder if Olivia checked with the fourth-grade teachers about the texts they use." I also noticed that when the student made that comment, which was audible to everyone in the room, Olivia looked at the other side of the room and continued talking. I noted, "Did she hear him say that?"

We had agreed that I'd observe for 45 minutes. Students sat on the rug for half an hour. Olivia talked about the book, prompted a few pair-shares, and then distributed copies. Still on the rug, she read the first (very short) chapter of the book aloud while students followed along, tracking the words with their fingers as she'd asked. When they returned to their desks, they were instructed to write a reflection on what they'd read. Olivia wrote sentence starters on the whiteboard and set the timer. Then they were told to read what they'd written with a partner.

While we waited for instructions on the next activity, I asked two students, "What are you learning?" And "Why do you think you're doing this activity?" When I observe instruction, if I have a chance to talk to students, those are the two questions I always ask. Sometimes I also ask, "How does this learning connect to learning you've done previously?" After listening to what students had to say, I returned to my computer to capture their words. Olivia had been watching me as I talked to the students, and I noted her furrowed brow. "Is she worried?" I wrote. Olivia and I were set to debrief her lesson after school that day, so I had blocked out 90 minutes in my schedule to process my notes and prepare for the conversation.

Objective Data and Subjective Interpretations

When we observe instruction, we capture as much raw data as we can, data that would be found on the first rung of the Ladder of Inference (see Chapter 11, "How to Coach Beliefs"). We use this data to debrief with a teacher and to create a scope of learning. However, there's value in gathering our assumptions and subjective evaluations. It's helpful to do this so that we can sort out the raw data from our assumptions.

Following an observation, I often summarize my assumptions, conclusions, concerns, and wonderings for myself—not to share with my client. I do this so I can remember what I was thinking and feeling and to differentiate between data and my interpretations. To be clear, there's nothing wrong with subjective interpretations. We all make them, consciously and unconsciously, and sometimes there's validity in those interpretations. The key is to be clear on what's interpretation and what's raw data.

Here are examples of the interpretive notes I made after Olivia's observation:

- The purpose of the lesson isn't clear. Does she create objectives for lessons?
- There was no activation of background schema or exploration of their prior knowledge—about any of the topics.
- There was no way to know what students learned. She needs to be able to identify their growth and learning after every lesson. What did she hope students would learn or gain from this lesson?
- Some vocabulary could have been front-loaded for the eight newcomer students.
- Thirty minutes is a long time for them to sit on the rug as evidenced by their squirming.
- Miguel seemed so uncomfortable sitting on the floor. He's a big kid, they were supposed to be sitting in their colored square on the rug, and he did not fit. He would stretch out his legs and then bump the girl in front of him, and she'd wiggle and complain. Twice Olivia said, "Miguel—crisscross apple sauce!" At which Miguel rolled his eyes, muttered that they weren't kindergartners, and tried to cross his legs. I know that Olivia did her student teaching in a first-grade class, and I wonder if she lacks knowledge about how to work with older kids.
- The transition back to their desks took seven minutes, which was longer than they need. Her directions for this transition were unclear.

- When Olivia prompted students to pair-share, she didn't give them instruction about who should start first. She didn't provide a mid-point cue to switch. She also didn't notice that a few students didn't have partners when they started the pair-share and that they ended up joining a pair and becoming a trio.
- The sentence starters that Olivia gave were all low level: "One thing I liked about this chapter . . . One question I had about this chapter . . ."
- Olivia didn't tell students that they'd be reading their writing to each other ahead of time. Several flipped their notebooks over and didn't read anything.

The two students I talked to didn't know what they were supposed to be learning in that lesson or why they were learning it. They did say they liked the story.

Let me be clear about my opinion of the lesson I observed: it wasn't bad. On the hopeful side, Olivia's relationships with students was positive, she quickly redirected wandering students during the transition, and her selection of a book that her majority Latine students could connect to was on point. Her classroom was also organized, and there was student work on the walls already. When a parent walked in as I was packing up, Olivia greeted him warmly by name and invited him in, even though it was also clear that she wasn't expecting him. But the lesson also revealed that Olivia had gaps around lesson design, creating relevance, assessment, routines and procedures, teaching English Learners, creating psychological safety, and understanding her students.

What I observed in Olivia's class were her *behaviors*. Some of my notes pointed to questions about her beliefs and ways of being, which I planned to explore. I was grateful to have a set of tools to use—the tools I'll share in this chapter—to categorize her behaviors, describe some of her struggles through a learning lens, and come up with a plan to refine those behaviors.

As I reflected on the observation and planned the debrief, I recalled observing teachers during my first year or two as a coach. I remembered being in their classrooms and feeling completely overwhelmed by what I saw. I felt like I noticed a thousand problems, I couldn't prioritize them, and I couldn't figure out a sequence for how to address them. Most of my notes reflected my interpretations and assumptions, rather than teacher or student behaviors. When I debriefed with teachers, I was often struck by how different our experiences had been. I'd open the conversation by asking, "How do you feel that lesson went?" and be shocked to hear them say, "I think it went pretty well!" The discrepancy between our assessments would throw me off, and I mentally added "lack of self-awareness" to the issues I'd listed.

I now understand that their response could have been avoided. For one thing, I now understand the risks with opening a conversation with "How do you feel . . . ," and I never use that stem (I'll give you some alternate suggestions shortly). More importantly, when I started coaching, I didn't know how to structure an observation or how to work toward alignment between my perception and a teacher's. I hadn't learned how to debrief a lesson, co-create a learning plan based on the data I collected, or get the teacher's buy-in to a plan I proposed.

The Purpose of Observations

Within a coaching context, the purpose of an observation is to support a teacher to develop their practice so that they can better meet the academic, social, and emotional needs of students. Within an evaluative context, the purpose is to assess performance against a set of established criteria. An administrator's responsibility is to observe, to support development, and to evaluate growth. Coaches are not evaluators, however, and so we need to reiterate that the purpose of evaluation is to help someone grow.

To conduct observations that will help a teacher grow, a Transformational Coach needs to use all the tools in their kit—all the strategies described in this book. As you continue reading about how to do observations, consider the places and opportunities to weave in strategies to coach beliefs and ways of being.

Should Observations Be Optional?

Olivia asked me to observe her, which was something she expected as a new teacher. Other teachers are apprehensive about observations or are strongly opposed to them. These responses are indicators of levels of trust—perhaps in the coach, perhaps in the broader context, perhaps in themselves. Observing teachers is invaluable. Your coaching will be severely limited in impact if you don't observe your clients performing the skills you're coaching them on. Consider any pushback or hesitation a sign to build trust. Your job will be to build enough trust for your client to let you in the door and then to make sure the observation becomes a trust-building experience.

Sometimes when teachers are really apprehensive, I say, "How about if I come in for 15 minutes and all I'll do is capture data on your strengths and what's going well?" In the debrief, I primarily take a supportive approach (see Chapter 5, "Fifty Questions to Ask"). Sometimes I'll do this three or four times before I shift into other approaches or ask reflective questions about the data I've gathered.

You can't force anyone to do anything—and if you do, you're not being a Transformational Coach. You can say, "It's an assumption that within coaching I'll observe you, just as you might listen to your students reading to hear their fluency so you can adjust your instruction." You can say, "I understand that this can feel really scary. Let's give it a try and see how it goes. I will ask for your feedback." You can say, "What would make this feel a little less scary?" And you can say, "I trust myself to guide you through a meaningful experience. Let's give it a try." Sometimes kind persistence is a useful coaching disposition.

Planning the Debrief

My goal for the debrief was to align on Olivia's areas for growth and to get her agreement on a sequence for her development. Given that she was a new teacher and that she had expressed receptivity to my guidance (and an awareness that she didn't know what she didn't know), I suspected that I could present ideas for a plan. With more experienced teachers, I would have co-constructed the plan. I also planned the debrief in consideration of what Olivia had asked for—a baseline evaluation—and by recalling her reference to the school's initiative around higher-order thinking and her commitment to being a culturally responsive teacher.

To arrive at my plan, I used the Gaps Framework (which you'll read about shortly) to organize my reflections on Olivia's areas for growth. Then I prioritized and sequenced Olivia's areas for growth and began creating a scope of learning. I reviewed the Adult Learning Principles (which you'll also read about in this chapter) to reflect on whether I was overlooking any aspects of Olivia's learning needs in my emerging plan. Then I reflected on a set of questions to help me plan the debrief conversation.

Guidelines for Conducting Observations

What follows are brief suggestions on effective practices for observations.

Pre-Observation:

- Communicate the purpose of observations. Are they expected as part of coaching work? Does someone else (administrators, credentialing programs) expect them to be done? What's the goal for doing them?
- Decide how long you'll observe for; observations of a 10–15 minute segment can be as meaningful as an entire period. I have come to find it more useful to do more frequent, short observations. You can gather a lot of data in 15 minutes, and the debrief can be more focused. That said, sometimes teachers want you to see the whole lesson, and sometimes you can accommodate that request to build trust.

- Make clear agreements: what time you'll be there, where in the classroom you'll sit or stand, what you'll focus on, how you'll gather data, whether or not you'll interact with students, how you'll take notes, whether you'll share those notes with the teacher or just a summary, and when you'll debrief.
- If you'll be capturing video, get your client's approval.
- Clarify whether you'll offer feedback and what that feedback will sound like.
- Discuss confidentiality agreements. Will anyone else see the data you'll gather or hear about it?
- If you plan on using a data-gathering tool, consider showing it to your client before the observation. The only exception to this is if you use the teacher-to-student tracking tool (available on my website and in *Coaching for Equity*).
- Normalize apprehensions or fears about being observed and provide space for your client to name their feelings.

During the Observation:
- Keep your word about agreements you made. Be a warm and neutral presence in the classroom. Keep your facial expressions generally neutral. Affirmative expressions (lots of smiles and nodding) can be problematic because if/when your opinions shift, your client may register this in your expressions.
- Take thorough notes. I prefer to use a computer because I'm a fast keyboarder, and if we've agreed, I can easily share them with my client.
- Don't intervene in anything that happens in the classroom unless someone's physical or emotional well-being is in danger. If a teacher "loses control" of the class, don't take over. If the teacher asks for help, you can provide it. Otherwise, you undermine the teacher's authority.
- Only use real-time feedback (providing suggestions or direction in the moment) if this has been agreed upon in advance.

After the Observation:

- Use the Gaps Framework; the Adult Learning Principles; and, optionally, the Inquiry, Systems, and Change Management Lenses (discussed in Chapter 15) to prepare a plan.
- Give yourself ample time to process and plan, usually two to three times the amount of observing time for preparing (a 15-minute observation requires 45 minutes for me to prepare for a debrief).
- Use the questions in Table 14.2 (later in this chapter) to plan the debrief conversation.
- Consider additional opening questions/statements such as:
  - Tell me about a moment in that lesson when you felt like students were moving toward mastering the objective.
  - What do you think students learned, and how do you know?
  - What did you notice about how students engaged with the lesson?
  - What did you notice about how students interacted with each other?
  - What did you notice about your emotions during the lesson?
  - If you were going to make a "best of" video montage of that lesson, what would be in it?
  - If you could do that lesson over, what would you change?
- Be prepared to answer the question "What did you think?" I often respond with any of the following:
  - I promise I'll share observations I made about both areas of strength and areas for growth.
  - I'm grateful for the time in your class and have some ideas about how to support you in your development.
- Be clear on the one or two priorities for growth that you want to elevate for your client. You'll need their buy-in to these, and they'll need to see how they align to their broader goals and areas for growth.

During the Debrief:

- Open by stating the purpose of the conversation and your intention. This can sound like, "The goal of this conversation is to share my observations and to align on next steps. My intention is to continue supporting you to live into the vision you have for yourself as a teacher and to meet the needs of our students."

- Know that anything can happen in a debrief and anticipate that strong emotions might arise for your client. You can debrief a lesson over multiple coaching sessions.
- Incorporate strategies to coach beliefs and ways of being.

A Note on Who Defines Goals

You might be wondering, when you coach a teacher, who defines the goals for the work you do together?

Ideally, you're working in a school or organization where leaders have developed a coaching framework. This means that goals for coaching are aligned to teacher professional practice goals, school initiatives, and student learning needs. For example, a district could be addressing academic literacy and social-emotional learning, and all coaching goals would be tied to those foci. Or a teacher's coaching goals might be directly aligned to the evaluation system. In some places, a teacher might be invited to select any aspect of their practice around which to create goals.

There may be a tension between a teacher's desire to direct their learning (given our core need of autonomy) and the perspective of leaders about what teachers need to improve on. In one school where I coached, teachers created a goal around anything they wanted and created a second goal aligned to the school-wide initiatives. This compromise was appreciated.

The question around goals also raises a question around who defines "good teaching." In some places, an evaluation tool defines this. I've also worked in places where there's no criteria for good teaching, a challenging and frustrating situation for teachers and coaches. If that's your situation, it can help to use resources such as Doug Lemov's *Teach Like a Champion* to align on the criteria for good teaching.

The Gaps Framework

Think of something you've always wanted to be able to do but right now you know you can't—riding a horse across the Mongolian plains, publishing a memoir, or being a superintendent. Let's say you want to ride a horse across Mongolia. You'll need knowledge about the Mongolian land and climate; you'll need skills to ride long distances; you'll likely need to learn a few words in Mongolian and something about communicating with people in that region. The gaps between your current abilities and where you'd need to be for your Mongolian adventure are likely quite large.

Anytime we struggle to do something or aspire to do something new or different, there are gaps between our current ability and our desired (or required) abilities. When a new teacher can't control their classroom, they likely have skill gaps (such as ensuring that all students are paying attention when they give directions) and knowledge gaps (such as effective strategies for getting students' attention). They may also feel stretched beyond capacity—working long hours, neglecting self-care and sleep, and perhaps taking care of their own children. If they're teaching students who don't share their racial background, for example, they may have cultural competency gaps. If they get frustrated when students don't pay attention and then get flustered, they may have emotional intelligence gaps.

Gaps are not deficits. They do not reveal fundamental flaws in who we are. Gaps are areas for growth. Conceptualizing these areas as gaps anchors us in a growth mindset when we're coaching. We *all* have gaps; we'll have gaps for as long as we live, because there's no person alive who has the ability to do everything. This framework is not about finding weaknesses. It's a tool to recognize potential and explore what lies in the way of fulfilling it. It's a way to categorize areas for growth, prioritize and sequence learning activities, and clarify next steps to close gaps.

Table 14.1 describes the six gaps categories and offers examples of what they can look like in practice.

Table 14.1: The Gaps Framework

Gap	Description	Examples for a Teacher
Skill	The ability to execute the technical elements of a task. Usually the application of knowledge.	• Identifying an appropriate learning target for a lesson • Front-loading vocabulary • Getting the attention of the whole class • Breaking down steps needed to solve complex equations
Knowledge	The theoretical or practical understanding of a subject. Can be information.	• What constitutes a polynomial • The preferred names of all your students • Strategies for redirecting behavior • Which texts have been used in prior and subsequent grades
Capacity	The time and resources to do something. Can be physical capacity.	• Having time to call students' parents • Having books to differentiate learning • Being able to attend a PD session on a Saturday morning • Having the physical energy (or ability) to attend evening school functions
Will	Desire, intrinsic motivation, passion, or commitment. Usually has an emotional tone.	• Loving your work • Wanting to serve a community • Aspiring to interrupt educational inequities • Committing to helping kids learn

Table 14.1: (Continued)

Gap	Description	Examples for a Teacher
Cultural competence	The ability to understand, appreciate, and interact with people with different identity markers or belief systems; the skill to navigate differences in identities.	• Understanding that eye contact has different meanings in different cultures • Correctly pronouncing students' names • Referring to "winter break," rather than "Christmas break" • Using students' preferred pronouns
Emotional intelligence	The ability to be aware of, navigate, and express one's emotions; the ability to recognize, empathize with, and navigate other people's emotions.	• Awareness of your anxiety when an administrator enters the class • Ability to draw boundaries around requests for help from colleagues • Skills to regulate irritation with a student • Skills to connect with a student

By presenting the gaps in Figure 14.1 as a pyramid, I'm implying a hierarchy: some skills really do rest on others. Instructional coaches often focus on knowledge and skill, but these elements depend on the foundational elements, those closer to the base of the pyramid.

Consider capacity. Let's say you observe a teacher delivering a lesson from the new ELA curriculum. It's a disaster. You might recognize skill and knowledge gaps, and you remember that this year district leaders rolled out seven new initiatives, that the teacher is also implementing a new math curriculum and a new classroom management program, and that he's also piloting an initiative to mainstream students with special needs. If you only coached him on instructional skills and didn't recognize his capacity gap, he may not improve. If you acknowledge and address his capacity gap, he may be able to grow in ELA instruction. Emotional intelligence and cultural competency are even more foundational.

Figure 14.1: The Gaps Framework

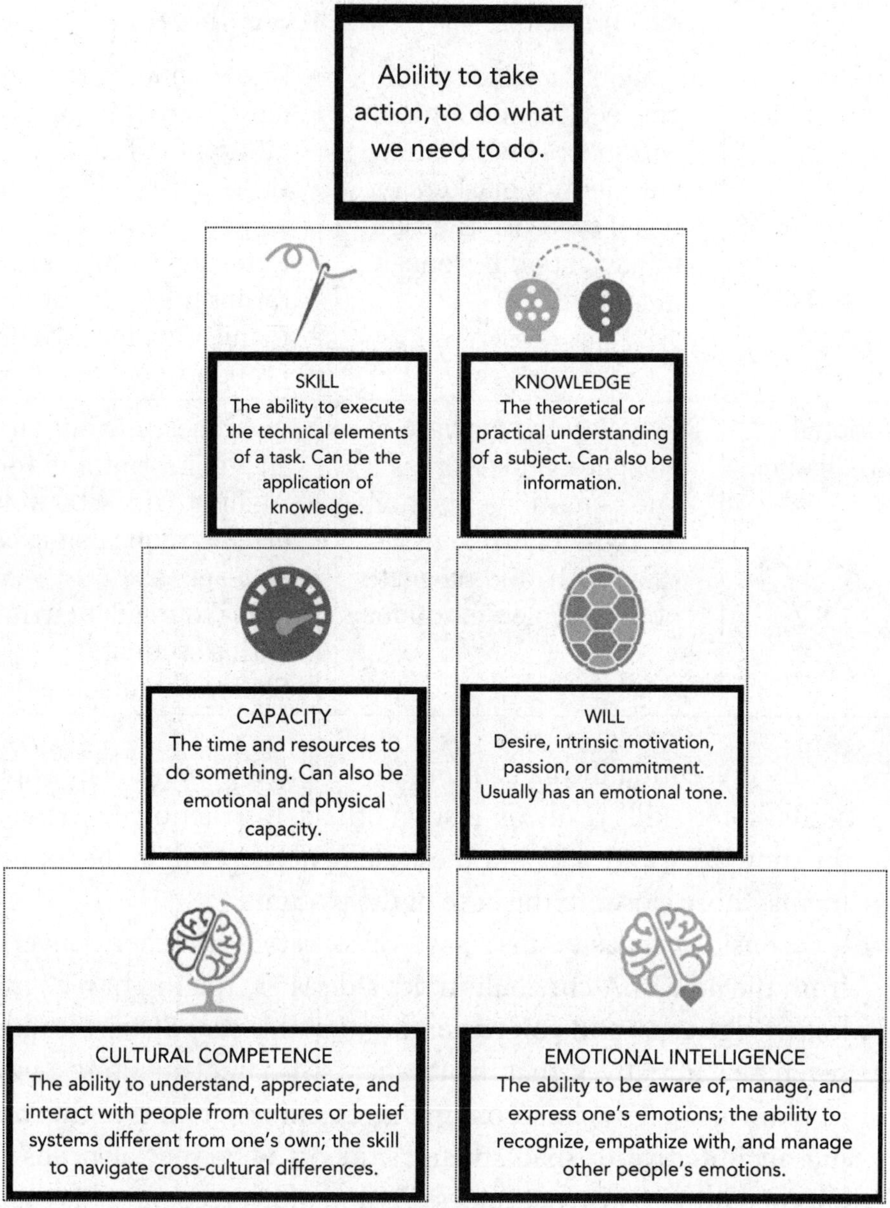

Ability to take action, to do what we need to do.

SKILL
The ability to execute the technical elements of a task. Can be the application of knowledge.

KNOWLEDGE
The theoretical or practical understanding of a subject. Can also be information.

CAPACITY
The time and resources to do something. Can also be emotional and physical capacity.

WILL
Desire, intrinsic motivation, passion, or commitment. Usually has an emotional tone.

CULTURAL COMPETENCE
The ability to understand, appreciate, and interact with people from cultures or belief systems different from one's own; the skill to navigate cross-cultural differences.

EMOTIONAL INTELLIGENCE
The ability to be aware of, manage, and express one's emotions; the ability to recognize, empathize with, and manage other people's emotions.

There are a number of ways to use the Gaps Framework. I'll explain how to use it as a thinking tool for yourself during a conversation and also as a tool for shared reflection with a client. Then I'll apply this framework to my observation of Olivia.

Using the Gaps Framework as a Thinking Tool During a Conversation

Imagine you're debriefing an observation. The teacher you observed begins by describing their experience: "I was prepared to introduce the new unit, and I was so excited about it, but the lesson flopped. I thought students would be engaged with the Do Now, but they were like, 'this is stupid, teacher.' I got flustered when they responded that way, and I think I rushed through the instructions for the first activity."

Where to begin? Using the Gaps Framework tool to consider what to say in this debrief conversation, you might wonder if the teacher's lesson required skills that she had never used before, perhaps lesson planning skills. You might also consider the teacher's knowledge about what students already understood about the topic. You might also wonder about her emotional intelligence—whether she recognized in the moment that she was getting flustered and whether she can self-regulate when she realizes this.

Thinking through the Gaps Framework helps me determine what to ask next and how to dig deeper. In this situation, I might ask the teacher, "How did you decide on the Do Now?" or "What student data did you use to sequence the elements of this lesson?" These questions probe the teacher's decision-making and help us get to the root causes of their struggles.

With a Client as a Tool for Shared Discovery

I also use the Gaps Framework as a tool for shared discovery. When Stephanie, the young ninth-grade English teacher I introduced in the previous chapter, complained that her students didn't turn in homework, I gave her a copy of the framework, explained the concept of the Gaps Framework, and asked her which gaps might be in play. She quickly and accurately concluded that her students didn't have the skills to complete the homework she assigned. The homework she assigned asked student to use skills that they hadn't yet built.

When I asked Stephanie what *her gaps* were when it came to teaching, she was thoughtful. "I have so many gaps," she said. "It's kind of a relief to see it this way because I recognize how many areas for growth I have. But I do have will!"

I frequently share the Gaps Framework with clients. I give them a copy of the graphic, invite their reflections on their own gaps and their students', and sometimes reference my own gaps as a coach, perhaps saying something like, "I'm working on the skill of holding silence." Being transparent around this framework is a way to pull back the curtain on the process of learning, to normalize that we all have gaps, and to generate a commitment to growth.

There may be times when you recognize gaps in your client's abilities but they disagree with your perception. For example, Greg, a new first-grade teacher, was frustrated about student behavior. When he asked what I thought he should do, I suggested that he work on building relationships with students. I believed I was seeing an emotional intelligence and a cultural competence gap.

"No, that's not the problem," he said. "The problem is that I don't know how to manage first graders. I think I'm using strategies that are more appropriate for older students." He believed he had a knowledge gap. In this case, because we were still building trust and I wanted to get to know Greg better, I followed his lead. We visited two other first-grade teachers and observed their strategies for redirecting off-task behavior and for creating a focused classroom. As we reflected on the visits, I emphasized the observations I'd made of the relationships between the teachers and students.

"Okay, I see what you're saying about relationships," Greg said, "I don't know if I agree with you, but I see what you're pointing at." I left it at that for the time being. He later came to see how relationships and managing students were two sides of the same coin.

When I coached Maggie, a new sixth-grade history teacher who was struggling, I suggested that she work on procedures and routines. She knew the routines that could keep her class running smoothly, but she wasn't consistent in requiring students to use them. I believed Maggie had a skill gap. When I made this suggestion, she said, "The problem isn't that I'm not consistent. The problem is that these kids don't respect authority here." Maggie paused. "I shouldn't have to tell them over and over that they need to walk into class and start the Do Now. Once is enough!"

Maggie's reflection revealed additional gaps and underlying beliefs, and I shifted to coaching her around her sphere of influence.

"Do you think there's *anything* that you can do to improve what's going on in your class?" I asked. I nudged Maggie to take responsibility for what she could do, and I also set about to gather data to help her see what I saw: that the way she explained routines was muddled, and that by not requiring students to use them, she sent confusing messages.

Often when I'm coaching, one thinking tool or framework leads me into using another. This is why we need a full coaching toolbox and knowledge of how and when to use each tool.

Using the Gaps Framework After an Observation

After an observation, you essentially create a proposal for next steps. There are two components in this process:

1. Categorize the gaps you observed.
2. Determine the criteria for prioritizing the gaps to close. (The criteria can be teacher goals, school priorities or annual initiatives, and indicators of effective instruction.)

Once you identify which gaps you're working on with your client, you will sequence the learning needed to close the gap. There's a lot of debate about how to sequence teachers' learning, and I'll contribute my perspective.

When I observe instruction and prepare a coaching plan, I consider the following sequenced components:

- *Emotional intelligence:* How does the teacher regulate their emotions? How do they relate to students? How does the teacher wield power in the classroom?
- *Social intelligence:* How has the teacher created a psychologically and identity-safe classroom for students? How do students interact with each other? How does the teacher respond to students who don't treat others kindly?
- *Cultural competency:* What indicators are there of the teacher's awareness of their own identity markers and how their identity affects their practice? Who does the teacher call on, praise, or reprimand? Are there patterns in those interactions related to students' identity markers? What else illustrates the teacher's equity awareness or lack of?
- *Purpose and objectives:* What is the learning target for the lesson? Is it "right-sized" and connected to prior learning? Is it relevant and important? Do students understand what mastery of the target will look like?
- *Lesson design and execution:* What's the quality of the lesson? Is it rigorous? Engaging? Is it based on grade-level standards? Is it well-paced? Is it structured and scaffolded?
- *Routines and procedures:* How does the teacher manage transitions, get students' attention, and give instructions? Are these done quickly, kindly, and effectively?
- *Assessment:* How often and in which ways does the teacher assess what students are learning during the lesson? What does the teacher do with the data that they gather during a lesson? How do they adjust the lesson based on formative assessments? Can they modify when necessary?

This is not the only way to sequence a learning plan for a teacher. Some might say, for example, that unless we start with the quality of lessons, other elements are irrelevant. I'd argue that a teacher can have relevant, rigorous lesson plans, but if they are intimidating and mean and they send the same Black boys to the office every day, lesson plans don't matter.

What's critical is that you are clear on the criteria for effective instruction and that you are intentional in sequencing the learning components that lead to it. Ideally, this is determined by a team of educators—perhaps by a Leadership Team or a group charged with leading professional development. When values and a theory of action aren't clear, then coaches sometimes address gaps either randomly or based on their own values and theories of action. This is a breakdown in systems.

Olivia's Observation and Coaching Plan

When I reviewed my notes from Olivia's observation, I didn't find evidence of capacity, will, cultural competency, or emotional intelligence gaps. I did come up with a substantive list of skill and knowledge gaps, which I sequenced in order of priority.

Olivia's Skill Gaps:
- Learning targets: creating lessons that have clear, doable objectives
- Making learning relevant: connecting new learning to past learning
- Lesson design: structuring the lesson, varying activities, scaffolding components
- Varying questioning strategies and increasing the rigor of questions
- Giving directions and checking for student understanding of directions
- Front-loading vocabulary and using other English-language development strategies for English Learners
- Setting up pair-shares and other group learning activities: providing clear directions and checking for understanding before releasing students

- Ensuring psychological safety when students are asked to share with each other
- Checking progress toward learning targets with formative assessments
- Transitions: creating clear routines
- Evaluating student learning at the end of the lesson: ensuring that the learning target was met by all students

Olivia's Knowledge Gaps:

- Determining curriculum (vertical alignment of texts)
- Purpose of read-alouds; how to actively engage students during read-alouds
- Literacy acquisition and fluency development
- Strategies for teaching English Learners (ELs)
- Developmental awareness: what's accessible or appropriate for fifth graders

The many skill and knowledge gaps I observed in Olivia's instruction are typical of those we see in new teachers, and I suspected that, as we worked together, other gaps might surface. Those gaps, I knew, would likely be located at the lower, foundational levels of the Gaps Framework pyramid. And they did surface. For example, as I coached Olivia around working with her EL students, I observed continuous low rigor for those students. Exploring those skill gaps revealed gaps around Olivia's cultural competency: she had persistent low expectations of her EL students and didn't understand the role that oral language played in the development of students' literacy at home. This work, in turn, revealed an emotional intelligence gap—in one conversation, Olivia shared that she felt hopeless about the situation for her EL students and fearful that they'd never catch up and would always be at a disadvantage. Eventually, we would work to close all these gaps—we'll get to that later in the chapter. For now, let's return to the 90 minutes I spent planning for the debrief of my initial observation.

Adult Learning Principles

Using the Gaps Framework to analyze the data you gather during an observation is the first step in preparing for a debrief. Step 2 involves reflecting on adult learning principles. These seven principles provide a cross-check to ensure that your emerging plan is aligned with what is known about how adults learn. This step also provides opportunities to flesh out the learning plan.

Research from across the fields of neuroscience, psychology, and sociology agree on what adults need in order to learn. This is often labeled "adult learning theory" or "adult learning principles." The seven adult learning principles are:

1. Adults must feel safe to learn.
2. Adults come to learning experiences with histories.
3. Adults need to know why we have to learn something.
4. Adults want agency in learning.
5. Adults need practice to internalize learning.
6. Adults have a problem-centered approach to learning.
7. Adults want to learn.

As with the Gaps Framework, you can use adult learning principles as a thinking tool during a conversation and as a tool to reflect on after an observation to determine next steps. I'll describe the seven adult learning principles and then explain how I used them to coach Olivia. For a longer explanation of adult learning principles, see Chapter 4 of *The PD Book*.

Adults Must Feel Safe to Learn

The principle: Our ability to receive new information is directly tied to our emotional state. Our bodies experience psychological threats as threats to our physical well-being and respond by fighting, fleeing, freezing, or appeasing. When our energy goes toward survival, our ability to learn shrinks. This is why you must build trust with your clients, address emotions, and attend to your own ways of being.

My reflection: Olivia and I had met only a couple of times prior to the observation, and I wondered how safe she felt with me. Although she had seemed open and eager for feedback, I also suspected that, like any novice in a field, she felt vulnerable being observed. I made a note to begin our conversation by inviting her to reflect on her feelings about being observed and about the debrief.

I noticed my desire to be direct from the get-go and jump straight into a discussion of her gaps. I suspected that if I did that, Olivia would appear receptive—she'd think that's what a "good" first-year teacher would do—but she might do better with another approach. I checked my urgency, reminded myself to trust in the process, and committed to building trust with Olivia in every conversation.

Adults Come to Learning Experiences with Histories

The principle: Clients show up for coaching with a wide range of previous experiences, knowledge, interests, and competencies. Making explicit connections between what we already know and what is new makes learning deeper and more permanent. This is true for the 23-year-old new teacher, for the second-career teacher, and for the veteran teacher. While teachers are usually aware of some of the ways their histories shape their present, much of what they bring is unconscious—and what is unconscious can become an obstacle. For example, a teacher new to your school who seems resistant to coaching may have had a negative experience with a coach at a previous school. Therefore, they may have assumptions about what coaching is and project those beliefs onto you. This principle demands that we get to know our clients so that we can maximize their strengths and skills and rewrite stories and shift behaviors that no longer serve.

My reflection: When I reflected on this principle, I wondered about Olivia's experience teaching English Learners. I also wondered about Olivia's previous experience receiving feedback on her teaching. I wondered if her master teacher had taken mostly directive coaching stances or facilitative. I wondered how that experience would influence how Olivia would receive the feedback I'd provide. This principle made me realize that I still didn't know Olivia very well. I decided to ask Olivia about how she receives feedback, and I committed to listening carefully for areas in which I could continue to get to know Olivia.

Adults Need to Know Why We Have to Learn Something

The principle: Many adult learners commit to learning when the "why" is clear—and meets personal and professional needs. Articulating the "why" prevents resistance, creates opportunity for learners to find points of connection, increases trust in the coach, and primes clients to be receptive to new ideas. Anyone who has taught middle school can visualize the hands that shoot up when a new topic is announced and the question that follows: "Why do we have to learn this?" Adults may not voice this question, but they wonder nonetheless.

My reflection: I suspected that Olivia wouldn't question the *why* of the learning I'd recommend, but I wondered if she'd agree with the sequence I suggested. I committed to explaining that sequence—but briefly, because I wanted to be sure that I was preserving her cognitive energy to focus on closing the gaps. Framing the "why" in relationship to student needs, I suspected, would help Olivia get on board. For example, I could say, "The eight newcomers barely wrote two sentences. They needed sentence frames or the option to speak their responses, in Spanish, to a partner."

Adults Want Agency in Learning

The principle: Adults crave autonomy and want some control over our learning—the key word here being *some*. To get the most out of coaching, adult learners need to be empowered to make decisions. Honoring adult agency means trusting your clients. It means recognizing that your clients know themselves and their students and that they can participate in decisions about their own learning.

My reflection: I had felt tempted to just present the plan to Olivia and direct her through it, but this principle reminded me to invite her input. Although she was a new teacher and we both knew that she didn't know what she didn't know, I still needed to create space for her autonomy. I also reminded myself that Olivia knew herself best and that I could trust her to make decisions about her learning. I wrote down questions to invite her into the decision-making process about which areas to work on first, and I activated my humility.

Adults Need Practice to Internalize Learning

The principle: Most adults don't learn simply by being exposed to new content—we need opportunities to apply knowledge and to practice new skills, and we need feedback on that practice. Coaching is the perfect place for practice to occur. But for the practice to be effective, coaching activities must be within the client's Zone of Proximal Development (ZPD), practice must be scaffolded, and coaches need to use a gradual release-of-responsibility model. This principle is a reminder of basic learning theory: what works in the classroom with students also works with adults.

My reflection: Each of the skill gaps that I wanted Olivia to work on closing was complex—each, I reminded myself, depended on multiple subskills. For example, for Olivia to give clear directions, she'd need to get the whole class's attention. She would also need to use nonverbal cues and provide written directions. As I broke the skills into subskills, I recognized more nuances of skills that become automatic and unconscious with experience, such as visually scanning the class to ensure all students are paying attention or checking for understanding to ensure that directions had been received. As I thought about all of these elements, I began sequencing them.

I realized that I needed to get clarity on Olivia's ZPD to be sure I was chunking the learning skills accurately and providing the kind of gradual release that would support her best. I reminded myself not to overestimate what a new teacher knows and to remember the complexity in skills, even in skills as routine as giving directions. I recalled times when coaching took longer than necessary because I hadn't recognized a weak foundational skill. As I planned for my work with Olivia, I generated questions that would help me assess her ZPD and plan for scaffolding the learning components.

Adults Have a Problem-Centered Orientation to Learning

The principle: Adults can be highly motivated to acquire new skills if we think these will help us solve an issue we're struggling with. When coaching focuses on problem-solving, clients will be more engaged and motivated. If you're coaching a disengaged teacher, consider what your client feels are the pressing issues. This builds trust, creates the potential for buy-in, and makes it more likely that clients will internalize new behaviors, beliefs, and ways of being.

My reflection: As a new teacher, Olivia would likely buy into the areas I proposed she work on. However, I wanted to check my assumptions and be sure that I was connecting the challenges that Olivia felt she faced to the skills I would guide her to learn. Sometimes with new teachers I'd felt so much urgency to help them close their many gaps that I'd been too directive and instructive, and had missed the opportunity to help them learn to drive their own learning; they hadn't become reflective decision-makers. I reminded myself that even though Olivia was new and young, it was essential that I build her critical thinking skills about her own learning. I wanted to pull back the curtain on my coaching because I knew this would empower her as a learner.

Adults Want to Learn

The principle: Humans want to learn from the minute we are born. When that cranky veteran teacher stomps into a PD session mumbling, "This too shall pass," it can be hard to see them as someone who loves to learn. But once, perhaps many years ago, they *did* love learning, and maybe the learner who's been dormant for decades could emerge again. At our core, adults want to learn and will engage in learning when conditions are right.

My reflection: I had no doubt that Olivia wanted to learn. Like many new teachers I'd coached, she was enthusiastic about coaching. However, this principle made me consider where Olivia might have the most will for learning—whether that would be working with English Learners or crafting rigorous learning targets. I made a note to explore this.

I also thought about whether Olivia might need some quick wins at the start of our coaching work. I wanted to think about how to amplify Olivia's desire to learn as she considered the lengthy list of gaps that I knew she needed to close. I decided to look for low-hanging fruit (such as building knowledge about how long fifth graders can sit on the rug) to boost Olivia's confidence in her ability to learn.

Planning the Debrief

I've created many versions of a debrief plan, some more elaborate than others. Table 14.2 is the plan I prepared for my work with Olivia. It contains the essential questions to consider as you plan for a debrief. On my website, you can download a copy of this tool with a blank "My Notes" column to use for your planning.

After observing a teacher like Olivia with a lot of skill and knowledge gaps, it can be helpful, in addition to planning the first debrief conversation, to sketch out a longer-term plan. You might map the sequence of

Table 14.2: Debrief Plan for Olivia Date of Observation: May 19, 2022

Focus	Reflection Questions	My Notes
Intentions	Who do I want to be? How do I want to show up?	I want to be encouraging, supportive, clear, and direct. I want to communicate confidence in Olivia's ability to grow. I want to communicate trust in the process.
Goal	What's the purpose of this conversation?	To align on the skills we'll focus on in coaching.
Buy-In	How can I make these goals relevant to my client? What student data might be compelling? How might closing skill gaps connect to the teacher's core values or vision for themselves as an educator?	I will share some pieces of observational data that I gathered—data on student experience. Olivia is so committed to being an effective teacher—this will help get her buy-in. I don't anticipate that she'll push back on my feedback, given that she's a new teacher and has been receptive to coaching.
Trust	What might I need to do to cultivate trust and ensure that my client feels safe to learn with me? Where will there be opportunities to highlight my client's strengths? How might power dynamics play a role in safety?	I want to be intentional about highlighting Olivia's strengths. She may push for critical feedback, but I know that everyone needs some validation when they take risks. As I share strengths, I'll name specific and precise behaviors that I observed. I will also invite Olivia to share her feelings about the observation and the debrief, and I'll be sure to use a lot of listening strategies. I'll also make sure I'm leaning into curiosity and compassion.

(Continued)

Focus	Reflection Questions	My Notes
Opening	What will I say to open the conversation?	"I want to acknowledge your willingness to have me observe as we're just getting to know each other. I recognize your commitment to students and to your own growth as a teacher."
Gaps	Which are the two or three gaps that I want my client to address? Why? What evidence indicates that those are significant gaps?	Learning targets (which will allow us to talk about rigor, pacing, and chunking), English Language Development strategies (a few simple strategies might make a difference quickly for her EL students), and expectations for students to sit on the rug for extended periods (a quick gap to close and allows us to discuss the developmental stage of fifth graders). I think Olivia will be on board with exploring these gaps, and they will have significant impact on student learning.
Agency	How and where can I give my client choice in their learning?	I want to share half of the gaps that I observed—all of them would be overwhelming. Then I want to ask Olivia which ones she feels most compelled to explore or which she feels like she already knows something about. I also want to give her choice about how we move forward—which activities might be most helpful (observing other teachers, receiving real-time feedback, etc.).

Table 14.2: (Continued)

Focus	Reflection Questions	My Notes
Tools	Given what I know about this client, which thinking tools might be most useful in the conversation? Do I have copies of these tools in case I want to share them?	I will make copies of the Core Emotions and the Spheres of Influence because I often give those to new teachers. I might also have a copy of the Gaps Framework, but I don't want to overload her with ideas in this debrief. So maybe I'll have the copies for next time.
The Three Bs	Where can I anticipate opportunities to coach my client's beliefs and ways of being in this debrief? Which of the gaps might elicit an exploration of beliefs?	I think I might need to unpack Olivia's assumptions about rigor. I'm not sure I'll do that in this conversation, as we'll have a lot to discuss, but I'm going to listen for indicators that her beliefs about students are impacting the rigor with which she's teaching. I hope to get a sense as to whether the low rigor stems from her inexperience with this age group or is related to her racial and class background. I'm also going to listen for how Olivia feels about herself as a new teacher. I'm curious about her expectations for herself and how she engages with emotions.
Next Steps	What might our next steps be? Which activities might help my client close their gaps?	I'd like to do some lesson planning with Olivia, focusing on learning targets and sequencing activities to meet those targets. I'd also like to co-observe an experienced fifth-grade teacher who can model lesson structure and pacing. Finally, I want to practice new ELD strategies with Olivia and observe her using them.

(Continued)

Table 14.2: (Continued)

Focus	Reflection Questions	My Notes
Closing	Which questions offer my client an opportunity to reflect on their learning in this conversation?	"What did you learn about yourself in this conversation? How did this conversation feel to you?"
Intentions	What do I hope my client will think and feel as this session ends? What do I hope to think and feel as this session ends?	I hope Olivia will feel excited about coaching and hopeful about her ability to make growth. I also hope she'll be glad she asked me to observe. I want to feel like I used a lot of Transformational Coaching skills and didn't just stay on the level of instruction and behaviors. I hope I feel energized and that my core need of purpose and meaning was met.

skills and knowledge that you'll address and consider a rough timeline. When I considered Olivia's gaps, I knew it would take us several months, meeting once a week, just to take a first pass at closing those gaps.

When I planned for this first observation debrief, I also knew that other issues would likely arise and I'd need to be responsive—which did happen two weeks after our first debrief conversation. When I showed up for that coaching meeting, I found Olivia in tears because her principal had stopped by unannounced and had left her critical feedback. We spent that session exploring power dynamics and strategies for communicating with administrators. That conversation pushed back the timeline for addressing Olivia's skill gaps, but it was important. But now I've gotten ahead of myself again. Let's return to the first observation and the debrief.

How to Coach an Open, Receptive, "Easy" Teacher

The conversation I had with Olivia about my observation was very similar to ones I've had with many teachers. As it was a long conversation, I'll summarize some parts.

When I opened Olivia's door after dismissal, she was sitting at her desk, staring out the window. She looked tired but smiled when she saw me. Skipping over greetings, she said, "Okay, tell me. Do I have a chance at being a good teacher? Am I hopeless?"

I pulled up a chair. "You've got a good chance," I said, smiling. I believed it and felt I needed to say something affirming. "Are you worried about what I thought?" I asked.

"I mean, yeah. You're my coach," Olivia said. "And I've only been teaching for two weeks."

"Makes sense," I said. I paused. "I want to start by asking you if you have any hopes or goals for this conversation we're going to have? Or any fears you want to share?" I almost immediately regretted inviting fears as that's where Olivia jumped in.

"I'm afraid you're going to tell me that there's so much I need to work on, and I'll feel overwhelmed."

"Thanks for sharing that," I said. "I'm going to be thoughtful about not inundating you, but let me know if you start feeling overwhelmed." I paused. "What are your hopes for this conversation?"

Olivia sighed and thought. "I guess I hope you've got something good to say and also that you give me actionable feedback. I really want to be a good teacher. Not just good—I want to be a *really* good teacher."

I nodded. "That sounds good," I said. "My hope for this conversation is that we align on the skills we'll focus on and also that I continue to get to know you. I recognize your vulnerability in inviting me to observe so soon, and I want to keep building our relationship." Olivia was watching me carefully. I took a moment to bring awareness to my body language and facial expressions and to consider whether they were open and relaxed.

"So what did you think?" Olivia asked.

"I gathered a lot of data that's helped me identify what I think are some high-leverage areas for you to work on. Before I share those, I want to name some of the strengths I saw. How does that sound?"

"Okay," Olivia said. "But I want you to know that I can take hard feedback. I want it."

"I hear that," I said. "One of the reasons for sharing strengths is so that you know what to do more of and to identify transferable skills. I noticed evidence of strengths in the areas of relationships with students and in creating a warm, organized, and comfortable classroom. I also noted that you selected a book that will be relevant to almost all of your students and that is identity affirming." I pause. "I'm curious how you felt during the lesson I observed?"

Olivia thought for a moment. "I guess I felt pretty good, considering you were there. I was nervous when you arrived, but then I relaxed. I was also a little worried during the read-aloud, because I noticed how many students were moving around. But overall I think I felt good." Her face relaxed a little.

"You seemed calm," I said. "Your voice was always steady, you spoke in a tone and volume that was appropriate for your students, you redirected the students who were wandering during the transition, and when Mr. Garcia came in, I noticed how you warmly welcomed him in Spanish and invited him to sit down."

"Oh yeah, I didn't know he was coming," Olivia said. "He's stopped by a few times. He told me that last year Felix had a teacher who was really mean to him and he didn't want to go to school. His dad is really on top of what's going on in school, and I don't mind at all that he wants to come in."

"That's great, Olivia," I said. "It can feel nerve-wracking to have a student's parent in class when you're brand new. That says a lot about how you can build relationships with families. And it's meaningful not only for Felix but for all students to see that you welcome parents. That's going to make all of them feel more secure."

"I hadn't thought about that," Olivia said. "That's good to know. I really want to have good relationships with caregivers. I feel like they're invaluable for me to understand my kids. I know that as a white woman working in this community there's so much I don't know. I see their parents as my teachers."

"Olivia," I said as I leaned forward, "I'm hearing your awareness that you need to build your cultural competency—that's super powerful—and that you have ideas about how to do that. This is also a strength for us to note."

"Okay," she said. "I'm glad to hear that. Can we get to the stuff I need to work on now?"

I smiled. "Yup!" I said. "Let's get into it."

I decided to begin with an entry point that Olivia had opened—with her observation that students were squirming on the rug. Whenever you can follow a client's lead, you'll be responding to their interests. Before sharing my observations, I asked Olivia a few questions to push her thinking about that moment—what had she noticed? What had she considered doing? What prevented her from making a shift in her lesson plan?

From that point, I went back to the start of the lesson. I asked about her objectives and what she hoped students would learn. She responded with embarrassment, saying, "My objective was to introduce the book, but I know that's not a strong learning target. I can't believe I made such a rookie mistake." I followed up with questions so I could assess whether she had the skills to design strong learning targets ("What would have been a stronger objective?") or whether this was an area for coaching. In asking these questions, I was determining Olivia's ZPD around writing learning targets. Olivia seemed to know how to create strong targets and said that she'd been rushing to finish the lesson plans and just hadn't thought enough about the learning target. I made a mental note to explore capacity and what she spent time on, as well as how she prioritized different elements of a lesson plan.

We talked through many of the observations I'd made. I checked in often to see if Olivia was feeling overwhelmed, but she insisted she wasn't. "I really want a baseline assessment," she said at one point, "so I want to hear it all."

"Okay," I said. "I also want to honor that you expressed concern about becoming overwhelmed. So I'll check in." Olivia nodded, said she appreciated that, and affirmed that she was feeling okay. After I shared almost every knowledge and skill gap that I'd suspected existed, I asked her where she felt it would make the most sense for us to start.

"I'm strangely relieved to see this long list," Olivia said. She'd been jotting down notes. "It's helpful to see what I need to work on."

"I'm glad to hear that," I said. "Where do you want to dive in?"

"I think there are things that I can work on by myself. Like, I know how to create strong learning targets. I know how to do that. Other things I really don't know how to do—like front-loading vocabulary for my English Learners or providing other options for them during writing time. I mean, I have a couple of ideas, but I need your expertise."

"Is there anything that feels like it could be a quick win?" I asked. "An easy skill to acquire?"

"I'm not sure," Olivia said. "What do you think?"

I made a few suggestions, and we landed on talking about pacing lessons. I realized that a conversation about Miguel sitting on the rug wasn't necessary. I simply said, "Thirty minutes is probably too long for fifth graders to sit on the floor. I'd suggest you halve that time." Olivia nodded and made a note.

It was relatively easy, as I'd predicted, to align on areas to work on in coaching. I also got insights into other areas to explore, such as when Olivia said, "I've decided I'll give myself five years to teach in this community, and if I can't serve these students well, then I'll quit and go teach in the suburbs." I wanted to know how Olivia defined "serving students well" and what might make her want to quit. This statement was an opportunity to coach her beliefs and way of being, and I planned to return to it as part of a larger conversation about who she wanted to be as a teacher.

During my conversation with Olivia, I made a few notes about the kinds of questions she was most receptive to. I noticed that while she appreciated the instructive approach I took a few times to fill in some knowledge gaps, she responded best when I asked questions that probed her thinking and decision-making.

Toward the end of our time, we listed next steps, which included observing how another fifth-grade teacher modifies lessons for English Learners, looking at her lesson plans together, and practicing giving instructions. We made clear agreements about who would do what by when, and then I shifted into closing the conversation. "I often end coaching sessions with the same two questions: What did you learn about yourself in this conversation? And how did you feel during the conversation?"

"Well," Olivia said, "right now I feel good. Tired, but good. I feel excited about coaching. I did feel a little overwhelmed, even though I didn't share that. But I'm glad I didn't tell you because I got through it. I feel like you kept things focused and manageable and it wasn't just a list of things I need to get better at. You were clear about how you were going to help me. Honestly, it was also good to hear things I'm doing well."

"I'm so glad to hear that," I said. "What did you learn about yourself?"

"I want to think on that," Olivia said. "But I feel like I shouldn't have been so nervous. I guess I was reminded that I can learn. I can do this."

"That's big," I said. "And I want say that it's okay to feel nervous about being observed. That's normal."

"I know," Olivia said. "I just don't know you that well."

"Exactly," I said. "And that's why we'll continue getting to know each other. I don't expect you to trust me right away." Olivia smiled. "In our next session," I added, "I'd love to hear more about your student teaching. Maybe we can spend 10 minutes or so on that. I think it would help me get to know you more."

"That would be great," Olivia said. "My master teacher was so different from teachers here, so I think it would be interesting to process that."

I agreed. I left our session noting that I'd met my intention to use a number of different Transformational Coaching strategies and recognizing that I felt energized and satisfied—like I'd done something meaningful.

Sometimes during conversations about beliefs and ways of being, I notice an urgency surge—I feel like I'm not having the "real" conversations that will create change for kids tomorrow. When these feelings of urgency arise, I remind myself to trust the process. Then I remember that every action emerges from a belief—and that when I coach behaviors, opportunities arise to get to the roots of behaviors and to explore the ways of being that sprout from those behaviors. I recognize the way the Three Bs are interconnected and that addressing one opens opportunities to address others and that this is how transformation happens—by holistically exploring who we are as humans.

My experience coaching Olivia was in some ways unremarkable. She was a quick learner, she was receptive to coaching around beliefs and ways of being, and her cultural competency and emotional intelligence were solid to begin with. I could say she was "easy" to coach. The majority of teachers, I've found, are a lot like Olivia, in that they want to learn what to do to meet the needs of their students, and they have what it takes to do that learning. And so, like Olivia, most teachers give us the opportunity to regularly use all of the Transformational Coaching frameworks so that we can support them to meet the needs of every child, every day.

Pause and Process

Reflect:

- How do the instructional coaching strategies in this chapter around coaching behavior compare and contrast to other instructional coaching strategies you've learned about?
- What elements of the observation and debrief process described in this chapter do you think you could implement? What feels challenging to implement?
- What's one thing from this chapter that you could start doing right away?

Next steps:

- Listen to *Bright Morning Podcast* episode 208 on using the Gaps Framework in conversation.
- Download the Gaps Framework from my website and make copies of it.
- Download the "Debrief Plan for an Observation" from my website and use it to plan a conversation.
- Download "How to Coach Behaviors" from my website, which provides an overview of this process.

CHAPTER 15

The Art of Transformational Coaching

Heart-Centered Coaching

Common misconception:	*Transformational Coaches know:*
Coaching is the application of a set of knowledge and tools.	Coaching is a skill and an artform that requires ongoing practice.

Coaching is an art. It requires that we use a wide variety of tools with refined skill to both prepare for and respond to whatever arises with our clients. We need to know about structures and forms, and we need to be innovative and creative when new challenges come up. Some tools are easier to understand and use than others—using a strength-based approach, for example, is fairly straightforward, while using the ACE Emotions framework takes greater will and skill.

In this chapter, I'll introduce you to the coaching lenses, the final framework in a Transformational Coach's tool set. Many years ago, I trained coaches in the Oakland schools in using the lenses. After practicing for a few months, one of the coaches I supervised confessed that she was struggling to apply the tool in the field. She dropped her head. "It's okay," I said. "Let me know in five years if you're still struggling." I quickly explained my flippant response, reassuring her that the Lenses take more than a few months to learn well. Of all the frameworks in this book, this is one of the most complex—and one of the most powerful.

The Lenses are worth learning to use. They push our thinking into places where the other tools don't go. They teach us to think strategically, systematically, comprehensively, and holistically. When you first start to use the thinking tools, you'll likely feel as if you had an intense physical workout. Your mind will be sore. The Lenses are a muscle to build—the more you practice and train, the easier they'll be. After a while, you'll internalize the assumptions and questions and find yourself using them without effort—but that might take five years of regular practice.

The Coaching Lenses

The Coaching Lenses are based on theories that attempt to explain human and organizational behavior. Most of the Lenses come from the National Equity Project, an Oakland-based organization I was fortunate to learn from in my first years as a coach. They created the Lenses of Inquiry, Adult Learning, Systems Thinking, Systemic Oppression, and Change Management. When I began using the Lenses, I saw that they were a game-changer. In the years since, I've added a couple of lenses—the Lens of Emotional Intelligence and the Lens of Compassion—in order to incorporate our full humanity. I also renamed the Lens of Systemic Oppression as the Equity Lens and modified others. I'm ever grateful to the National Equity Project for this work (and all their work) and for permission to print the lenses.

Here's a quick overview of the Coaching Lenses:

- *What*: A framework to think through a complex situation from many angles.
- *Why*: To expand how we see the world; to interrupt our habitual ways of thinking and interpreting evidence; to surface the root causes of a problem and determine a strategic course of action.
- *How*: As a tool to reflect on an observation or a conversation, as a tool to plan a coaching conversation, as a tool to incorporate into a consultancy protocol, or as a tool for thinking during a conversation.

How to Use the Lenses

Let's say you have just walked out of a coaching conversation in which you debriefed an observation and the conversation didn't go as you'd hoped. Perhaps you feel more confused about what's really going on for the teacher, and you aren't sure how to proceed. You go back to your office and pull out the Coaching Lenses.

Each lens is comprised of a set of *assumptions* and *questions*. The assumptions are simple statements that represent the key ideas that inform each lens. The questions for each lens arise from the assumptions. These are not necessarily questions to ask a client. They are questions that deepen reflection and analysis.

Sitting at your desk, you read over the assumptions to anchor in the key concepts for a lens. As you read, you begin getting new insights into what's going on for the teacher, or perhaps additional wonderings arise. Then you read the questions for the lens—and consider them as they relate to the dilemma with the teacher. As you read the questions, more insights or questions come to mind. You might jot down notes on your emerging understandings and capture questions to continue exploring, and maybe you come up with a question or two to ask your client.

You read through each lens, because even though one might feel most relevant to the situation, you know that it's only by looking through each lens that you approximate a comprehensive understanding of the situation. You know that every situation requires that you examine it from multiple perspectives. You also recognize that the Lenses are interrelated and also overlap—you jump back to lenses you've already read and make new connections.

While certain aspects of the situation you're in become clearer, you also feel humbled. You may even feel awed by the complexity of the situation. You remind yourself to trust the process, and then you get up from your desk and take a walk. Later you'll identify next steps—questions to ask the teacher when you meet again, maybe additional information to gather from the site administrators. But first you need to let your reflections sink in and clear your mind.

An Overview of Each Lens

You'll find the complete set of Coaching Lenses in Appendix C and on my website where the downloadable version is nicely formatted. For now, this brief overview of the lenses will give you a sense of the content.

- *The Adult Learning Lens*: This lens is based on the principles of adult learning (see Chapter 14). It suggests that problems of change are problems of learning, and to respond to problems of change we must understand how to guide adult learners.
- *The Change Management Lens*: When we look through the lens of change management, we consider pathways to change. We're reminded that beneficial change is possible, and we explore options for enacting change as we consider individual and systemic factors at play.
- *The Inquiry Lens*: The Inquiry Lens invites us to ask questions and seek understanding. It emphasizes that the way we define a problem dictates how we define the solution. The Inquiry Lens compels us to gather evidence and data in order to make decisions. It reminds us that there's

usually more to the picture than what we initially see and that data helps us check our assumptions. The Inquiry Lens urges us to slow down, step back, and look again at what's going on.

- *The Systems Thinking Lens*: Systems thinking helps us explore how individual elements of a situation are interconnected. This lens reminds us that everything we observe is the result of a complex set of interactions, and we must understand them if we want to intervene. This lens compels us to look at the pieces, the whole, and the interactions to understand the system and to change it. Systems thinking also explains that all energy moves in cycles and that if we can identify the phase that a system is in, and understand conditions for change, we might be able to move it into a different phase of the cycle.

- *The Emotional Intelligence Lens*: The EI Lens anchors us in the centrality of the human experience and reminds us that whenever we seek solutions to a dilemma, we need to consider the emotions of everyone involved. It prompts us to attend to the foundational components of emotional intelligence.

- *The Equity Lens*: The Equity Lens brings us into the current reality of systemic oppression. It reminds us that our identity markers and identity experiences locate us in relationship to power and privilege. It reminds us that equity issues are always present in any situation and that it's our responsibility to see and surface them, as well as to address them.

- *The Compassion Lens*: The final lens is an invitation to work from and with love. It reminds us that compassion is our true nature, that we must have self-compassion before we can truly act with compassion for others, and that compassion is a powerful mechanism for change.

Using the Coaching Lenses to Plan

Mahesh was a sixth-grade English teacher at a K-8 school in the Bay Area that had adopted a project-based learning (PBL) approach. He was born and raised in Queens, New York, to Indian immigrants. He'd been teaching for

10 years and served also as the department head, which meant he was on the Leadership Team. His instruction was traditional—spelling tests on Fridays, a lot of teacher-directed learning, and a focus on "the basics." His students often performed well on standardized tests and seemed to appreciate his consistency and organization.

Administrators envisioned phasing in PBL, and so during that first year, teachers were allowed to pick a few strategies to try. Mahesh and I had met a handful of times. During those sessions, he was cordial but seemed guarded. He expressed concerns about PBL's effects on student readiness for high school or college. As we moved into the second year of implementation, I was charged with coaching teachers on their first-semester unit plans and ensuring that they included PBL. All teachers had been asked to email me their first-semester unit. When I looked at Mahesh's plans, I saw no evidence of PBL. They looked like the same plans he'd worked from five years previous.

I noticed my mind gearing up for battle. I noticed my thoughts that Mahesh was "resistant." I noticed my feelings of frustration and fear—I worried that I didn't know how to coach Mahesh, that the site administrators would be disappointed in me. I was also concerned about Mahesh's status on the Leadership Team—would he sabotage all our efforts to infuse learning with more student-centered experiences?

I decided to use the Lenses to see if I could gain more understanding of the situation before our meeting. I used the simple process you'll read in Table 15.1. You can download a blank template of this table from my website.

When I use the Coaching Lenses to reflect on a situation, as I did with this one, I feel like I've been lifted above the dilemma and offered an expansive view. I often feel humbled, my curiosity grows exponentially, and I always discover, if not a clear road map, many options for paths to explore.

Ideally, you'd be able to engage in a reflection like one I did regularly as part of preparing for coaching conversations. The more you sit with these lenses and think through them, the more available the concepts will be to you during conversations.

Table 15.1: Analyzing a Situation Through the Lenses

Adult Learning (AL) Lens	
Reflection Prompts	**Analysis**
One or two assumptions that help me understand the situation	• Problems of change are problems of learning. • People must feel safe to learn.
Insights from this assumption	The assumptions from the AL lens feel relevant here. I wonder if Mahesh feels safe as a learner with me. I wonder what he needs to learn in order to incorporate PBL.
One or two questions from the lens that feel relevant	• Where are the gaps? Skill? Knowledge? Will? • What strengths can be built on?
Questions I could ask this client	• I'm curious to understand, when you consider the skills required for PBL, what you feel you know how to do? • I'm curious about your will to teach PBL. On a scale of 1–10, where's your will level?
Change Management Lens	
Reflection Prompts	**Analysis**
One or two assumptions that help me understand the situation	• Building on strengths can lead to positive change. • For successful change to occur, there needs to be leadership, vision, skills, incentives, resources, and a clear plan of action.
Insights from this assumption	I wonder if our plan of action is clear enough; I wonder if Mahesh has the skills or feels the incentive to implement PBL. I want to surface Mahesh's strengths.

(Continued)

Change Management Lens	
Reflection Prompts	Analysis
One or two questions from the lens that feel relevant	• What are the opportunities for leveraging change? • What incentives are in place for people to change?
Questions I could ask this client	• What would need to be true for you to be willing to incorporate PBL? What would you need to know or understand? What support would you need? • What's your understanding of why we're implementing PBL?

Inquiry Lens	
Reflection Prompts	Analysis
One or two assumptions that help me understand the situation	• The way we pose the question determines the nature of the answer. • The way we define the problem dictates how we define the solution.
Insights from this assumption	I've been thinking that Mahesh is the problem—that his resistance to implementing PBL is the problem. This has led me to come to conclusions about what's going on for him.
One or two questions from the lens that feel relevant	• Who is defining the problem? • From which perspective am I seeing this situation?
Questions I could ask this client	• I'm curious how you see the situation. To me it looks like you're not willing to implement PBL, but I want to understand your perspective.

Systems Thinking Lens	
Reflection Prompts	**Analysis**
One or two assumptions that help me understand the situation	• Whatever is happening in a moment is exactly what is supposed to happen in the system as it is. If we understand these interactions, we can intervene to change them. • Conflict and tension in a system are necessary and natural.
Insights from this assumption	Mahesh is part of a system. I haven't thought about the larger system and considered the leverage points in the system as a whole. I also recognize that Mahesh's reluctance to implement PBL might be beneficial if it reveals other tension points in the system.
One or two questions from the lens that feel relevant	• How did this system generate the behavior we're seeing? • If we shift our perspective, what might we understand about this situation?
Questions I could ask this client	• What do you think we could have done differently in the roll out of PBL?

Emotional Intelligence Lens	
Reflection Prompts	**Analysis**
One or two assumptions that help me understand the situation	• Emotional intelligence allows us to speak about emotions, ask for help, and establish boundaries. • Emotional intelligence is the foundation of emotional resilience, adaptability, and flexibility.
Insights from this assumption	I hadn't thought about how Mahesh's EI is at play here. I hadn't considered what he was feeling or how his emotions might be contributing to his experience. I also hadn't thought about how my feelings are affecting the situation—I hadn't recognized that I've been frustrated with Mahesh.

(Continued)

Emotional Intelligence Lens	
Reflection Prompts	**Analysis**
One or two questions from the lens that feel relevant	• What indicators are there that people are aware of their emotions? • Where is fear present?
Questions I could ask this client	• Tell me about how you've experienced the rollout of PBL. What feelings have come up for you in this process? • What are your fears about PBL?

Equity Lens	
Reflection Prompts	**Analysis**
One or two assumptions that help me understand the situation	• Systemic oppression manifests in economic, political, social and cultural systems, and in interpersonal relationships.
Insights from this assumption	I wonder how his identity experiences might be at play. Mahesh came from an upper-middle-class background, and his students are all low income, and I wonder about how this affected his beliefs about instruction, management, and student needs. I also wonder about the cultural and racial differences between Mahesh and his students and how those play out in his classroom. Finally, I recognize that there are many differences between when I consider our race, ethnicity, linguistic background, gender, class background, religion, and the regions where we grew up, among others. I wonder how these differences might be shaping how I coach Mahesh and how he feels about me.

Equity Lens	
Reflection Prompts	**Analysis**
One or two questions from the lens that feel relevant	• How safe is it for people from marginalized communities to share their truths? • What comes up for me around coaching and leading across difference?
Questions I could ask this client	• I want to acknowledge the difference in our identity markers. I'm curious how you think this difference might be in play, or your identity experiences, in this situation? • I'm curious about your comfort level with speaking your truth here. I'm wondering if you feel like you're heard or if you feel safe to share your perspectives. • I'm curious how you think your identity shapes who you are with your students?

Lens of Compassion	
Reflection Prompts	**Analysis**
One or two assumptions that help me understand the situation	• Curiosity, humility, and trust foster the development of compassion.
Insights from this assumption	I wonder how I can deepen my compassion for Mahesh. I wonder if my compassion has been wavering as I've become frustrated with him.
One or two questions from the lens that feel relevant	• How can listening help us cultivate compassion? • How do we support others to discover their best qualities?
Questions I could ask this client	• How can I support you?

The Art of a Transformational Coaching Conversation

In the following conversation that I had with Mahesh, you'll read how my reflection showed up in what I said. I hope you'll also see evidence of the many Transformational Coaching strategies that I've described. If you want to actively engage with this text, you could make notations in the margins of the strategies you've read about, such as the use of a thinking tool or framework, a listening strategy, or a response strategy.

I've chosen to keep this conversation almost exactly as it transpired (it was one I recorded and so this is almost a literal transcript) because it captures what so many initially difficult coaching conversations can feel like. We didn't get to an easy place quickly. I want you to know that sometimes it takes persistence and commitment to get to a transformational outcome.

Mahesh wasn't one for small talk, so as soon as we were seated and my notebook was open, I began. "Thanks for emailing me your unit plans last week. Although to be honest," I continued, "I was a little confused because I didn't see any PBL strategies and you know that my job is to coach PBL."

Mahesh's expression was unreadable. After a moment, he said, "I don't really know why you're surprised." He paused. "You were there when we looked at the data at the end of the year. Our kids couldn't write! We implemented PBL and did a disservice to our kids. Frankly, I was scared when we looked at the sixth graders' writing assessments. I did as I was told and let them do a lot of journaling last year. Then at the end of the year, when we gave them a basic prompt, they couldn't write one coherent paragraph. That was startling."

Mahesh had been speaking rapidly, and I was nodding and jotting down phrases. He stopped, and I let the silence sit between us. I knew

Mahesh wasn't finished and wanted to let him share everything on his mind. I hoped this might help us build trust. "Tell me more," I said, "I want to hear it all."

"Look," Mahesh said, leaning forward. "I've been told to make data-driven unit plans. So I looked at my data and decided I'm going to teach them how to write. I'm starting with the five-paragraph essay, basic sentence structure, and a review of grammar rules." I was nodding in a way that I hoped indicated that I was listening, but not necessarily agreeing.

"Okay," I said. "That's helpful to understand." I was about to ask another question, but Mahesh continued.

"That kind of instruction works," he said. "I know it's out of fashion to have spelling tests on Fridays, but it works. I learned that way; you probably did too. Reading fiction is nice, but I don't want to end up with another year where we're shocked that kids can't write. So I put this unit plan together. If you need me to change it, I'll change it. But I just don't see how they're going to learn to write."

I made a note to return to Mahesh's comment about how we learn; I suspected this could be an entry point to a conversation about beliefs, assumptions, and equity. "Thanks for sharing that and helping me understand the decisions that you're making," I continued. "What I'm hearing is that last year you followed the suggestion to try different strategies and you didn't see the results you wanted to see. And so this year you're making different decisions."

I paused. "Is that correct? Am I missing anything?" I really wanted to check my understanding and also open up the door for Mahesh to share anything else.

"Yeah," Mahesh said, his fingers twirling his moustache. "But the only thing that might be missing is that we did not hit the mark. Kids aren't leaving sixth grade on grade level." Mahesh had been speaking rapidly. He leaned back and sighed and then in a slower cadence, he said, "We must do something different."

I put down my pen and nodded. "Your commitment to our students' success is inspiring," I said, speaking slowly. "I appreciate that you're holding us all to high standards, and yes, I was also disappointed with the results last spring. I'm curious to hear more about what you feel, if anything, went well last year in terms of our attempt to implement new strategies."

Mahesh shook his head, which I wasn't sure how to interpret. He leaned forward again and made eye contact. "When there was a push to make sure that what we put in front of students is relevant to them, I was on board," Mahesh said. "They need to be able to see themselves in our curriculum. I also support developing their critical thinking. I liked that project where they had to find someone in their community to write to, and they had to watch the news and talk about what they want to change. I supported all that." Mahesh stopped and looked away.

I wasn't sure whether to ask a follow-up question. It felt like a long silence passed before Mahesh continued. "Then I had conferences with students, and they shared their ideas, and I was like, 'Great, now go write that down—everything you just said to me.' And then students started saying, 'I don't know how to spell the word 'community,' and there were tears and frustration, and I got papers with no words on the page." Mahesh shook his head. His brow was furrowed. Other teachers often thought he was angry, but I held back on interpreting his expression.

"I was shocked," Mahesh continued. "They're in sixth grade, and I'm not supposed to focus on spelling. I'm not supposed teach them to write strong paragraphs. I'm supposed to just help them to connect to their feelings and what they want to change in the world? We cannot have students exiting sixth grade without being able to write a basic five-paragraph essay," Mahesh said with intensity in his voice.

I knew I was hearing strong emotions and wanted to invite Mahesh to explore them, but I wasn't sure how he'd respond to that invitation. I decided to take the risk.

"I want to acknowledge the way that you pay attention not just to academic success but also to our students' emotional experience," I said. "Mahesh," I said and then paused, "if I ever ask a question that doesn't feel helpful, feel free to tell me that, but I think I'm hearing some strong feelings, and I'm curious if it would be helpful to explore those for maybe three minutes?"

I watched Mahesh's expression carefully but couldn't read his reaction.

"Okay, how do I feel?" He looked upward and rubbed his chin. "Well, I don't feel happy. I feel a little frustrated. I also feel unsure of where this conversation is going. I don't want to be in trouble for my unit plans. So I just want to know what you want me to do. Yeah, I'm frustrated about last year. I care a lot for the kids. I'm not going against anything, but you can just tell me what you want me to do."

Mahesh drank water and wiped his mouth. I considered the different ways I could respond and decided to continue holding space for emotions.

"I really appreciate your honesty," I said. "I hear sadness. I hear frustration or anger. I also hear a little bit of fear in your words—perhaps about what might happen to our kids if they're not prepared and perhaps about whether you're in any kind of trouble. I want to acknowledge that. I promise I will be clear about where we're going in this conversation. But I'm curious what you're hearing in what you're saying?"

Mahesh raised his eyebrows and took a deep breath. "I guess I'm hearing that I have more feelings than I thought. I thought I was just frustrated. I'm hearing that I'm not willing to step away from my belief that every kid needs to know how to write by the time they leave sixth grade." Mahesh stopped and took a deep breath and then continued. "I'm also saying," his voice got louder, "that if we're going to do project-based learning, cool; I just need to know how to teach the skills kids need. If they didn't have to take a test at the end of the year to demonstrate that they know how to write, sure, I'd show up every day and sing songs. I will do whatever I'm asked to do, but our accreditation is based on student test scores. I don't want to be an F school. If someone shows me how to do PBL and also raise proficiency in reading and writing, I'm down. But I have not seen that yet." Mahesh crossed his arms over his chest and leaned back.

I smiled slightly. I wondered if Mahesh was trying to bait me into a debate. "Mahesh," I said, trying to speak in a tone that wasn't as serious as his, "I actually don't believe that if it wasn't for the test, you would just sing songs every day. I've heard you sing. I don't think anybody would put up with that." Mahesh laughed, and I smiled.

I waited for a moment and then continued. "But I'm hearing your deep commitment to the kids and to who we are as a school." Mahesh nodded.

"I also think I'm hearing that you're recognizing that you and all of us have skill gaps," I said. "We don't know how to do PBL in the way that we want to. And you said, 'Show me and I'm down with it.' So I'm hearing that you're not necessarily opposed to the idea of reflective writing and writing for real-world audiences. You just want to be sure that they're prepared for seventh grade." I paused for a moment and then added, "Am I getting that right?"

Mahesh had been nodding as I was talking. "Yeah," he said. "That's it. Just show me the data that PBL is moving our students, and I will do your project-based learning."

I smiled again. Mahesh may have been trying to provoke me, but I wasn't biting. "Okay," I said. "I hope that after a few conversations, you might say, 'I'm willing to do project-based learning,' rather than 'do *your* project based learning.' Because I hear you'll do it because it's a mandate but not because you're truly invested in it. I hope to help you see how PBL can serve our students in many ways and that you'll feel like, yeah, I really want to do this."

I was a little apprehensive about sounding like I was going to try to convince him—this put us into a dynamic that could become tricky, but Mahesh responded quickly, "Okay, yeah, okay," he said. His tone was more open than I'd heard, and I felt there was truth in his response.

"Do you think that could be a possibility?" I asked.

Mahesh thought for a moment and then said, "Yeah, I guess I'm a little distant because it was not my idea to do this. We were shown all this data from another school that did PBL, and I was like, okay, that's great. But we can't just copy and paste what someone else did. And I voiced that it may not work out for us given our context. I admit that I have not been on board from the beginning."

Mahesh was sharing what I'd suspected but hadn't really explored with him. "How do you feel like your concern or doubt has been received, even just by me?" I asked.

"I think you've always heard my concerns," Mahesh said, "but I have no idea if the principal is listening to me. When he said, 'hey, we are switching to PBL, here's the data from this other school that has done it,' I voiced a concern. I wish that we were talking more about the science of reading—I have older kids who have no basic phonics understanding, but whatever. If we're adopting PBL, okay."

"Let me ask you something," I said. "At the beginning of last year when we began project-based learning, what was your expectation for how long it would take in order to see that it was working? How long did you imagine giving it a chance?"

Mahesh seemed to be thinking. He was quiet and then said, "I wanted to see some kind of result in the year."

I nodded. "Okay," I said, "I'm curious if you saw any data that indicated that perhaps that we were on the right path?"

"Well, I have some kids who said, 'This is the first time I've been interested in looking at the news,'" Mahesh said. "Some kids seemed really excited to share about their families. I heard them say, 'This was fun.' So the fact that some of them thought it was fun, that's something. I like for kids to have fun at school. If school is miserable, you're not coming back."

I wanted to ask Mahesh more about his experiences in school as a child—I wanted to know him better, but he continued. "I think when we looked at comprehension, there was steady growth. We did some nonfiction reading about local governments, and they liked that. I still snuck in some test-taking skills to make sure that they could express their understanding on the exams. But they were missing some core skills—like they couldn't spell 'community.' That still bothers me. And they couldn't write a paragraph with an assumption, evidence, and commentary. Sure, there was some stuff that was positive, but it was frustrating that they couldn't express their opinions in writing."

Mahesh's tone of voice had significantly shifted. I heard much more of a conversational tone and less adversarial tones. I wanted to be careful with making assumptions about his tone of voice, however, but registered the softening. "Okay, Mahesh," I said. "Check me on this, but I think what I'm hearing is that some things worked and there were some holes. Kids need to know how to spell 'community,' maybe they need some direct phonics instruction, and they may need test-taking skills. They need to know how to construct a paragraph that expresses their opinion. They need to be able to write in many genres."

Mahesh was nodding enthusiastically.

I continued: "So what I'm hearing you say is that the way we implemented project-based learning last year had some gaps. I'm curious if you think that we could close those gaps?" I paused. "Is there any reason that we would not be able to teach kids test-taking skills or phonics?"

Mahesh leaned over the table and propped his chin on his hand. He took a deep breath and said, "I think we could. Yeah, we could definitely do that if we focused. I think the stuff I was doing under the radar is stuff everybody on my team can do." Mahesh made eye contact with me, it felt like, to see my response. I nodded.

"We need to give kids multiple-choice comprehension tests on what they're doing," he said, "because kids take multiple-choice tests. So we could build in comprehension skills and grammar within these big, ambiguous, project-based things. But I don't know how to do that with this PBL structure."

Mahesh frowned and looked down. After a moment, he continued. "I know the stuff that I've used before to teach grammar, but I don't know if you've got to do it in a clandestine way. I'm willing to change it if this is not the best way, but I have only seen kids learn something when this instruction is systematic, intentional, and structured. I haven't exactly seen learning happen when kids can just decide when and how they figure out spelling, when and how they figure out grammar."

It seemed like Mahesh was experiencing cognitive dissonance—a conflict between his beliefs. I still felt like there was distrust between us, and so I wanted to keep indicating that I was listening, that I wasn't judging him. "So I'm hearing a number of things," I said. "You want permission to supplement PBL and to bring this to your department and talk about doing this systematically. You want to see data throughout the year that says that we're working toward closing skill gaps for our students." Mahesh was nodding as I spoke.

"I'm also hearing you talk about skill gaps that teachers have about how to ensure that grammar and spelling are part of project-based learning," I paused. "Do you feel like I'm missing anything key about what you need in order to feel confident going forward using project-based learning?"

"Permission to supplement mainly," Mahesh said. "And the acknowledgment that other teachers on my team need to teach these core skills."

I wanted to explore Mahesh's willingness. I couldn't tell how big his will gap was. I said, "Okay, so I'm curious, on a scale of 1 to 10, what's your level of willingness to teach PBL? Ten is like, you're really willing." I paused, and then quickly explained: "Actually, there are two parts to this question. First—how willing are you to give PBL a chance? And second—how many years are you willing to give in order to see impact? Because I'm concerned if you have an expectation that we're going to see dramatic change in one year." I stopped talking, realizing that I'd piled on too many questions and my own opinion.

Mahesh sat up straight. "Am I willing to do it? Yeah," he said. "I have never been unwilling to change. I'm not an obstinate person. I am a person who will change it when I see it. I just am uncomfortable when we do things because we saw shiny things happening at another school and then we say, 'Oh, it's going to take a really long time to see results for kids.' My job is to see results for kids. I get that it's an unrealistic expectation to see something dramatic in one year, but I wonder if we can see *something* at least. We should at least be tracking student learning better so we can see if there's any growth."

I let there be a moment of silence and then took a deep breath. "I just want to acknowledge that I hear your doubt," I said. "I hear your fear. I also hear that you're not clear on why we adopted this model." Mahesh shook his head.

"What I heard you say," I continued, "is that 'we saw something shiny at another school,' so I'm hearing that you don't understand the decision-making that we went through or the data that we looked at or the 30 years of research on the impact of PBL. I'm hearing the need for more information about how we came to this decision and the need to know that we're going to be tracking student progress more carefully. Did I miss anything?"

Mahesh's expression was puzzled. "I didn't know there was 30 years of research about this," he said. "That wasn't in the PD. That week was all about 'here's the curriculum, here's what you're doing, you're going to be doing it this way,' and we had so many community building activities, which I felt like was a waste of time. I've been teaching here for 12 years, and we know each other."

I also remembered that along with small talk, Mahesh disliked icebreakers. I smiled. "I really appreciate that feedback because I helped to design and facilitate that training," I said. "When I helped plan that session, I really wanted to get teachers into learning how to do PBL and not go into all of the why. But I'm hearing it would have been helpful for you to know the reasoning behind the decision. I'm hearing you say, 'I can't just trust you.' That's totally fine." I paused, observing Mahesh's expression, which was unreadable again.

"Mahesh, I want to invite you to continue being doubtful," I said. "Bring your skepticism. We need it. It'll help us get better. I want you to raise these questions as we go along. How does that sound?"

Mahesh looked surprised and a little confused. "So you're saying I can raise questions and there won't be this weird look like, *Why are you asking this question when we are going to be doing this anyway?*"

I smiled. "Yes, please raise the questions. Let's talk about when and where and how you raise them so that I can respond to them," I said. "I remember once we were about to jump into practice in a PD session and you raised your hand and said, 'Our kids don't know how to write a paragraph so I don't understand why we're doing this thing on mapping community resources.' Mahesh looked down at his hands, his expression a little sheepish.

"I want to address your doubts and concerns," I said. "And in a whole-staff PD session, I have to think about the needs of the whole group. So I think about where you can best raise issues that deserve substantive time and space." I paused. "How do you receive that?" I asked.

Mahesh sighed and rubbed his hands together. "Okay, yeah, it sounds like . . . I mean, I've led PD sessions, so I know what it's like when someone throws something out there and it takes us off track." Mahesh shifted his weight in his chair. "But I haven't felt like there's time to ask questions," he continued. "I've felt like I've been told, 'We're doing it, we're doing it, we're doing it.' And then we're asked, 'Are there any questions?' but not all questions are acceptable—not questions about why we're doing this or what do you think of this, just questions about do you know what you're supposed to do." Mahesh sighed loudly. I nodded, hoping to indicate that I was listening. I resisted the urge to speak.

"So when am I allowed to ask real questions?" Mahesh said. "Or say this isn't working? I haven't experienced any open dialogue."

I felt relieved to hear Mahesh share this. I felt honest when I said, "I appreciate that feedback. And I think you're right. We haven't had enough open discussion time." I paused.

"I'm thinking about our leadership team meetings and the role you could play," I said. "I think you could help identify the data that we could collect every week on how our students are progressing on a whole number of indicators. Like you said, we need systematic, intentional, and structured ways to track and ensure progress toward our goals. I'm wondering if you could help identify the metrics that we need to track."

Mahesh was nodding and making eye contact. "And also," I continued, "I'm wondering if you could collect questions about PBL that are coming up for teachers. And then maybe ever so often we could answer those. I'd be curious if you think this needs to happen every week or two or once a month? And do you think we should answer questions in person or whether we do it through the Monday Message email?"

Mahesh looked surprised. "I think that's a good idea," he said. "I think we should be able to write down questions, no matter what they're about, and submit them anonymously. You could answer them during our Leadership Team meeting," Mahesh paused, and then added, "Those meetings are not very useful anyway."

I felt a shift in Mahesh again, as if he was trying to bait me. I felt like he kept testing me to see if he could trust me. I said, "What I'm hearing is that you want to hold us accountable. Just as administrators are trying to hold teachers accountable for integrating these instructional PBL practices, you want to hold us accountable for providing data that indicates that we're on track. I'm also hearing some systems implications—we need to strengthen or create systems for monitoring student learning and for hearing teacher feedback and questions. And I'm hearing the need for PD on topics related to PBL because you've raised some skill gaps."

Mahesh was nodding. "I guess that's right," he said.

I decided to shift into coaching Mahesh on his way of being. I wanted him to think more expansively. I asked, "I'm curious if you can imagine 10 years in the future. How do you want to remember yourself as a leader during this school year?"

Mahesh's face relaxed into a smile. He said, "I want to remember that I spoke up when our data didn't match what we say we want for kids. I want to remember that I jumped into PBL with both feet and got better at it. I want to remember that I felt really proud of the data at the end of the year and that kids felt proud of themselves."

I let his words sink in, and then asked, "How does it feel to name those desires?"

"I think what got me was thinking about the actual kid part. I could have a great day, but it doesn't matter if the kids didn't learn anything. It feels good to keep thinking about their experience and how we're setting them up to be successful."

"So anchoring in student experience and outcomes," I said.

"Yeah, that is 90% of the job for me," Mahesh said.

I nodded. I wanted to continue affirming Mahesh's commitment to kids. "I consistently hear you expressing things that make me think that it's 100% of the job to you," I said. "You focus on what kids need." Mahesh's expression was open, and I hoped I was laying the foundations for him to feel safe to engage in coaching with me. "Mahesh," I continued, "our time is coming to a close, and I respect your time, but I'm curious if you feel like there's a question that you wish I had asked you today about your feelings about project-based learning?" I asked this question to give him an opportunity to say anything else on his mind, but I also included the continued invitation to share his feelings—not just his thoughts. I had noted that several times when I'd asked him about his emotions, he'd shared thoughts. I wanted to keep cueing that emotions were welcome.

Mahesh rubbed his chin. "I appreciate that we talked about the problems with PBL," he said, his volume lower than in most of our conversation, "but I wish we'd talked a little more about what I need to do. I have my unit plans, but do you want me to change them? Is this a good start? Do you want me to add on PBL? I wish we'd gotten around to talking about what I'm supposed to do."

I was grateful to hear this—it seemed like an indicator that he was ready to focus on what was within his sphere of influence and that he trusted me more. "What I'm hearing," I said, shifting my tone of voice to a register that might have more authority in it, "is that you're ready to have that conversation about your unit plans and that you might be willing to explore how to supplement your plans with some PBL elements. Does that sound accurate?" I used active listening to ensure that I was understanding correctly.

"Yeah," Mahesh said without hesitating. "I am definitely willing to add to my unit to make it more of a project thing, and I'd love to know how to address my students' skill gaps."

"Okay," I said. "I hear your willingness to incorporate PBL, and you want to be sure that you're addressing students' skill gaps. So here's what I want to ask you to do before we meet next time, because I think that you can answer the questions you just asked me. I think that given your years of teaching and knowledge of our students, you could revise your unit plan so that it incorporates PBL and addresses the skills you see that students need. I don't think you need me to tell you how to do that." I paused trying to register Mahesh's response. I wanted him to own the problem; I wanted him to access his agency. "How does it sound," I continued, "if for our next meeting, you revise your unit plans, and then I'll provide feedback and answer any questions about PBL that come up in your planning?"

"Yeah, I can do that," Mahesh said. "I need a little bit of time, but yeah, I'll do that."

"Mahesh, I really appreciate your thoughtfulness and courage," I said, pausing and taking a breath, "and your willingness to try new things and to take a leadership role in implementing PBL in our school. I have a feeling this will be a better year for everyone."

Mahesh nodded. I still couldn't really read his expression, but his face looked relaxed. "Well, thanks," he said. "I guess I could be more proactive on the Leadership Team, especially if you're willing to let me raise my questions."

I nodded. "That would be great. That's the place to raise them, and I love thinking about how you can expand your leadership," I said.

Mahesh closed his notebook and stood up. "Good meeting," he said. I wasn't sure how to interpret that but decided to take it at face value.

"Glad you feel that way," I said. We made a quick agreement about our next meeting time, and I decided to skip my usual end-of-session reflection questions given that Mahesh seemed ready to close up. "Thanks, Mahesh," I said as we walked out.

He nodded. "Thank you."

Reflecting on a Coaching Conversation

Most of the time, what I plan to say in a coaching session differs from what I actually end up saying. If you re-read the questions I generated for my session with Mahesh, you'll see many that I never asked. This is the art of coaching—this is how we meet someone where they're at, how we respond to the human we're working with. We prepare a plan and use it when it serves the client.

Even though I didn't ask Mahesh all the questions I'd come up with, my work with the Lenses wasn't wasted. My reflection allowed me to show up with true curiosity and guided me into the questions I asked. When I sat down with Mahesh, I realized that I hadn't anticipated that he would be as guarded as I experienced him. Registering his fear, I knew I'd need to prioritize building trust. To do this, I had to acknowledge the urgency that came up for me—school was starting so soon, I wanted to make sure his unit plans were strong—and I had to trust the process. I used a lot of active listening stems to ensure that I was understanding his perspective, to help him hear what he was saying, and to build our relationship. I was also aware of the power dynamic—I was sure he perceived me as having more power, and I wanted to avoid getting into debates about PBL versus basic skills, but I also wanted to be clear that our school was moving toward PBL and it wasn't optional.

This is how real coaching works. We create lists of questions to reflect on and surface in future conversations, and then, more often than not, in a conversation further down the road, you'll recognize an entry point to one of those items on the list. And because of previous work, the question you want to ask is already formed and ready to be asked. Reflection is practice; when you plan conversations and reflect on them afterward, ideally in writing, you create the possibility for new behaviors. When you role-play a conversation with a colleague, you create more possibility.

During the conversation with Mahesh, I considered raising my wonderings about equity. But reverberating loudly in my mind was the adult learning principle that we need to feel safe to learn. I chose to wait. I recognized the need to build a foundation of trust before exploring identity and equity. When I sensed Mahesh's defensiveness, I reminded myself to meet him where he was; and because he was in a place of fear, I worked to create a space in which he'd feel seen and heard, accepted, and trusted.

I was also acutely aware of the way Mahesh seemed to engage with emotions. I noted that when I invited his reflection on his feelings, he shared thoughts. I wondered about his awareness of his feelings, his understanding of emotions in general, and of how he thought about their role in his experience. During the conversation, I paid attention to Mahesh's body language, facial expressions, tone of voice, and the volume and pace of his speech—all data on how he might have been feeling. At the same time, I reminded myself to be cautious about drawing conclusions, as there was so much I didn't know about Mahesh yet, and also because of our different cultural backgrounds. My curiosity about Mahesh's emotional intelligence helped me anchor in humility and helped me feel empathy for him.

The Inquiry Lens had helped me commit to understanding Mahesh's perspective and decision-making. Sometimes when teachers raise challenges like this one, when they have disagreements, coaches adopt a debate stance—they try to convince a client by reasoning. "I'm going to tell you," they seem to say, "why you're wrong, and I'll find a way to shut you down and make you do what we want you to do." When a coach is in debate mode, the coaching is over. Given the power differential between a coach and a client, the conditions for learning are no longer present. Note that for yourself: stay out of debate mode. And know that if you slip into it—and this is easy to do—you'll need to learn how to get yourself out. Sometimes that sounds like saying, "Let me pause for a second. I realize I was going in a direction that might not have helped." And then find a different direction to go in, one that centers your client and helps you understand them.

Another area for deeper reflection that became clear during our conversation was around systems issues. I heard how the systems in our school (and the lack of systems) had generated Mahesh's seemingly problematic behavior—we hadn't done a good job of gathering teacher input or feedback on the adoption and implementation of PBL. We also didn't have strong data-gathering systems or procedures for data analysis. And Mahesh's concerns about accreditation were valid—the larger system in which we were embedded mattered. Reflecting on my session with Mahesh, I turned first to the Systems Thinking Lens—and it helped me come up with a proposal to address some of the breakdowns and gaps in our PBL implementation.

During our conversation, I thought about the assumption from the Change Management Lens that building on strengths can lead to positive change. This influenced my choice to surface and validate Mahesh's strengths. I also remembered a question from this lens that asks about the vision that people are working toward. I wondered whether the vision for PBL at our school was clear, which again made me think about our implementation of this initiative.

Reviewing the Coaching Lenses before our conversation rooted me in a place of compassion and curiosity and in the vision I hold for who I want to be as a coach. The assumptions and questions I had internalized guided me through our conversation and allowed me to use additional Transformational Coaching tools and strategies. As I reflected on the conversation afterward and used the Coaching Lenses once again to gain deeper insight, I saw how my efficacy was a result of a lot of practice with these frameworks, as well as of a commitment to a way of being.

Things We Don't Talk About, Yet

Over the following school year, Mahesh cautiously incorporated a number of PBL best practices. He also integrated basic skill building—as did the whole sixth-grade team. Student assessments validated the direction we were headed as a school. I met with Mahesh twice a month, and, as our relationship grew, our sessions became increasingly comfortable, frequently punctuated by laughter and friendly jousting.

About a year after the conversation you just read took place, Mahesh and I sat down to talk about the upcoming year, and he raised our conversation a year prior.

"I've thought about that meeting a lot," he said. "I came into it feeling defensive and full of excuses." He smiled. He smiled a lot more now when we met. "But," he continued, "I didn't hear you saying that I had to change my unit plans. I didn't feel like you were fighting me. I didn't feel like you were telling me that I was wrong."

Mahesh paused. "I think in that conversation I felt like we were on the same side. Like we were both trying to figure out what's best for kids. I was surprised that you asked things like, 'what do you think we should do?' and that you thought I had good ideas. You didn't seem to just be trying to placate me into compliance."

"No, I wasn't," I said. "I know that wouldn't have worked." I smiled.

"We're always going to have different perspectives about how to do things," Mahesh said. "I know that my childhood and background inform how I see things and how I think we should do things." I was nodding. We'd had a couple of long and intense conversations about the role of identity in shaping our beliefs and behaviors. "But," he continued, "I saw that you truly wanted to figure out the problem together. I realized administration did too, but I'd been defensive with them as well."

"We've all been building trust," I said. "Trust takes a minute when we work in hierarchical organizations in which we've had experiences of not being seen or heard."

"That's what made it easier for me to take your advice," Mahesh said. "When you gave me information, or asked me to try something I felt uncomfortable with, I tried, I guess, because I trust you."

"I'm so grateful that you're sharing these reflections with me, Mahesh. They're helping me understand you better and know what works for you in coaching. I'm wondering if there's anything else from that conversation a year ago that stands out?"

Mahesh rubbed his chin. "This feels awkward," he said, "but what really helped was when you said you heard fear—you said you heard that I was afraid. I was surprised, but I realized I *was* feeling afraid. I also appreciated that you heard how much I care about our students. Sometimes I think I'm seen as a difficult teacher, but I really care."

"Thank you for sharing that," I said. "I did hear your fear and your love."

"It *is* love," he said. "It feels awkward to use that word, but it's the right one."

I nodded. "I know it can feel uncomfortable to talk about those feelings. I wish we talked about love more," I said.

I suspected I saw a mix of humor and doubt in Mahesh's expression. "I'm still trying to get more comfortable with small talk," he said. "Give me a little more time before you start asking me about love too, okay?" He smiled.

"Got it. Thanks for the feedback," I said. I was thinking about the principles of adult learning and wondering how to apply those in coaching people toward love. I was also thinking about the power of compassion as a force to change the world.

I smiled. "I'll stay within your comfort zone for talking about strong emotions—and I'll think through a plan to scaffold you into discussions on love."

Mahesh laughed and shook his head. We'd talked a lot about the importance of scaffolding in our coaching sessions. "I'm not going to say what I'm thinking right now," Mahesh said, "It's way too cheesy. But I'll just say that I appreciate you, Elena."

I smiled. "I love you too, Mahesh."

Pause and Process

Reflect:

- What insights into Transformational Coaching do the Coaching Lenses offer you?
- What further insights into Transformational Coaching do the conversations with Mahesh offer?
- Which of the coaching lenses surprised you or might offer you a new way forward in your work? What's one way you might start incorporating the Coaching Lenses into your coaching?
- How did this chapter help you develop your vision for who you want to be as a coach?

Next steps:

- Listen to *Bright Morning Podcast* episode 209 on using the Teacher-to-Student Interaction tool.
- Download Table 15.1, "Analyzing a Situation Through the Lenses" and use it to reflect on a coaching situation.
- Download "The Coaching Lenses" from my website. Select one you would like to use in planning for an upcoming coaching conversation.

CONCLUSION:
ALL YOU NEED IS LOVE

*A*rise is an invitation—an invitation to coach and lead in a human-centered, compassionate, wildly optimistic way. Think about the word *arise* for a moment. How do your body, heart, and spirit feel thinking about the word? Does it make you want to take action, or perhaps to surrender to a current in the air and let yourself soar?

I hope I've created the conditions in which you can reflect on who you are and who you want to be. I hope I've helped you see that you have far more influence (or perhaps even control) over how you experience life and over the impact you have on others.

I've always been a relatively optimistic person, but as I get older, I am becoming even more optimistic. I think this is because, through my work, I've seen so many people learn and grow. I've seen people release the racist beliefs in which they were socialized, change habitual ways of being and behaviors, and acquire skills to engage with their emotions. I've also seen that as a result of all of this learning and change, schools have become more humane, caring places—for the big and little people who enter them every day.

I hope that as you use Transformational Coaching strategies, you'll connect more deeply to your own agency, you'll see your ability to make changes in your Three Bs, and you'll see other people and communities change. Many of us have been conditioned into a mental model in which we think that change is so hard and that it takes so long, and yet I've witnessed radical changes in behaviors, beliefs, and ways of being in a short amount of time. Know, however, that change isn't linear. Remember to trust the process, keep reflecting on and refining your practice as a coach, and you'll see change.

What do you want to remember from this book? I encourage you to make a short list of big takeaways. Here are the things I want to remember from my journey as a Transformational Coach:

- Humans have emotions, and they can be an ally in our growth.
- I don't have to work through all those human emotions alone—a therapist is a great help.
- No one can learn from you if you think that they suck.
- Every action emerges from a belief.
- I can choose who I want to be.
- LOVE IS ALL THERE IS.

My ultimate hope is that this book has helped you connect more deeply to love—to love for others, for yourself, and as our ultimate calling and assignment. I hope you sensed the current of love beneath everything I write. Perhaps, in order to be a Transformational Coach, in order to enact the art of Transformational Coaching, all you need is love.

REFERENCES

Aguilar, Elena. *Coaching for Equity: Conversations That Change Practice*. San Francisco: Jossey-Bass, 2020.

Aguilar, Elena. *Onward: Cultivating Emotional Resilience in Educators*. San Francisco: Jossey-Bass, 2018.

Aguilar, Elena. *The Art of Coaching Teams: Building Resilient Communities That Transform Schools*. San Francisco: Jossey Bass, 2016.

Aguilar, Elena, and Lori Cohen. *The PD Book: Seven Habits That Transform Professional Development*. San Francisco: Jossey-Bass, 2022.

Bowman, Barbara T., James P. Comer, and David J. Johns. "Addressing the African American Achievement Gap: Three Leading Educators Issue a Call to Action." *Young Children*, vol. 73, no. 2, 2018.

Bohan, Suzanne. "Day I: Three East Bay ZIP codes, life-and-death disparities," *East Bay Times*, December 2, 2009 (updated August 15, 2016), https://www.eastbaytimes.com/2009/12/02/day-i-three-east-bay-zip-codes-life-and-death-disparities.

Canadian Council for Refugees. "Anti-oppression." Accessed May 2, 2023. https://ccrweb.ca/en/anti-oppression.

Chugh, Dolly. *The Person You Mean to Be: How Good People Fight Bias*. New York: Harper Collins, 2018.

Cisneros, Sandra. *The House on Mango Street*. New York: Vintage, 1991.

Cullors, P., Ross, R., and Tippet, K., host. "The Spiritual Work of Black Lives Matter." *On Being* Podcast. 18 Feb 2016. Retrieved from https://onbeing.org/programs/patrisse-cullors-and-robert-ross-the-spiritual-work-of-black-lives-matter-may2017.

Darling-Hammond, Linda, Ruth Chung Wei, Alethea Andree, Nikole Richardson, and Stelios Orphanos. "State of the Profession: Study Measures Professional Development." *Journal of Staff Development*, vol. 30, no. 2, 2009, 42–50.

Echeverría, Rafael, and Julio M. Olalla. *The Art of Ontological Coaching*. Boulder: Newfield Network, 1993.

Freire, Paulo. *Pedagogy of the Oppressed*. New York: Seabury Press, 1968.

French, J. R., Raven, B., and Cartwright, D. "The Bases of Social Power." *Classics of Organization Theory*, vol. 7, 1959, 311–320.

Gladwell, Malcolm. *Outliers: The Story of Success*. New York: Back Bay Books, 2011.

Goldhaber, Dan, Leslie Lavery, and Roddy Theobald. "Uneven Playing Field? Assessing the Teacher Quality Gap Between Advantaged and Disadvantaged Students." *Educational Researcher*, vol. 44, no. 5, 2015, 32–56.

Grissom, Jason A., and Christopher Redding. "Discretion and Disproportionality: Explaining the Underrepresentation of High-Achieving Students of Color in Gifted Programs." *AERA Open,* 18 January, 2016.

Hargrove, Robert. *Masterful Coaching*. San Francisco: Jossey-Bass, 2003.

Javdani, Shabnam. "Policing Education: An Empirical Review of the Challenges and Impact of the Work of School Police Officers." *American Journal of Community Psychology*, vol. 63, no. 3–4, 2019, 253–269.

Jeon, Lieny, Cynthia K. Buettner, and Anastasia R. Snyder. "Pathways from Teacher Depression and Child-Care Quality to Child Behavioral Problems." *Journal of Consulting and Clinical Psychology*, vol. 82, no. 2, 2014, 225–235.

Keltner, Dacher. *Awe: The New Science of Everyday Wonder and How It Can Transform Your Life*. New York: Penguin, 2023.

Kendi, Ibram X. *How to Be an Anti-Racist*. London: One World, 2019.

Kendi, Ibram X. *Stamped from the Beginning: The Definitive History of Racist Ideas in America*. New York: Nation Books, 2016.

Klopfenstein, Kristin. "Advanced placement: Do minorities have equal opportunity?" *Economics of Education Review*, vol. 23, no. 2, 2004, 115–131.

Maté, Gabor. *The Myth of Normal: Trauma, Illness, & Healing in a Toxic Culture*. New York: Avery, 2022.

Schwartz, Richard. *No Bad Parts: Healing Trauma and Restoring Wholeness with the Internal Family Systems Model*. Boulder: Sounds True, 2021.

Senge, Peter. *The Fifth Discipline Fieldbook: Strategies and Tools for Building a Learning Organization*. New York: Doubleday, 1994.

Smith, Edward J., and Shaun R. Harper. "Disproportionate Impact of K-12 School Suspension and Expulsion on Black Students in Southern States." University of Pennsylvania Center for the Study of Race and Equity in Education, 2015.

Sutcher, Leib, Linda Darling-Hammond, and Desiree Carver-Thomas,. "A Coming Crisis in Teaching? Teacher Supply, Demand, and Shortages in the U.S." Learning Policy Institute (2016). Accessed February 28, 2018. https://doi.org/10.54300/247.242.

Tatum, Beverly Daniel. *Why Are All the Black Kids Sitting Together in the Cafeteria? And Other Conversations About Race*. New York: Basic Books, 1999.

Todd, Andrew R., Kelsey C. Thiem, and Rebecca Neel. "Does Seeing Faces of Young Black Boys Facilitate the Identification of Threatening Stimuli?" *Psychological Science*, vol. 27, no. 3, 2016.

U.S. Department of Education Office for Civil Rights, "Data Snapshot: School Discipline," *Civil Right Data Collection,* March 2014.

Wulsin, Lawson, Toni Alterman, P. Timothy Bushnell, Jia Li, and Rui Shen. "Prevalence Rates for Depression by Industry: A Claims Database Analysis." *Social Psychiatry and Psychiatric Epidemiology*, vol. 49, no. 11, 2014,1805–1821.

Zohar, Danah. *Rewiring the Corporate Brain*. San Francisco: Berrett-Koehler, 1997.

APPENDIX A

Transformational Coaching Mini-Rubric

A rubric guides you toward mastering a complex set of skills. What follows is a short version of my Transformational Coaching Rubric, which is available in its entirety on my website. The mini version is a distillation of the complex art of Transformational Coaching and includes the essential competencies. The longer version is triple the length and contains all of the competencies and indicators required for enacting Transformational Coaching with fidelity.

A TRANSFORMATIONAL COACH'S BELIEFS: Why We Do What We Do		
Domain	**Competency**	**Indicators**
Beliefs about Self	I have to start with myself	I attend to, reflect on, and develop my own behaviors, beliefs and ways of being.
		I prioritize meeting my core human needs and caring for myself.

(Continued)

A TRANSFORMATIONAL COACH'S BELIEFS: Why We Do What We Do		
Domain	**Competency**	**Indicators**
Beliefs about Client	My client has agency	My client can solve many of their own problems given the right conditions.
	My client can be effective	I create the conditions for my client to learn, grow, develop, and transform. I guide clients to access the knowledge and wisdom within them.
Beliefs about Transformational Coaching (TC)	Transformational Coaching serves a mission to ensure that all students thrive	Transformational Coaching is a structure and process through which to create equitable schools in which every child's needs are met, every day.
	Transformational Coaching is a model that creates the conditions for change	People change when the conditions are right; those conditions can be created.
	Transformational Coaching focuses on equity	Equity issues are present in every situation.
		Power and privilege must be explored for change to happen.

A TRANSFORMATIONAL COACH'S WAYS OF BEING:
How We Show Up

Domain	Competency	Indicators
Emotional Intelligence	Emotional Self-Awareness	I am aware of how the way I express emotions affects others.
	Emotional Self-Management	I engage in processes to understand my emotions and engage with them in a healthy way.
	Social Awareness	I am able to accurately read my client's emotions, including how they feel about me.
	Relationship Management	I am intentional about building, maintaining, and repairing trust.
		I communicate empathy and appreciation for my client.
Dispositions	Compassion	I hold unconditional positive regard for others.
	Trust in the process	I understand that although I may not see indicators of change in my client, change may be underway.

A TRANSFORMATIONAL COACH'S BEHAVIORS: What We Do

Domain	Competency	Indicators
Foundational Abilities	Cultivating Agency	I stay out of fix-it mode and communicate confidence that a client can solve their own problems.
	Navigating Power Dynamics	I position myself not as an expert, but as the facilitator in a process whose role is to provide guidance on a learning journey.
Listening	Transformational Listening	I cultivate awareness of where my mind goes when I'm listening and use strategies to return to presence when I wander.
Responding	Intention to make every conversation count	I know that every conversation is an opportunity to create a more just and equitable world.
	Thinking	I think through different Thinking Tools to select a response to what my client says.
	Language	I use a wide variety of coaching stems with my client.
	Use of Silence	I am comfortable holding silence in a conversation.
	Active Listening	I use active listening throughout a conversation and when it may provide my client with an opportunity to more deeply understand themselves.
	Coaching Stances	I primarily use facilitative coaching approaches.

A TRANSFORMATIONAL COACH'S BEHAVIORS:
What We Do

Domain	Competency	Indicators
Coaching the Three Bs	Coaching Ways of Being	I guide my client to acknowledge and accept their emotions, cultivate compassion for themselves and others, and expand the stories they tell.
		I guide my client to identify and explore how their core human needs are or are not being met.
		I coach my client to align their behaviors, beliefs, and ways of being to their core values and to enact their core values.
		I guide my client to identify their own strengths.
		I recognize when fear is in play. When it is, I invite my client to explore their fear.
		I coach a client towards resilience at any opportunity and through a variety of methods.
		I coach the person and not their problem.
	Coaching Beliefs	I motivate a client to explore their beliefs and can create a safe-enough space for them to do so.
		I guide a client through the Exploring Beliefs Framework and the Ladder of Influence to recognize and explore current beliefs and help them create new ones.
		I coach towards identity awareness by using the Wheel of Power and Privilege and a range of coaching strategies and stances.
	Coaching Behaviors	I use the Gaps Framework to inform my coaching decisions and with my client for their self-awareness.
		I use the Coaching Lenses and the Adult Learning Principles to make decisions about how to guide and sequence my client's learning.

APPENDIX B

The Core Emotions

(Adapted from *Wise Mind Living* by Erin Olivo)

Core Emotion	Fear	Anger	Sadness	Shame
Common terms for this emotion	Agitated	Aggravated	Alienated	Besmirched
	Alarmed	Agitated	Anguished	Chagrined
	Anxious	Annoyed	Bored	Contemptuous
	Apprehensive	Antagonized	Crushed	(of self)
	Concerned	Bitter	Defeated	Contrite
	Desperate	Contemptuous	Dejected	Culpable
	Dismayed	(other than	Depressed	Debased
	Dread	for self)	Despairing	Degraded
	Fearful	Contentious	Despondent	Disapproving
	Frightened	Contrary	Disappointed	Disdainful
	Horrified	Cranky	Discouraged	Disgraced
	Hysterical	Cruel	Disheartened	Disgusted
	Impatient	Destructive	Dismayed	(at self)
	Jumpy	Displeased	Dispirited	Dishonored
	Nervous	Enraged	Displeased	Disreputable
	Panicked	Exasperated	Distraught	Embarrassed
	Scared	Explosive	Down	Guilty
	Shocked	Frustrated	Dreary	Hateful
	Shy	Furious	Forlorn	Humbled
	Tense	Hateful	Gloomy	Humiliated
	Terrified	Hostile	Grief-stricken	Improper

(Continued)

Core Emotion	Fear	Anger	Sadness	Shame
Common terms for this emotion	Timid	Impatient	Hopeless	Infamous
	Uncertain	Indignant	Hurt	Invalidated
	Uneasy	Insulated	Insecure	Mortified
	Worried	Irate	Isolated	Regretful
		Irritable	Lonely	Remorseful
		Irritated	Melancholic	Repentant
		Mad	Miserable	Reproachful
		Mean	Mopey	Rueful
		Outraged	Morose	Scandalized
		Resentful	Neglected	Scornful
		Scornful	Oppressed	Sinful
		Spiteful	Pessimistic	Stigmatized
		Urgent	Pitiful	
		Vengeful	Rejected	
			Somber	
			Sorrowful	
			Tragic	
			Unhappy	

Core Emotion	Jealousy	Disgust	Happiness	Love
Common terms for this emotion	Competitive	Appalled	Agreeable	Acceptance
	Covetous	Dislike	Amused	Admiration
	Deprived	Grossed out	Blissful	Adoring
	Distrustful	Insulted	Bubbly	Affectionate
	Envious	Intolerant	Cheerful	Allegiance
	Greedy	Nauseated	Content	Attached
	Grudging	Offended	Delighted	Attraction
	Jealous	Put off	Eager	Belonging
	Overprotective	Repelled	Ease	Caring
	Petty	Repulsed	Elated	Compassionate

Core Emotion	Jealousy	Disgust	Happiness	Love
	Possessive	Revolted	Engaged	Connected
	Resentful	Revulsion	Enjoyment	Dependent
	Rivalrous	Shocked	Enthusiastic	Desire
		Sickened	Euphoric	Devoted
		Turned off	Excited	Empathetic
			Exhilarated	Faithful
			Flow	Friendship
			Glad	Interested
			Gleeful	Kind
			Glowing	Liking
			Gratified	Passionate
			Harmonious	Protective
			Hopeful	Respectful
			Interested	Sympathetic
			Joyful	Tender
			Jubilant	Trust
			Lighthearted	Vulnerable
			Meaningful	Warm
			Merry	
			Optimistic	
			Peaceful	
			Pleasure	
			Pride	
			Proud	
			Relieved	
			Satisfied	
			Thrilled	
			Triumphant	

APPENDIX C

The Coaching Lenses

The Coaching Lenses are based on theories that attempt to explain human and organizational behavior. Most of the Lenses come from the National Equity Project, an Oakland-based organization I was fortunate to learn from in my first years as a coach. They created the Lenses of Inquiry, Adult Learning, Systems Thinking, Systemic Oppression, and Change Management. I added the Lens of Emotional Intelligence and the Lens of Compassion. I also renamed the Lens of Systemic Oppression as the Equity Lens and modified others. I'm ever grateful to the National Equity Project for this work (and all their work) and for permission to print the lenses. You'll learn more about using the lenses in Chapter 15.

Here's a quick overview of the Coaching Lenses:

- *What*: A framework to think through a complex situation from many angles
- *Why:* To expand how we see the world; to interrupt our habitual ways of thinking and interpreting evidence; to surface the root causes of a problem and determine a strategic course of action
- *How:* As a tool to reflect on an observation or a conversation, as a tool to plan a coaching conversation, as a tool to incorporate into a consultancy protocol, or as a tool for thinking during a conversation

Adult Learning	
Assumptions	**Questions**
• Problems of change are problems of learning. • People must feel safe to learn. • Adults want to be the origin of our learning. • We must meet adult learners where they are; they can only be where they are. • Adults come to learning with a wide range of previous experiences, knowledge, interests, and competencies. • Adults want and need feedback.	• What is the gap between current reality and the goal? • What is the goal or objective? What does exemplary performance in this role look like? How has that been communicated? • What progress has been made towards this goal? • What is going well? Which strengths can be built on? • Where are the gaps? Skill? Knowledge? Will? Capacity? Emotional intelligence? Cultural competency? • Is there evidence of prior learning? • Does the will for learning exist? • Is this a safe space for learning? • How can the learner fully own their learning? • How can I understand where the learner is on their learning path?

Change Management	
Assumptions	**Questions**
• Beneficial change is possible in any situation. • Building on strengths can lead to positive change. • Change can be studied, understood, and influenced. • For successful change to occur, there needs to be leadership, vision, skills, incentives, resources, and a clear plan of action. • People need will, skill, knowledge, capacity, and emotional intelligence to change.	• What are the conditions for change in this situation? • What's working in this situation? • Which strengths can be built on? • Where are the opportunities for leveraging change? What threats to change are present? • What is the vision that people are working toward? • Which skills do people need to achieve the vision? What knowledge is necessary? • Do people have the skills and knowledge necessary to implement change? • Does the will for change exist here? Where? • What incentives are in place for people to change? • What resources are available to support change?

Inquiry	
Assumptions	**Questions**
• The way we pose the question determines the nature of the answer. • The way we define the problem dictates how we define the solution. • The questions we ask are as important as the answers we find. • People can create their own knowledge and solutions. • Seemingly intractable problems can be addressed. • When you own the question, you take responsibility for the answer. • Evidence and data are critical to making informed decisions. • Multiple forms of data, including authentic and qualitative measures produced by multiple constituencies, are necessary for effective decision-making. • Knowledge is socially constructed. • We never know everything we need to know, but we need to act anyway.	• Who is defining the problem? • What do I think is the problem? What do others think is the problem? • Whose question is this? • What data do we have on this problem? Which problems does that data say we should address? • From which perspectives am I seeing this situation? What other perspectives would help me understand this situation? • How is this situation connected to other things?

Systems Thinking	
Assumptions	**Questions**
• Everything we observe is the result of a complex set of interactions.	• How is the current system designed to produce the results we're seeing?
• Whatever is happening in a moment is exactly what is supposed to happen in the system as it is. If we understand these interactions, we can intervene effectively to change them.	• How did this system generate the behavior we're seeing?
	• What are the relationships between things here?
• If we understand a system's structure, we can identify possible leverage points to change it.	• Where is the energy in this situation? Where are the stuck points?
• Conflict and tension in a system are necessary and natural.	• If I do this here, what would happen over here?
• To change systems, we must understand the big picture, consider an issue fully, and resist the urge to come to a quick conclusion.	• If I do this now, what will happen immediately? What will happen in the long term?
• We must consider the short- and long-term consequences of an action.	• What are the unintended consequences of a particular action?
• All systems have delays. Change in one part of the system does not result in immediate change elsewhere.	• If we shift our perspective, what might we understand about this situation?

Emotional Intelligence

Assumptions	Questions
• Human beings have emotions. We can learn from them, and they can be guides, or they can become obstacles. • When we have awareness of our emotions, we can make choices about how to respond to them. • We can learn skills to regulate or manage our emotions. • Recognizing emotions in others is essential for individual and collective well-being. • We can learn skills to respond to the emotions that others express so that we can manage our relationships. • Emotional intelligence is the foundation for effective communication. • Emotional intelligence allows us to speak about emotions, ask for help, and establish boundaries. • Emotional intelligence is the foundation of emotional resilience, adaptability, and flexibility. • Emotional intelligence is what allows us to meet our core human needs and to thrive.	• Where is there evidence that emotions are at play? • What indicators are there that people are aware of their emotions? • How are people expressing their emotions? • How are people managing uncomfortable feelings? • Where is fear present? • How are people tuned in to the emotions of others? • How do they respond to the emotional expressions of others? • How are power dynamics influencing emotions? • How is conflict dealt with? • How are my emotions influencing the situation?

Equity

Assumptions	Questions
<ul><li>Inequities based on identity markers (including race, class, and gender) are prevalent in our education system.</li><li>Oppression and injustice are human creations and can be undone.</li><li>Systemic oppression negatively affects the educational process in countless ways.</li><li>Oppression and systematic mistreatment (such as white supremacy, racism, classism, sexism, and homophobia) are more than the sum of individual prejudices.</li><li>Systemic oppression has historical antecedents: it is an intentional disempowering of groups of people based on their identity in order to maintain an unequal power structure that subjugates one group over another.</li><li>Systemic oppression manifests in economic, political, social, and cultural systems and in interpersonal relationships.</li><li>Systemic oppression and its effects can be undone through recognition of inequitable patterns and intentional action to interrupt inequity.</li><li>Discussing and addressing equity will be accompanied by strong emotions.</li></ul>	<ul><li>How are inequities playing out right here, right now? (In this relationship, classroom, school, group, organization, and district?)</li><li>Who has power here? What is that power based on?</li><li>How are power relations affecting the truth that is told and constructed at any given moment? How do power relations reflect dominant systems of oppression?</li><li>Who is at the table? Who isn't? How does this reflect dominant culture?</li><li>Whose safety is prioritized when there's space to share truths?</li><li>How safe is it for people from marginalized communities to share their truths?</li><li>Do others see where they are in relationship to privilege and power given their identity markers?</li><li>How are my identity markers giving me access to power and privilege?</li><li>What comes up for me around coaching and leading across difference?</li></ul>

Compassion	
Assumptions	**Questions**
• Compassion is the ability to suspend judgment of ourselves and others, appreciating that each of us makes choices based on the information and skills that we have at any given time. • Compassion is acting on empathy. • Compassion for another starts with compassion toward one's self. • Curiosity, humility, and trust foster the development of compassion. • We can use compassion to dismantle destructive beliefs and behaviors. • Human nature is compassionate; conditions can arise that block our ability to be compassionate, but we can find our way back.	• How are others experiencing this situation? What are things like from their perspective? • How do we support others to discover their best qualities? • How do we help others explore the consequences of their actions and learn from them? • How can listening help us cultivate compassion? • Where do we see people treating each other with kindness? How can we create more spaces where people treat each other with kindness? • How can we return to a state of compassion when we notice we are activated? How can we help others do this? • How can compassion help us to dismantle systems of oppression? • How can we cultivate compassion in ourselves?

INDEX

Care, expression, 165
Caregivers, relationships, 429
Catalytic approach (facilitative stance), 150, 155–156
Cathartic approach (facilitative stance), 150, 153–155
Cathartic coaching, appearance, 154
Cathartic question, 170
Challenges, classification, 238
Change, conditions (creation), 46–47
Change Management Lens, 405, 346
  assumptions/questions, 461, 483
  usage, 441t–442t
Character, 38
Children
  behaviors/beliefs/ways of being, negative impact, 284
  Black/Brown children, educational outcomes, 352
  care, ability, 33–34
  experience/outcomes, impact, 276
  fate, teacher contribution, 326–327
  multiple-choice comprehension tests, usage, 452
  service, 32–34
  teacher commitment, appreciation, 82–83
Chödrön, Pema, 234
Choice, opportunities (providing), 216
Chronic stress, presence, 215
Chugh, Dolly, 372
Cis-gendered males, superiority, 195–196
Cisneros, Sandra, 397
Clarifying question, 170–172
  incorporation, 156
  temptation, 171
Clarifying stems, 172
Clarity, 280
  need, 172
  offering, 241
Classroom
  focused classroom, creation, 412
  level, transformational coaching (impact), 51–52

management
  issues, creation, 127–128
  techniques, 287
  pre-observation, 403–404
  problems, prioritization issues, 401
Classroom observation, 342–344
  baseline evaluation, 403
  conducting, guidelines, 403–406
  debrief, planning, 422–426, 423t–426t
  debrief session, 405–406
  Gaps Framework, usage, 413–415
  goals, definition, 406
  interpretive notes, examples, 399–400
  objective data, usage, 398–401
  option, 402
  process, 397–406
  purpose, 401–402
    communication, 403
  questions/statements, consideration, 405
  subjective interpretations, 398–401
Clients
  agency, 45–46
    coaching, 100
    cultivation, 80
  awareness, 364
    guidance, 296
  belief, 472
  buy-in, 276
  coach beliefs, 45–47
  conversation control, options, 99
  core values
    knowledge, 309
    usage, 311
  discomfort, 368–369
  effectiveness, 46
  emotions, description, 251–252
  energy, usage, 99
  feeling, indicators, 123
  focus, maintenance, 152
  growth, 120
  knowledge gap, 152